The Tragedy of Zionism

THE TRAGEDY

OF ZIONISM

Revolution and Democracy

in the Land of Israel

BERNARD AVISHAI

Farrar Straus Giroux / New York

Copyright © 1985 by Bernard Avishai
All rights reserved
Printed in the United States of America
Published simultaneously in Canada by
Collins Publishers, Toronto
First edition, 1985
First paperback edition, 1986

Library of Congress Cataloging in Publication Data
Avishai, Bernard.
The tragedy of Zionism.
Bibliography: p.
Includes index.
1. Zionism—History.   2. Labor Zionism—History.
3. Israel—History.   I. Title.
DS149.A88   1985   956.94'001   85–10235

Portions of this book have appeared,
in somewhat different form,
in The New York Review of Books

For my father,

BEN SHAICOVITCH,

of blessed memory

Contents

I believe that the national character of Judaism does not exclude universalism and modern civilization; on the contrary, these values are the logical effect of our national culture . . . The Biblical story of the creation is told only for the sake of the Sabbath ideal. It tells us in symbolic language that when the creation of the world of nature was completed, with the calling into life of the highest organic being on earth—of man—the Creator celebrated His natural Sabbath. Then, at once, began the workdays of history.

MOSES HESS
Rome and Jerusalem

Men make their own history, but they do not make it just as they please; they do not make it under circumstances chosen by themselves, but under those directly encountered, given, and transmitted from the past. The traditions of dead generations weigh like a nightmare on the minds of the living.

For just when living men seem engaged in transforming themselves and things, in creating something that has never yet existed—precisely in such periods of revolutionary crisis—some anxiously conjure up the spirits of the lapsed revolution to their service, and borrow from their names, battle cries, and costumes in order to present the new scene of world history in a time-honored disguise . . .

KARL MARX
The Eighteenth Brumaire
of Louis Bonaparte

The Tragedy of Zionism

Prologue

I first traveled to Israel on June 19, 1967; I was eighteen years old. Along with everybody else in suburban Jewish Montreal, I had been deeply alarmed by the Arab siege that began in May, when Egypt blockaded the Straits of Tiran. By June 1, Israeli reserves had been called up for weeks and we knew there would be war; I recall my father punning, cheerlessly, that Hitler had swum to Egypt and "become *nasser*" ("wet" in Yiddish). On June 1, some acquaintances of mine from McGill University presented themselves to the Israeli consulate and volunteered to do farmwork or other manual labor until the soldiers could go home. Immediately—rashly, perhaps—I decided to join them, though to everyone's astonished relief the war was over before most could leave.

My father had emigrated from Bialystok to Canada at the age of eleven. He had been a Zionist Organization executive during the fifties—the "only Canadian," so he put it, to have witnessed the 1947 partition vote from the gallery at the United Nations. Self-taught, strongly drawn to politics, my father had often expressed the regret that he had not followed those *chalutzim* ("pioneers") in his Zionist youth group who had founded kibbutz Kfar Menachem in 1936. He would say that this "mistake" had forced him to lead a misplaced life in the Montreal needle trade. My mother, who had died in 1966, had been an affectionate and unstable woman,

Montreal-born, and had never shared my father's intense passion for Israel; indeed, the two had been estranged for as long as I could remember. Yet "Zionism" had been something of a sacred word for her, too. During my childhood, the banter of mealtime would die away quickly if some reporter on the radio mentioned Ben-Gurion or the Suez Canal. "Zionism" had been our answer to Quebec's ultramontane priests, to Adrien Arcan and Father Coughlin, to Arthur Godfrey's "restricted" hotels in Florida. The modern Hebrew I had learned at school seemed of a higher order than the ordinary speech of Jewish Montreal—English, puppy-Yiddish, and whatever French had to be learned "for business."

In retrospect, a man of my father's strong ambitions was probably more suited to commerce than to any kibbutz; he certainly seemed soothed when, before I left Montreal that summer of 1967, I promised to return in the fall to begin my sophomore year. Still, arriving in Israel as mobilization gave way to euphoria, I thought I discerned what my father had once found inviting in Zionism. Israel was strong, warming, lustrous, green; in every way, it seemed a more vigorous version of the large Polish-Jewish clan to which I was, and remained, devoted. My uncle in Tel Aviv, a singularly mild man, would linger for hours over the daily *Ma'ariv*, with its pictures of "Jewish boys" hauling away captured Soviet tanks. (The week before, in Montreal, my father had taken out a map to show me how Israeli forces had attacked the Gaza Strip—"with a pincers movement," he had said proudly.) Few of us gave much thought then to the Arab towns that would have to be ruled. We thought that a just war had brought lasting peace; that Israelis had exercised the former, and that Jews deserved the pleasures of the latter.

On June 28 I went to Jerusalem for the first time, taken there by a friend of the family, a paratrooper who had fought for the Old City just days before. All morning we walked around the ridges overlooking the Old City; not yet disturbed were markers made of piles of stones and helmets, on places where his friends had been killed. In the baking noon sun, we drove our straining Citroën *deux chevaux* up to the old Mandelbaum Gate, the checkpoint that had divided the Israeli city from the Jordanian since the 1948 war. We'd expected to be stopped there, and had practiced how to con the guard into letting us go on to the Old City. But we found no checkpoint and no guard. Anxiously we flipped on the radio—to hear that the city had been declared united and annexed to Israel just twenty minutes before. The announcer played "Jerusalem of Gold," and tears rolled down my companion's cheeks.

It seems curious to me now, but I think that summer in Israel made me ashamed of my origins in a way restricted hotels never could. Israel implied something continuing, redemptive, dramatic. It gave the promise of an authenticity North American Jews seemed to lack. In Israel, I concluded vaguely, there was no "alienation."

By 1970, I was married to my high-school sweetheart and had started graduate school in Toronto: Hobbes, Mill, the labor theory of value, subjects remote from that paratrooper's conscience. In fact, I remained hopelessly preoccupied with my impressions of Israel and of him. I ruminated guiltily about the virtues of constancy. For the first time, I read voraciously about the death camps. I was eager to get on with what my wife and I called our "lives." Then, in 1971, my father died. I began to ask myself if I, too, would make his mistake. Might a Jewish homeland indeed compensate for the loss of a Jewish home? In the spring of 1972, my wife gave in. We packed our books, sold our wedding gifts, and moved to Jerusalem.

.

There was satisfaction at first in solving together the mysteries of the Hebrew press, visiting antiquities, and farming the land of a friend I had made in 1967. Israel was growing, prosperous— America's darling—and we were happy to share in its prestige. We imagined ourselves contributing to something uncommon, one's own, yet strangely universal. (It was a time when one thought of one's powers as a "contribution.") The word "Zionism" was still pretty much an abstraction for us, but it stood for a great many novel pleasures, especially the grateful praise we got from older Israelis, whose pasts seemed so much more turbulent and brave than ours. We dug in, bought an apartment, went to work. The following summer our son was born, and we named him for my father.

The birth proved an unexpected turning point, however. Embarrassing though it was to acknowledge, we had always assumed our children would turn out something like us. It had never occurred to us that among our son's first words would be Hebrew words. Not that we were unreceptive to Israel's Hebrew culture, which seemed only the more charming and estimable the more we acquired of it. The problem was that, in acquiring it, we could not keep up any

Zionist's pretension to have always possessed it. Hebrew culture seemed complex and intimate, something Israelis had in common with each other, not with "Jews." What my wife and I had in common was, after all, the English language. As it was, we had barely suppressed the desire to hear it, speak it, and write it. Now we wondered if our child would ever want to read all those books we had packed.

The dilemma forced us to reexamine the normative justifications of Zionism—the classic theoretical claims of Zionist writers against Jewish life in the Diaspora. But these claims failed, or so I discovered with regret, when one seriously tried to apply them to our own doubts, or, indeed, to the predicament of other American and Canadian Jews. There is much more to be said about old Zionist theories; it has taken some time to think them through. Yet even then I remember thinking about what Achad Haam, one of the important mentors of early Zionism, had written about Eastern Jews who moved west to France and Germany: that having surrendered Hebrew and Yiddish culture to French and German, i.e., for the sake of "political freedom," they had then suffered from feelings of "cultural enslavement." In Israel, during the summer of 1973, I came to appreciate the force of his insight, though—and who could ignore the irony?—it was our English spirit that was effacing itself for Hebrew.

One tries at first to dismiss the implications of uncomfortable logic. We redoubled our efforts to become "real" Israelis. We blamed our unhappiness on city life; we blamed ourselves for not participating more in the classic tasks of revolutionary Zionism—kibbutz, army, life on the land. Then, that fall, there was another, more terrible war. Our doubts were submerged in the spontaneous solidarity of that time, in guard duty, and in mourning. Inevitably, however, even after joining the "right" kibbutz, we became increasingly convinced that we were living among foreigners—fine people, but not our own. I remember watching American and British programs in the kibbutz lounge, feeling panic, like one in exile: my home, alas, seemed more with the dissolving images on the screen than with the comrades breathing next to me.

During the spring of 1975, when our son started to seem another such comrade, we bolted back to Jerusalem; then—in the fall—home to Canada. The word "Zionism" still evoked in me—as in many

American and Canadian Jews who have lived in Israel—pride in Israel's existence and an abiding sense of loyalty to Israeli friends. It meant mutual aid in dark moments, a personal way to read history, also a measure of self-accusation. But all these "Zionisms" were the product of love, not of moral reason. In any case, they are not what I mean by Zionism in this book.

.

Zionism was a revolutionary movement. Most of Zionism's cadres came, not from the West, but from the Russian Pale of Settlement, where the Jews had lived—in Karl Marx's vivid phrase—"in the pores" of Russian and Polish peasant society. By the end of the nineteenth century, the Eastern European Jews numbered in the millions, and a great many of them were at once excited by the ideals of secular emancipation and deeply frustrated by the force and persistence of European anti-Semitism. It was in this context that Zionist writers competed with other radicals, and with each other, to reach the Eastern Jews with a number of original theories about why and how the Jewish people might take its place in the modern world by building a national home—preferably, but not necessarily, in Palestine, the ancient "Eretz Yisrael."

While it is true that Zionists did not have nearly the influence of the much more numerous advocates of other radical ideas—emigrationists, Yiddish proletarian nationalists, socialists, and anarchists—they proved to be in significant ways the most ambitious and ideologically sophisticated of them all. Like Jews who left for the Western democracies, Zionist pioneers were willing to suffer the pains of emigration; like the Yiddish nationalists, most pioneers were unwilling to give up either on Jewish national life or on socialism for the sake of liberal freedoms. Still, there was a hardheadedness to their idealism. After 1897, yearly Zionist congresses occasioned many debates about what practical goals the Zionist movement could have. To be a Zionist meant taking sides in these debates and choosing among the various moral arguments put forward by Zionist writers. Indeed, there can hardly have been a practical revolutionary movement whose activists depended more on complex ideological claims—just because Zionist goals seemed so distant and the number of people who shared them so small.

By 1918, when the British Army conquered Palestine, Zionism's most important internal debate had for the most part been settled in favor of Labor Zionism, which aspired to the slow colonization of that country by means of Hebrew-speaking collectives. Remarkably, it took no more than another generation for Labor Zionism to put down the fundamental institutions of its revolution in Palestine: the political parties, the "Histadrut" trade unions, the public corporations, and the communal farms. During much of that time, in Palestine and abroad, the word "Zionism" itself was largely understood as the evolution and impact of Labor Zionist institutions. Even such non-socialist Zionist leaders as Chaim Weizmann, the president of the World Zionist Organization between the world wars, put their efforts into consolidating Labor Zionism's institutions. Eventually these were critical for Palestinian Jews to become sufficiently powerful to create the state of Israel.

.

After the state of Israel was established in 1948, the Zionist movement came to seem the predictable response of world Jewry to anti-Semitic persecution. It is obvious why: in its first months, Israel provided a home for a majority of the 300,000 European Jews who outlasted Hitler. International support for the establishment of the state grew out of revulsion against the Nazis' nearly successful attempts at exterminating Europe's Jews; indeed, who has not been at least a little consoled that so soon after Jews seemed nothing but casualties, Zionists could exercise power and sovereignty? During the fifties, Israelis absorbed more than half a million refugees from the Arab states and, in the face of Arab enmity, succeeded in making a developed country. American and Western European Jews who do not live in Israel have been properly proud of these accomplishments. They have credited Zionism with them, and have supported Zionist organizations.

Yet it would be wrong to confuse Israel with the movement that produced it. Israel is a state in the normative sense, a country, a home for its citizens, and not merely a cause for people who identify with historic Zionism. Israel has a Hebrew-speaking majority and is, by all Zionist criteria, the Jewish national home. Most Israeli Jews call themselves "Zionists" when they mean to call attention to their patriotism. But if Israel is a democratic state, its four million citizens must be counted as individuals. Curious as this may seem, many of Israel's citizens were never Zionists in any rigorous sense, or—as in the case of Israeli Arabs—Zionists at all.

Moreover, when one makes the effort to distinguish the actual institutions of the Zionist revolution from the intentions of Zionist theorists—and distinguish both from the state's political constitution—it becomes obvious that Israeli democracy was never fully organized. Israelis enjoy many civil liberties, but the state also enforces important laws and economic regulations which contradict democratic ethics. What American Jew, for example, would want to live in an America without civil marriage, or in which only certified Christians were permitted to buy certain properties? In judging why Israeli leaders gave priority, not to democratic norms, but to building the Hebrew nation, one can hardly minimize the shock of the death camps or the consequences of the Arab revolt. But some of the reasons for Israel's failures as a democracy are internal to the logic of the Zionist revolution, and in any case, the mitigating circumstances of the 1940s do not justify current law.

Labor Zionist pioneers had wanted to build a democratic society like the one envisaged by their mentors, those secular Jewish intellectuals of Eastern Europe who yearned for emancipation, socialism, and safety. In the Yishuv, the revolutionary institutions of Labor Zionism understandably discriminated in favor of Jews and excluded the interests of Arabs and others, but the pioneers considered these arrangements temporary and took for granted that the national home would, in becoming a state, enact a democratic constitution. During the 1950s, however, Israel's first Prime Minister, David Ben-Gurion, consolidated the Israeli state by absorbing into its bureaucratic apparatus some of the most exclusionary Zionist institutions, which he thought would help settle new waves of Jewish immigrants. Ben-Gurion's improvisations in building the state were certainly never designed to accommodate the plural society Israel finally became under his tenure.

Prospects for completing Israel's democracy only grew dimmer after 1967, following military victory and the conquest and occupation of the West Bank and Gaza. Until the Lebanon invasion of 1982, certainly, greater and greater numbers of Israelis, perhaps the majority, came to accept a conception of Zionism that was utterly nationalist, self-absorbed, and bent on "redeeming" the land of biblical Israel. None of this may be as confounding to Israeli democracy as the actions taken in Zionism's name since 1977, when Menachem Begin was first elected Prime Minister. Occupation has given rise to what has seemed, at least superficially, the official revival of Zionist pioneering. Some 45,000 Jewish settlers have established homes all over the West Bank and have helped to frustrate the search for political compromise with the Palestinians.

The replacement of Begin by Shimon Peres has allowed that search to be cautiously renewed. But can any Israeli leader reverse the annexation of Jerusalem, or annexationist trends in the West Bank and Gaza which preempt moderate Palestinians and Jordanians? Meanwhile, the settlements have intensified the alienation of Israeli Jews from all Palestinian Arabs—not only the residents of the occupied territories, but also the Israeli Arabs who comprise one sixth of the state's enfranchised population. The civil rights of both the Israeli Arab minority and of Israeli Jews who dissent from Orthodox law have been obscured by the settlers' messianic rhetoric. Even young Israelis who do not support annexation of the occupied territories have begun to think of Zionism as a mandate, if not properly the means, to unite the ancient land; indeed, more and more have become cynical about democratic practices.

.

In calling this book *The Tragedy of Zionism,* I do not mean to suggest that Zionism is some historical misfortune. Rather, that Labor Zionism is a good revolution that long ago ran its course, that it stopped short of its liberal-democratic goals, and that recent efforts to reinvigorate Zionism in Israel have only brought Israelis more misfortune. Israeli political life may be admirable when compared with the regimes of its Arab neighbors, but any such comparisons are cold comfort to those Israelis—the people with whom American Jews have the most in common—who are properly anxious that their liberties not only may not be extended but may be ruined. How many Israeli youngsters will learn to appreciate democratic standards so long as they view themselves as engaged in a revolutionary Zionist struggle against a major part of their country's citizens? Democratic ways of thinking would come easier with peace, no doubt, though a commitment to democratic values may also be peace's prerequisite. Still, the prospects for peace cannot be advanced by any new Zionist achievements. If the West Bank (including Arab Jerusalem) and Gaza remain a part of Israel there will be more wars. At best, Israeli Jews will be faced eventually with the choice of expelling many more Palestinian Arabs, or living with them in an unequal society. Neither result is inevitable, but neither can be precluded by more military victories.

To be sure, Labor Zionism's tragedy is that of all revolutionary movements. No vanguard group has ever fully anticipated the political force of its theories and practices. Ironically, peace is now farther away than it might have been just because most new immigrants to Israel since the 1950s have revolted against Labor Zionism's economic power and social theories, and have in consequence voted for Labor's most reactionary rivals. Labor Zionists cannot properly be blamed for having tried to impose their vision on all the people who became Israelis—Sephardi Jews, Soviet Jewish refugees, Orthodox. Yet Labor Zionism's failure to do so only underscores how misguided is the impulse to meet the challenges of post-Zionist Israel with obsolete strategies for pioneering settlement or idle talk about "ingathering" Western Jewry from their "flesh pots." Thirty-seven years after Bonaparte, Frenchmen who could not shed the promise of Brumaire inadvertently cleared the field for Louis Napoleon. Israel was founded thirty-seven years ago; will it be said of Israelis, too, that outdated Zionist ways of thinking helped to obscure what might have been historic Zionism's great achievement, namely, a democratic Jewish state?

.

A few words about this book's method. Since its inception, the World Zionist Organization had been dominated by a number of successive and quite distinct tendencies. In Part One, I have considered how each emerged, keeping as much as possible to the events which determined the course of the movement as a whole. At times, particularly in the first three chapters, I have given rather careful attention to some of the Zionist arguments which predated Labor Zionism, and I have also reproduced the voices of their proponents. There are good reasons to have done both, not the least of which is the habit of many people in Israel and America of claiming Zionism for purposes few historic Zionists would recognize. Also, Israeli political discourse is never without references to these early Zionist theories—actually, to abstracted parts of them. Israelis speak of historic Zionists the way Americans speak of the Federalists, or Frenchmen speak of Rousseau and Voltaire.

However, the main purpose of Part One is to explain how the Zionists' debates impinged on the evolution of Labor Zionist institutions. My argument is written and footnoted in the manner of a historical essay, and some of my specific interpretations of the work of Zionist thinkers, particularly the connection between Achad Haam and A. D. Gordon, may break new ground. I have tried to take a fresh look at many historic events. Yet I have not written a history of Zionism or of Zionist ideas. Rather, historical illustrations are used to explain Zionist institutions more fully, to depict the action of Zionist ideas in a succession of episodes upon which the Zionist revolution turned. I have certainly not meant for anybody to consider the career of Zionist ideas as if from the past forward; indeed, my introduction to Part One only touches on the social, economic, and moral conditions of the Eastern Jews. Rather, I've examined some of the origins of Zionism only to help illuminate what Israelis now think or claim, or to help explain the political and legal world in which Israelis live.

In Part Two, I've endeavored to show how Labor Zionism became preoccupied with the struggle for a Jewish state despite the fact that statehood was not a critical element in Labor Zionist ideology. I have attempted to explain how Labor Zionist institutions successfully, and humanely, confronted the challenge of an Arab majority in Palestine—and how those very institutions antagonized the Sephardi immigrants whom the state of Israel hoped to assimilate during the 1960s. My main purpose in Part Three has been to consider the changes in the moral perceptions of Israelis since 1967, and to outline some of the diplomatic changes brought on by the occupation of the West Bank and Gaza. In a concluding chapter about the 1984 elections, I have tried to examine the impact of the occupation on Israeli democracy.

Finally, there is a cautionary saying from the Mishnah: *"Gilah tefach v'chisah tefachaim,"* which is to say, "He shows his palm and hides the content of both hands." Those who are reading about Zionist leaders for the first time should take this to heart: Zionists appear here mainly as personifications of their ideologies, and who knows what really causes a man to act? Yet if I have failed to do justice to the people beneath the ideologies, it is not for want of admiration. Nor does my argument suggest how any Israelis or American Jews have failed Zionism. On the contrary, my point is that it may finally be time to retire everybody's Zionism, time for more democracy, for what some Zionists used to call "normalcy."

PART ONE

Revolution: The Making of

Zionist Institutions

Introduction / The Jewish Problem

People who want to appreciate the weight of democratic values within historic Zionism must first try to imagine how Zionist ideas appeared to the Jews for whom they were intended. Zionism arose in Eastern Europe during the twenty years following the pogroms of 1881. How insubstantial its claims must have seemed to the embattled Eastern European Jews of the Pale of Settlement!

The pressures on the Eastern Jews had been building for half a century, since czarist ministers began to oust them from the countryside and drive them to the cities. Though Napoleon had emancipated the Jews of his empire in 1807, eighteen years later, in 1825, Czar Nicholas I intensified persecution of the million and a half Jews who lived in his. Nicholas had been dismayed by Jewish sympathies for Napoleon's occupation.[1] He was determined to centralize control of the Russian Empire and russify its peoples. Czarist ministers repressed the kehilloth, the semiautonomous Jewish Municipal Corporations which had been supported by wealthy Jews and by levies on every Jew's income. By 1835, czarist officials were conscripting thousands of Jewish boys every year for a virtual lifetime of military service—a form of forced conversion.

The economic initiatives of the 1840s added burdens. In forcing Jews out of the liquor trade, the czarist state expropriated the livelihoods of tens of thousands of Jewish agents, manufacturers, and wholesalers. Heavy railroad construction, some of it financed by a small, rising class of Jewish bankers, damned to poverty more thousands of Jews engaged in the carriage trade. Alexander II's emancipation of the serfs in 1861—along with his crushing of the Polish revolt in 1863—further endangered thousands of Jews who had been acting as agents to the nobility or as rural moneylenders— occupations which had long before earned Jews the unyielding hatred of the peasantry.

Thus, more and more Jews, whose total population numbered about 3.5 million by the middle of the century, faced social and economic ruin. Tens of thousands made their way to the cities, desperate to practice some acquired craft or trade. Odessa was an obvious place to go, but thousands of Jews also began to populate the provincial cities of Poland. In 1802, for example, the Jewish population of Minsk was 2,176; by 1847 it had reached 12,976. In faraway Dvinsk, the figures for these years are 749 and 2,198. The Jews were not only highly visible in such cities but were on their way to becoming the new majority.[2] Czarist officials had not foreseen this, or how much trouble would be caused by so many literate, restless people: having adjusted to urban life, young Jews were increasingly drawn to the ideals of secular enlightenment and political liberty.

The Jews' hopes for liberal emancipation were disappointed when, in March 1881, Czar Alexander II was assassinated by an anarchist group, the Narodnaya Volya ("People's Will"), which included several Jews. After the assassination, anti-Semitism became Alexander III's great obsession. "It was the Jews who crucified Our Lord," he announced, "and spilled His precious blood." The Czar was convinced, as were many of his ministers, that Jews remaining in the countryside exploited the confused, disorganized, and unemployed Russian peasants whom Alexander II had freed from serfdom—though most of those 50 million peasants were impoverished by the sharp practice of the aristocracy. The chief procurator of the Holy Synod, Constantin Pobedonostsev, one of the leaders of the slavophile movement, held that Jews were a foreign growth on the Russian body politic, were purveyors not only of a subversive religious creed but of "materialism." The Jews, he said, would undermine the bond of family between the Czar, the Russian people, and the Mother Church.

Pobedonostsev subsidized the influential conservative and national press in an insidious campaign of Jew-baiting. The number of Jews active in revolutionary movements, though not small, was wildly exaggerated. Weird conspiracies were ascribed to Jews, precursors of the *The Protocols of the Elders of Zion*, which would appear mysteriously twenty years later. In this climate, Jews began to fear that those whom the state could not assimilate would have to disappear. An apocryphal story began to circulate that Pobedonostsev had already arrived at a formula that would doom them: one third by assimilation, one third by expulsion, one third by murder. One should note here that Russia's industrial proletariat increased more than sixfold between 1860 and 1913; only 8 or 9 percent were Jews, though a disproportionately large number of them joined—and led—proletarian movements. Still, Jews were far more concentrated in trades: 50 percent of the Russian work force in petty capitalism were Jews, most of them becoming more and more marginal to the industrializing cities where they had sought to make a new life.[3]

.

The 1881 pogroms started in April. By the end of that year, 215 Jewish communities had been attacked by mobs; about 100,000 Jews were left without means of gaining a livelihood. In Minsk, fully a fifth of the city—1,600 buildings—was razed. Deaths numbered in the hundreds, and the pogromists seemed particularly bent on abusing Jewish women. These deeds humiliated all Jews; but particularly young men so recently caught up in the struggle for enlightenment and, in consequence, unable to find solace in prayer or in a traditional faith in Judaism's superiority. (One Yiddish song of the day included the haunting words: "Brides taken from their grooms, children from their mothers: Shout, children, loud and clear . . . you can wake your father up, *as if he were asleep for real.*") In May 1882, Minister of the Interior Nikolai Pavlovich Ignatiev promulgated the May Laws. Once in the cities, the laws decreed, Jews could not return to the countryside, and those who remained in villages—perhaps two fifths of the total Jewish population—could expect little protection from the Czar's provincial governors. Jews could expect harassment from the police and, indeed, could be expelled to the cities by summary verdicts of rural courts made up of half-literate *muzhiks.*

In developing the May Laws, the czarist ministers may have been acting as much out of their fear of the pogromist mobs as out of their anti-Semitism. It was easy to imagine restive peasants eventually turning their ire on the Czar and the aristocracy—a strong reason to evacuate the Jews from the countryside more quickly, and ruthlessly, than before. In any case, the flow of Jews to the cities now turned into a flood. By 1897, the Jewish population of Minsk was 47,562; it was 32,400 in Dvinsk. In Minsk, the Jews finally comprised 52 percent of the whole population; in Bialystok, 63 percent. Nor did the Russian urban capitalists welcome these new arrivals. Even Jewish capitalists continued to prefer Russian workers over destitute Jewish craftsmen. One did not have to give the Russian peasant what the Jew expected: Saturdays off, a wage sufficient to educate a son, and a bar mitzvah present for that son.

In time the total Jewish population swelled to nearly 5 million, and hundreds of thousands were intimidated and went hungry. Young Jews felt themselves caught between the lure of modern life and a new age of barbarism, unable to go forward and unable to go back. Most were seized with the desire to act dramatically in defense of Jewish interests; indeed, thousands seemed bent on fulfilling Pobedonostsev's prophecy: they became increasingly impatient, radical, nationalist. Yet their miserable life did not make the value of a Zionist movement seem obvious. To many, the ideal of a Jewish national home in biblical Eretz Yisrael only mocked their condition.

.

What excited most of these people was not any movement but an impulse to motion—that is, the passage of ships from Odessa to New York. Between 1881 and 1914, 2.5 million Jews emigrated from the Russian Empire. Of these, 2 million settled in America and only 30,000 made their way to Palestine. American democracy was, and remains, Zionism's great rival in providing for the safety of Jews. The raw numbers do not reflect the divided feelings of the emigrants or the relative merit of any particular decision. The emigrants who considered themselves the most fortunate—about half a million—found homes in Vienna, Berlin, Paris, or London, places where the emancipation and enlightenment of Jews resulted from what seemed long-standing rights. Who knows where most of these people would have chosen to go had they not believed that they needed to earn a livelihood in the American boom? Indeed, many were merely following the example of pluckier relatives; in *Call It Sleep*, Henry Roth compares those immigrants to the boats they landed on, "backing water, drifting slowly and with cancelled momentum."[4]

Yet for the intellectuals among the emigrants, America, too, meant the more abstract promise of emancipation. After all, America was an English-speaking world which might be liberal in spirit. What readers of Tolstoy had not heard of Dickens and Abraham Lincoln? Once in New York, Irving Howe writes, the intelligentsia was bristling with texts: "Mention of Nietzsche brings the talk back to Wagner's music, Gorky's novels, Zola's realism; 'all these things had to be decided upon . . . by people who understand them, more or less.' "[5]

Some Zionist doctrines were imported by the immigrants, and they competed with the *Jewish Daily Forward's* Yiddish socialism to challenge liberal values and the urge to assimilate. The images attaching to Zionism—of Hebrew Jews living in the Promised Land —were revered in sweatshops and mills. But doctrines, too, were stations on the way to America.

It was America, not Zionism, which appealed to that minority of Orthodox Jews who, in leaving the Pale, were not seeking the uncertainties of modernity. America was a huge, expanding country whose citizens came from everywhere and which demanded less religious conformity than even the most tolerant countries of Western Europe. Immigrant rabbis, to be sure, were appalled by what Roth called America's "side-walk-and-gutter generation." But the Orthodox had a vivid sense of themselves within their Torah culture; they had laws, ritual commandments, and an oral tradition of rabbis who interpreted both. They needed only freedom to establish the homeland Heinrich Heine said they carried "on their backs."

Pious Jews traditionally worshipped the idea of a return to the land of Israel; Eretz Yisrael provided them with a reference point on a kind of spiritual map. However, the map corresponded to no actual territory, unless it was to the distant, destroyed world of harvests, prophets, and sacrifices, now honored as liturgical symbols. Though every year Jews concluded the Passover seder with the fervent prayer to be "next year" in Jerusalem, this was an expression of a corresponding hope: that the peace of Jerusalem, or what the rabbis now called the "higher Jerusalem," would finally extend to Minsk, Kishinev—or, indeed, Brooklyn.[6] Messianic rhetoric—including prophetic calls to "ingather the exiles"— eventually influenced Zionist politics. When Zionism was getting started, however, it was part of what obstructed the development of Zionist thought.

The Jews who actually lived in Jerusalem were addled and shabby representatives of their Orthodox brethren in Eastern Europe. Most went there not to live but to die. Jews who were born in Jerusalem enjoyed a certain prestige—perhaps the right to wear a gold coat on the New Year instead of a black one. But their lives were centered on the schools, yeshivas, and synagogues, and they certainly enjoyed no moral advantage over scholars at such great centers of Jewish learning as Vilna. The founders of the Mea Shearim quarter in Jerusalem supported themselves by making souvenirs, sachets of "holy earth," penholders of olivewood. The cabalists of Safad and many Hasidic sects lived mainly from funds collected in Europe, usually (ironically) on the night of the first Passover seder. However, there were no Zionists among Palestinian Jews until secular Jewish immigrants founded colonies on the coastal plain during the 1880s. Only then did some religious Jews leave Jerusalem to establish such Zionist colonies as Petach Tiqvah.

Meanwhile, Eastern European rabbis expelled from rabbinic schools students with secularist or nationalist leanings. The rabbis regularly condemned and obstructed the meetings of secular Hebrew groups, and their animus grew more fierce after 1897, when —following Theodor Herzl's call for a Jewish state—the influence of Zionism spread rapidly. For the rabbis, this was an impudent attempt to defy God's will. The daily prayers stated that Jews had been exiled "for their sins." Zionism seemed the product of heretical questions. As if to confirm this, many Zionist writers vehemently repudiated traditional law. The rabbis were the very bane of early Zionism, worse than the left-wing Yiddishists with whom it was at least possible to argue for secular nationalism. The socialist-Zionist Nachman Syrkin wrote in 1901 that the Jewish masses were being "stultified by ignorance, Orthodox obscurantism, and Talmudic idolatry," that Jewish Orthodoxy—"which Heine described brilliantly not as a religion but a misfortune"—was the chief obstacle "to culture, knowledge, emancipation," and "to the illumination of the socialist and national ideal."[7]

1 / Political Zionism

Their desire for emancipation raises the question of whether the early Zionists were disposed to democratic ideals. In fact, Zionist theorists were preoccupied with other questions. They sought to define the problem—what most Zionists frankly called the "Jewish problem"—which emigration to a national home solved but which seemed impossible to resolve by more conventional means, including the struggle for democracy. This is not to say Zionists were indifferent to democratic norms. If the Jews were to repair to a national home, they asked themselves, by what political and moral principles should it be governed? How could individual Jews exert political power? Obviously it was impossible to address such questions without taking into account how democratic norms might be applied. Ordinary Zionist cadres wanted their revolutionary organizations to be as democratic as possible—to be voluntarist, open to new recruits, and tolerant of dissent; all were eager to avoid factional splits.

Still, no Jew identified with the Zionist cause for the sake of "democracy." Like "peace" or "normalcy," democracy was an ultimate good. A belief in, say, individual liberty or majority rule did not, in any case, distinguish the Zionist from the Jew who went west, went underground, or joined the Yiddish proletarian organizations.

Thus, to understand how much democracy the Zionist movement would ultimately create for the state of Israel, one must examine the way Zionist institutions evolved in Europe and the Yishuv before the state came into being. One must begin with the attitudes of the early Zionist writers, and with the skepticism with which their ideas were greeted. The fate of Israeli democracy was by no means determined by the course of early Zionist attitudes. Yet the institutions out of which Israeli democracy had to be organized owed much to them.

i

For the early Zionists, democratic values were embedded in a number of prior questions, many of them complex and charged with emotion. Zionists asked themselves if they should choose Palestine or some other country, if they should start collective farms or promote private enterprise. Another question was even more fundamental: Should immigration be organized en masse, by a sovereign Zionist "corporation," though any such method of settling the Jewish national home was bound to produce a mix of European languages there? Or should priority be given to supporting small groups of cultural pioneers who were devoted to evolving modern Hebrew, however gradually? Should Zionism wait for support from the imperial powers or go it alone in small vanguard groups?

During Zionism's formative period, there were two major efforts to provide answers: "political" Zionism and "cultural" (or "practical") Zionism. The dominant trend, which developed mainly in Eastern Europe in response to political Zionism, was cultural Zionism. The cultural Zionists succeeded in defining the goals which the Labor Zionist parties would eventually implement. The first trend in Zionism, political Zionism, appealed mainly to Western European intellectuals and contributed little in the way of an ideology to the people who built up the Yishuv. Political Zionist prejudices were absorbed into Zionist myth as the Yishuv moved inexorably toward self-determination during the 1930s. Only after they were thought— rightly or wrongly—to anticipate the bitter lessons of World War II did they put cultural Zionism in eclipse.

The political Zionists favored the vigorous pursuit of an international charter which would enable Jews to emigrate en masse to Palestine or some other available territory. Political Zionists saw

Jews as vulnerable to Gentile persecution; their suspicions about anti-Semitic tendencies among Western European intellectuals were especially acute. A Jewish state, political Zionists thought, would provide a strategic base for self-defense. Yet their emphatic desire for a state superseded their attachment to the ancient land of Israel. What political Zionists daydreamed about was national sovereignty in a territory separate from Europe, a new land where Jewish self-respect could be nurtured. They craved international recognition for Jewish national rights. They considered territorial claims, like all national claims, to be self-conscious symbols of Jewish power and renewal; their use of national symbols—a flag, an anthem—suggested regained national élan.

When the political Zionists finally settled on—few actually settled in—Palestine, they claimed the whole land and demanded the support of the Great Powers of Europe and even of the Ottoman Empire. Political Zionists viewed Jews as a permanent minority in a natural order that made national antagonisms inevitable and crushed weakness. To declare oneself a Zionist was therefore a crucial decision for the political Zionist: it made one take a stand, made one more the creature of progress and *Realpolitik*. Correspondingly, political Zionists thought Zionist leaders should speak as if from a government-in-exile and offer a kind of citizenship.

Still, the political Zionist demand for "historic" rights to Palestine was not intended actually to determine the routine of an individual settler's daily life there. Most political Zionists ignored the quotidian, or thought about individuals in relation to the market economy, which, most thought, determined one's struggle for existence in a natural way. Political Zionists were reluctant even to pronounce about such personal matters as the settler's language and culture. More important than providing a home for Hebrew life, they thought, was giving the lie to Gentile anxieties about the "homeless" Jews in their midst.

This is not to say that political Zionists were immune to the appeal of social democracy, or of any other political economic program which could make the market society work more fairly for the national good. Once the Yishuv was a going concern, people who had been political Zionists supported Hebrew education, even in the Diaspora. But for political Zionists the main point of politics was creating the state apparatus itself, which would preside over individuals and embody their general will. Indeed, the arguments of the political Zionists usually relied heavily on such psychological categories as "will," "pride," and "recognition." They spoke frankly of "symbols," "honor," "normalcy." They were keen to show physical courage. Their claim for a state derived from the conviction that "power," the exercise of sovereignty, was a kind of psychological therapy for people made unattractive by a want of self-confidence.

Intriguingly, political Zionists often accepted as true some of the anti-Semite's most outrageous stereotypes of the Jew. It was the undignified Jew, after all, who most needed the help they sought to provide. (Arthur Koestler wrote that he had become a Communist out of hatred for the poor and a political Zionist out of hatred for the Yid.) Accordingly, political Zionists were often unable to articulate precisely what Jewish principles were to be defended—apart from an assertion that the Jewish people should survive. Political Zionism promoted such things as dueling fraternities, songs and marches, and a rather atavistic notion of nationalism. In some cases, political Zionist ideas were at variance not only with the ideals of democratic pluralism but with the ideals of normative Judaism as well. Indeed, political Zionists spoke of an "organic," uniform bond among Jews. They dismissed as trivial and fractious the rivalries among Orthodox, Reform, secularist, and proletarian Jews. Though political Zionists did not frown on pluralism in principle, only a few, including Theodor Herzl himself, could conceive of civil tolerance among people who did not share each other's cultural dreams. Why be a Zionist if the liberal state could work?

The political Zionists were most persuasive, obviously, when physical dangers to Jews were great enough to preclude questions about what made the Jews a people apart from Gentile anti-Semitism. The Gentiles, or so political Zionists claimed, would never let Jews assimilate. Individual Jews might try to do so, but common prejudice would drive them all together and teach them that they were, after all, necessary to one another. This conviction was often the product of a personal disappointment; it is not surprising, then, that many of the mentors of political Zionism—Leo Pinsker, Herzl, and Vladimir Jabotinsky—were themselves people who had tried to assimilate and, unexpectedly, failed.

ii

Leo Pinsker was raised in Odessa, that most cosmopolitan of Russia's cities. His father, Simcha Pinsker, was a Hebrew scholar and *maskil* (or enlightened Jew) who had admired the reforms of Alexander II. Leo was given a secular Russian-language education, acquiring only a smattering of Hebrew at home. He then attended the University of Moscow and, in 1844, acquired a degree in law. Several years later, increasingly frustrated by the prohibitions against Jewish lawyers pleading in court or entering the state's legal service, Pinsker turned to medicine. He became a physician specializing in psychological disorders, and indeed, it was in treating the depressions of his patients that Pinsker appropriated the principles which would later influence his political thinking about the Jewish problem.

That his Jewish origins prevented him from following his preferred career did not lead Pinsker away from his assimilationist course. He certainly kept aloof from the swelling Jewish ghettoes. In 1863 he joined the Society for the Spread of Enlightenment among the Russian Jews, a group actively committed to russification of the Jews. Even the vicious Easter pogroms in Odessa in 1871 failed to sway him. He continued to believe that models for Jewish emancipation in Germany and France could be made to apply in liberalizing Russia. It took the events of 1881 to make Pinsker realize that Jewish life in Russia might be doomed.

After the pogroms, writing furiously, Pinsker produced *Auto-Emancipation*, a polemical pamphlet in which he totally repudiated his former faith in Russian liberalism. Now, far from advocating cultural assimilation, Pinsker invited the Jews to imagine themselves citizens of a Jewish state, outside the reach of hostile Gentiles. The Jews were inherently indigestible, Pinsker thought, not because they were culturally distinct—he casually denied that the Jews could be said to share "a common language and common customs" —but because the Jews suffered from a kind of moribund quality typical of people who have lost the approving recognition of others.

The essence of the problem as we see it lies in the fact that, in the midst of the nations among whom the Jews reside, they form a distinctive element which cannot be assimilated, which cannot be readily digested by any nation . . . The Jewish people has no fatherland of its own, though many motherlands; it has no rallying point, no centre of gravity, no government of its own, no representatives. It is everywhere a guest, nowhere at home.[1]

Pinsker began *Auto-Emancipation* with an epigraph—really a truncated version of the sage Hillel's most famous saying: "If I am not for myself, who will be for me? And if not now, when?" (He omitted the part that goes: "If I am for myself alone, what am I?") The Jews had lost pride in their "nation," and thus the will to live; their misfortunes, he wrote, "are due above all to their lack of desire for national independence."

On the face of it, the opposite claim was more plausible: Pinsker's dream of national independence—indeed, his willingness to con- sider himself part of the Jewish nation at all—was due "above all" to anti-Semitic persecution. But this is to underestimate the original- ity of Pinsker's approach and, in any case, what made the political Zionist tradition he initiated distinctive. For Pinsker, nations were produced by subtle fellow feeling, by psychological, not cultural, ties; nations emerged inevitably from the world's competitive, abra- sive conditions, its "inherent, national antagonisms." The ideal of international harmony was nothing more than a dangerous illusion. Indeed, the Jews' phlegmatic posture in the middle of this war of all against all was their "mark of Cain," which "repels non-Jews and is painful to the Jews themselves."

The Jews, Pinsker wrote, were "a ghostlike apparition of a people without unity or organization, without land or any bond of union, no longer alive and yet moving among the living." Jews had to over- come the moralistic hallucinations that kept them from seeing what (he thought) Darwin saw: that only the fit survive, that weak- ness inspires attack.

Auto-Emancipation, which was first published anonymously in Berlin in 1882, made few specific recommendations about how to achieve a Jewish state. It was as if the mere statement of Pinsker's diagnosis would shock his patients into self-correcting actions. The geographic location of the new Jewish state was certainly a matter of indifference to him, though he had a particular disdain for "ancient Judea," the place where "our political life was once interrupted and destroyed." All he insisted on was that the land be "productive" and "well-located" and big enough to settle "millions." It might be a part of North America, or a sovereign pashalik of Asiatic Turkey. Pinsker gave little thought to whether the Jewish home would be a democracy, or to any other constitutional arrangements. He was also uninterested in linguistic and cultural matters. As to organization, Pinsker proposed that Jews have a directorate, along with "an associated body of capitalists," to secure the assent of other European governments: "The struggle of Jews for unity and independence . . . is calculated to attract the sympathy of people to whom we are rightly or wrongly obnoxious."

It seems worth reiterating that, for traditional Jews, persecution and dishonor are not necessarily the same experience. Jews who had suffered persecution were honored in legend, and their words were often absorbed into the liturgy. Yet *Auto-Emancipation* caused a sensation in some of the secularist Jewish circles of Odessa. In the wake of the pogroms, several hundred vanguard intellectuals had founded a Hebrew cultural society and underground movement which they called Hibat Zion—"the Love of Zion"—an organization devoted to Hebrew education and national revival. Could such values ever be fostered in Russia? Though its author was unknown, *Auto-Emancipation* soon became the basic manifesto of Hibat Zion's leaders—including M. L. Lilienblum, Hermann Zvi Shapira, and Emanuel Mandelstamm. These men had been inclined toward a "territorial solution" in Eretz Yisrael. They ignored *Auto-Emancipation*'s opposition to settling in ancient Judea and welcomed its general and forceful arguments for Jewish independence and colonization of a national home.

Lilienblum, Hibat Zion's preeminent writer, had become fascinated, like so many other enlightened Jews, with the prospect of reshaping traditional Jewish texts to fit liberal and scientific premises. He had wanted to make of the Jews' legal and literary tradition a reservoir of material for modern ethics. Typically, Lilienblum had briefly involved himself in Russian letters, but even before the 1881 pogroms he had lost faith in Russian culture. He had immersed himself in Hebrew, writing essays, biography, and occasional poetry. After the pogroms, Lilienblum realized that the future of Jewish life and certainly of a Hebrew renaissance was in jeopardy. But where else could modern Hebrew be evolved?

When the identity of *Auto-Emancipation*'s author was revealed, Lilienblum was particularly impressed that so privileged a Jew as Pinsker would cast his fate with ghetto Jews. He prevailed upon Pinsker to take on the leadership of Hibat Zion and use what influence he had to raise funds and help develop the political structure of the movement. In 1884, Pinsker convened Hibat Zion's first large meeting at Kattowitz. Hibat Zion's membership rose to a peak of about 14,000 in 1885—mostly in loosely connected, underground cultural circles which met in the homes of various writers and activists—an impressive figure, but small as compared with proletarian movements also in formation at that time.

iii

In the wake of the pogroms, groups of young Jewish intellectuals loosely associated with what would become Hibat Zion went to Eretz Yisrael in a spontaneous show of revolutionary zeal; they founded Rishon Le'Zion and Zichron Yaacov. Joining them after the Kattowitz conference were more youngsters from Kharkov and St. Petersburg—and also from Rumania, where independence from the Turks had given rise to anti-Semitic legislation. Many of those young settlers had been inspired by Tolstoyan ideals; they had said, vaguely, that they wanted to become a Hebrew peasantry and live an autonomous style of life "on their native soil." In fact, they quickly became dependent on Hibat Zion help; those who were intensely idealistic did the least well.

The most interesting of the early settlers, certainly the most celebrated, were the Biluim. They were also Zionism's most spectacular failure. In 1881, prodded by Israel Belkind, students in Kharkov conceived a plan for a model community in Palestine. It not only would be Hebrew-speaking and nationalist in spirit but was to be organized along collectivist lines. Belkind's group viewed Jewish agriculture as a moral duty, one that would permit them to transform the country and win sovereignty by degrees. Young men were to be instructed in the use of weapons; like the Guardians of Plato's Republic, they would forswear private property and devote their "strength, power, and courage to the good of the society."[2] When they finally set out for Palestine in June 1882—under the slogan *"Beit Yaacov L'Chu V'Nelcha"* ("House of Jacob, let us arise and go": hence the acronym BILU)—several members of the group remained in Constantinople to petition for favors from the Ottoman sultanate. But instead of the three thousand cadres they had hoped to attract, only about fifty finally assembled in Palestine. In 1884, the Biluim founded a permanent settlement in Gedera. Half their number abandoned it within two years.

The Biluim may have been perceptive to see that the national ideal would require a collective economic base to flourish, but their ideas were too abstract and their party organization too feeble to support them through their many personal hardships. Besides, there was as yet no established class of Jewish landowners and capitalists in Palestine against which the Biluim might pit their proletarian ideals. There was too little wealth in Palestine's Jewish economy and too little incentive to create it. Settlers were bound to get lonely, tired, sick; only direct material rewards, it seemed, could strengthen their resolve. The Palestinian settlements that did prosper were not the products of such rigorous ideology but of a combination of private enterprise and philanthropy.

Like the Biluim, the colonists of Rishon Le'Zion and Zichron Yaacov were destitute soon enough. But unlike the Biluim, they successfully sought out conventional sources of help. In 1882, Yosef Fineberg, a member of Rishon Le'Zion, convinced Pinsker to join in a delegation to Baron Edmond de Rothschild of Paris. Though the baron had been deeply moved by the consequences of the pogroms in the East, he was hardly a Jewish nationalist; Rothschild was, if anything, keen to convince his Gentile associates that being Jewish did not mean being disloyal to one's country. Yet he agreed to a series of subsidies for Fineberg's colony, and his donation inaugurated a twenty-year involvement with other settlers as well. Before he was through, Rothschild spent £1.5 million, far more than anything the Hibat Zion groups could have raised on their own in Russia and Poland. Rothschild's subsidies were, from the beginning, indispensable to Hibat Zion's program of colonization. Indeed, the First "Ascent," or "Aliyah," of Jews to Palestine would have been impossible without him.

.

The reliance of Hibat Zion on Rothschild money set the stage for what would later be seen as Zionism's first internal dispute. From the beginning, Rothschild made it clear that his support for

Palestinian settlement—he called them "my colonies"—was philanthropic, and that he expected the colonists to make their settlements
commercially self-sustaining. He insisted that viniculture be their
basic industry, in part because he was involved with the wine trade
in Europe. Nor did he take chances with the settlers: to see that his
conditions were met, Rothschild stationed personal representatives
in Palestine, and these people increasingly saw themselves as managers of the colonial enterprises.

It should be noted here that by 1890 the number of Jewish agricultural settlers in Palestine was climbing to 3,000. By 1891, the
year of Pinsker's death, there were at least fifty-three societies of
Hibat Zion, all with dues-paying members. The Odessa committee (the only one to gain legal status) consistently claimed about
4,000 members—or about one third the total. Still, Hibat Zion's
total income had never reached more than 40,000–50,000 rubles per
annum—a hopelessly small sum considering that it took about 3,000
rubles to settle one family on the land.[3] Fourteen colonies in Palestine were growing dependent on Hibat Zion to some extent, and new
lands would be acquired at Hadera (between Haifa and Jaffa), at
Mishmar Hayarden, Motsa, Metulla.

Inevitably, Rothschild's notion of private enterprise contradicted
the cultural ambitions of new colonists. Rothschild's demand that
Hebrew nationalism be put on a low flame offended many of Hibat
Zion's supporters in Russia. The fact that Rothschild wanted the
colonists to turn a profit can hardly be held against him, but wine
making was precisely the kind of industry to crimp the colonists'
cultural goals. Unlike the fruit, vegetable, and dairy farming by
which the Biluim had hoped—and later failed—to build Jewish
self-sufficiency, viniculture tied the settlers to the world market.
Worse, it entailed the intensive use of Arab labor. Jewish colonists
quickly discovered that they could not speak much Hebrew to each
other while they were overseeing Arab workers.

Rothschild's involvement was thus both a godsend and an embarrassment for Hibat Zion. The colonies did exist, but they were
not really carrying out the mandate Hibat Zion members in Eastern
Europe had set for them. In 1889, in his landmark essay, which he
called "This Is Not the Way," Asher Ginzberg, a young intellectual
from Odessa, articulated the mounting reservations felt by Hibat

Zion activists regarding the First Ascent. Writing under the pen name Achad Haam ("one of the people"), he observed that, although the colonies should have become a place for political action, they had made only economic gains. Were materialist gains for individuals also material gains for Hebrew culture? Now, Achad Haam maintained, the national ideal was still a "tender and young plant," and (extending the metaphor in a somewhat disagreeable way) he charged that overfeeding would kill it. He seemed unperturbed by the failure of the Biluim—it is not clear how much he knew about them—and he called for idealistic men and women who would forswear private advantage for the "national ideal."

In 1891, and again in 1893, Achad Haam joined Hibat Zion fact-finding missions to Palestine, and if anything, these only strengthened his views. His faith in voluntarism was somewhat shaken—the failure of the Biluim finally hit home—but Achad Haam saw all too clearly the dangers of an economy based on viniculture. By now about 15,000 settlers had entered Palestine. Achad Haam worried about an Arab majority whose proportion of the population might be increased if the colonies continued to abide by Rothschild's conditions. He implied that a new way of settlement would have to be found that would establish Jews in the land without making them dependent on greater numbers of Arab inhabitants. This would be good politics, but also good for the Hebrew language. Nothing irked him more than the prospect of Jewish settlers adopting Arabic as the language of work. "The Arabs are not wild men of the desert," Achad Haam wrote in "The Truth from Eretz Yisrael": "If in the course of time the Jewish holding in the country develops to such an extent that it encroaches on the native population, the latter will not easily give up its position."[4]

During the years that followed, Achad Haam grew increasingly hostile to the materialism of the First Ascent and disenchanted with a Hibat Zion leadership which saw itself constrained to support it. More and more, he went his own way, founding first an elite literary circle called the Bnei Moshe ("Son of Moses") and later becoming editor of a new Hebrew journal, *Ha'Shiloach* (the name of a spring in Jerusalem whose waters, so the Torah says, "flow slowly"—implying that the work of Hebrew culturists could not be rushed). It was just about this time—in 1896—that the Eastern European Jews got wind of Theodor Herzl.

iv

Herzl's name is so closely connected with the reputation of Zionism that it is astonishing to discover how far removed he was from the crucial Zionist debates that were conducted among the Eastern European Jews from 1881 on. We shall see that, eventually, Herzl gave the stalwarts of Hibat Zion a desperately needed new structure, the "Zionist Congress," and the means to raise funds from sources other than philanthropists such as Rothschild. For a while, he united all Zionists by the force of his passion. Yet Herzl's views could not be called original. Indeed, they conformed so closely to Pinsker's that Herzl immediately inherited many of Pinsker's critics, including Achad Haam. (Herzl's initial impatience with his critics may be explained, in part, by his never having heard of Pinsker or Achad Haam. Nor could he have named any of the Yishuv's colonies at the moment he declared himself a Zionist.)

Herzl was born in Budapest in 1860, and was brought up speaking German by parents whose Reform Jewish practice was vague and mechanical. Before he was a teenager, the family moved to Vienna, where *Kultur* and steam power were thought to be transforming the world. "I have pondered a great deal on the purpose of human existence," Herzl wrote in a high-school essay, "[and] all the clever frauds of men like Moses, Jesus, and the Count of St. Germain have already been exposed by the human spirit. It will undoubtedly soon unravel the last and final secrets of the human order."[5] Such views give added meaning to the wry remark of Moses Hess—Karl Marx's mentor, who late in life became a prophet of Hebrew nationalism —that the Jews' Reform movement in Germany had only "the negative purpose of establishing *disbelief* as the foundation of religion."[6]

Vienna's Jews numbered something under 10,000 when the Herzls moved there. Hess was certainly right, if ungenerous, to imply that by their Reform Judaism they had renounced the communitarian works of Eastern Orthodoxy in favor of an individualist faith. Most "Germans of the Mosaic persuasion," as many called themselves, became avid champions of religious privatism, searching traditional Jewish law for precedents that could be thought compatible with the freedoms of civil society. "The Jews," Heine wrote, "may console themselves for the loss of Jerusalem and the Ark of the Covenant, for this loss is but a trifling when compared with the Bible, the indestructible treasure they have saved." Moses had been the first to demand that slaves be freed, Heine asserted, and their law prescribed shaming servants who refused freedom by puncturing their earlobes: "O Moses, our teacher, Moshe Rabbeinu, exalted enemy of serfdom, I pray thee furnish me with hammer and nails that I may nail our willing slaves, in their liveries of black, red and gold, by their long ears to the Brandenburg gate!"[7]

After 1881, however, another kind of Jew was coming to Vienna; Eastern European Jewish immigrants fleeing the pogroms would increase Vienna's Jewish population to nearly 100,000 by 1899. Neither the city's Gentile bourgeoisie nor Vienna's upper-middle-class Jews—among whom the Herzls now counted themselves— could ignore this state of affairs. Families such as the Herzls found their Russian and Polish co-religionists philistine and kept their distance, trying to get closer to the aristocracy. The young Herzl in particular seemed drawn to the style of the aristocracy, which he thought a way of joining the nobility—as the historian Carl Schorske put it, "an aristocracy of spirit as a surrogate for an aristocracy of pedigree or patent." Herzl became a dandy, as if to ward off vulgar Jewish materialism. He dreamed of becoming a kind of local Disraeli, and set his sights on elegance, chivalry, service.[8]

Herzl studied Roman law at the University of Vienna. While a student, he joined the Burschenschaft Albia, a strongly nationalist dueling fraternity. In 1883, when that group participated in an anti-Semitic ceremony to commemorate Wagner's death, Herzl protested and was forced to withdraw. That the fraternity struck him off its rolls was a source of deep consternation for him. Herzl had not intended to make a stand for the sake of the Jews so much as to honor civility itself. Indeed, his views toward the Jews were still highly ambivalent: he considered many Jews deformed by the ghetto and unfit for public life. The year before, the year of the czarist May Laws in Russia, Herzl expressed a restrained solidarity with the Eastern European Jews, but also a condescension toward them. He had serenely noted in his diary that Jews everywhere would best be absorbed by intermarriage: "Cross-breeding of the occidental races with the so-called oriental one on the basis of a common state religion, this is the great desirable solution."[9] He had read Eugen Dühring's anti-Semitic book The Jewish Question, and with minor equivocations echoed the author's condemnation of "the crookedness of Jewish morality," the Jews' lamentable "lack of ethical seriousness." Then he added a prophetic afterthought: "An infamous book, [but] it is so well written, in such a deliciously pure and excellent German . . . When such vile stuff is expressed so sincerely, when Dühring with a mind so well-trained and penetrated with a deep universal learning is capable of writing it—what then are we to expect from the ignorant rabble?"

Herzl earned his degree in 1884, and his parents, who had always coddled him, now rewarded him with an extended European tour. It was on this trip that he first tried his hand at writing, composing a series of highly subjective travel essays which impressed the editors of the *Neue Freie Presse*, Vienna's most prestigious daily newspaper. The *Neue Freie Presse* published several of the pieces and invited Herzl to join its staff on his return. Thereafter, Herzl's life became a struggle to succeed in the stuffy, narcissistic, and increasingly anti-Semitic circles he frequented. (It was during this time that Karl Lueger first ran for mayor of Vienna on an openly anti-Semitic platform.)

To a large degree, Herzl did succeed. He became a well-known critic and man-about-town. Yet Herzl's great ambition was to become a successful playwright, what he thought was Vienna's most honored profession; in this he failed. His sense of frustration was exacerbated by the success of his university classmate and one-time protégé, Arthur Schnitzler. Gradually, Herzl became prone to melancholy, which grew worse in an unfortunate marriage. It seems he came to regard his wife, Julie, as the kind of spoiled and uninspired Jewish woman he ridiculed relentlessly in his plays. (Their domestic rift, which was worst during their early years together, took a toll on their children. All three fought mental illness most of their lives. The oldest, a daughter, committed suicide. Herzl's son converted to Christianity on the twentieth anniversary of his father's death; later, he too committed suicide. The youngest, Trude, died in a Nazi concentration camp.)

In 1891, the *Neue Freie Presse* appointed Herzl to the coveted post of Paris correspondent. At first the honor and the change of scene cheered him, but soon he was caught up in a deeply disturbing rush of events. In 1892 France was shocked by the Panama Scandal, a commercial bubble fraud in which several Jews were implicated. The Paris mobs now proved themselves as openly anti-Semitic as the ones Karl Lueger had been stirring up in Vienna. Insults were everywhere hurled at French Jews; Jewish shops were attacked. As the provocations reached a peak, several Jewish officers in the French Army answered those affronts in duels. This all impressed Herzl enormously. He had written in his journal some years before that he would himself like to challenge the likes of Lueger; now, for the first time, he noted that Europe was "enemy territory."

None of this is to imply that Herzl was as yet thinking in terms of Jewish nationalism. As late as 1893, his solution to the Jewish question was the mass conversion of Jewish children to Christianity. He toyed with the idea of contacting the Pope and inviting him to preside over such a ceremony at Vienna's St. Stephen's Cathedral; Herzl felt that honor demanded that he remain Jewish, but the children, at least, would be saved. Meanwhile, Herzl's literary work continued to betray traces of Jewish self-hatred. In 1894, Herzl wrote what he thought was his best play, *The New Ghetto*, which was full of anti-Jewish stereotypes—lives revolving around social climbing, marriages made for profit, stock-market manipulations. (Only one Jew, a man named Jacob, considers his people's honor and dies fighting a duel. In its original version, the play closed with a line insinuating that Gentiles would not let Jews live until Jews learned how to die noble deaths—though Herzl cut this line out of the published version after Schnitzler scolded him for it.)[10]

In 1895 Herzl witnessed Paris in an uproar again, this time over the trial of that unlikely spy (and more unlikely Jewish martyr) Captain Alfred Dreyfus. Shortly thereafter, Vienna's Burgtheater turned down Herzl's new play. "In a flash," or so he wrote, the idea of a Jewish state came to him and he began frantically to jot down some ideas outlining his plan. In May 1895, he requested an interview with Baron Maurice de Hirsch, who was then funding the settlement of Jews in Argentina. Like Pinsker, Herzl sought to get backing for a national corporation to settle Jews en masse somewhere outside the continent. But Hirsch was unreceptive both to Herzl's proposals and to him. So Herzl decided to compose an address to Edmond de Rothschild, and began by trying out his views in a series of appeals to Dr. Moritz Güdemann, the Chief

Rabbi of Vienna, who gave him some encouragement. It is from these ideas that Herzl constructed his most famous polemic, *The Jewish State*.

.

The Jewish State begins with a cursory analysis of anti-Semitism —a lightning rod for "commercial rivalry" and "an outgrowth of the emancipation of the Jews."[11] Herzl wrote that wherever the Jewish question did not exist, it would arise with any new Jewish immigration (a view that does not compare favorably, perhaps, with Jean-Paul Sartre's justly famous observation that where the Jews do not live, anti-Semites are disposed to invent them). The answer, in Herzl's view, was a separate "Society of Jews," to be led by a "Jewish Company." All would be achieved absolutely in accordance with the law. There would be a concurrent movement of Christians into the positions relinquished by Jews; the outflow would be gradual, without any disturbance, and its very inception would signal "the end of anti-Semitism."

Jews, Herzl wrote, would be strong enough to form a state, a "model state," if they were granted sovereignty over "a portion of the globe adequate to meet rightful national requirements." How should Zionists proceed? Herzl's three principles for action amounted to a completion of Pinsker's plan: The Jewish state could be organized in any free territory, perhaps in Argentina, or preferably, but not necessarily, in Palestine. The state would be secured by public (i.e., international) law, "entirely within the framework of civilization." Finally, the state would absorb in an orderly manner European Jews en masse. The poorest Jews would go first; they would put down the agricultural and industrial infrastructure. The middle class would come next, followed by men of property, and finally— chasing men of property—the intelligentsia.

What of the agricultural settlements that already existed in Palestine? Herzl found little in them to approve. "It is silly," he insisted, "to revert to older levels of civilization." Little farms were outdated. If the land had to be cleared of wild beasts, for example, there could be a "grand and glorious hunting party," not individuals going out with spears. ("Drive the animals together and throw a melinite bomb into their midst.") Buildings, too, should be built in the modern style, using the latest technology. Why go back to the land? The world that increasingly threatened Jews had at least put greater powers at mankind's disposal: "The electric light was certainly not invented so that the drawing rooms of a few snobs might be illuminated, but rather to enable us to solve the problems of humanity by its light."

Jews who wished to remain in Europe could do so; indeed, Herzl argued that they, too, would benefit from the disappearance of large numbers of poorer Jews from their midst. Herzl called for the formation of a "corporate body," which he clearly intended to lead, and which would oversee the entire operation—a virtual government-in-exile. He would personally call on the Sultan, and wrote that "in return [for Palestine] we could undertake the complete management of the finances of Turkey." Herzl even designed a flag under which he would initiate the negotiations; it was to be a "white flag with seven gold stars," a banner to rally all those willing to join in the "campaign of enlightenment."

There was not much in the way of democratic ethics in *The Jewish State*, for Herzl's major concern was to unite the Jewish masses in a struggle for pride and power. What was important to him was the corporation, the international charter. His claim of territory would be accompanied by a plan for evacuation and by the trappings of sovereignty. He wanted unity, not the divisive forces engendered by democratic procedures. What is a nation if not a group of individuals who can be stirred by the same marvelous idea at the same time?

Herzl's idea of the Gentile also seemed a stereotype—invariably powerful, ruthless, and cavalier in personal affairs but ready to sacrifice himself for reasons of state. Herzl thought Jews could learn something from this. Does there not come a point when a healthy people—the Jewish people, too—stands and fights, whatever the consequences? Like many Viennese intellectuals of his day, Herzl was thrilled by the élan of mass movements and by military ceremonies, which, he thought, provided a unifying moment for nations. Incidentally, Herzl knew no Hebrew or Yiddish. During the time that he was ruminating on the first draft of *The Jewish State*, Herzl's only cultural inspiration, at least the only one suggested by his autobiographical writing, was his attendance at a performance of Wagner's *Tannhäuser* at the Paris Opera. Yet what more suitable muse for a man of Herzl's sentiments than Wagner? The opera may well have reinforced his evolving conviction that the bonds of German culture were too subtle and too profound to be dissolved by liberalism, that intellectuals and especially artists could be more anti-Semitic than "ignorant rabble."

Consider *Tannhäuser* as Herzl might have then: the opera's enormous sin of the flesh, the passions which find expression in longing eulogies to Venus. Think of the litanies of priestly accusations against Tannhäuser, who for all his contrition seems the more heroic for his reckless desire and self-imposed solitude. The opera tells the story of a man finally saved by Christian grace and a woman of impeccable Germanic virtue. One did not have to be a faithful Christian to be touched by such high romance; in a way, lapsed Christians could be moved most perfectly by it. But Herzl may well have wondered if non-Christians could ever do justice to it, especially people from his stereotyped Jewish world of contracts and manipulated demands for tolerance. What did Christian sinners have to do with Jewish family law? What did rabbinic debates have to do with a pagan world of flesh and forgiveness? Herzl seemed to have accepted at least some of Wagner's claims against the Jews: that the materialism of Jewish businessmen and the spoken Yiddish language would corrupt the organic ties binding the German folk together. Who, in any case, was in a better position than Herzl—a literary celebrity—to know that German bonds were real and, for Jews, real barriers? The superior German, or so Wagner argued after Nietzsche, made himself free by transcending Christianity. Herzl might well have grudgingly agreed that German intellectuals should not—or would not—bother with what he took for Christianity's more tribalistic, legalistic forebear.

In imagining the Jewish people detached from Wagner's atavistic German folk, Herzl implicitly freed himself from the secularized Jewish liberalism of his youth. The Jews were to be a separate nation, not just a mass of individuals respectful of contract, tolerance, self-interest, and private faith. Yet to be a nation, Herzl inferred, Jews must be possessed of organic bonds, too; they would have to become conscious of these in order to exert power in a state. And when Herzl began to specify just what was organic to the Jews, it was clear how deeply he lacked what the Jews in Eastern Europe took for granted: Hebrew, *Yiddishkeit*, a knowledge of the classical texts. Ironically, Herzl could at best envision a Jewish society that would be a paragon of the very liberal virtues he had claimed to reject in becoming a nationalist.

His statement of this vision would come in 1902, in his utopian novel *Old-New Land*. The "New Society," as Herzl called the Jewish state, would—in contrast with France and Germany—be inherently cosmopolitan, scientific, multilingual, and cooperative. It would be a home for fitness, theater, and open-spiritedness, while old Europe declined into reaction, chauvinism, and panic. The Jews would become the Jews of Passover (the one traditional festival Herzl cherished); they would perfect themselves as Heine's symbol for just response to unjust treatment. Owners would bequeath factories to workers; prisons would educate and heal broken lives. An underground tram would run up a tunnel to the top of Carmel Mountain; a hydroelectric canal would join the Dead Sea to the Mediterranean.

In *Old-New Land*, the Jews of the New Society would be an example for African peoples. ("All nations need a home.") As to the Arabs who lived in Palestine, most could be "spirited" across the Jordan River. Yet Arabs who remained in the New Society would be full citizens of it—indeed, like Reshid Bey, the Moslem character in the novel who quickly adapted to the New Society's operas and salons:

> "Would you call a man a robber who takes nothing from you but brings you something instead? The Jews have enriched us, why should we be angry with them? They dwell among us like brothers. Why should we not love them? I have never had a better friend among my co-religionists than my friend David Littwak here . . . He prays in a different house to the God who is above us all. But our houses of worship stand side by side, and I always believe that our prayers, when they rise, mingle somewhere up above, and then continue on their way together until they appear before Our Father."

Or consider how Littwak, Herzl's protagonist, describes the New Society to a visitor, Kingscourt:

> "There is no army in the New Society," David replied.
> "Woe's me," jeered Kingscourt.
> David smiled. "What would you expect, Mr. Kingscourt? Nothing on earth is perfect, not even our New Society. But we have no state like the Europeans of your time. We are merely a society of citizens

seeking to enjoy life through work and culture. We content ourselves with making our young people physically fit. We find athletic and rifle clubs sufficient for that purpose, even as they were thought sufficient in Switzerland. We also have competitive games—cricket, football, rowing —like the English . . . Jewish children used to be pale, weak, timid. Now look at them! . . . But you must be tired from your trip. First you must rest, and this evening, should you be so inclined, we shall go to the opera. Or to the theater—to the German, English, French, Italian, or Spanish theater."

"*Schwerenot!*" shouted Kingscourt. "Is all that here?"[12]

Achad Haam, who gave the book a scathing review in *Ha'Shiloach*, noted with a surprise equal to that of Mr. Kingscourt that there was no Hebrew theater in the New Society.

Interestingly enough, *Old-New Land* implied that the Jewish nation would do without an army. What could Herzl have meant by this? The political Zionist tradition, so keen to make Jews militant, was surely not going to abjure the force of arms, and the *levée en masse* was a logical step up from his cultural ideal. In fact, Herzl's attitude toward the military is not clear. He did not think Zionism would immediately provide an answer to physical attacks or military threats against the Jews. Even after learning the details of the Russian pogroms Herzl did not suggest self-defense training for Zionists or the establishment of military organizations—though, eventually, Herzl did encourage the founding of Zionist dueling fraternities at the University of Vienna. Perhaps Herzl simply could not imagine a Jewish state, or any state for that matter, existing outside some larger imperial system. In his day, sovereignty derived as much from the diplomatic recognition of the Great Powers as from any independent fighting force. Surely the New Society, which would be founded in the colonial hinterlands, would have to be protected by whatever imperial power it had concluded an alliance with.

v

Though *The Jewish State* had an immediate impact on Hibat Zion circles—what Eastern European intellectual, looking west, could match Herzl's dash and connections?—Herzl at first tried to launch Zionism entirely on his own. In the summer of 1896, he finally secured a meeting with Baron Edmond de Rothschild, whom he called the kingpin of his entire plan. But the baron soon made up his mind that he wanted nothing to do with Herzl's project and reiterated to Herzl what he had made clear to the settlers of the First Ascent: that his help was meant to be philanthropic and in no sense an endorsement of Jewish nationalism. The meeting between Herzl and the baron took place just at the time when the Dreyfus Affair was raising the specter of a Jewish fifth column in France. Rothschild was deeply offended by Herzl's pretensions to be leading a movement which seemed to presuppose access to the Rothschild fortune.

As things turned out, Rothschild's brusque dismissal of Herzl proved a blessing in disguise, for it forced Herzl to take account of his most reliable constituency, the Hibat Zion intellectuals who were the originators of Zionist thought. These people were still little more than a distant abstraction for him in the summer of 1896. But *The Jewish State* had stirred them up. If his plan for a Jewish government-in-exile was to be more than a forlorn hope, Herzl now realized he had no alternative to calling for grass-roots delegations to a large meeting of all Zionists. At first, Herzl intended to convene this first congress in Munich. Rothschild's opposition to this step was echoed by Dr. Güdemann, who having reconsidered his earlier support for Herzl now reminded his congregation that the "idea of a return to Zion" was a symbol for the messianic ideal, not a political platform. To underscore Güdemann's point, as well as to preempt any effort to impugn their patriotism, the leaders of the Israelitische-Kultusgemeinde of Munich, the largest Jewish Community Council of Bavaria, demanded that Herzl hold his congress elsewhere. Herzl relented, and finally announced a plan to convene it in Basle, Switzerland, in August 1897. His call reached Hibat Zion groups during the summer and fall of 1896.

Herzl's shift in strategy did not mean that he was ready to abandon his authoritarian attitudes. He still fancied himself the maestro and the Jewish masses his players; he wanted a congress he could control. (On his way to Basle, Herzl noted in his diary that he headed an army of "schnorrers, boys, and schmucks.") In fact, however, the Zionist congress was his first taste of those developed forces for Zionism which would ultimately control him, including young and scruffy activists from Odessa, Kiev, Bialystok, and

Kharkov. To be sure, the congress was a success, at least insofar as it consolidated the forces for a Jewish national home and captured the attention of the press in Western Europe. In Basle, Herzl founded the World Zionist Organization. But these were not the only results Herzl had had in mind. Herzl had hoped for support mainly from men of property and high standing. He also wanted to attract famous Western Jewish intellectuals, more people like the Paris-based Hungarian writer Max Nordau, Herzl's only quick convert and eventual collaborator. Neither of these hopes was rewarded. Only a quarter of the delegates were men of business, industry, or finance; more than half were minor writers, professionals, and students—overwhelmingly middle class in outlook, rooted in Eastern Europe, and short of funds.

To his credit, Herzl was sufficiently nimble-minded to grasp how Zionism's future rested with the Russian Jews. Their nature, he presently wrote, "is simple and unbroken though they have not withdrawn from modern culture." At least they were not "tormented" by any thoughts of assimilating; indeed, they were on the right track, endeavoring to learn what was good from all peoples.[13] And having discovered the power of their commitment, Herzl took his revenge on Rothschild. In October 1897 he published a scandalous (and as always revealing) attack on the baron in *Die Welt*, the new Zionist journal he edited. Herzl "thanked" Rothschild sarcastically for splitting with his movement.

> Mauschel [i.e., the kike] is spineless, repressed, shabby—when the Jew feels pain or pride, Mauschel's face shows only miserable fright or a mocking grin—he carries on his dirty deals behind the masks of progress and reaction; with rabbis, writers, lawyers, and doctors, who are only crafty profit-seekers.

Zionism, Herzl continued, must break with the Jewish high bourgeoisie. "We are viewed as a nation of hagglers and crooks," Herzl wrote, "because Mauschel practices usury and speculates on the stock exchange."[14]

Eventually Herzl realized that Zionism's money would have to be collected from the Eastern European masses. He accepted into his movement any Jew willing to contribute the smallest pittance— a "shekel," as he put it. In 1899 Herzl founded the Jewish Colonial

Trust, a development bank, each share selling for just one pound sterling. To these remarkable achievements Herzl added a relentless round of diplomatic engagements. Nor did he ignore Zionism's internal structure. He continued to convene annual congresses.

But though Hibat Zion intellectuals had previously managed to organize little more than their thoughts, their feelings for Herzl could not be anything but ambivalent. Many were overwhelmed by his personality and would have crowned him their king. The congresses had meant the beginning of a new era. What Yiddish writer from the Pale could think so grandly of a "world" organization and a national bank? Yet there was more to their spirit than some "simple and unbroken" nature, as Herzl put it, which presumably made them good material for Herzl's leadership. It remained to be seen in what way Herzl's ambitions would affect the Yishuv. Indeed, some intellectuals from Hibat Zion were uncertain that Herzl could even grasp the dreams which would make any Jew want to live there.

2 / Cultural Zionism

After the First Zionist Congress, the outlines of two adversary concepts of Zionism began to emerge. If political Zionists such as Herzl and Nordau were persuaded that the Jews could never be assimilated in modern Europe, the cultural Zionists were dismayed precisely by the number of Jews who seemed willing to assimilate wherever they could. This is not to say that the cultural Zionists were insensible to anti-Jewish repression. On the contrary, since they were mainly of Eastern European origin, the pogroms of 1881 had been deeply demoralizing for them, and many had suffered at firsthand a more palpable anti-Semitism than anything yet experienced by Western European Jews. Yet the cultural Zionists were more secure in their Jewish identity than people such as Herzl. They were rooted, however uncomfortably, in their parents' Torah culture. They grasped that defying hostile Gentiles did not in itself assure the freedom to be Jews.

i

The cultural Zionists were influenced by such enlightened Eastern Jewish writers as Alexander Zederbaum-Erez, the founder of the Hebrew journal *Ha'Melitz* (*The Advocate*), the novelist Peretz Smolenskin, and the historian Simon Dubnow—not all of whom were or became Zionists. Most had experienced an intensely traditional childhood in the *shtetl* (the Jewish town), followed in many cases by a dislocating move to the rapidly industrializing cities of Poland and Western Russia. They yearned for the prestige of scientific rationalism and were looking for a way to combine its premises with the study of classical Hebrew texts, rabbinic literature, and what they took to be traditional ethics and aesthetics. They hoped to produce a "modern" Judaism which could not be dissipated, as Orthodoxy was being dissipated in the cosmopolitan atmosphere of Berlin, Paris, and even Odessa. Indeed, they thought they could recast the Jewish tradition in national terms.

If political Zionists wanted Jews to take up the challenge of more powerful men, the cultural Zionists wanted an answer for Judaism, which, they reasoned, had been put on the defensive by more powerful ideas. Achad Haam asked, "Can the Jewish people shake off the inertia of repressive legalism, regain direct contact with the actualities of life, and yet remain the Jewish people? Can one bring humanism into Jewish life without disturbing Jewish continuity?" Simon Dubnow, a friend and rival of Achad Haam, recounted in his *Autobiography* how the vernacular of science and social theory—"cause and effect," "senses," "evidence," "motion," "progress," "happiness"—replaced the language of Orthodoxy. Reading the work of Auguste Comte, Dubnow wrote: "I had in my grasp for the first time a complete system of scientific ideas to displace religious and metaphysical systems."[1] He took an especially dim view of Hasidism or any mysticism dependent on fundamentalist teachings.

Such enlightenment is never the product of disappointed faith alone. There were material reasons for the skepticism of Dubnow's milieu, the most important one being that the Jewish corporations in the countryside (the kehilloth) had been all but destroyed. Moreover, the practice of Jewish law did not so much presuppose faith as engender it: since Sinai, the rabbis taught, the God of Abraham, Isaac, and Jacob revealed His grace only to those Jews who observed the commandments of the covenant; yet the routines of industrial life made it inevitable that increasing numbers of Jews would flout Orthodox laws. Jews had to work on Saturday; it was hard to get kosher meat. There was decreasing support for Torah education, and in consequence, divine authority became obscure. "Humanity has only one sacred Bible," Dubnow wrote, "the links in the chain of knowledge, proceeding from mathematics and astronomy to biology and sociology."

Why did Eastern European Jews impatient with Orthodoxy not turn to Reform Judaism? As practiced in Berlin, Paris, and Vienna, this was a companion faith to the ideals of scientific rationalism and civil society—the Judaism of the "home," where citizenship, as the philosopher Moses Mendelssohn had put it, was "in the street." However, there was no realistic prospect of civil reform in the czarist empire, where the struggles of various nationalities against russification seemed so much more urgent. After 1881, certainly, Eastern European Jewish intellectuals—even those who valued cosmopolitanism—could hardly imagine blending into some larger Russian society as russified individuals. So instead of pursuing Reform Judaism, they grew fascinated with their own social history, the history of the Jewish people, the more so as the pioneering works of Jewish historical scholarship—the studies of Leopold Zunz, Moritz Steinschneider, and, finally, Heinrich Graetz—were translated from German into Russian, Yiddish, and Hebrew.

With the Eastern Jews concentrated in the cities—in Odessa, Vilna, even Warsaw—it was particularly the Yiddish novelists and Hebrew poets, men like Sholom Aleichem and Y. L. Peretz, who fostered Jewish nationalism in works that evoked many details of the folk culture. Indeed, the Eastern Jews' spiritual habits had evolved into a culture they thought immanently national. Orthodox seclusion had produced a common aesthetic sense, a year shaped by festivals and a singsong Hebrew liturgy. There was an oral tradition of legends and heroes, a diet of permitted foods, not to mention the unifying intellectual experience of studying the classical texts and rabbinic literature.

Impressed by this ambience, the people who became cultural Zionists perceived the Jewish predicament, not from what was ominous about the Gentile world, but from what was most compelling about the Jewish tradition—language, text, prophesy. Jews, they reasoned, should retain and modernize much of what made the Jewish culture of the Pale distinctive. How wonderful if Jews posed scientific questions in Hebrew! And cultural Zionists were their own best evidence that this was possible, if not in the Pale, then why not in a national home, in Eretz Yisrael, where Jews could be secularists without undermining Jewish survival?

As Jewish migration out of Eastern Europe increased, cultural Zionists—many of whom were first associated with Hibat Zion—supported Hebrew colonies in Palestine. Eventually most opposed Herzl's plan to found a Jewish state, however, for they argued that the more adventurous goal of Zionism—in any case, the prior goal—was to create out of the matrix of Eastern Jewish life a modern Hebrew nation. Cultural Zionists acknowledged that once a Hebrew nation came into being—out of schools, farms, publishing houses—political and military action might eventually liberate it. They did not disdain political independence in the abstract. But the question of any political negotiations or of building a militia seemed premature to them and also ran the risk of confusing the means with the end. Political and military force could not create the new language, or establish an autonomous cultural life worth fighting for.

Though Eretz Yisrael had been a symbol of national disgrace for Pinsker, the culturalists wanted that sense of continuity which they thought would come from communing with the places of Jewish national origins. Palestine was, after all, the place where the Hebrew language was born. King Solomon was wise there; Judah the Maccabee was brave there. In Hebrew, "wisdom" and "bravery" would always bring to mind the connotation of Solomon's wisdom, Judah's heroism. Of course, the cultural Zionists did not want to preserve the many mystical allusions to the power of Eretz Yisrael that were implied by liturgical Hebrew, or preserve any of the other nuances implying messianic longing and fundamentalist faith in God. Yet how better to banish these from Hebrew than by using the language for modern forms of work precisely where the language was born? Where better to demystify the Hebrew language than in the land of the Bible?

Still, the cultural Zionists were interested in territorial claims only insofar as land would permit them to build from the ground up the social institutions that would aid in revamping Hebrew culture. Unlike the politicals, they did not lay claim to the *whole* land of Palestine for reasons of political symbolism. They took it for granted that political borders might eventually circumscribe the new cultural settlements, but cultural Zionists thought it was more important to concentrate on winning the right of individual Zionist cadres to immigrate or on buying more land for settlement. Nor was there any need, so early on, for international recognition or for a Great Power charter—certainly not for Zionism to begin its task. Indeed, the cultural Zionists doubted that Zionism would become a mass movement at all. What was needed, they asserted, was a good-sized number of Jews to lay the groundwork over many generations, people whose achievements would inspire the Jews of the Diaspora.

The cultural Zionists, finally, had a tendency to be communitarian, even illiberal in economic matters, for they saw private enterprise as bound to absorb Arab labor and, in consequence, bound to preclude Hebrew revival. Yet they were much more inclined to democratic ways of thinking than the political Zionists, if only because they viewed Jewish cultural renewal, not as something that would stem from the power either of a great leader or a militant organization, but rather as the compounded action of creative individuals—workers, scientists, and artists—in voluntary association. Their democratic ethos did not incline the culturalists to be sympathetic toward Arab claims against Jewish settlement in Palestine. The culturalists imagined superseding Arab civilization with a Hebrew-speaking Jewish majority.

Being radical secularists, the culturalists had no more respect for Arab or Moslem religious culture than for Jewish Orthodoxy. Still, no culturalist seriously considered—as did Herzl—transferring the Arab population across the Jordan River. Generally speaking, culturalists remained open to bi-national arrangements with Palestine's native inhabitants. In any case, they took the Arabs much more seriously than did the politicals. This was not a matter of greater or lesser militancy. The culturalists simply grasped that all people, Jews and Arabs included, will fight most ferociously when they have a cultural life to lose. Achad Haam wrote:

> It is not only the Jews that have come out of the Ghetto, Judaism has come out too. For Jews the exodus is confined to Western countries and is due to toleration; but Judaism has come out (or is coming out) of its own accord wherever it has come into contact with modern culture. This contact overturns defenses of Judaism from within, so

that Judaism can no longer remain isolated and live apart. The spirit of the Jewish people strives for development; it wants to absorb those elements of general culture which reach it from outside, as it has done in other periods of history . . .

For this purpose, Judaism needs but little. It needs not an independent state, but only the creation in its native land of conditions favourable to its development: a growing settlement of Jews working without hindrance in every branch of culture, from agriculture and handicrafts to science and literature . . .

This Jewish settlement, which will grow gradually, will become in the course of time the centre of a nation, where its spirit will find more perfect expression, and go forth to all the communities of the diaspora and breathe new life into them, preserving their unity . . . And when our national culture in Palestine has attained that level [which cannot be contained by its political origins] we may be sure that it will produce men in the country people who, on a favourable opportunity, will be able to establish a state which will be a *Jewish* state, and not merely a state of Jews.[2]

ii

Asher Ginzberg, who was to become Achad Haam in 1889, was born in 1856 near Kiev. He was the son of a rabbi in the Chabad movement, one of the few Hasidic groups that attempted to reconcile mysticism and Talmudism; from his autobiographical fragments, we learn that he earned the right to pursue his particular passion for mathematics at the age of eleven, though he had to give up smoking cigarettes to seal the agreement. During his adolescence, largely in secret, the young Ginzberg read emancipationist literature. He began with the work of the Jewish enlightenment scholar and positivist philosopher Kalman Shulman and thereafter immersed himself in the fundamentals of British empiricism: John Locke, David Hume, and their successors, such as John Stuart Mill.[3] (Much later in his career, notoriously jealous of his prerogatives as editor of *Ha'Shiloach*, Achad Haam was asked by a colleague to surrender a section of the journal. Achad Haam replied, "Even if Herbert Spencer were to ask me to place a section of the paper entirely at his disposal I should refuse!"[4])

Little else is known of Ginzberg's systematic reading as a young man except for his encounter with the works of certain German idealist philosophers—Herder, who made great claims for "national spirit," was probably among these—whom Achad Haam claimed not to admire. In 1886, at the age of thirty, Ginzberg moved to Odessa, with the vague hope of joining in the struggle to modernize Judaism. He had found the countryside suffocating and was greatly impressed by the vitality of the new movements growing up in the Russian cities. Almost immediately, he joined Hibat Zion and supported its work, and three years later he launched his literary career in opposition to Pinsker's reliance on Rothschild.

Throughout that career, Achad Haam continued to look at Jewish modernization in much the way he had looked at scientific progress in his youth. He avidly followed the Russian positivists. But Spencer was perhaps the most important influence on him, especially the notion that our languages and cultures are "organic" growths which struggle for existence—grow in complexity and flourish or decline—much like any other "organism": Beginning with a barbarous tribe, Spencer wrote, "progress has been and still is towards an economic aggregation of the whole human race"; the fittest cultures survive and absorb the rest, become models for the rest.[5] "Modern" cultures, indeed, were the most fit to survive, for they operated by the same principles as those of scientific communities. Presumably they were governed by open debate, evidence, tolerance, proof. Modern societies lived according to rational principles, which lead to technological progress; their governments, Spencer had reasoned, subjected men and women to the rule of law precisely for the sake of "improvement." In the final stage of history, social scientists would refine to a greater degree the laws that are good for the greatest number, and citizens would support them, and the habits of reason, almost instinctively.

In such essays as "Emulation and Self-effacement," written in 1894, Achad Haam seemed to develop his ideas about "Jewish spirit" directly from Spencer's blunt postulates regarding evolution and culture. Achad Haam did not believe that Jewish culture was to be compared with that of Spencer's barbarians. But it was not quite fit for survival, either. He was troubled by Jewish backwardness—its repressive legalism and metaphysical conceptions of God's will—but he was even more worried about the consciousness of Jews who remained cultural minorities in such improved countries as Germany, France, and England. Here, in Achad Haam's view, Jews learned modernism in a discourse foreign to what he called

the "Jewish form"; they became "self-effacing imitators" of the superior form; indeed, they had a "genius" for cultural imitation, and
hence became subservient to foreign spiritual forces.

Instead, Achad Haam believed, the Jews should emulate in a
"competitive" way superior scientific and artistic cultures without
losing their unique language. Hibat Zion's challenge was to direct
and channel the Jewish genius for learning from other, higher
civilizations, to give Jews the means to apply the creativity of universal culture to Judaism. "Backward people," he wrote, "must appropriate for their community that spiritual force which is the
cause of their self-effacement, so that the community will no
longer look with distant awe on the foreign life, but reveal its
own spirit or personality in those ways in which the [higher] model
revealed its own."[6]

How, given Spencer's criteria, had modernity "overturned Jewish
defenses" from *within*? Achad Haam's answer led to an even more
intriguing line of argument, which he eventually articulated in
"Judaism and the Gospels":

> Herbert Spencer anticipates, as the highest possible development of
> morality, the transformation of the altruistic sentiment into a natural
> instinct, so that men will be able to find no greater pleasure than in
> working for the good of others. Similarly Judaism, in conformity with
> its own way of thought, anticipates the development of morality to a
> point at which justice will become an instinct with good men, so that
> they will not need long reflection to enable them to decide between
> different courses of action according to the standard of absolute justice,
> but will feel as in a flash, and with the certainty of instinct, even the
> slightest deviation from the straight line . . . Judaism associated its
> moral aspirations with the "coming of the Messiah," and it attributed
> to the Messiah this perfection of morality.[7]

Obviously Achad Haam did not go along with the conventional
wisdom of the enlightenment critics he admired, which was that
Judaism, like all "theological" cultures, would simply have to be
replaced by the principles of science. Judaism was not yet fit for
survival; yet there were rationalist tendencies in the Jewish tradition
Achad Haam appreciated—particularly in talmudic debates about
Mosaic law, which had themselves been inspired by the ways of

the "higher" Hellenic civilization after the destruction of the Second Temple. Indeed, Maimonides, the twelfth-century philosopher and physician Achad Haam particularly admired, had defended Jewish law as a training for the faculties of reason, something akin to Aristotle's injunction to practice "the mean." "Follow reason and reason only," Achad Haam quoted the sage, "and explain religion in conformity with reason, for reason is the end of mankind and religion is only the means to an end."[8]

Under the influence of Maimonides, Achad Haam noted, rabbinic assemblies of the Middle Ages incorporated secular knowledge in regulations dealing with eating, drinking, and care for the dead. They justified such eclecticism by talmudic injunctions to preserve life, "a higher value than the Sabbath." Insofar as classical Judaism assumed practice of the law to be the vehicle for messianic redemption, Achad Haam considered both as anticipating progress through reason. Can it be that he did not regard the Jewish spirit as bound up in a theological culture at all?

For Achad Haam, the Jewish spirit was, first of all, to be found in the Hebrew language; as Spencer might have put it, Hebrew was the major empirical product of Jewish social life. In 1912, after the Yishuv had developed much further, Achad Haam visited a collective farm and recorded:

> So soon as the Jew from the diaspora enters a Jewish colony in Palestine he feels that he is in a Hebrew national atmosphere. The whole social order, from the Council of the colony to the school, bears the Hebrew stamp: they do not bear traces of that foreign influence that flows from an alien environment and distorts the pure Hebrew form. This preponderance is, albeit, half complete; extending only to the children. But the process of *free* development has only just begun, and is going on. [9]

The material substance of Jewish spirit—its "flesh," Achad Haam wrote in another later essay—was the Jewish people itself.[10] But Jewish spirit could not be perceived, much less developed, in men and women who did not speak Hebrew or, correspondingly, share deeply in the Jews' traditional culture. Even people who were born Jews would fail to appreciate Jewish national life without Hebrew. Since Orthodox law no longer held the Jews together, only the Hebrew language could do so. And as if to prove the

point, Achad Haam's essays were studded with allusions to rabbinic Hebrew literature: he compared the mistakes of the Essenes
to the record of the Pharisees; he brooded over the political acumen
of Moses; he marveled how the Jewish spirit "progressed" from
exodus, to law, to messianic ideals.

Far from being inimical to scientific and secular modes of thinking, however, the social spirit embedded in Hebrew seemed to
Achad Haam particularly open to them; this, in part, was what
made Jewish tradition worth saving. Consider if nothing else those
principles inherent in the Jewish spirit which Achad Haam thought
consonant with Spencer's moral vision, the messianic ideal, which,
presumably, allowed the Jews to imagine moral instincts as natural
habits. According to Achad Haam, Jews were such promising
candidates for the moral sentiments of modernity that he simply
dismissed Nietzsche's blond "superman" as vulgar and, instead,
pronounced the Jews a "superpeople"—as it were, a secularized
version of the biblical notion of the chosen people. The modern
Jewish spirit affirmed law over brute force and thus superseded the
Israelite's affirmation of God over paganism.[11] (He wrote this in
1898, four years before Herzl's protagonist in *Old-New Land*
bragged about how Jews now looked like the Swiss, rowed like
the British, worshipped theater like the Viennese.)

In Achad Haam's view, the Jewish spirit had even anticipated
the fundamentals of the scientific outlook. He believed that the
monotheism of the ancient Jews implied consciousness of the
unity of nature. What distinguished the scientific mind from the
primitive one if not the conviction that commonsense perceptions
were in no way sufficient to account for most phenomena, that
there were hidden unities behind mere appearances? Judaism, with
its disdain for idols and idol making, had been the first culture to
put itself at odds with common sense. Thus, Achad Haam wrote,
were he asked to impart the essence of the Torah all at once—
"on one leg," as the sage Hillel had put it—he would not have
answered, as Hillel did, that one should refrain from doing to
one's neighbor what one finds obnoxious. Rather, he would merely
have cited the ancient prohibition against making graven images.[12]

There was even a special role for the rabbinate in Achad Haam's
scheme. The rabbis prepared the Jews for the days of messianic
justice by refining the law and presiding over its practice. The best

rabbis stimulated progress, he believed, by deriving legal principles out of their people's common experiences, and codified and interpreted the historical record. Unlike the Christians, rabbis did not imagine the possibility of individual redemption; rather, the rabbis concerned themselves with the peace of the whole community. They "balanced gains and losses, from the point of view of social development," he wrote, and so seemed the precursors for a kind of utilitarianism. Indeed, the traditional claim of the rabbis that their legal system was revealed did not impress Achad Haam so much as the way their debates influenced the secular frame of mind. Their readiness to abrogate any commandment for the sake of saving a human life implied that traditional rabbis were incipiently humanist, and Achad Haam pointed with particular pride to the rabbis' pragmatism, say, in granting divorces to disgruntled wives as well as to husbands.

.

This was certainly an enviable version of Judaism. The Jews seemed possessed of principles which Achad Haam took to be the underpinnings of a scientific, universal culture. Yet he was not complacent about this, and for good reason since, if Jews were precursors, then contemporary Europe threatened Jewish survival in an unprecedented way. It was not that Europe was "enemy ground"—as Herzl put it—upon which Jews were forbidden by anti-Semites to assimilate. The problem was rather that parts of Europe—i.e., the Western countries in which positivism and progress seemed irreversible—would be seductive to Jews as the perfected version of their own principles. Modernity would thus beckon Jews even more powerfully than it did other peoples. Achad Haam feared that, in consequence, Jews would be tempted to abandon the Hebrew language, forfeit their "spirit," free themselves not only from practice of the law but from knowledge of the law.

Not surprisingly, Achad Haam thought that assimilating Western European Jews had begun to lose their self-respect precisely because they had lost the sense of what the Jewish people, in contrast with individual Jews, had contributed to the universal culture. Outside the imagined national home, the secular Jew becomes a "slave" to someone else's conceits, styles, and opinions. In contrast, the Jews of the East still do not have political freedom. But neither had they "sold their souls" for it.[13] "I know why I remain a Jew,"

Achad Haam wrote, "or rather I can find no meaning in such a question any more than if I were asked why I remain my father's son. I can say just what I please about traditional values and beliefs without thereby being afraid that I may cut myself adrift from my people . . . My feelings and opinions are my own. And this freedom of spirit—scoff who will—I would not exchange for all the civil rights in the world."[14]

iii

The great Hebrew revivalist of the First Ascent, Eliezer Ben Yehuda, had settled in Palestine in 1881. Unlike most of his contemporaries, Ben Yehuda did not settle on the land but led a group of collaborators in founding the Hebrew Language Council of Jerusalem, which compiled the Yishuv's first modern Hebrew dictionary. The agricultural settlers deeply admired the dictionary and used it as best they could. In 1893, in Jaffa, the Alliance Israélite Universelle opened Palestine's first secular school to offer instruction in the Hebrew language.

Achad Haam was jubilant. The Jaffa school, he wrote, would prove the efficacy of national Judaism: "What would happen if, after some years, hundreds of young Jews who had been educated in a purely Hebraic spirit on the ancestral soil should stand before our Western brethren without demonstrating any inferiority of knowledge or manners and other signs of culture?" Still, he was not easily satisfied. After visiting the Jaffa school in 1893, he said of the pioneers whose fate it was to discharge his dream: "You only have to hear how the teachers and students stammer together for lack of words and expression to feel that this 'speech' cannot arouse respect or love of the language . . . The children, with their sensitivity, will feel the artificial bonds which Hebrew speech imposes upon them."[15]

It should be noted here that, as the language of scholarship, Hebrew was virtually unknown to Jewish women and was not the language of family life. It was the language of the Torah, the commentaries, and the new enlightenment. Moreover, Hebrew was stern, austere, and exquisitely regular—the medium for heroism and national experience as grasped by readers of the classic texts. Hebrew was always considered something of a divine trust, which is why the most radical atheists in the East remained Yiddishists and perhaps one of the reasons why they failed to become Zionists. Unlike Hebrew, Yiddish had for centuries expressed the homilies, the jokes, and the poignancies of the family circle. It was the language of inner space: ambition, lust, trade, heresy. The Yiddish spirit was by its very nature more tolerant of individual foibles. The problem was that it made Zionism seem unrealistic, if not downright pretentious.

For Achad Haam, at least, the classical quality of Hebrew, its association with the ancient trials, was a part of its strength. Hebrew was the stuff from which Jewish national literature—as distinct from "ghetto literature"—had been composed and was thus the better vehicle for voluntarism and high-minded idealism.

> An attempt is being made to invest Yiddish—that German-Jewish jargon which the Jews of Central and Eastern Europe have spoken for some centuries—with the dignity of a national language . . . Its partisans claim it is the language of the majority of Jews and is spoken by nobody else but Jews . . . But no nation with a long history and a great literature has ever picked up a new "national language" in a foreign country . . .
>
> It is with the nation as it is with the individual. A man must hear [his national language] in the cradle; it must be part of his being before he knows himself; it must grow up in him along with his own self-consciousness. Similarly, a nation's language must belong to it from the start, must precede the full development of its national consciousness, and must be so linked with the whole course of its history as to be inseparable from its memories . . .
>
> There is one language and only one that always has been, is and forever will be bound up with our national existence, and that is Hebrew.[16]

That analogy to the cradle might well have given the Yiddishists more ammunition against him. What Achad Haam hoped for, in any case, was that a second generation of settlers in Palestine would grow up speaking mainly Hebrew and, in consequence, be empowered to carry out the Zionist project. As he put it in a letter to his colleague in Hibat Zion Menachem Ussishkin, Jews could not hope to create a "spiritual center" in Palestine until Hebrew speakers became "a majority of the population, own[ed] most of the land, and control[led] the institutions shaping the culture of the country."[17] It would be absurd to raise the prospect of a Jewish state, for example, before 100,000 Hebrew-speaking Jews lived in Palestine; people whose roots were in the land, whose claims were the claims of use, and whose goals would seem "practical" to European powers and potential Jewish settlers alike. A Jewish majority, presumably, was also the only way to ensure that Hebrew would be the language of work, that reasonable people would come to think Jewish national rights fair. It was a process, Achad Haam believed, which might take one hundred, even two hundred years.

It is worth stressing that Achad Haam's belief in a spiritual center was not a bow to Orthodoxy. Achad Haam believed that a Jewish nation would eventually grow from Palestinian roots, acre by acre, cowshed by cowshed. Because it was a *secular* nation that he wanted, Achad Haam could imagine no other place for it than the ancient land of Israel—Jerusalem, Mount Tabor, the Sea of Galilee. Daily work on the ancient soil would emancipate Hebrew speakers from metaphysical conceptions of these places. Indeed, in order to stop hankering after the "higher" Jerusalem, Jews would have to live in the "lower" one.

> I went first, of course, to the Wailing Wall [Achad Haam wrote after his first visit to Palestine]. There I found many of our brothers, residents of Jerusalem, standing and praying with raised voices—also with wan faces, strange movements, and weird clothing—everything befitting the appearance of that terrible Wall. I stood and watched them, people and Wall, and one thought filled the chambers of my heart: these stones are testaments to the destruction of our land. And these men? The destruction of our people. Which catastrophe is greater? . . . Destroy a land, and a living people shall rebuild it. But destroy a people, and who will arise, and from whence comes its strength?[18]

For Achad Haam, the city of Zion was no symbol of Jewish unity or dignity. Its Orthodox men were evidence of how much remained to be done by Zionists who wanted either. He could not have imagined children of the new Hebrew stirred by the idea of a "holy" land.

iv

Almost immediately, Achad Haam regarded Herzl's version of Zionism with much the same disdain that the Viennese critic Karl

Kraus would show for Freud's psychoanalysis: as "the disease that presumes itself the cure." But the Zionist movement came to life during the high tide of European imperialism. Herzl thrived on this world of machinations and grand designs, and promised that diplomacy would create political opportunities for Jews. Even before the First Zionist Congress, he was courting German princes and English lords, expecting to dazzle them into supporting an international charter for Zionism. He certainly dazzled most Eastern European Jews, who, in any event, could do little else than react to his initiatives.

Achad Haam's opinion mattered. *Ha'Shiloach* was by now the most important Hebrew journal in Eastern Europe, and Achad Haam was the preeminent teacher and critic of the movement. The poet Chaim Nachman Bialik called him the star around which the lesser planets revolved. Few of the Eastern Zionists had thought about modernism as deeply as Achad Haam; if only intuitively, many sympathized with Achad Haam's view of how the nation would be the product of a Hebrew revival. Also, they appreciated his call for a secular culture and his support for the colonies of Eretz Yisrael. They shared his apprehension that assimilation would follow from any more conventional form of Jewish "progress." (Achad Haam's disciple in Bnei Moshe, Chaim Weizmann, who would later become the first President of Israel, recalled in his memoirs going to the First Zionist Congress as a spokesman of the Russian-Jewish masses, "who sought in Zionism self-expression and not merely rescue." Though still a student, Weizmann thought Herzl's views "mechanical."[19])

Still, Achad Haam was virtually alone among the Eastern European Hibat Zion veterans in rejecting Herzl from the start. Most of Achad Haam's colleagues—including Peretz Smolenskin, the editor of the Hebrew journal *Ha'Shachar* (*The Dawn*), and Nahum Sokolow, the editor of Warsaw's *Ha'Tzfira* (*The Alarm*)— embraced Herzl's leadership, converted by the promise of a new movement presided over by a man of reputation in the West. They appreciated the new horizons that Herzl opened up, the press attention, the dignity of emotion suggested by his bearing. Political Zionism was exciting and Herzl was charismatic. Some Eastern European Jewish intellectuals had learned to be wary of strong leaders during the Pinsker era, but they were willing to give Herzl a chance, or at least to view him as a foil through which their own, more authentic Zionism would gain clarity and practical significance.

In spite of his reservations, Achad Haam did go to the First Zionist Congress. There, Nordau greeted him in Herzl's name and asked solicitously if he was a Zionist. Achad Haam retorted, "Yes, I am a Zionist." Achad Haam participated in deliberations leading to a declaration in favor of a "national home," not a Jewish "state" as Herzl had demanded in *The Jewish State*; and he put forward the idea that the Zionist congress begin a program of secular cultural education. Still, when Achad Haam returned to Odessa, he confessed that he had felt at Basle like "a mourner at a wedding feast." He wrote a deft portrait of Herzl, the bitterness of which seemed as much an expression of his own powerlessness as of ideological disagreement.

> The Western Jew is unhappy, because after leaving the ghetto and seeking to attach himself to the people of the country in which he lives, his hope of an open-armed welcome is disappointed. He returns reluctantly to his own people and tries to find within the Jewish community that life for which he yearns—but in vain . . . He has already grown accustomed to the broader social and political life; and on the intellectual side, Jewish cultural work has no attraction because Jewish culture has played no part in his education from childhood and is a closed book to him. So in his trouble, he turns to the land of his ancestors and pictures to himself how good it would be if a Jewish state were established there—a state arranged and organized exactly in the pattern of other states. Now he could live a "full, complete" life among his people, and find "at home" all he sees on the outside, dangled beyond his reach.
>
> But as the Western Jew contemplates this fascinating vision, it suddenly dawns on him that, even now, before the Jewish state is established, the mere idea of it gives him almost complete relief. He has the opportunity for organized work, for political excitement . . . and has thus regained his "human dignity" without overmuch trouble or external aid: the pursuit of the ideal is enough to cure him of his moral sickness. And the higher, and the more distant the ideal, the greater its power of exaltation.[20]

Achad Haam was not so bold in temperament as to confront Herzl or Nordau directly at any more Zionist congresses. After 1897, Herzl dominated the Smaller Actions Committee of the World

Zionist Organization and held himself accountable to no one from the old Hibat Zion. Besides, Achad Haam knew that the movement as a whole was too weak to survive open division. He chose to bide his time on the sidelines, reckoning that he could do no more than go into a kind of official opposition until enthusiasm for Herzl began to wane.

In opposition, Achad Haam wrote even more feverishly about Judaism, Zionism, the Jewish spirit; he succeeded in defining his effort as the other Zionism, "practical" Zionism, a fully formed alternative he hoped would survive Herzl's failures. That Herzl *would* fail he had no doubt. What Achad Haam feared was that Herzl would meanwhile sacrifice what he couldn't understand for the diplomatic coup he could never deliver.

v

Herzl admired the enthusiasm of the Eastern European delegates but argued with increasing impatience that preoccupation with secular Hebrew culture betrayed a kind of atavism. Nordau was soon calling the practical Zionists Jewish "Boxers," an allusion to the Chinese rebels, who were thought to be fighting against the forces of progress. Herzl wrote in 1900 that while the practical Zionists and political Zionists could agree that Eretz Yisrael should belong to the Jewish people, they couldn't seem to agree on much else. He ridiculed the Hibat Zion settlements as "philanthropic, experimental stations."

> The practical Zionists want to start going even before the land belongs to us. The political Zionists, on the other hand, say: First it has to belong to us and then we will go there. To be sure, even the practical Zionists do not go there right away. They merely send some people there to till the soil. These are the *settlers for show*. That looks great from a distance; it is a pretty sight. Then they can go and tell people that the Jews are not all peddlers and bankers. Their evidence: there are Jews who cultivate the soil and grow wine.[21]

Some Eastern Zionist leaders did not take this lying down, though the masses remained under Herzl's spell. They sought to educate Herzl to the actual conditions of their situation and redoubled their efforts to harness the growing strength of the radical socialist youth movement in Russia and Poland. "It is a fearful spectacle,"

Weizmann wrote to Herzl, "and one that obviously escapes Western European Zionists, to observe the major part of our youth—and no one would describe them as the worst part—offering themselves up as a sacrifice [to police repressions of the Social Democrats] as though seized by a fever."[22] The culturalists also continued to carry on with the tedious, often frustrating strategy of colonizing Palestine, establishing small, dense settlements, rather than waiting for any imperial support.

Through the intervention of freelance court intriguers, Herzl contrived to meet an assortment of German princes, leading, eventually, to an interview with the Kaiser, who while sympathetic proved unhelpful. Herzl tried frantically to press his case for a Jewish home in Palestine with the Turkish Sultan. He even paid the Sultan's retainers thousands of pounds drawn from the World Zionist Organization's funds. But the bribes led nowhere. Herzl's plan to produce an international charter remained always, it seemed, just beyond reach, and Eastern Zionist leaders grew weary of them, however popular Herzl remained with the Jewish masses.

In September 1902, the Russian Zionists called a conference of their own at Minsk. Here, they put cultural revival at the forefront of the agenda, and even threatened an independent course. Achad Haam, the keynote speaker, declared, "The foundation of a single great school of learning or art in Palestine . . . would do more to bring us near our goal than a hundred agricultural colonies," though one could not do without the colonies. In the end, the Minsk conference set up a cultural commission charged with a broad mandate to pursue secular Jewish education. (The demand for cultural work would be reissued at the Fifth World Zionist Congress.) Later in September, Achad Haam published his review of Herzl's novel *Old-New Land*, in which he excoriated the author for his vision of a Jewish utopia without Hebrew—just when Herzl's negotiations with the Sultan collapsed. Max Nordau wrote a bitter rejoinder to Achad Haam's review, while Weizmann, Martin Buber, and many other Eastern Zionists came to Achad Haam's defense. The situation became so polarized that a student Zionist writer, Shmaryahu Levin, felt impelled to intervene. "Herzl builds and you destroy," he pleaded with Achad Haam in a letter. "Cease from destruction and begin to build."[23]

In desperation, Herzl traveled to Moscow to meet with Count

Vyacheslav von Plehve, the czarist Minister of the Interior who had fomented the Kishinev pogrom of 1903. Herzl thought he could convince Plehve to intercede with the Sultan, and, impressed by Herzl's style, Plehve did give Herzl some vague promise to permit Zionist activity in Russia. Understandably, however, many more Eastern European Zionists liked that style much less after they heard of the meeting. About a thousand Jews had been killed in Russia in various pogroms during the years since the First Zionist Congress.

One final shock remained, and it made reconciliation almost inconceivable. After the failure of his campaign to win from the Sultan a charter for Jewish settlement in Palestine, Herzl had turned to Joseph Chamberlain, the British Colonial Secretary. He had proposed to establish a Jewish colony near El-Arish in North Sinai, which at a more propitious moment could serve as a staging area for Jewish settlements farther north. Since Herzl had hoped that success would stifle the growing criticism of his actions in Eastern Zionist circles, he had made rash and lavish commitments to Chamberlain, promising to secure the area for the British Empire and populate it with "industrious and progressive" Jews. Herzl had professed a great admiration for Cecil Rhodes, the autocratic British colonizer of South Africa, and left Chamberlain in no doubt that the Zionist movement he led could be depended on by British missionaries and entrepreneurs.

Impressed, Chamberlain had sent Herzl off to a meeting with Lord Cromer, the British minister in Egypt, who was, for all practical purposes, the de facto ruler of that country. But for all of Herzl's carefully prepared arguments—perhaps because of them—Herzl's meeting with Cromer had gone badly. His plan to divert water from the Nile to the Sinai, like some of his other grandiose ideas, struck Cromer as entirely too controversial. In the beginning of 1903, Cromer had vetoed Herzl's plan, complaining of the strain it put on relations with Egyptian Arabs. However, Chamberlain now demonstrated a curiously intransigent faith in the Zionist cause. While its leader was in Russia meeting with Plehve, Chamberlain revived an older offer of a huge tract of land in East Africa, adjacent to Lake Victoria.

Herzl, whose health was deteriorating, immediately persuaded himself that Chamberlain's offer could be the basis for an interim solution, a "night station," as Nordau came to call it, for the Jewish masses awaiting their ancient home. Herzl was tired and dejected and anxious for a breakthrough. He realized, of course, that he was putting himself further at odds with the Eastern European faction. Menachem Ussishkin, a leader of the Russian Zionists, had had a tense meeting with Herzl earlier in the year to demand greater support for the colonial bridgehead already established in Palestine. Now Herzl would be proposing the virtual abandonment of these colonies.

In spite of his apprehensions, Herzl pressed ahead at the Sixth Zionist Congress, which was called for August 1903. The session was, if anything, worse than he had anticipated. What had been opposition was turning into sanctimonious defiance. Even Eastern Marxists like Ber Borochov rallied to Ussishkin and to Weizmann, who orchestrated denunciations of the African proposal. Herzl, they claimed, was proposing a "public apostasy," his version of realism an "estrangement from the moral ideal." The Russian members of the Actions Committee handed Herzl a declaration opposing the "Uganda" plan and then left the hall, though Herzl won a narrow majority to set up a commission to study Chamberlain's proposal further. Later, in December 1903, an overzealous anti-Ugandist made an attempt on Nordau's life. The would-be assassin cried out, "Death to Nordau, the East African." The assault was roundly condemned, of course, but the Russian Zionists more and more couched their criticism of Herzl in demands for greater democratization of the Zionist executive.

In fact, what had been a six-year coalition was finally coming apart. The Russian delegation remained in the WZO, though mainly because they knew they could defeat the East Africa plan during the course of the coming year; by the time of the Seventh Zionist Congress, they reasoned, they would have a majority to direct Zionism's resources to the Palestinian colonies. Herzl died shortly thereafter, in 1904, just before he would have lost control over the movement whose institutions he had made. Achad Haam wrote: "He died at the right time. His career and activities during the past seven years had the character of a romantic tale. If some great writer had written it, he too would have had his hero die after the Sixth Congress."[24]

·

After the Seventh Congress, Israel Zangwill, the noted English writer, who had been instrumental in bringing Herzl to Chamberlain, accused the Russian Zionists of "religious sentimentalism." He then broke with Congress Zionism and founded a "territorialist" movement bent on pursuing the Uganda offer. Zangwill got nowhere with his new movement, and in any case, his poke at the Easterners' purported religiosity entirely missed its mark; indeed, what religious Zionists there were at the early congresses had supported the Uganda scheme, for they saw no reason why they could not practice the Orthodox faith in Africa as well as anywhere else. What the secular majority of Easterners already grasped, rather, was that the Palestinian Jewish colony was by now much more than some hypothetical instrument of cultural revolution. To support its gradual development had become, as it were, a practical matter.

Herzl's disciple, a meek man named David Wolffsohn, succeeded to the chairmanship of the Smaller Actions Committee later in 1904. His election belied the real shift in power that was under way. The politicals did not fare well during the years after Herzl's death: Weizmann, Levin, and Nahum Sokolow joined the executive after 1904 and openly criticized Herzl's strategy of diplomatic action, which left few resources for Palestinian settlement. They forced the WZO to use its funds to consolidate Hibat Zion's achievements. Meanwhile, Wolffsohn refurbished the Jewish Colonial Trust, raising subscriptions amounting to some £4 million. In 1908, prodded by the demands of the WZO executive, he founded the Palestine Land Development Company, with a share capital of £50,000. Faithful to his mentor, Wolffsohn carped at the "waste" of Zionist money on uncertain colonial projects. Nonetheless, he shared his power.

Weizmann had moved to England in 1906. There he began a career as a research chemist while continuing to work actively for Zionist goals. He successfully solicited support from liberal politicians in Manchester and London, and also gained the backing of the *Manchester Guardian* newspaper for the Jewish national home. In 1908, Achad Haam moved to England as well, to become the representative of the Wissotzky Tea Company. He closely advised Weizmann in further efforts to secure British political favor for various Zionist projects, particularly for the Yishuv, whose population had grown rapidly and now numbered perhaps as many as 15,000 settlers. The rest of the Zionist executive remained in Vienna.

Herzl's remaining supporters on the WZO executive still hoped to carry out his political Zionist plans. Nordau, for example, was briefly seized by an enthusiasm for the so-called Young Turks, who gained power in Constantinople in 1907. For his part, the cautious Wolffsohn correctly supposed that Enver Pasha's regime would no more countenance negotiations with Zionists than did the Sultan. In any case, no serious overtures to the Turks were undertaken. In 1911, a new cabal of Eastern Zionist leaders—Weizmann, Levin, Sokolow, and Viktor Jacobson—finally pushed Wolffsohn off the executive. They called themselves "synthetic Zionists" and claimed to be combining the best elements of practical and political Zionism. But Wolffsohn was perfectly aware that the designation was a kind of subterfuge. The new executive of the WZO was entirely committed to the idea that Hebrew settlement in Palestine should precede political action to secure an international charter. This was straight out of Achad Haam.

The new executive elected as president Otto Warburg, a compliant German delegate who had lived in Palestine and had even helped to found the Bezalel School of Art in 1905. Nordau was not fooled, either, and, in 1911, withdrew from Zionism altogether. This cleared the way for the culturalists to bring to bear the full force of the WZO in support of the Hebrew-speaking colonies of Eretz Yisrael.

3 / The Conquest of Labor

The victory of cultural Zionists at the Seventh Zionist Congress ensured that the fate of the Zionist cause would be determined by Jewish settlers in Palestine. Thereafter, no substitute land for Eretz Yisrael was entertained at any congress, and the World Zionist Organization executive had several million pounds at its disposal with which to endow colonial efforts directly. Still, the methods by which Jewish settlers could gradually advance the national ideal remained at issue. Having won control of the WZO executive, such disciples of Achad Haam as Chaim Weizmann and Nahum Sokolow had to confront the difficulties inhibiting colonial work of any kind.

In Palestine, there was the "materialism" of the Rothschild settlers to contend with. In Eastern Europe, Zionism remained a rather small movement, particularly when compared with socialist-Yiddishist groupings like the Allgemeiner Yiddisher Arbeterbund—the "Bund"—which had been founded in 1897, the same year as the WZO. Zionists also found themselves in competition with Jewish activists drawn to a non-sectarian Marxism. Even if cultural Zionism's plans for Palestine could be made practical, who among the Eastern Jewish youth would want to try to implement them?

i

In the *shtetl,* Jewish workers had deeply resented the propertied men of the Jewish Municipal Corporation, the kehillah. Sholom Aleichem spoke for many when he wrote: "May the devil take their parents, the blood-suckers, flayers of the poor." When Jews were forced into cities like Odessa, old grudges melded with the socialist promise of proletarian action, and by 1895, dozens of politically conscious union cells—the *kassy*—had been formed throughout the Pale, most of them spontaneously and with little common organization.

During the next several years, the *kassy* attached themselves to a clandestine Jewish trade-union movement and, eventually, to a Jewish-led strike movement, becoming the cutting edge of Russian socialism. The Zionist writer Ber Borochov estimated that Jewish workers' unions organized no fewer than 2,276 strikes between 1895 and 1904, and many of these strikes included Gentile workers.[1] In Minsk, in 1895–96, 100 percent of all bristle workers, 75 percent of all binders, and 40 percent of all locksmiths were organized, as were 20 percent of the Jewish workers in Bialystok and 40 percent in Gomel. One strike-movement leader, Scholem Levin, reports that he drank a good deal of vodka in meetings at which he tried to persuade Russian workers not to scab. "Neither of us achieved anything," he wrote after a particularly frustrating round. "They could not make me a drunkard, and I could not make them class-conscious."[2]

As Borochov's statistics implied, the proliferation of their strikes betrayed a weakness of the Jewish unions that had little to do with competition from Russian workers. Jewish workers were striving against a vast number of "bosses" who were, in fact, Jewish craftsmen themselves—tailors, tanners, and small textile brokers. Could such people be expected to satisfy their workers' wage demands, however just, any more than abolish Russian anti-Semitism or compete against the new state factories? Remarkably, the frustrations of the Jewish strike movement hardly discredited socialism or unionism in the eyes of most young Jews. The unions cheered workers whose livelihoods as hands in small shops were threatened by unemployment from larger capitalist enterprises. The union meeting seemed to many a kind of reincarnated prayer quorum (or *minyan*), and indeed, the socialist views of many young Jews, though fervent, were hopelessly dogmatic. One Russian socialist intellectual, Vera Zasulich, complained to Georgi Plekhanov that the Jewish youth from the Pale of Settlement often acquired a whole world outlook from a few books, that they were "boring."[3] As if to vindicate that verdict, the historian Ezra Mendelsohn records a bristle worker asking a strike agitator what would happen if the Messiah were to come before "we achieve freedom and introduce socialism."[4]

By 1900, some 30 percent of those arrested for political offenses in czarist Russia were Jews.[5] On the whole, the various left-wing movements stood up for Jewish rights and fought against the police, the censors, the monied classes. Lenin's elite Russian Social Democratic Workers' Party (founded in Minsk in 1898) made a denunciation of anti-Semitism one of its first actions and, indeed, included many Jews in its ranks and even in its leadership. Opposition to anti-Semitism in no way implied sympathy for Jewish nationalism; the Bundists would learn that hard lesson when they broke irrevocably with Lenin in 1903. Yet Weizmann may have been thinking of his own brother when he wrote to Herzl that young Jews were offering themselves up to socialism as if "seized by a fever."

.

Zionists could not dismiss the challenge of socialist principles to the creation of a Jewish national home. Jewish socialists called on Jews to stay in Russia, and they implied a style of internationalism next to which the dialectics of cultural Zionism seemed, if not boring, then reactionary—a surrender to "bourgeois rabbis." How, young Zionists asked themselves, would it be possible to make Zionism seem more relevant and less escapist to its natural constituency of young Jewish workers? In fact, many Eastern European Zionists, people who had been cultural Zionists active in Hibat Zion, had absorbed socialist ideas into their ways of thinking. Some of them, like Borochov, began to use Marxist methods of reasoning to show how Jewish proletarian action would not only prove futile in Russia but would also prove the only practical method for settling Palestine.

The product of this intellectual effort was socialist Zionism or Labor Zionism, whose first important exponents were Nachman

Syrkin and Borochov himself. The works of Syrkin and Borochov never inspired a mass movement in the East, but then Zionism was the cause of a minority, and a small number of activists could change its course in a fundamental way. What Syrkin and Borochov did inspire was the founding of Poale Zion, the "Workers of Zion" —the first Labor Zionist party, which grew quickly from 1903 until the start of World War I. Some 5,000 young men and women trickled into Palestine between 1905 and 1914 (especially after the failure of the uprising in St. Petersburg); about 1,500 cadres of this Second Ascent contained members of Poale Zion, including David Ben-Gurion, Yitzchak Ben-Tzvi, Yitzchak Tabenkin, Berl Katznelson, and Zionism's first major writer of fiction, Yoseph Haim Brenner. The other major theorist of Labor Zionism, Aaron David Gordon, had never been a member of Poale Zion, but he helped to found the more culturalist, non-Marxist party, Ha'Poel Ha'Tzair ("The Young Worker") after coming to Palestine in 1904.

.

In Palestine, or so all Labor Zionists argued, proletarian action seemed justified as much for national reasons as for political-economic ones. The farmers of the Rothschild settlements had built up an increasingly solid economic foundation; their plantations were growing year by year. But the hiring of Arab labor seriously threatened progress toward the national ideal: as Achad Haam had pointed out, Jews who hired Arabs didn't learn Hebrew, at least not well enough to participate in the development of a secular national culture. Moreover, an agricultural economy cannot always be booming. If the hiring of Arabs depressed wages in hard times, Jewish workers, no matter how idealistic, would end up leaving Palestine. This was no great hardship for the plantation owners, but every such departure was demoralizing to the Jewish workers who remained behind.

Small wonder, then, that pioneers came to associate independence from "materialist" farming with the national ideal itself, and to view Zionism and socialism as mutually reinforcing:

Big land-owners are the ruin of Palestine [one pioneer wrote back to his friends in Europe]. With big land-owners Palestine will be closed to the Jews, because big land-owners will never take Jews as workers instead of cheap Arab labour. They say that the Arabs are poor workers. That is not true. Arabs are just as good as the European workers . . . [Besides,] if private individuals will buy the land, speculation will at once start, and a crash will be inevitable . . . Nationalization of the land is essential for the success of the enterprise.[6]

There were other problems in the Yishuv which socialist ideology seemed particularly fit to address. The Ottoman administration of Palestine grew more hostile to Zionism as the Yishuv began to seem viable. It was comforting for the settlers to think about a march of history, of the future without reactionary empires and atavistic nationalisms. Moreover, the reality on the ground of Palestine was that, by 1907, Arab raiding parties had forced settlers to found a self-defense organization, a corps of guards known as Bar Giora ("the sons of Giora"), to be followed in 1909 by a more tightly organized militia, Ha'Shomer ("the Watchman"). Though most of the initial Arab attacks were carried out by Bedouins more tempted by loot than by any political feelings, there were already stirrings of more sophisticated anti-Zionist feelings—by Arab *effendis* and peasants who, as Achad Haam had predicted in 1893, "would not willingly give up their position." To remain calm in this increasingly violent situation, the settlers required an ideology that explained how national antagonisms might be transcended by socialist fraternity. Labor Zionism claimed that, in any case, socialism allowed Zionists to achieve their aims in a way that did not subordinate Arab workers or add the antagonisms of class to whatever tensions might emerge between the Arab nation and the Jewish one.

Besides, Labor Zionists held that the capitalist Diaspora posed special risks to Jews, which would push them to Palestine. Bourgeois life corrupted Judaism and robbed Jewish workers of the chance to enjoy participating in all sectors of a developed economy; capitalism made the Jewish people a class remote from manual labor. The Labor Zionists argued that socialist principles were the only way to foster Hebrew and thus achieve "self-realization." Incidentally, though depressions in Palestine's agricultural economy threatened incoming pioneers, Jewish proletarians did have more leverage in Palestine than they had had in Russia. Arab labor came even cheaper than Russian, but there was a chronic shortage of skilled Jewish labor in Palestine, which made the Rothschild settlers and other Jewish property owners increasingly vulnerable to Jewish unions.

Socialism made sense for more personal reasons, finally. As the Biluim had taught a generation before, the delight of creating a new Hebrew environment did not compensate for the indignities of economic dependency. Zionist pioneers, after all, had not spurned New York only to work in Palestine as the instruments of some other Jew's profit. Rather, the pioneers desired the means to direct their own lives in a way consistent with the national ideal. It fell to the Labor Zionists to provide them with their first model collectives —the *kvutzot*, kibbutzim, and *moshavim*—and thereafter to organize the collectivist industrial base which led the whole Yishuv to unanticipated political struggles.

ii

In 1898, when Nachman Syrkin wrote "The Socialist-Jewish State," he knew almost nothing about conditions in Palestine. His purpose was to formulate a position within Zionism that could appeal to Eastern European youth, and at the same time answer that "bourgeois-Zionist" Theodor Herzl. Yet, as if by intuition, Syrkin hit on principles that would ultimately permit the settlers to do without Arab labor and survive Turkish repression and Arab resistance. Many Jewish students could not attend Russian universities because of quotas. It was Nachman Syrkin's good fortune to have come of age in comparative liberty, among other Russian Jewish students—Chaim Weizmann, Leo Motzkin, and Shmaryahu Levin —who attended Berlin universities. In Berlin, these young emigrés developed considerable self-assurance, the czarist persecutions always on their minds. Most participated in the Russian Jewish Scientific Society, a small Jewish debating group where they thrashed out the respective merits of socialism, Bundism, and Zionism.

In her lively and adulatory memoir about her father, Marie Syrkin relates an anecdote about these debates which had been told her by Shmaryahu Levin; it is so revealing, one hopes it is true. It seems that one Marxist radical undertook to convince his fellow students, once and for all, that, "objectively," Zionism had no place in the future cultural life of European socialism. The international division of labor, he argued, necessitated internationalist sentiment, not new, "artificial" divisions of culture such as the ones promoted by Zionism. "Take this coat," he roared, holding up his tattered jacket. "The wool was taken from sheep which were pastured in Angora; it was spun in England, woven in Lodz. The buttons came from Germany, the thread from Austria—" At this point Syrkin sprang to his feet, gesticulating wildly: "And the rip in your sleeve no doubt came from Kiev!" (There had been a pogrom in Kiev a few months before.)[7]

The Zionists won that round. But Syrkin nevertheless despised Herzlian Zionists for their belief in capitalism, their admiration for the European aristocracy, and their connection to imperialist courts. In contrast, socialism would give Jews the opportunity to increase their political power, improve their economic lot, and "raise their spiritual level." At the same time, Syrkin feared that the situation of the Jewish middle class would only be made worse by class struggle, which would unleash a wave of anti-Semitism dangerous to all Jews, working class and middle class alike. Socialism, he wrote, would solve the Jewish problem "only in the remote future": the more various classes of society were "disrupted," the more "unstable" life would become, the greater would be the danger of the ruling classes using anti-Semitism to divert proletarian revolution.

Anti-Semitism, Syrkin implied, was a necessary feature of modernization itself, like dull work at a power loom: "The classes fighting each other will unite in a common attack on the Jew." The dominant elements of capitalist society, i.e., the men of great wealth, the monarchy, the Church, and the state, would seek to use the religious and racial struggle as a substitute of class struggle.

·

Syrkin was not an orthodox Marxist. He abjured historical materialism and, indeed, claimed to oppose all determinist views of social development. (He devoted two doctoral dissertations to proving the force of voluntarism in history, and he wrote in one of them: "Every attempt to conceive history according to one uniform plan must be considered erroneous, a barren and unscientific undertaking."[8]) In "The Socialist-Jewish State," which proved to be his most influential polemic, Syrkin wrote: "All defensive, creative, and ideological activities are realized not through the class struggle but in spite of it. Zionism is a creative endeavour of the Jews and it stands, therefore, not in contradiction to the class struggle but beyond it."[9] Still, Syrkin's view of the Diaspora was almost as rigid as that of a Marxist. He could not bring himself to denigrate the power of internationalist sentiment and, in a way, reserved a higher place for it in his moral scheme than Zionism itself. The characteristic of nationality, he wrote, "is neither language, nor religion, nor state, but the consciousness of historic unity." That consciousness is contingent on historical events and must, someday, be superseded by cosmopolitan ideals. "The creation of one humanity with a common language, territory, and fate, this conception is the greatest victory of the human mind over the accidental and unknown in history, a dream which the greatest spirits of all eras have shared."[10] Nationalism, he wrote, "is only a category of history, not an absolute."[11]

There were the seeds of a contradiction here, whatever the manifest dangers of capitalism to Jews. If, as Syrkin implied, Jewish nationalism was but a product of class conflict, one might just as soon work toward a classless society in Russia as go to Palestine. But to the extent that Syrkin's ideas were internationalist, they only helped allay the fears of pioneers regarding Arab opposition to their cause. Syrkin was himself blind to the prospect of a Palestinian Arab nationalism in conflict with the Zionist project, precisely because he had linked all nationalism—including Zionism—to the progress of the international class struggle. He expected that any opposition to Zionism from other oppressed peoples within the Ottoman Empire would shortly be dissipated by the settlers' socialist, anti-imperialist achievements.

The Jews, Syrkin insisted, would form a majority in socialist Palestine, but would build the land in accordance with the principles of socialist fraternalism. "In those places where populations are mixed," he mused in "The Socialist-Jewish State," "friendly transfers of population should ensue. "The Jews should receive Palestine, which is sparsely settled and where the Jews are already a part of the population."

> The best and most honorable way to secure the land is in alliance with the other oppressed nationalities in the Turkish Empire through a common stand against the Turks. This does not mean that the Turks should lose their national independence but only that other people

in the Ottoman Empire should regain theirs. Macedonians, Armenians, Greeks, and other non-Moslem people should be liberated from the Turkish yoke wherever they form a national majority.[12]

Zionists would even support other "revolutionary elements" in the Ottoman Empire with funds from the national bank. Zionists should count on the support of progressive movements in turn.

To be sure, Zionists had not yet found a common language with Arab peasants, and Syrkin did not include Arabs in his list of potential revolutionaries. Yet Syrkin's reasoning led to the conclusion that the principles of cooperation were the same for Arabs as they were for the other nationalities. In any case, opposition to Zionism was presumably a sign of Arab backwardness. All proletarians should embrace Zionism; people who had not done so had simply not achieved proletarian consciousness.

.

Syrkin was a relentless critic of the Orthodox rabbinate. Jews had to be socialists because their "revolutionary monotheism"— "its social solution, its historical heroism, its humane hopes"—was inherently incompatible with the "egoism" of bourgeois society.[13] Syrkin was a secular Jew consciously in the mold of Moses Hess— the man, Syrkin wrote, who "recognized the eternal striving of man toward perfection, toward historical change and creation." Nor was he less caustic than Hess about the Reform synagogue:

> The assimilatory process forced Jews to find a connecting link between the old tradition and the new Judaism, between the lamentations of exiles by the waters of Babylon and the "prayers" of Jewish stock-brokers who strolled contentedly by the waters of the Spree. This task was willingly assumed by theologians. The synagogue, like the Church, has a healthy stomach; it digests all that its preservation demands.[14]

To mitigate the influence of middle-class Jews, Syrkin hoped to pit Zionist workers against the culture of capitalist society. In a separate Jewish workers' state, in a separate territory, a proletarian culture would be fashioned to compete with Reform Judaism's intellectual syncretism. Curiously, the revival of Hebrew was not of particular importance for Syrkin; though he was competent in Hebrew, and committed to it over Yiddish, he wrote mainly in German. The point was to create a proletarian culture, to link the universal aspirations of the working class to the ancient visions of the Jewish prophets. One might even say that Syrkin's vision of a socialist-Jewish state amounted to a left-wing version of the New Society Herzl proposed in *Old-New Land*. Syrkin, too, wrote as if Zionists could constitute themselves entirely outside the system of conventional nation-states; as if Jews should leave Europe not only to save themselves but to give Europeans a taste of their own highest possibilities.

Alone among the important Labor Zionist thinkers, however, Syrkin proved less than adamant about founding the socialist-Jewish state in Palestine. In 1905, at the Seventh Zionist Congress, he joined forces with Israel Zangwill, the leader of the territorialist faction which was formed to pursue the Uganda offer. Syrkin announced to the congress: "The Socialist Zionists see in the fixation of the Zionist Program on Palestine a limitation of Zionism in fact and principle, for Palestine cannot afford the minimum conditions for the realization of our goal, and will result in small-scale colonization and similar undesirable consequences."[15]

Given the ambivalence of Syrkin's connection to Palestine in 1905, it is remarkable how prescient "The Socialist-Jewish State" of 1898 proved to be, how cannily it addressed the problems which the Palestinian pioneers would eventually confront in the Yishuv— and in a language they admired. Syrkin correctly perceived that Jewish workers would not come to Palestine out of despair. If socialism solved the Jewish problem "only in the remote future," capitalism could not be counted on to create a Jewish problem in America in the foreseeable future. Thus, Syrkin argued like Achad Haam (but more hardheadedly) that the Yishuv should draw the masses to it by holding up a higher moral standard.

> Since the entire effort at colonization will be taking place in an underdeveloped country, wages will be depressed far below any level of subsistence that a European Jew could find acceptable . . . It is inconceivable that people would agree to work for the creation of an autonomous state based on social inequality, for this would amount to entering a contract of social servitude.[16]

Indeed, better than any of his contemporaries, Syrkin appreciated the danger to the Yishuv posed by unrestrained market forces. If these should prevail, he wrote, "most of the workers would be recruited from the native population because they would work for less," and colonization would increasingly become just a business venture: "Jewish immigrants would be forced to leave, and the groups intending to follow would be stopped by fear. The entire movement would begin to disintegrate almost before it had begun."

Syrkin added that the Yishuv's economy could not expand quickly enough without what he called "socialist accumulation": "Within the limits of petty capitalism, it is not possible to mechanize agriculture and create large industries." The Jews, he continued, were an undeveloped people. In order to realize maximum benefit from machinery, the greatest productivity from labor, large-scale enterprise was essential. The land should be the common property of the group that "works and builds on it, with community-owned machinery."

> The houses, factories, and means of production will also be owned by the groups of settlers . . . When the first settlement has been securely established it will make payment to the National Bank . . . and as soon as the first colony returns the financial outlay, a second colony will be founded until mass-immigration is achieved.[17]

After the Seventh Congress, when he joined Zangwill's territorialist movement, Syrkin grew aloof from left-wing Zionist politics; he was unimpressed by the gradualism of men such as Weizmann and Levin. He moved to New York in 1907, and only after 1909 did he reenter the Zionist fold, agitating and writing from the Lower East Side. His early pamphlet sufficed to maintain his reputation among the Poale Zion cadres of the Second Ascent; indeed, they continued to revere him as the man whose work had taken their scattered thoughts and presented them with a program for practical action.

During the First World War, Syrkin supported the founding of a Jewish legion within the British Army, and he endorsed the idea of establishing a Hebrew University in Palestine. Eventually he became active in American Jewish affairs: he was elected as a Zionist to the first American Jewish Congress, then to the American Jewish delegation which attended the Versailles Peace Conference.

Poale Zion held an international conference in 1918, at which Syrkin took his place among the old guard. When Lenin formed the Third International, Syrkin voted in a losing effort to get Poale Zion to seek membership in it. His party eventually split, and he joined the left faction, which petitioned Moscow for official recognition over the majority's objections. The request was denied, of course, but Syrkin apparently considered a suggestion that he travel to the Soviet Union to appeal to the Communist leadership. (Curiously enough, the suggestion had come from David Ben-Gurion, who wrote Syrkin: "There must only be found a man who will raise the Socialist-Zionist banner in Russia with pride and power.")

In 1920, finally, Syrkin went to Palestine for the first time. Although Arab disturbances in Jerusalem marred his visit, Syrkin reveled in the growing kibbutz movement, and particularly in the formation of Ha'Mashbir, the wholesale cooperative for consumer goods. He approved of the founding of the Histadrut, the General Federation of Hebrew Workers, and was deeply moved when its leaders acknowledged him as one of their mentors. Syrkin used his celebrity wisely, warning the pioneers in their newly established collective farms, the kibbutzim, not to become so obsessed with economic autarchy that they forgo opportunities to sell their goods to Arabs. Some settlers had expressed the fear that this would be a form of colonial exploitation, and it fell to Syrkin to remind the pioneers that exploitation occurs in production and not in exchange.

Back in New York, Syrkin heard about the violent riot of Arabs against Zionist leftists in Jaffa in 1921. He died in 1924.

iii

If for Syrkin capitalism made the Diaspora dangerous, for the idiosyncratic Marxist Ber Borochov it suggested historical laws which made immigration to Palestine inevitable. Borochov was born in a Jewish town in the Ukraine in 1881; his family were staunch members of Hibat Zion. As a young man, Borochov not only made an energetic study of Marxism but compiled the Jewish Pale's first bibliography of contemporary Yiddish literature. He was among the first to apply quantitative methods to the study of Jewish class structure. When Lenin rejected the idea of Jewish autonomy in 1901, Borochov left the Russian Social Democratic Workers' Party; by 1906 he had become a leading member of Poale Zion in Russia.

At the Sixth Zionist Congress, Borochov emerged as a bitter opponent of the Uganda proposal. He defended his opposition to the plan with what can only be called Marxian coyness; and yet in doing so formulated a defense of a Jewish national home in Palestine which was to be enormously important to settlers who came out of Poale Zion, especially to the leftist radicals of the Third Ascent, who went to the Yishuv after World War I. "We do not claim," he wrote in "Our Platform," in 1906, "that Palestine is the sole or best territory. We merely indicate that Palestine is the territory where territorial autonomy will be obtained. Our Palestinianism is neither theoretical nor 'practical' but predictive."[18]

In his most famous essay, "Nationalism and the Class Struggle," written in 1905, Borochov adopted the central premises of Russian Marxism and applied them to Zionism. It was in view of those premises that his "prediction" made sense. "In the social production which men carry on," he wrote, "they enter into definite relations that are indispensable and independent of their will; these relations of production correspond to a definite state of development of their material powers of production."[19] What propelled history, Borochov continued, were class conflicts; in the "bourgeois stage," the conflict between the capitalist and the worker.

In addition to the standard Marxian notions of "relations" and "means" of production, Borochov made an original and innovative claim: he contended that there were "conditions" of production, consisting essentially of the national territory, that conditions of production helped to account for the differences between peoples' linguistic and spiritual expression. Moreover, conditions of production varied considerably from one territory to another: "They are geographic, anthropological, and historic . . . a sound basis for a purely materialistic theory of the *national* question." Other Marxists—Plekhanov for one—had accounted for national differences in terms of geography. But Borochov went further, associating conditions of production with the nation's presumably inherent struggle for survival. "The assets of a social body," he wrote, "lie in its control of its conditions of production; the national struggle is waged not for the preservation of cultural values but for control of 'material possessions.' "

Thus, a nation defended its territory in order to survive, to preserve the "feelings of national kinship" deriving from shared "conditions of production." To be sure, this national "feeling" was reactionary when its bourgeois proponents did not link it to the class struggle; in that case, it was merely "nationalism." But the nation *might* be of fundamental value to the working class under certain conditions, especially when the national conditions of production were denied. In any case, the proletariat must be interested in nationalism as a focus for political action: "If the general base and reservoir of the conditions of production, the territory, is valuable to the landowning class for its land resources and as a base for political power . . . then it has value for the proletarian— i.e., as a place in which to work."

Significantly, it was not Borochov's view that national consciousness would disappear, even in a classless society: "Every serious student must consider as far-fetched and hazardous the contention that national differences will be eradicated simultaneously with the eradication of class differences." In making conditions of production a fundamental category of Marxist analysis, Borochov seemed rather to imply that nation was as important a category of analysis as class: both were rooted in material reality. Consequently, or so Borochov concluded, workers of a nation might justifiably do whatever was necessary to survive as a national proletariat.

In "Our Platform," Borochov applied his materialist view of nationalism to the Jewish question:

> Our point of departure is the development of the class-struggle of the Jewish proletariat. Our point of view excludes a general program of the Jewish people *as a whole*. The anomalies of the entire Jewish nation are of interest to us only as an objective explanation of the contradictions of the Jewish proletariat . . . We [Jewish workers] defend our cultural needs and economic needs, wherever we are. We fight for the political, the national, the ordinary human needs of the Jewish worker.

The Jews, Borochov argued, were in a uniquely vulnerable position in Eastern Europe; in the *Galut*, the Diaspora, Jewish workers depended on the proletariat of what Pinsker called the "host" people. The Jewish class struggle, meanwhile, was directed against a bourgeoisie with little economic power and, since it was largely Jewish, no political power at all. A solution would be found only "when the Jews find themselves in the 'primary' levels of production." Only then will the Jewish proletariat "hold in its hands the fate of the economy of the entire country, the sectors of the economic life where the fabric of the society as a whole is woven." Indeed, Borochov thought he discerned a law of history that other Marxists had missed:

> We may state quite simply that a national struggle takes place wherever the development of the forces of production demands that the conditions of production belonging to a social group be better, more advantageous, or that in general they be expanded.

That may not have been putting it simply, but Borochov was suggesting an insight which many young Jews found to be enormously shrewd: When Jewish workers found themselves economically disadvantaged—i.e., vulnerable to the forces of the larger economy—they might be expected to gain a new "strategic base" within the international division of labor, as much for the sake of the class struggle as for their own sake. Genuine nationalism in no way obscured class-consciousness, Borochov insisted. It manifested itself only among "progressive elements" of oppressed nations; indeed, it was "the purpose of national demands to assure the nation normal conditions of production, to assure the proletariat a normal base for its labor and class struggle."

Borochov conceded that the first choice for most Jewish emigrants from Eastern Europe was America. But this was not the right choice, he argued, since Jewish workers in New York, for example, were employed almost exclusively in the production of consumer goods and "performed no essential functions in the *primary* levels of production."

> [The immigrant] is incapable of paralyzing the economic organism in a single stroke as can the railroad or other workers who are more advantageously situated in the economic structure . . .
>
> Upon his arrival, [he] seeks to enter the first levels of production, the levels of constant capital. Through their concentration in the large

cities, however, Jews retain their former economic traditions and are condemned to the final levels of production, the labor-intensive manufacture of consumer goods. Thus the need of the Jews to develop their forces of production and become a normal proletariat remains unsatisfied.

Why should Jewish immigrants to America not count on gainful employment there? In a later essay, "The Economic Development of the Jewish People," Borochov wrote that intense competition among market entrepreneurs would result in the increased use of machinery, the concentration of industrial capital, reduced wage bills, and so on. There would thus be a steady growth in that part of investment capital devoted to what Marx called "constant" capital —machinery, plant, materials—and a proportionate diminution of that part devoted to "variable" capital—i.e., to labor. Following Marx, Borochov called this the tendency of the "organic" composition of capital to rise, and he predicted both a general decline in the rate of profit and cyclical crises which would become more and more intense. Borochov concluded that the rise of the organic composition of capital would not only bring about widespread and increasing unemployment but that it would first hit workers— particularly Jewish workers—concentrated in enterprises where the proportion of variable capital is high. Since Jewish labor was concentrated almost exclusively in the production of variable capital —i.e., as in the small capitalist trades of the Jewish workers of the Pale—Jewish labor would be displaced by non-Jewish labor.

> Marx divides modern capital into two categories: *constant* capital (land, factory buildings, raw materials, coal, machines) and *variable* capital (human labour-power) . . . The Jews as a whole participate but little in the production and distribution of constant capital . . . That constant capital grows at the expense of variable capital is one of the most important generalizations in Marxian economic theory . . . the fact that machines displace the worker . . .[20]

Borochov correctly identified an important development in the political economy of Eastern European Jewry. But had he read Marx's *Capital* more patiently—or read Adam Smith's *Wealth of Nations* at all—it is doubtful he would have drawn the conclusions he did from which he inferred the inexorable forces of Zionist emigration and settlement. For one, capitalist advance did not have to result in the absolute impoverishment of workers. To be sure, successful capitalists might become richer and richer *relative* to the workers they employed; there might be a "relative impoverishment." (Marx had wryly anticipated how this, too, hurts: "Put a castle next to a house," he wrote, "and the house becomes a hut.") But a rise in the organic composition of capital did not mean that wages could not rise substantially, or that severe unemployment must be chronic and increasing. In fact, a general rise in the organic composition of capital could mean unprecedented enrichment for everybody.

Enrichment presupposed other developments: unions would have to be formed to fight for wage hikes; entrepreneurs would have to be skilled in science; credit would have to be organized. But the mere fact that New York machines were able to do the work of immigrant Jewish weavers from Lodz was no reason to expect, as Borochov did, the drift of indigent Jews to Palestine. On the contrary, if machines made things faster and in larger quantities, and if Jewish workers and their children displaced by machines moved to new industries and professions in spite of anti-Semitism, then real wages—for American Jews and everybody else—might rise to a level much higher than before. Just such an age of improvement was about to dawn on the Jews of America, led by, of all people, the Jew-baiting inventor of the Model T.

Borochov did not foresee this. His solution was for Jews to find some underdeveloped land which they could develop by means of labor-intensive enterprises. It would be best, he thought, for Jewish workers to get a strategic base in Palestine, where the economy was still primitive; where the kinds of skills Jews possessed would allow them to participate more handsomely in the class struggle than in America. The national territory, he thought, would give Jewish workers just what America could not: "National competition is possible only within the national economic territory; no nation can compete successfully unless it has a strategic base."

Naturally, many young Zionist pioneers embraced Borochov's vision; life in Palestine was difficult, and the pioneers liked to think Jewish workers had no alternative but to come there sooner or later. Indeed, the pioneers began to talk about "reversing the pyramid" of Jewish occupations in their national home, about concentrating in that part of the economy—i.e., agriculture—which was the "primary condition of production." In this way, they joined Tolstoyan notions of making a Hebrew peasantry with a "structural" analysis of Palestinian economic life. Also, radical socialism appealed to the pioneers' democratic sensibilities, since the small, mainly agricultural collectives they envisioned would be directed by the whole community in common, would be a classless society— "from each according to his ability, to each according to his need."

Still, it is doubtful that Borochov provided a serious rationale for Jews leaving the Pale to concentrate in labor-intensive production. Just why, for example, he thought it impossible for Jews to become railroad workers in America he left unexplained. Perhaps he implicitly agreed with Syrkin that anti-Semitism would prevent this. Certainly he thought—wrongly—that the capitalist economy was constantly contracting, not expanding, and that this would create difficulties for any immigrant group. Borochov also seems a victim of his own sleight of hand regarding his use of the term "primary conditions of production." Territories, of course, may be important to the development of any nation insofar as it needs to evolve somewhere in the world. But this is an arguable anthropological point, surely, not a reason to expect a strike of farm workers to have more effect than a strike of garment workers. In fact, the pioneers could not more paralyze the Palestinian economy in a single stroke than could the Jewish garment workers in America; and had they been able to, their power would have had nothing to do with Eretz Yisrael's historic role of providing ancient Hebrews with their primary condition of production.

Perhaps Borochov had an agenda which he was unable to articulate or unwilling to acknowledge: that the loss of Eretz Yisrael, after all, like the abandonment of the rural-life Yiddish in Eastern Europe, did not make the Jews vulnerable so much as make *Judaism* vulnerable. Was Borochov's reasoning merely Marxist in form but cultural Zionist in content? It seems clear that Borochov's Jewish workers did *not* become a nation in Palestine in order to become a more vital proletariat; they became a proletariat in Palestine in order to become a more vital nation. Borochov's very notion of a strategic base seemed an encoded endorsement of Achad Haam's notion that Jewish culture, to survive, must be the product of every branch of production, "from agriculture and handicrafts, to science and literature."

Borochov never saw Palestine. He agitated for Poale Zion until the war, and then he traveled to America. In 1917 he went back to Russia to participate in the Revolution and organized a small Zionist brigade that fought in the Red Army. Exhausted, he died in December of that year.

iv

Aaron David Gordon was perhaps the most important of the early Labor Zionist theorists, distinguished from the others by his actually living in Palestine. Gordon's ideas emerged out of his direct experience with colonial conditions. His political party, Ha'Poel Ha'Tzair, was remarkably resistant to the more ambitious plans of Eastern European socialist doctrine. Yet it became the moving force behind the establishment of the first agricultural collectives.

Gordon was born in 1856, the same year as Achad Haam, in an obscure corner of the Pale—Troyano, near Vilna. His father saw to it that he received a religious education but, unlike Achad Haam's father, did not attempt to discourage him from secular studies. Gordon married at twenty-two and spent much of his subsequent life working as an overseer on the nearby estate of a wealthy relative. Here, he developed a *narod's* attachment to the soil and also had the time to indulge his interest in Russian literature, including Tolstoy, Lermontov, Belinsky, Mikhailevsky, and Gorky.[21] Gordon fathered seven children, but unfortunately only two survived. By no means did he cut himself off from Judaism during this period, especially after the pogroms. He remained active in his town's dwindling kehillah. However, by the age of thirty Gordon had reached something of a dead end. He had little faith in Orthodox law, but less regard for the Jewish enlightenment, the Haskalah, which he thought merely derivative, inauthentic. His ambivalence regarding Orthodox Judaism was made worse by his son, who became an intolerant adherent to religious law and who finally broke with him in bitterness.

What transformed Gordon's attitude toward Hebrew secularism was Achad Haam's collection of essays *At the Crossroads*, which was published in 1895. Thereafter, Gordon saw to it that Hebrew-language study was made compulsory for boys and girls alike in his town. By 1903, Gordon had broached to his family the possibility of settling in Palestine. His determination grew stronger the following year in the wake of the death of his parents and the sale of the estate which employed him. Gordon acknowledged to his wife that the responsible thing was to emigrate to America, not to Palestine; he was now forty-eight years old. But he had underestimated her. She persuaded him to go to Palestine, alone to begin with, and to send for his family later. At the end of 1904, Gordon set out for the "glowing Hebrew landscape" of Palestine's coastal plain. His son now disowned him completely.

Soon after his arrival in the Yishuv, Gordon published a number of essays, which won for him immediate and wide acclaim, although perhaps as much for the curiosity evoked by his age as for the originality of his thoughts. Having come to Palestine before the anti-czarist uprising in St. Petersburg, the "old man" became a culture hero to many Poale Zion youngsters who had followed only after becoming jaded by the failure of the 1905 revolution. Gordon exhorted Jewish intellectuals and tradesmen to transform themselves into agricultural workers, and he demanded that Jewish capitalists, particularly the Rothschild plantation managers, hire Jews—and only Jews—in the Zionist economy. He called for a boycott of any Jewish enterprise which failed to hire Jews; he even provided for the possibility of strikes against the Rothschild colonies in the name of the national ideal.

Gordon coined the slogan "conquest of labor" (*"kibbush avodah"*) and he used it in a novel way. Indeed, he invested it with nuances favored by the culturalists, blending traditional Jewish notions with a rhetoric reminiscent of Russian anarchism. Many settlers were taken with Gordon's ideal of the collective life, with its unselfishness, its emphasis on nature and harmony. And though Gordon's party lacked Poale Zion's more general socialist program, Gordon's principles appealed to many of the Poale Zion pioneers who grew more nationalist in Palestine and, at the same time, recognized the necessity of collectivizing production on the land. They appealed all the more after Gordon led the way in founding the Yishuv's first collective farm.

In 1907, the Zionist executive appointed Arthur Ruppin, an accountant, as their representative in Palestine. They could not have made a better choice. Ruppin was both flexible and incorruptible, and set out to consolidate the Zionist administration with energy. It was Ruppin who, in 1908, set up the Palestine Land Development Company, the PLDC, the most ambitious undertaking of which was the Kinneret farm, which cost £5,000 and employed over thirty Jewish workers. The farm was to serve as a model for how the Zionist organization would purchase and administer land. But Ruppin had not realized how Labor Zionist sentiment had influenced the new immigrant workers. In 1909 there was a strike at the Kinneret farm, and many of the workers claimed that they should be given political autonomy as well as greater material reward. Nor was the strike Ruppin's first warning; the work was hard, and malaria was rampant among the settlers. Ruppin had estimated that half the 5,000 young Jews of the Second Ascent left after only a short stay.

At first Ruppin thought he could defuse the Kinneret strike by getting rid of the manager, an agronomist named Bermann. "The workers repeatedly made the point," Ruppin wrote, "that the manager, with his salary and personal expenses on journeys, etc., was an intolerable burden for the farm. His *bourgeois* standard of living, in contrast with the miserable accommodation and food for the workers—who were mostly better educated than he was—created a social gulf which Bermann had further aggravated by his domineering behavior." The strike ended in time, but as Ruppin later acknowledged, it represented a much deeper malaise, "profoundly important for the future development of the country."

It became increasingly obvious to Ruppin that cultivating the self-respect of workers would be a prerequisite for making Hebrew society grow. But how? "There are few things sadder to imagine than the state of mind of the old colonists . . . The older generation had grown weary and sullen with the labour and toil of a quarter of a century, without the faintest hope for the future or the slightest enjoyment of the present. The younger generation [meanwhile] . . . wished but one thing, namely to leave agriculture, which could not provide their parents a secure living, and to find a 'better' occupation in the outside world."[22] Coincidentally, Achad Haam revisited

Palestine around this time, and he put the predicament in which Ruppin and the workers found themselves with characteristic acuity:

> There are laborers who have already attained the ideal of becoming independent farmers, but are still counted as laborers because they maintain a connection to their former "party." Most were settled by the Jewish Colonization Association on the tenant-farmer system in the Lower Galilee. Their holdings are comparatively large, and they have neither time nor need to work for others; on the contrary, they themselves need labor at certain seasons and, having become employers, do not always employ Jewish labor!
>
> This last phenomenon gave me much food for thought. Among these young farmers I know some men who had been regarded as the pick of the laborers, not only from the point of view of efficiency, but in their character and devotion to the national ideal. If these men could not stand the test, then perhaps it is really impossible for anybody to stand it. But when I put this problem to laborers who had not yet become farmers, they replied that these comrades of theirs, having become farmers, had lost their proletarian sentiments. Then I asked further: "If so, where is the solution? You yourselves tell me that most of your comrades came to Palestine in the hope of becoming farmers in the course of time, and as the hope grew fainter the number of new arrivals grew less. But then laborers come with hope of becoming farmers and, as soon as they achieve their ambition, lose their idealism and employ non-Jews on their land, what is the good of 'conquering labor,' of all your efforts?"
>
> To this question the laborers nowhere gave me a satisfactory answer.[23]

Obviously Achad Haam had not spoken with the Kinneret strikers —among them Berl Katznelson—who increasingly demanded *collectivist* arrangements within the PLDC.

Gordon and several other "most capable workers" had already started up a model cooperative at nearby Umm Juni, which they called Degania; this was a *kvutza*, or group, a forerunner of the kibbutz. The members of Degania had asked Ruppin for support, but now they also insisted that the Kinneret farm be run along cooperative lines. They suggested that the manager's job be eliminated and that the farm be placed in the hands of a workers' committee. Ruppin balked. To get PLDC support, he told Degania leaders, they would have to employ an expert manager and pay members according to their work. As for collectivizing the Kinneret farm, that would be "out of the question." But Gordon and the other workers would not be deterred, and meanwhile, the Kinneret farm went on strike again. Finally, in 1911, Ruppin relented. "I was impressed with their seriousness," he admitted. Fascinated, if skeptical, Ruppin gave the cooperative movement most of what it wanted—a decisive step, the first act of cooperation between the practical Zionists in the Diaspora and the Labor Zionists in Palestine.[24]

Incidentally, the leaders of Degania did not relax their ideology just because they had won a political victory. They shared everything—earnings, food, clothes, the Arab mud huts which were their first homes. They also shared the mosquitos, and bugs, the night watches against Bedouins and robbers, malaria, typhoid, sandfly fever—everything, that is, except their beds, for they lived the first several years in chastity. They refused to employ hired labor, to handle money except in their dealings with the outside world, and even to mark their shirts before going to the communal laundry for fear that the inclination toward possessiveness would slowly corrupt them.[25]

·

It was during those early days at Degania that Gordon wrote his most influential essays. He, too, urged the Jews to have a distinct "spirit," continued and fulfilled in such practical actions as forming collectives. In primitive times, Gordon wrote, the Jewish spirit issued from the bond between the Jews and their God; now it must produce a subtle, modernist culture that bound the Hebrew language to the collectivized land of Israel. This culture would be produced by a Jewish majority that used Hebrew to evolve its secular and scientific style of life: "In the center of all our hopes we must place work. Our entire structure must be founded on labor."

Gordon's emphasis on the dignity of physical labor, which the early kibbutz movement raised to an obsession, has established him in Zionist memory as a much more stridently anarchist thinker than he was in fact. For unlike Bakunin and Tolstoy, Gordon never believed physical work was an end in itself. He viewed labor in the manner of a positivist, as Achad Haam saw "flesh" producing "spirit." Labor produced commodities, and it put one in direct contact with the earth. But labor also produced national experience; indeed, it found its highest expression in national art and literature.

"All that we wish for in Palestine," he reflected, "is to work with our very own hands at all things which make up life, to labor with our hands at all kinds of work, trades and crafts, from the most skilled to the coarsest and most difficult." As laborers, Jews could consider themselves possessed of an authentic, living culture. "Work," he said, "would heal us."[26]

> What is the character of the culture we propose to create? We call this culture the regeneration of the spirit—not only a living spirit that fills and vitalizes the entire body, that in turn receives from the body its life force, but it is an aristocratic sort of spirit setting up its abode within the confines of its heart and mind. It is a culture concerned with ideas.
>
> A living culture embraces the whole of life. Whatever a man creates for the sake of life is culture: the tilling of the soil, the building of homes, the paving of roads, and so on . . . Here is the foundation of culture, the stuff from which it is made. What a man feels, what he does, thinks, lives while he is at work—arrangement, method, shape, the way a thing is done—these are forms of culture. Together with living nature underlying all these forms, there is molded the spirit of culture. Higher culture draws its nourishment from science, art, imagination and opinions; from poetry, ethics, religion. Higher culture is the butter of culture in general, of culture in the broadest sense. But is it possible to make butter without milk, or will man make butter from milk belonging to others—his own butter?[27]

It is worth noting that Gordon's hope was to "heal" Judaism as well as Jews. The pioneers, as the early folk song put it, were to "rebuild themselves in the building of the land." But they were not to do so only as individuals; their immediate major task was the revival of the national language: "All must work; all must learn Hebrew."[28] Indeed, Gordon was an avid supporter of the Hebrew University and was shocked to discover that his own reputation for proletarian radicalism dampened enthusiasm for it among some members of his own party. Gordon wrote that the university would house the "spiritual possessions" that had kept Jews together since the dispersion. He dismissed as mere "idol worship" the notion that working Eretz Yisrael would become the basis of some new, ecstatic religion. "The Jewish pioneers are not planting some new seed in Palestine," he wrote, but transplanting a "full grown tree with many roots and branches, which must blossom and live again in its original soil."[29]

Notwithstanding its proletarian dimension, the conquest of labor was thus a product of the Jewish spirit, as Jewish as the Sabbath, not an internationalist cause. Collectives were justified as socialism was justified, but the *kvutza* also drew on traditional messianic feelings so recently eclipsed by enlightenment perceptions. The *kvutzot* certainly never became instruments for the multinational, anti-imperialist revolution the young Syrkin had proposed they become, and were in no sense microcosms for the project of Arab-Jewish bi-nationalism. Gordon assumed from the start that Arabs, or any other Gentiles for that matter, were excluded from the Hebrew national project of which the *kvutza* was but a part.

This is not to say that members of the collectives were insensible to the injustice of excluding the Arabs. But as Achad Haam had seen in 1893, Arab labor represented a threat to Hebrew, hence a threat to Zionism. Gordon was apprehensive that private Jewish farmers would exploit Arabs and turn the Yishuv into a collection of tense latifundia: "Whatever relations exist between the classes are in the main economic, and the struggle between them is an economic struggle. [In the Rothschild settlements] the employers are Jews and the workers are members of different nations." But the former failed to see, he continued, that the struggle was also a political one.

> The workers are natives; the employers are foreigners. If we do not till the soil with our very own hands, the soil will not be ours—not only not ours in a social, or national sense, but not even in a political sense. Here we shall also be aliens . . . who traffic in the fruit of the labor of others.[30]

Gordon did not believe that a conflict between Jews and Arabs was inevitable. "Through the power of truth," he wrote, "we shall find a way for a life of partnership with the Arabs. Cooperative life and work would become a blessing for both peoples." In retrospect, however, such assertions, however sincere, seem oddly wistful and unconvincing. Indeed, when he was not delivering exhortations to cooperation, Gordon was quite capable of perceiving the clash of interests between Arabs and Jews: Arab peasants were not about to form *kvutzot*, and Arab intellectuals who might well have tried to organize the puny Arab proletariat in the towns would not have done so to make room for Jews. Gordon conceded this in advance:

> Some hold that when we come to Palestine to settle upon the land we are dispossessing Arabs who are its natural masters. But what does this term mean? If mastery of the land implies political mastery, then the Arabs have long ago forfeited their title. If we discount the rights acquired through living on the land and working it, the Arabs, like ourselves, have none other than a historic claim upon the land . . . As for rights accruing from occupation and from work, we, too, live and work upon it. Between us and the Arabs the real difference is based on numbers, not on the character of the claim.

Thus Gordon reduced the hope for cooperation in Palestine to a challenge thrown down to the Arabs to compete peacefully for the land. He had no doubt that Jews could win the competition. Jewish pioneers would be "strengthened by the added numbers" from throughout the Diaspora. If the Arabs took this to mean a power struggle, so be it. But Zionism would prevail, not by subduing the Arabs—their claims were as legitimate as those of the Jews—but by establishing Jewish cooperatives, such as Degania, and then pressing for open immigration. Meanwhile, Zionist collectives would everywhere encroach on Arab towns. Jews would become a majority. Arabs would improve their lot and, having progressed, acquiesce in Zionism.

Moreover, Gordon's (and Syrkin's and Borochov's) emphasis on numbers, the faith in a Jewish majority, is critical for an understanding of the way the Labor Zionist movement came to view democratic standards. Unlike the British liberal tradition, in which the ensuring of minority rights was particularly important, Zionism arose in Eastern European countries where the principle of majority rule was itself an idea of considerable novelty. Zionism would be *ipso facto* democratic, Gordon believed, so long as Jews outnumbered Arabs in Palestine and continued to resist the temptation of exploiting Arab labor. As for Zionism's internal affairs, the Labor Zionists took democracy to be principally a process for electing leaders and ratifying decisions—where all important public purposes had already been decided according to the logic of their revolution. The pioneers who shared Gordon's rhetoric associated freedom with the demand to run their own collectives, with the right of all workers to debate decisions regarding production. The WZO ran things in the Diaspora, and their secretaries ran things in their *kvutzot*. Labor Zionists could not imagine how democratic protections against the tyranny of the majority applied to them—or to Arabs—except insofar as Jews were quintessentially the persecuted people.

Many pioneers were, it is true, much more nonconformist than Jews in Europe, especially regarding sexual matters and questions of literature. Amos Elon recounts the story of a member of a collective who was found with a bullet through the head, a revolver in one hand and a copy of *The Brothers Karamazov* in the other.[31] The pioneers were in rebellion against the Jewish family, against the law, against the stereotype of the Jewish weakling. Still, it cannot be said that their dissenting impulses carried over to a general critique of state power or the celebration of the individual. On the contrary, the settlers presumed that all Jewish afflictions, like world sorrow, would soon be overcome by new men, i.e., the landed Jews to emerge from the Hebrew revolution; that anyone who did not want his shoulder at the wheel of revolution would not have come. Similarly, the ideal of "pioneerism"—what came to be called *chalutziyut*—entailed revolutionary solidarity. Once decisions were taken by the majority, the minority was expected to toe the line. The song that would eventually become the anthem of Labor Zionism, "*Techezakna*" ("May Your Arms Be Strengthened"), puts the matter rather bluntly: "May your spirit not fall, may you rise up in good cheer. Come all, one shoulder together, to the aid of the people."

·

A contemporary of Gordon's observed that he worked the fields of Degania, where he died in 1922, not with the bearing of a proletarian, but with the fervor of pious Jews during the *Neila*, the concluding prayer service of the Yom Kippur liturgy:

> He toiled with reverence and love, his slender body moving to and fro in his work, his lean hand rising and falling vigorously with each digging of the hoe, with heavy streams of perspiration dropping down his face and upon his white beard . . . His eyes had the same quality one perceives in him who has done that which is acceptable in the eyes of God.[32]

For Gordon, unlike Syrkin and Borochov, a revamped *halachic* life may well have been the central goal: Zionism would resemble the old Orthodoxy insofar as it would exist in a routine of public actions and the anticipation of mutual improvement. If only in this sense, the labor movement Gordon inspired was far more the creature of the Pale's traditional messianic universe than might at first seem evident from the left-wing rhetoric and anti-rabbinic sentiments the Zionist settlers so proudly expressed. People engaged in the revival of Hebrew were precisely the last to lose sight of the fact that the word in Hebrew for labor, "*avodah*," was also the word for worship. The Israeli critic Gershon Shaked put it this way: "The ideal of *halacha* was transformed by modern Zionism into the ideal of *hagshama* or 'realization.' Socialist-Zionists interpreted religious observance into human-socialist activism."[33] Rabbi Abraham Isaac Kook, another contemporary of Gordon's living in Jaffa, and a disciple of the Orthodox Zionists, conceived of the advent of the Zionist labor movement as a strengthening of the vessels for *Ruach Elohim*, the "spirit of God." "The secularists will realize in time," he assured himself, "that they are immersed and rooted in the life— land, language, history, and customs—bathed in the radiant sanctity that comes from above." Kook would say: "We lay *tfilin* [phylacteries], the pioneers lay bricks."

v

A final way of grasping the influence of Labor Zionism is to examine just why Orthodox Zionists such as Rabbi Kook were drawn to it. Rabbi Kook was not falsely proud, after all: he did assume that Gordon's Hebrew collectives would prove a stage in the redemption of the Jewish people, over which the Palestinian rabbinate would ultimately preside. Indeed, the Orthodox Zionists defined themselves in a long-standing relationship with Labor Zionism, exploited the *chalutzim's* political successes, and lived off their produce. If nothing else, Kook's attitude was evidence for Labor Zionism's industrial power. There is no Torah, the sages said, where there is no flour.

Orthodox delegates had made up a tiny minority of the early Zionist congresses—never more than 8 percent—and they were considered apostates by the majority of the Eastern European Orthodox communities. Yet they were misfits within Zionism, too—

political Zionists for convenience, but not in principle. They associated with Herzl's idea of a Jewish state, imagining a world without Gentiles, not unlike the kehillah—except that military power would ward off pogromists. Unlike Herzl, they imagined that Orthodox law would be incorporated directly into the state's constitution, and they disdained Herzl's celebration of sovereignty as a challenge to the all-sovereign sovereign. Still, they had no more affinity for the culturalist rebellions of Achad Haam's disciples. Indeed, from 1897 on, the religious Zionists strongly opposed the efforts of Ussishkin and Weizmann to set up Zionist committees promoting secular Hebrew education and culture.

Having been made increasingly aware of their anomalous position within Congress Zionism, the Orthodox delegates had called a conference for Vilna in the spring of 1902. This was the founding meeting of Mizrachi, an abbreviation of *Mercaz Ruchani,* or "spiritual center." That Orthodox Zionists should have used this phrase, "spiritual center," which was by now commonly associated with the ideals of Achad Haam, seemed—and may still seem—ironic. But this was just the effect the Orthodox delegates wanted to achieve. They were staking a claim of their own on the Jewish spirit and were determined to deny it any modernist nuances.

Mizrachi's moving force from the start was Isaac Jacob Reines, a man of great passion but little vision beyond the need to scotch the influence of the secularists. More important for the movement's ideological development was Zeev (Wolf) Jawitz, an accomplished scholar whom the Vilna delegates had named to write Mizrachi's first public proclamation. Jawitz went somewhat beyond his original mandate, which was to justify the political Zionist activity of religious delegates; not only did he proclaim the need for a refuge, he welcomed the culturalists' challenge as an opportunity to recast *halachic* Judaism in a way congenial to Palestinian settlement. "In the Diaspora," he wrote, "it is impossible for the soul of the nation, which is its holy Torah, to exist in full force and for its commandments to be fulfilled in their essential purity."[34] Buoyed by Jawitz's manifesto, Mizrachi leaders called their first large convention in Lida for the spring of 1903. During the year thereafter, they succeeded in organizing some 210 branches in the East, though Mizrachi failed to make much of an impact among cadres actually bound for Palestine.

Just how much the Orthodox Zionists were willing to see in Zionism the chance to rebuild a world apart—the kehillah, the yeshiva, rabbinic rule—was evidenced later in 1903, at the Sixth Zionist Congress. We have seen that, Jawitz's exegeses notwithstanding, most Mizrachi delegates voted to pursue the Uganda offer. After Herzl was out of the way, however, Mizrachi began to confront the power, "Palestinism," and gradualism of the culturalists. In 1908, Rabbi Yehuda Leib Fishman was sent to Palestine to explore how Mizrachi's proselytizing work could be initiated, and Fishman was particularly encouraged by Rabbi Abraham Isaac Kook, the Chief Rabbi of Jaffa. For his part, Kook welcomed this new trend in Zionism and together with Fishman took over the Tahkemoni school in Jaffa, the first of many schools which would constitute Orthodox Zionism's educational infrastructure. It was mainly with schools that Mizrachi fit into the interstices of the Zionist settlements.

Mizrachi continued to oppose secularist cultural programs in the WZO: in 1911, at the Tenth Zionist Congress, Weizmann and Sokolow pushed through a new program to promote secular education in all countries where the WZO maintained offices. Rabbi Reines and his powerful young associate Meir Berlin (Bar-Ilan) walked out in protest. Later Berlin would write:

> Church and state are kept separate, treated as separate provinces. Our case is different. Torah and traditions are not a man-made constitution but God's own law. We can have no partial acceptance, for this destroys the sanctity of the Torah [which] more than touches upon state and public life. It provides rules and regulations governing these aspects of life . . . The very sections of our laws which deal with man's relations to his conscience and his Maker also offer general and specific guidance on the conduct of the state and social life, and also our relations with other countries—how to wage war with them and how to live at peace with them. Neither . . . have we ever had laws that were of an exclusively "secular" nature.[35]

Rabbi Kook was stranded in Switzerland at the outbreak of World War I. He made his way to England, where he met Weizmann. Without conceding his new Zionist faith, Kook increasingly acknowledged the symbiosis of labor and *halacha*, and determined that he would make it his life's work to convert the pioneers to *halachic* norms. Kook wrote:

> Secular Jewish nationalism is a form of self-delusion: the spirit of Israel is so closely linked to the spirit of God that a Jewish nationalist, no matter how secularist his intention may be, must, despite himself, affirm the divine. An individual can sever the tie that binds him to life eternal, but the House of Israel as a whole cannot. All of its most cherished national possessions—its land, language, history and customs —are vessels of the spirit of the Lord.

Indeed, the redemption of the Jews in Eretz Yisrael would have a messianic result. Later Kook concluded: "All the civilizations will be revived by the renaissance of our spirit. All quarrels will be resolved, and our revival will cause all life to be luminous with the joy of fresh birth."

Most laboring pioneers resented the influence of Orthodox values on their early lives and thought Orthodox Zionism a contradiction in terms. They were willing to see *halacha* as a stage in their intellectual development. But Labor Zionists and practical Zionists now defined their nationalism in such secular categories as "historical consciousness," language, literature, spirit, aesthetics, and music. Many were philosophical and historical materialists, and if they thought seriously about Jewish religion, it was to reconstruct its principles in terms of nationalism. Rabbis would not rule. Weizmann wrote:

> I have never feared really religious people . . . It is the new secularized type of Rabbi, resembling somewhat a member of a clerical party in Germany, France or Belgium, who is the menace, and who will make a heavy bid for power by parading his religious convictions. It is useless to point out to such people that they transgress a fundamental principle which has been laid down by our sages: "Thou shalt not make of the Torah a crown to glory in, or a spade to dig with." There will be a great struggle . . . something which will be perhaps reminiscent of the *Kulturkampf* in Germany, but we must be firm if we are to survive; we must have a clear line of demarcation . . . Religion should be relegated to the synagogue and the homes of those families

who want it; it should occupy a special position in the schools; but it shall not control the ministries of the state.[36]

Still, the tension was by no means without ambiguities on both sides. The pioneers created an economic infrastructure to which the Orthodox community adhered. The Orthodox sustained the traditional culture without which the Labor Zionists' secularism was merely an abstraction. Secular culture was young and the Hebrew revival easier said than done. If nothing else, the secularists needed something to be against, to be emancipated from—if not the texts, then the liturgy or the law. Only God, the sages said, can make something from nothing.

Nor would the pioneers prove immune to the weird flattery Kook's blessings implied. His notion that the Labor Zionists were inadvertently preparing the ground for "redemption" added a dimension to the Zionist work which pioneers could live with; some were much more comfortable with the messianic flavor of Zionism than Weizmann would have liked. In fact, Mizrachi imparted a certain added legitimacy to Labor Zionism. At the very least, it reinforced the pioneers' view that, even in taking actions to reject the Torah culture, they were taking responsibility for the continuity of the Jewish people. Jawitz's notion that commandments could be carried out in their "essential purity" in the land of Israel appealed to the pioneers' romanticism. Of course, the notion that *mitzvot* had a special purity in the land of Israel, that the Messiah would come faster because of it, struck many non-Zionist Orthodox Jews as vulgar. Yet, in a way, Mizrachi's Zionism always made more sense to the labor pioneers who rejected it than to the Diaspora Orthodox who were supposed to accept it.

4 / Class to Nation

Until the Second Ascent, the Zionist movement was centered in
Eastern Europe. Syrkin and Borochov had articulated powerful
ideas about the fate of the Jews in the Diaspora which the young
activists of Poale Zion assumed to be right and which even influenced the thinking of non-socialist Zionists. In the East, Zionism
increasingly meant a revolution against bourgeois egoism, against
the risks of class conflict, against the rabbinic caste. But those who
actually went to Palestine quickly learned that Labor Zionist criticism of the Diaspora, however elegant, was insufficient to explain
how Jewish immigrants might build the Yishuv. Only after 1905
did Labor Zionists such as Gordon come to grips with problems of
settlement, economy, and politics in their new home; they understood that ideas were no substitute for power, and that what all
settlers lacked was political organization.

Though the outcome was in no sense determined, out of the
conflicting currents within the Yishuv, democratic-socialist institutions took root, especially between the Balfour Declaration in 1917
and the rise of European Fascism. The challenge, Gordon argued,
was to defeat the capitalist ethos of the First Ascent and, in so doing,
to transform the World Zionist Organization's priorities. There
would have to be collectives, worker self-management, a struggle
for Hebrew education. To remain a democratic cause, Zionism

would have to both create a Hebrew majority and refrain from subjugating the Palestinian Arabs; Zionism would fail, Gordon held, if Arabs became the pioneers' hewers of wood and carriers of water.

i

Of that group of people who organized the Second Ascent, none was more remarkable than David Ben-Gurion, who was the driving force behind the Achdut Ha'Avodah movement—the "Unity of Labor"—which eventually provided the core of the Mapai Party (the "Israel Workers" Party). By 1935, Mapai dominated the agencies of the WZO, and from then on its purposes became indistinguishable from Zionism itself. In Ben-Gurion, Zionism acquired a leader of world-historical stature. Like other such figures—Gandhi comes to mind—Ben-Gurion now presented the national movement he led as embodying a universal morality.

Ben-Gurion was born David Gruen in Plonsk, Poland, in 1886; his father, Avigdor Gruen, was a stalwart follower of Hibat Zion. David, who received his early education in his father's *cheder* (a one-room Hebrew school), was a strong-minded boy, but there is no evidence that he was ever at odds with his father's views; as an adolescent David helped found a Zionist youth society. In 1904, he moved to Warsaw to join Poale Zion. This was the era of the Uganda controversy and David joined the faction which staunchly opposed any territorial solution other than Palestine. He emigrated to the Yishuv in 1906 and, as a gesture of commitment, swore never to speak Yiddish again. Like other pioneers who were repudiating their origins, he took the Hebrew name Ben-Gurion, meaning "Son of Lions." He found work as a farmhand, first on the coastal plain, then in the Galilee.

In 1906, in Ramle, Ben-Gurion participated in the conference which established Poale Zion in Palestine. It is noteworthy that Ben-Gurion's understanding of Zionism was already so clearly inclined toward the primacy of pioneering that, although he had been in the Yishuv less than a year, he vociferously objected to the subordination of the Palestinian branch of the movement to the Russian. He demanded that Poale Zion acknowledge that its Palestinian cadres were the vanguard of the movement. He would later state the matter this way:

The Hebrew worker came here not as a refugee, clutching at any reed offered him. He came as a representative of the whole people; and as a vanguard pioneer in the grand enterprise of the Hebrew revolution did he capture his position in the labor market.

In all his deeds and activities, be they small or large, in his work in village and town, in the creation of his own agriculture and industrial economic structures, in conquering language and culture, in defense, in fighting for his interests at work, in satisfying his class interest and national interests—in all this the Jewish worker is conscious of the historical task destined to be carried out by the working-class preparing the revolution which makes labor and work the dominant elements in the life of the country and the people.

The Hebrew worker combined in his life work national redemption and class war, and in his class organization created the content of the historical aims of the Jewish people.[1]

In 1910 Ben-Gurion moved to Jerusalem and, in collaboration with his lifelong colleague Yitzchak Ben-Tzvi, began to edit *Ha'Achdut* (*Unity*), the organ of Poale Zion in Palestine. But he would not remain at this post for long. In 1912 Ben-Gurion went to Constantinople to study law; he did so in the hope that he would eventually represent Labor Zionist interests to an Ottoman administration which, since the Young Turk revolt, had become somewhat more reform-minded. Despite his absence from the Yishuv, his qualities did not go unappreciated, and in 1913 he was elected to the Central Committee of Poale Zion. He later attended the Eleventh Zionist Congress in Vienna.

Inevitably, the outbreak of the First World War put an end to Ben-Gurion's studies, and though he had become openly pro-Ottoman, he was nonetheless expelled from Palestine in 1915 by the commander of the Turkish forces; the Poale Zion program had been judged inimical to Turkish interests. Ben-Gurion made his way to Alexandria, where he met an obscure Zionist militant and writer, Vladimir Jabotinsky, who was then engaged in the formation of a Jewish legion to fight under British auspices. Chaim Weizmann, now in England, encouraged Jabotinsky's effort, though he thought Jabotinsky "overlaid with a certain touch of the theatrically chivalresque, a certain queer and irrelevant knightliness." For his part, Ben-Gurion opposed the idea of a legion, fearing Turkish retaliation against the Yishuv; he did not think that it was in the interests of Labor Zionists to side with either Britain or Turkey. Rather than remain in Egypt, Ben-Gurion traveled to North America to proselytize among left-wing Jewish trade-union activists for the Labor Zionist collectives in Palestine. It was while Ben-Gurion was delivering speeches in New York that the British government made a sweeping commitment to Weizmann in London, which by promising to transform the rights of Jewish settlers in Palestine compelled all Zionists to make common cause with the British against the Turks.

.

The British government promulgated the Balfour Declaration on November 2, 1917. Its terms endorsed the aim of the First Zionist Congress to secure a "national home" for Jews in Palestine, and were the culmination of months of negotiation between Weizmann (who was still advised by Achad Haam) and the British Foreign Secretary, Lord Arthur Balfour. By the end of 1917, it seemed likely that Turkey would be defeated, and that Palestine would come under British occupation along with territories that would become the modern states of Syria and Iraq, and the territories of the Arabian peninsula—the Hejaz, as it was then called. The Balfour Declaration committed the British government to stationing forces in Palestine, to further its own interests in the region, but also to help secure Zionist aims.

In view of how quickly the Zionist cause came into conflict with British interests, it may now seem perverse that Balfour promoted so obscure a cause. But in 1916 and 1917, one of the principal aims of British policy was to persuade the United States government to enter the war against Germany. Though America had entered the war before Balfour's undertaking to Zionism was sealed, great thought had been given in the British Foreign Office, especially during 1916, to the positive potential impact of a pro-Zionist undertaking on American Jews; indeed, Justice Louis D. Brandeis had persuaded Balfour that President Wilson would particularly view with favor a Jewish Palestine under British protection; an important consideration when negotiations with Weizmann began. Nor did Balfour think he could ignore the goodwill of the Russian Jewish masses as long as the Russian Army fought on under Kerensky.

For his part, Weizmann—who had been mobilized and was engaged in war research—succeeded in converting to Zionism some of the most prominent British political figures. Prime Minister Lloyd George admired him for his contribution to the national effort; C. P. Scott, the editor of *The Manchester Guardian*, became a close friend, as did other influential liberals in Manchester and London. Weizmann even succeeded in winning over some of the Tories in Lloyd George's coalition government, not least of whom was Lord Balfour himself. ("Are we never to have adventures?" Balfour asked the Lords. "Are we never to try new experiments?"[2]) Weizmann was justly proud of having secured the political charter for Zionism which Herzl had failed to obtain. Nor was his achievement lost on the rest of the Zionist movement. After Balfour's undertaking was made public, Weizmann occupied a commanding position in world Zionism, especially as the influence of Zionists in Berlin and Vienna faltered along with Germany's power. Among Berlin Zionists were extraordinary personalities, such as Kurt Blumenfeld, the man who later won over Albert Einstein to the idea of a Jewish national home. But it was Weizmann who took on the responsibility of organizing the Zionist commission which the Balfour Declaration mandated as part of an anticipated British occupation.

Significantly, the Balfour Declaration was not welcomed by all sides. It came as a betrayal for the Arab leaders who had themselves allied with the British. Two years before, Sir Henry MacMahon—then High Commissioner for Egypt—had promised the Hashemite Sharif of Mecca, the Emir Hussein, that Hussein's sons would rule those territories their forces would help wrest from the Turks. It was precisely on the basis of this understanding that Hussein encouraged his sons to fight with T. E. Lawrence on the British side, and Hussein assumed that the territories in question included Palestine and other lands that were traditionally considered to be part of southern Syria. Nor was the Balfour Declaration the first example of British furthering its war aims by making irreconcilable commitments. At the very time MacMahon was negotiating with Hussein, Sir Mark Sykes, an assistant secretary of the War Cabinet, was promising control of Damascus and Beirut to the French. Hussein certainly had no inkling of a British tilt to Zionism, or of the prospect of permanent British rule over any Syrian territory. And it should be stressed that there had already developed in Damascus a Syrian national movement of urban notables and intellectuals, many of whom had been trained by Western missionaries. Syrian nationalists were not now prepared to welcome either French imperialism or a Hashemite king. Certainly no Arab, Syrian, or Hashemite took seriously Balfour's guarantees of "civil and religious rights" for Palestine's 700,000 Arab residents.

.

Ben-Gurion was not much impressed by those guarantees, either; he discerned a rich new opportunity: "Britain has made a magnificent gesture, she has recognized Zionist claims to the existence of a Jewish nation and has acknowledged the Zionist right to settle in the whole of Palestine."[3] Moreover, since the British army commanded by General Edmund Allenby was poised to attack Palestine, Britain's "gesture" implied more than a favorable diplomatic climate for Zionism. There would be British soldiers to enforce Zionist claims where Turkish forces had suppressed them. Still, the Balfour Declaration did not lead to complacency on Ben-Gurion's part, and for good reason. On November 17, just two weeks after the WZO had its charter from Britain, Kerensky was brought down in St. Petersburg. Trotsky, who had for years railed against "the hysterical sobbings of the romantics of Zion," was now Foreign Minister of the new Soviet government. There were three other Jews in Lenin's ruling inner circle. Tens of thousands of Russian Jewish radicals—Borochov among them—had dreamed of such a government for a generation and had participated faithfully in the Revolution; anti-Semitism was officially outlawed.

Unlike Borochov, Ben-Gurion was by now a confirmed Palestinian; and at a time when few Russian Jews could be expected to fight for the Yishuv, Ben-Gurion enlisted in Jabotinsky's Jewish Legion and exhorted friends in the Palestinian labor movement to do the same. Yet the competition between Zionism and Russian socialism had suddenly come to a head in the most dramatic way possible, and Ben-Gurion was not about to take the success of his cause for granted merely because of British backing. Britain, Ben-Gurion wrote, had not "given" Palestine to the Zionists, and could not do so even if the whole land were conquered and the whole world agreed. "Only the Hebrew people can transform the right of settlement into a tangible fact; only they, with body and soul, with their strength and capital, must build their national home and bring about their national redemption."

Ben-Gurion's views were not yet terribly influential, but they are worth noting here because they coincided neatly with the practical Zionist ideas of Weizmann and the mainstream of the WZO. While the veteran political Zionist Max Nordau (who had withdrawn from Zionist affairs in 1911) did not miss the new opportunity to reaffirm Herzl's old call for mass emigration to a "Jewish state"—"at least half a million young men and women, to settle there at any cost, to toil there, to suffer there if need be"—Ben-Gurion and Weizmann both rejected the idea that Britain had simply handed Palestine to the Zionist movement. They certainly continued to abjure the call for a Jewish state as pretentious and provocative. Weizmann's chief aide, Nahum Sokolow, wrote: "It has been said and is still obstinately repeated by anti-Zionists again and again that Zionism aims at the creation of an independent 'Jewish State.' This is wholly fallacious. The 'Jewish State' was never part of the Zionist program."[4] Achad Haam went so far as to suggest inviting the Arabs into a joint venture:

> The Balfour Declaration does not affect the right of the other inhabitants who are entitled to invoke the right of actual dwelling. Palestinian Arabs, too, have the right to a National Home, have the right to develop national forces to the extent of their ability . . . In such circumstances it is no longer possible that the national home of one of them could be total. The management of the whole has to be directed in agreement with the interests of all.[5]

In fact this last proposal of Achad Haam's proved too much. Their rejection of a state did not mean that such people as Weizmann and Ben-Gurion were proposing to give up on the idea of a national home in the full sense. It was one thing to reject Nordau's unrealistic demand for mass Jewish immigration; it was quite another to give up on the idea of an eventual Jewish majority. Achad Haam's vision of cooperation between Jewish pioneers and Palestine's Arab inhabitants was perhaps consistent with the cultural Zionists' democratic sentiments. But it was also the product of an idealism which, Ben-Gurion knew, could be cultivated only from afar. Achad Haam's prior vision, that of a Hebrew nation, was after all not yet a tangible fact in Palestine. For Ben-Gurion, that nation could emerge only from a Hebrew working class that would eventually become dominant in Palestine; he came to use the slogan "from class to nation."

For his part, Weizmann complained that Achad Haam's pessimistic, supersensitive temperament had finally got the better of him. "Whatever you got was much," Weizmann wrote of his mentor, "or at least, big enough." Increasingly Weizmann echoed the ideals of the Labor movement, though he never considered himself a part of it. He wrote: "It is essential to remember that we are not building our National Home on the model of Djika and Nalevki"—typical ghetto districts of Warsaw. (In 1923, Weizmann declared to a Palestinian audience: "After the Mandate there will be no political successes for years; those political successes that you want you will have to gain by your own work in the Emeq, the Valley of Jezreel, in the marshes and the hills, not in the offices of Downing Street.")[6]

ii

Though Weizmann now disregarded Achad Haam's skepticism, he moved with dispatch to reach an understanding with the Hashemites, the only Arab leadership remotely open to British designs. In June 1918, Weizmann met with Hussein's oldest son, Faisal, who had been designated to become King of Syria. Weizmann sought to establish Jewish rights in the land, including the right to immigrate and purchase new estates. Faisal did not object; he seemed to think that he could preempt the establishment of a British government in Palestine if he offered protection for Zionism under a united Arab state. Weizmann sensed Faisal's ambitions and, though he could not endorse them, believed that agreement with the Hashemites was the only way to secure Arab approval for more Jewish immigration. In 1919, a formal agreement was signed.

But the mainstream Zionist commitment to a Jewish majority was, in any case, hardly less objectionable to Arab nationalists than Nordau's "state." It was naïve of the two leaders to have undertaken an agreement which failed to address the aspirations of Arab nationalists in Damascus. Granted, the Arab national movement had gained no official recognition from the French and British authorities, but it was represented in the Syrian General Congress, a consultative body with considerable political influence. When the agreement between Weizmann and Faisal was revealed in the winter of 1920, it provoked a storm of opposition from the Syrian and Palestinian nationalists in the congress. They accused Faisal of being in Zionist pay and threatened to sweep away any Hashemite too closely identified with "imperialism" or with the Zionists. Only the Christians of Beirut urged Faisal to accept French protection, but they were motivated, as the Hashemites knew perfectly well, by the fear of domination by pan-Islamic radicals.

Moreover, what had begun as political opposition on the part of the Syrian congress turned violent in the spring of 1920. It was then that the Yishuv got its first taste of siege: a group of marauders murdered a leader of the Jewish Legion, Captain Joseph Trumpeldor, along with six other Labor Zionist Jewish settlers at Tel Chai and Metulla. During the summer of 1920, the congress finally forced Faisal into rebellion against the French; the rebellion was crushed by the French Army, and Faisal was expelled from the country. In December 1920, the League of Nations mandated British rule in Palestine and, with the mandate, the terms of the Balfour Declaration. Weizmann was deeply satisfied. But in Palestine the disturbances continued, beginning with rioting in Jerusalem and culminating on May 2, 1921, with a melee in Jaffa in which forty-eight Arabs and forty-seven Jews were killed. (Significantly, that riot began when a group of Jewish Communists, men and women, demonstrated for working-class solidarity on May Day and passed out leaflets to Arab workers exhorting them to revolt against their own traditional elites. The Arabs thought the demonstration hostile to them and were particularly offended, it seems, by the sight of women in short pants. The Labor Zionist laureate, Y. H. Brenner, was one of the Jewish victims, though he had had nothing to do with the Communist demonstration.)

Just before the May Day fighting, Winston Churchill, then Colonial Secretary, had visited Palestine. Though he had privately expressed disdain for Jewish socialism, he came away determined to enforce the provisions of the Balfour Declaration. But the Arab riots impressed him more than Zionist determination, and he instructed the British administration in Palestine to react sharply to the bloody turn of events. The High Commissioner, Sir Herbert Samuel —a noted British Jew who had been instrumental in promoting the Balfour Declaration—temporarily suspended Jewish immigration; Sir Thomas Haycraft, the Chief Justice of Palestine, held public hearings on Jewish national aims.

In February 1922 Churchill proposed that Palestine be granted a legislative council, to which would be elected twelve Arab representatives and three Jews, with British-appointed representatives holding the balance of power. Had Churchill's proposal been implemented, Zionist hopes for a Jewish majority would have been greatly compromised. However, Weizmann, who believed that Jewish settlements were dependent on British police protection, acquiesced in the plan. Indeed, it was the Arab leadership who opposed the council, fearing that acceptance would further legitimize British rule.

Britain followed with more restrictions on Jews. In June 1922 Churchill issued a White Paper whose purpose was to clarify the somewhat contradictory aims of the Balfour Declaration. The White Paper linked all further Jewish settlement to the "absorptive capacity of the land," which was itself left rather vague. Churchill agreed that Jews might live in Palestine by "right" and not by the "sufferance" of the Arabs, but "Jewish nationality," the White Paper said, would not be imposed on the Arab inhabitants. Weizmann had no quarrel with Churchill's concern for Arab civil rights, but the new restrictions on Jewish immigration clearly represented a capitulation —the first of many—to Arab opposition to what they began to call the "Zionist invasion." Would restrictions on the purchase of land come next?

Churchill had already proposed that the area of Palestine east of the Jordan River be closed to Zionist settlement entirely. This was part of his effort to install Hussein's second son, Abdullah, as king of a new British protectorate known as Transjordan— compensation to Abdullah for surrendering the throne of Iraq to Faisal after the older brother had been driven from Syria. The Zionist executive, which included such militants as Vladimir Jabotinsky, had reconciled itself to that plan, too, but all Zionists were increasingly fearful that restrictions on settlements might be imposed west of the Jordan as well. The failure of the British to impose a legislative council in Palestine was the only victory for the Zionists during this period—and that was not of their own making.

iii

Between 1918 and 1923, the year the White Paper took effect—and, incidentally, the year Nordau died—the gates of Palestine had been thrown open to European Jews; there had been virtually no restrictions on immigration. Yet, as Ben-Gurion had anticipated, fewer than 35,000 Jews came to the national home, and most of the people who made up this Third Ascent came from the Soviet Union only after 1920, that is, after the Soviet government began to repress all expressions of Hebrew nationalism, both secular and religious. Ben-Gurion's battalion reached Palestine in 1918; still in uniform, he felt increasingly distant from the Jewish Pale and began to agitate for a united workers' party in Palestine.

There was always something impulsive about him, but Ben-Gurion was not an impatient man. What seemed to drive him now was the intelligent conviction that the Labor Zionist movement would either unite to exploit the opportunities afforded by the Balfour Declaration or lose the initiative to others. By 1918 the number of organized Jewish laborers in Palestine was about 5,000. Of these people, about 1,500 were agricultural laborers and 500 were settled in *kvutzot* and kibbutzim—not imposing numbers, though one should not be misled by them. The 5,000 pioneers might provide a nucleus which, if properly shaped, would become the revolutionary center around which future immigrants would cohere. Ben-Gurion's point was that the Labor movement could not become that nucleus unless it was organized to include workers in the cities, "to get the *kvutza* out of its loneliness and exclusiveness." Moreover, time was running out. "We did not see any progress in our efforts," he later acknowledged, "since no mass movement was already created around us."[7]

Ben-Gurion's insistence on the need to create a mass movement helped bring about a Zionist workers' conference at Petach Tiqvah in 1919. It was here that Poale Zion and affiliated socialist groups joined together to found Achdut Ha'Avodah, the first united Labor Zionist party. Ha'Poel Ha'Tzair, which still represented mainly agricultural collectives—Hebrew culturalists, anarchists—remained aloof from the new organization. But Achdut Ha'Avodah was not deterred. It quickly developed trade unions, labor exchanges, workers' kitchens, a sick fund, schools, and a bureau of public works. Berl Katznelson explained.

> Union is not going to make us one sect, one religion, one sociological church, and neither is it going to be a mere political party. The central aim of a political party in our day is to gain political power, and change

the society by seizing the institutions of the government. Consequently, a party concentrates its activities on propaganda, on elections, on administration and "politicking" . . . We desire to create life itself in its wide scope and all its different aspects. This can be done only if we take care of all the details of the laborer's life, by permanent "*chalutziyut*" . . .[8]

Just what Achdut Ha'Avodah meant by "*chalutziyut*" (again, "pioneering") had perhaps been best elucidated by Ben-Gurion some years earlier: "One can hardly find a revolutionary movement," he wrote, "that goes deeper than what Zionism wants to do to the life of the Hebrew people." Ben-Gurion was calling not only for proletarian action but for a cultural revolution as well.

It is a revolt against a tradition of many centuries, helplessly longing for redemption. We substitute a will for self-realization, an attempt at reconstruction and creativity in the soil of the homeland. We call for a self-sufficient people, master of its own fate. Instead of a corrupt existence of middlemen, hung up in midair, we call for an independent existence as working people, at home on the soil and in the creative economy.[9]

Alas, men do not make history just as they please. After the founding conference, from the end of 1919 to the end of 1920, about 10,000 Jewish immigrants came to Palestine but few joined Achdut Ha'Avodah, and even fewer joined Ha'Poel Ha'Tzair. What deterred them? It seems that although there was but a small measure of national stridency in Ben-Gurion's version of the Labor Zionist's vocation, this proved enough to deter ultra-left Zionists who came to the Yishuv charged up by the Soviet Revolution. The newcomers tended to be more radical, more internationalist_than the Labor Zionist parties. Many were affiliated with Tzeirei Zion, the "Young of Zion," which modeled itself after the Bolsheviks. The leaders among the newcomers—dynamic young men such as Menachem Elkind and Yehuda Almog—demanded the separation of what they called "national-political" and "economic" activities. Their demands were modeled on the examples of the Soviets: that is, they called for the formation of militant trade unions in all industrial sectors, from which Hebrew workers would fight for a class dictatorship.

Ben-Gurion was not averse to the primacy of the working class, nor to a tight, centralist method of leadership: in 1920 he and the other leaders of Achdut Ha'Avodah rejected the call by some rank and file for greater democratization of the leadership, a call to bar members of the party secretariat from also sitting on the party's trade-union General Council. What worried Ben-Gurion about the newcomers' industrial strategy was that it might lead to the inclusion into their unions of non-Zionists, Jewish Communists, and even Arabs. Worse, non-Zionists might gain control of the various trade unions, and with power devolving on trade unions alone, the Labor Zionist nationalist agenda itself could be jeopardized. Might the Labor movement even cease agitating for Hebrew education and Jewish national autonomy?

Even the leaders of Ha'Poel Ha'Tzair, who had rejected Achdut Ha'Avodah's invitation to merge into one party, began to realize that control over the Yishuv's Labor movement might fall into the hands of people not sufficiently steeped in the meaning of *chalutzi-yut*. But how to absorb newcomers who would not join the Labor Zionist parties into the Labor Zionist project? Ironically, the solution came as a result of the newcomers' own initiatives. Elkind and Almog began to press for a broader laborers' organization, in which their own viewpoints would be more fairly represented. But this was the very demand Ben-Gurion and Katznelson seemed to be waiting for. Achdut Ha'Avodah determined that all workers could indeed join in one unified class organization—so long as its central governing institutions were directly elected by, as it were, all laborers—not by trade-union organizations, where non-Zionists might gain control. Throughout 1920 Achdut Ha'Avodah—still the most conspicuous and well organized of the workers' parties—worked tirelessly for direct elections to a general body and promoted itself as the only party worthy of governing it.

There were some 7,000 organized workers in Palestine by the end of 1920. Approximately 4,500 voted for delegates to a founding convention—about 11 percent of the total adult population of the Yishuv. Achdut Ha'Avodah got 42 percent of the vote; Ha'Poel Ha'Tzair 31 percent. The minor leftist groups were hardly a factor. In December 1920, all the socialist political parties met in Haifa. The result was the formation of the Histadrut (*Histadrut Ha'Klalit shel Ha'Ovdim Ha'Ivriim B'Eretz Yisrael,* the "General Federation of Hebrew Workers"). Membership in the Histadrut was designed to be as inclusive as possible. There were to be regular elections. The founding resolution stated that the organization was open to all workers who did not "exploit the labor of others."

•

The Histadrut undertook a policy of land settlement run along collective lines, which would at once embrace the burgeoning kibbutz movement and negotiate work contracts and working conditions. It set up vocational training centers, encouraged cooperative production and mutual aid; it provided for security through participation in the Haganah, the unified defense organization. The Histadrut set up reception centers for new immigrants. It supported schools devoted to Hebrew-language education.[10]

Ben-Gurion was appointed joint secretary-general of the Histadrut in 1920 and immediately set to writing the organization's constitution. This was perhaps the most important theoretical contribution to Zionism among the many important ones he made. His purpose was to implement the established Labor Zionist agenda, but Ben-Gurion faced some immediate problems of organization which called for great tact and pragmatism. The first related to the fact that, notwithstanding the Yishuv's agricultural sector, it was petty capitalism—a shifting capitalism of workshops, farms, and trade—that dominated the Jewish economy. The young militants in the Histadrut still insisted on a kind of trade-union federalism which —like the *soviets*—promised class struggle at every place of work. Ben-Gurion was at a loss to see how the demands of the militants could be implemented in such an underdeveloped economy.

In the end, Ben-Gurion employed the Histadrut's inclusive principle of membership to formulate a different kind of trade unionism —a kind of citizenship in the Palestinian Jewish working class. Upon joining the Histadrut, a Hebrew laborer would be formally affiliated according to occupation. In fact, however, membership in the Histadrut would continue to be based on the kind of direct, individual membership corresponding to the freedom with which workers voted in the general workers' election of 1920. Each Histadrut worker, that is, would belong to a generality of workers, which would be led by the majority party in future Histadrut elections. The young militants accepted this plan.

A second problem pertained to collective management of Zionist means of production. By 1923, the year Ben-Gurion's constitution was ratified, there were seventeen workers' cooperatives "owned" by World Poale Zion and owing nothing to the Histadrut. Ben-Gurion wanted to forestall the emergence of a privileged class of Zionist veterans with a higher standard of living than the newer immigrants'. At the same time, Ben-Gurion did not want to diminish Zionist economic power. He worried that unless the Histadrut could accumulate capital and dominate investment in the Yishuv, there was a danger that a comparatively wealthy group of capitalist settlers would begin to import wasteful consumer and luxury goods while basic industry was starved. Following Syrkin's ideas, Ben-Gurion believed that a united Labor movement should scrutinize initiatives for investment and dictate pricing policies. Could the workers' organization compete with capitalists and not begin to exploit other, incoming workers?

Ben-Gurion's master stroke was the Chevrat Ovdim—literally, the "Society of Workers." He proposed that the Histadrut itself invest in primary industries and make Chevrat Ovdim the primary holding company. The body of shareholders in Chevrat Ovdim would be precisely coextensive with the membership of the Histadrut. In a way, the Histadrut would constitute itself as an economic state within the larger Palestinian economy, and any Jewish worker who became a citizen would "own" an equal part of the state's corporations. Meanwhile, the trade-union activities of the Histadrut, its strikes and economic demands, would shape the development of the private sector. The Histadrut would also provide those services which theretofore had been the responsibility of the various political parties.

Ben-Gurion's constitution effectively divested all the parties, including Achdut Ha'Avodah, of their major service functions—i.e., the sick funds and marketing cooperatives which had been part of their appeal. Thus, Histadrut became an incipient welfare apparatus for all Hebrew workers. Services were then supported from workers' dues, as in a "big commune," and these went into a general fund which connected the individual worker more directly to the generality of workers than to any particular trade union. Unity, Ben-Gurion thought, would emerge not only from common proletarian action but also from mutual aid. Political parties would have to compete—and compete they did—to gain control of the Histadrut and, through the Histadrut, of the Jewish Yishuv.

.

After Ben-Gurion's constitution was ratified, the work of organizing Zionist industrial and service enterprises entered a new stage. These included Solel Boneh, the construction firm; Bank Ha'Poalim, the Workers' Bank; and Tnuvah, the agricultural marketing cooperative. All these enterprises were manifestations of a profound egalitarianism, at least insofar as the subjective feelings of the workers were concerned. The wages paid to Histadrut managers were essentially the same as those paid to all workers. Most important, all profits of the Chevrat Ovdim corporations were plowed back into industrial investment. The Zionist worker could say plausibly that he owned everything, that the whole Yishuv consumed his dividend. For thousands, the Histadrut represented the general will, the symbol of a new social contract.

Of course "equality" of ownership was only a fiction. There was no equality of control of industry as there was, say, equality of obligation to perform military service in the Haganah or some other union-mandated volunteer activity. Indeed, Ben-Gurion spoke of the big Jewish commune mobilized according to "military discipline," not democratic idealism. In an address to the Achdut Ha'Avodah council in 1921, Ben-Gurion said:

> If we decide just on paper that the public must obey our orders, it will remain ineffective so long as the economy does not bind the people . . . and this will be possible only if we create a collective economy . . . How else are we going to enforce discipline unless we control the economy? . . . All members of Achdut Ha'Avodah must obey without demur the management of the labor army with regard to where they will reside, what occupation they will pursue, and how their work will be organized.[11]

To his credit, Ben-Gurion implemented his militant socialist ideal in a nonsectarian spirit and without a trace of personal corruption. The parties of the Histadrut submitted to regular elections, though, as Ben-Gurion's own prestige grew, Achdut Ha'Avodah's continual dominance became more and more a foregone conclusion. Democratic tendencies among the immigrants were reinforced by the constitutional norms of the British Mandate, at least during the twenties and thirties. Residents of Palestine were guaranteed most of the fundamental rights embodied in British common law: freedom of speech, of religion, of assembly, of party organization, of the press.

Nevertheless, the formation of the Histadrut and Chevrat Ovdim created a fundamental tension between democratic norms and the various socialist programs which by their very nature entailed an unlimited concentration of economic power. In 1921, Jews were invited to elect a Vaad Ha'Leumi—or "National Council"—under the auspices of the Mandatory government. Ben-Gurion's coalition immediately moved to control it. The Histadrut soon won control of the Haganah as well. In the Histadrut, there were no checks on executive authority beyond the General Council. The rank and file had little direct voice in major questions—except by voting for the various party slates in regular elections. Dissenting views were tolerated, if not welcomed; but with the British and Arabs watching, there was an unspoken consensus that these views should be voiced behind closed doors. In contrast, leaders who refused to accept Histadrut discipline were apt to lose their positions; workers might lose their jobs or be subjected to ridicule.

To be sure, the Hebrew revolution could probably not have succeeded under conditions of greater pluralism. The British and the Arabs were, indeed, watching. What should be noted, however, is that the Histadrut's standards were never designed for a democratic state. They were a kind of "dictatorship of the proletariat," fit for the first stage of a socialist revolution. Again, it is one of the fundamental tragedies of Zionism that Ben-Gurion could not move far enough beyond the Histadrut's political economy when he organized the Jewish state.

iv

Some 35,000 new immigrants arrived in Palestine between 1919 and 1923. About a third had been members of Labor Zionist parties abroad, but 60 percent of them joined Histadrut-sponsored collectives and unions. The World Zionist Organization had no alternative but to support the Histadrut once its success had become apparent. The indefatigable Arthur Ruppin, still heading the Palestine Land

Development Company in Jaffa, supported Histadrut settlements with loans of up to £3 million. Within the Histadrut, Ben-Gurion's Achdut Ha'Avodah grew to preeminence. But the problem of extending the influence of Labor Zionism into the public realm outside the Histadrut grew more complex, particularly owing to changes in patterns of Jewish emigration the following year. In 1924, the United States Congress passed the Johnson-Lodge Immigration Act, which severely curtailed Jewish immigration to America. Between 1924 and 1929, some 80,000 Jews arrived in Palestine from Central Europe, mainly from Poland, where recent anti-Jewish measures had provoked panic. Although 40 percent of these immigrants would soon leave, defeated by the rigors of pioneering, more than 45,000 stayed: they made up the so-called Fourth Ascent.

The Polish settlers were different in kind from their Russian predecessors; many had been small capitalists, and between 35 and 45 percent arrived with funds they could invest. Indeed, they were keen to establish and extend a market economy without much insight into how capitalism's booms and busts posed risks to the Yishuv's absorptive capacity. Between 1924 and 1926, more than 80 percent of the £12 million invested in the Yishuv was from private sources, and more land was purchased by private Polish and American real-estate corporations than by the Jewish National Fund. By 1927, about a third of all Jewish laborers in the Yishuv, some 11,000 people, were employed by 2,478 different, private Jewish enterprises. The power of the Labor Zionists seemed increasingly imperiled by the new capitalist competition.

Then, in 1927, a severe depression hit the Yishuv, stifling the new entrepreneurs and the growth they caused. Unemployment rose in all but the cooperative agricultural enterprises. Sensing a new opportunity, the Histadrut leadership now organized many more immigrant workers in the private sector, stiffening demands that private entrepreneurs hire only Hebrew workers. Nor did the Histadrut stop there. With Weizmann's cooperation, a plan took shape whereby the Jewish National Fund and the World Zionist Organization would take over some of the failing commercial enterprises, particularly the large private real-estate corporations, and lease more land to the Histadrut collectives. To be sure, the Histadrut's own industrial enterprises had suffered during the depression:

Solel Boneh became insolvent and closed temporarily. But once Achdut Ha'Avodah used its tight organization and concentrated economic power to take direct control of the Histadrut's industrial activities, most of the Chevrat Ovdim corporations survived and, indeed, fared better than private companies.

The party's good showing in hard times convinced the entire Jewish community that Achdut Ha'Avodah alone, the organized party of labor, could lead the Yishuv into the political arena. Ben-Gurion, Berl Katznelson—who began to edit the Labor daily *Davar* in 1925—and the radical kibbutz leader Yitzchak Tabenkin emerged as the spokesmen for what increasingly seemed like a Jewish worker-nation in the making. *Davar* became the Yishuv's semiofficial voice. Other important leaders included Chaim Arlozorov, David Remez, Moshe Sharett, and Eliezer Kaplan. In 1930 Achdut Ha'Avodah was powerful enough to absorb its old ideological rival, Ha'Poel Ha'Tzair, and they merged to form Mapai, *Mifleget Poale Eretz Yisrael*, the "Workers' Party of Israel," which would dominate the political life of the Yishuv and the state of Israel for two generations.

.

Mapai was not without rivals on the left. The most serious challenge came from the kibbutz radicals of the Ha'Shomer Ha'Tzair Party—the "Young Guardian"—young men and women who had been greatly influenced not only by Borochov's Marxism but also by German romanticism. Ha'Shomer Ha'Tzair professed antipathy to the family, hence to Jewish legalism, and they justified their rebellion by means of Freud's theories. Some were particularly taken with Martin Buber's "I-Thou" philosophy. In 1927, Ha'Shomer Ha'Tzair formed the ulta-left kibbutz movement, Kibbutz Ha'Artzi, and alone among the Labor Zionist parties continued to support the Third International. (The latter continued to repeal all overtures from Zionists, of course, and movement leaders condemned the purges during the 1930s; but Ha'Shomer Ha'Tzair grew increasingly Stalinist during World War II and did not deviate from a pro-Soviet line until after the founding of the state of Israel.)

By 1927, Ha'Shomer Ha'Tzair had attracted a good number of the Tzeirei Zion activists of the Third Ascent who had been out-maneuvered by Ben-Gurion in the Histadrut. During the late twenties, the Histadrut was directing capital investments to urban enterprises. But Ha'Shomer Ha'Tzair activists evoked memories of the Biluim with their agrarian, collectivist program. Under young leaders such as Meir Ya'ari, they grew more and more preoccupied with small-scale socialist communities, and particularly with refining the institutions of collective child-rearing. One particularly quaint interpretation of Freud inspired them to expose teens to the works of high culture (classical music, painting) especially at puberty, in the belief that this would help sublimate antisocial sexual urges.[12] During the 1930s, until the founding of the state of Israel, Ha'Shomer Ha'Tzair would try to sustain proposals for bi-nationalism with the Palestinian Arabs and would be joined in this by Hebrew University intellectuals, including Martin Buber and Judah L. Magnes, who had formed Brit Shalom in 1929. But Ben-Gurion himself did not at first reject the idea of bi-nationalism over an independent Jewish state, and in consequence, Ha'Shomer Ha'Tzair remained within the Histadrut, deep in Mapai's shadow. Ha'Shomer Ha'Tzair had won only 16 seats out of 87 in the original Histadrut council of 1920; it never improved much on that showing.

In fact, though the eccentric cultural experiments of Ha'Shomer Ha'Tzair kibbutzim have received a great deal of attention, they were marginal when compared with the great cultural event of the period: the flowering of Mapai's secular Hebrew literary and artistic culture, the product of the first generation of people who lived in what Achad Haam had called "the national Hebrew atmosphere." Spoken Hebrew absorbed the highly sophisticated political rhetoric of the Russian and Polish immigrants. In Hebrew, one could speak of a man's fate in the manner of Dostoevsky, speak of political power in the manner of Pilsudski. Nor was the new culture ever far removed from Labor Zionism's revolutionary ideals. Poets such as Natan Alterman and Avraham David Shlonsky eulogized the Labor movement in such journals as *Ktuvim*. Thousands of Hebrew children were educated to a standard of *chalutziyut* in movement schools and kibbutzim. Nursery rhymes have been called the unwritten diary of a nation. The Yishuv's children sang:

> *Ha'auto shelanu gadol v'yarok,*
> *Ha'auto shelanu noseah rachok,*
> *Ba'boker nosea, ba'erev hoo shav,*
> *Meivee hoo l'Tnuvah beitzim v'chalav!*

("Our truck is green and big,
Our truck goes far away.
It leaves in the morning, and returns at night,
It brings eggs and milk to Tnuvah!")

The only immigrant Jew who could not appropriate Labor Zionist culture, it seemed, was Achad Haam himself. He had left London for Tel Aviv in 1922, only to find that the world of the Histadrut both eluded and ignored him. His ideas had helped inspire a generation of Labor Zionists, but his attitude toward socialism and indeed all types of messianism had always been ambivalent: certainly a big commune was not what he had had in mind for the Yishuv. In any case, he was by now an old man, and the warmth and fellowship of the collectives were for the young.

Achad Haam still commanded the deep respect due to one of the great mentors of Zionism: the street where he lived was emptied and made quiet between two and four o'clock in the afternoon so that he could rest from the heat. Yet behind his sun-bleached walls, Achad Haam was constantly depressed. In 1923 he wrote his friend and rival, the historian Simon Dubnow:

I am crushed and broken and sunk in a dejection which I can never shake off . . . I live here among my dearest and most intimate friends; affection and respect are lavished upon me from all sides, my children are very near at hand, and for the present I can study in peace and quiet: and all of this in Palestine, of which I have dreamt all these years. And in these ideal conditions I sit and long for London!

I don't mean for the friends I left there—there may be three or four such—but just for London, for its busy streets and market places, for the gloomy city in which I spent so many years without light and air . . . These longings, painful enough in themselves, trouble me still more because they seem to be a sure sign of some disease of the spirit: otherwise such a thing would not be possible.[13]

Achad Haam lived to see the leaders of the World Zionist Organization found the Hebrew University in 1925. He died in 1927.

v

The dominance of Mapai in the Histadrut both firmly established the main current of Zionism as socialist, thus preempting Mapai's minor left-wing rivals, and put into eclipse any party representing the Jewish propertied or small capitalist classes in Palestine. It absorbed the religious Zionists, as much through its power as its messianic ideology. But there was one rival strain of Zionism which Labor Zionism's triumph seemed to strengthen, precisely because that rival self-consciously defined itself as Labor Zionism's foil. This is the movement known as Zionist Revisionism, whose antecedents can be traced back to the rhetoric of political Zionism and whose great leader was the complex figure Vladimir Jabotinsky.

Jabotinsky wrote prose in eight languages, poetry in four, and translated Dante and Poe into Hebrew and Hebrew poetry into Russian. More important, Jabotinsky was the first military hero of the Zionist revival, the commander of the Jewish Legion, and the theoretician of Jewish militarism. Revisionism challenged Labor Zionism in the peculiar way it tried to endow this militarism with a moral prestige greater than that of Hebrew socialism. "We ought not to be deterred by the Latin word 'militarism,'" Jabotinsky insisted, for this merely is "the natural defense effort of a people that had no homeland and was facing extinction": "If this is militarism then we ought to be proud of it."[14]

Jabotinsky was born into a middle-class and largely assimilated Jewish family in Odessa. He came from a kosher home but, as he said, one which inspired no "internal connection with Judaism." He grew up in the eighties and nineties, but Jabotinsky's family, which was impoverished after his father's death, kept the young Vladimir aloof from Bundism and Zionism, even after the pogroms of 1881. Jabotinsky had nothing to do with Hibat Zion, though he studied Hebrew sporadically. He was more drawn to Russian letters, and his work impressed some important writers. (Indeed, Maxim Gorky would later praise Jabotinsky's literary skill and lament its sacrifice to Zionist activism.)

In 1898, Jabotinsky went to Bern, then to Rome to study law. In Italy, he grew to idolize the saga of the Risorgimento, and in the wake of the Kishinev pogrom of April 1903, it appears that his latent Jewish feeling was awakened and fused to an admiration for Garibaldian militarism. Jabotinsky returned to Odessa and organized a self-defense force. Soon thereafter, he attended the Sixth Zionist Congress as a Russian delegate, arriving with the conventional opinions of the Eastern European Zionists. He dutifully opposed

Herzl's Uganda scheme and always professed absolute devotion to Palestine. Still, Jabotinsky was overwhelmingly impressed by Herzl's manner at the Sixth Congress and, after Herzl's death, revered his memory. In 1906, at the Third Conference of Russian Zionists at Helsinki, Jabotinsky endorsed equal rights for the Jews within the Czar's empire. But soon after, he seems to have been persuaded that political Zionists should be thinking of ways to escape Russia, not liberalize it. By 1908 he wrote that it was undignified for Jews to be steeped in Russian literature, or any literature for that matter that contained so much anti-Semitism.[15]

Once he was converted to Zionism, Jabotinsky made an intensive study of Hebrew, though, like Herzl, he became fixated on what he took to be the cowardice and atavism he identified with the ghetto. Moreover, he disdained agricultural pioneering as philistine and rejected its socialism as a form of typical Jewish weakness; for him the socialist "gave off the smell of garlic." As early as 1910, Jabotinsky conceived of a more elegant example for the Jews to emulate: the radical individual who would fit into Herzl's state and recognize the benefits of centralized power. Jabotinsky saw no contradiction between individualism and nationalism, because the former seemed to him more an aesthetic principle than an argument about the commonweal. Liberty was precious because artists and writers needed it, or at least the illusion of it, to re-create the world in imagination without inhibition. Jabotinsky would later identify such individualism with the Futurist school of art and literature—a prelude to Italian Fascism.[16]

As to the real world, not surprisingly, Jabotinsky thought that liberal tolerance was a "laughingstock," a kind of "childish humanism." As early as 1910, in what he took to be the spirit of Hobbes, Jabotinsky had written that society was a play of natural antagonisms, a battle of all against all. "Justice exists," he wrote, "only for those whose fists and stubbornness make it possible for them to realize it."[17] Indeed, much as he admired them, Jabotinsky could never have been satisfied with Herzl's aristocratic notions of self-emancipation. More than fifty Jews were killed in Kishinev; Jewish women were raped. This was dishonor Jabotinsky could touch and feel. When he wrote that the Jews ought to learn from Gentiles—"our teacher and master, the *goy*"—to give blood for the sake of honor, he, unlike Herzl, seems to have meant it. He was political Zionism's heir but also its first genuine article.

        .

   As a war correspondent in Egypt in 1914, Jabotinsky discovered that hundreds of young Zionist pioneers had been deported by the Turks. He organized them and other volunteers from around the world into the Zion Mule Corps, which eventually saw action at Gallipoli. Thereafter, Jabotinsky set himself the task of building up a larger Jewish force, which would fight in the British Army to liberate Palestine from the Turks. This, he thought, would validate Jewish political claims to Palestine after the war was won. Jabotinsky persevered and by August 1917 had organized the Jewish Legion.

   Jabotinsky's unit played a minor role in Allenby's final push into Palestine, though no more minor than the role played by Faisal's forces; it played a major role in the formation of Jabotinsky's political consciousness. In his autobiography Jabotinsky wrote that the Great War had redeemed him: "What would I have done if the world had not broken into flames? . . . Perhaps I would have gone to Eretz Yisrael, perhaps I would have escaped to Rome, perhaps I would have founded a [Russian] political party."[18] When Joseph Trumpeldor was killed at Tel Chai, in March 1920, Jabotinsky was made head of the Haganah in Jerusalem. He commanded the Jewish volunteer forces during the first Arab disturbances in April. These events—Trumpeldor's death, Arab rioting—shocked him, but not as much as what he felt was the bland response of the British authorities. The High Commissioner, Sir Herbert Samuel, attempted to place the blame for the rioting on Arabs and Jews alike. Jabotinsky was jailed along with the Arab rioters, then amnestied together with them in July. Adding insult to injury, Jabotinsky thought, Samuel adjudicated a lingering property dispute in Beisan in favor of the Arab claimants.

   In March 1921, Jabotinsky was elected to the Zionist executive. This was a time of tireless activity for him. However, British policy continued to distress him. In the spring of 1921, Samuel elevated Haj-Amin-al-Husseini to the position of Mufti of Jerusalem, though it was well known that Haj-Amin had participated in the anti-Zionist riots the year before. (Haj-Amin had not even been elected by his peers, as was the custom; Samuel chose him from a list of possible candidates which included several moderate figures, apparently hoping that Palestinian nationalists would be more compliant if their most extreme spokesman was brought into the administration of the Mandate.) Samuel's actions persuaded Jabotinsky that the British could not be depended on to carry out the provisions of the Balfour Declaration—not, at least, in the face of stern Arab opposition. That suspicion was reinforced by the Haycraft Report of 1921 and the Churchill Memorandum of 1922, both of which stressed the rights of Palestinian Arabs and curtailed those of the Zionist settlers. Although Jabotinsky endorsed the Zionist executive's decision to acquiesce in the prohibition of Jewish settlement east of the Jordan River, he began to express resentment for the apparent meekness of the executive. Jabotinsky particularly opposed Weizmann's willingness to accept a Palestinian legislative council in which Jews would be greatly outnumbered. In submitting to these indignities, Jabotinsky thought, Zionist leaders were abandoning the very self-respect and toughness which, for him, Zionism was supposed to produce.

Besides, Jabotinsky reasoned, Britain either shared interests with Zionism or she did not. If she did—and Jabotinsky's theory of power suggested that she must or she would never have supported Zionism in the first place—then demanding from the Mandatory government that it live up to the Balfour Declaration could do no harm. If, on the other hand, Britain did not share interests with the Zionists, accommodating British reservations on behalf of the Arabs would do no good. To Weizmann, this kind of *Realpolitik* seemed childish. The Yishuv grew by accommodating the Mandate authorities over political questions which did not undermine Zionist efforts to buy land and settle new immigrants. Jews were now arriving in greater numbers than ever before—not great enough to defy British rule, to be sure, but great enough to intimate the prospect of a future Jewish majority. Moreover, the Jews needed British protection. There was no serious possibility of defying Britain, however worrying its backsliding on the Balfour Declaraton had become. ("Political work," Weizmann lamented, "was precisely what Jabotinsky was unfit for.")

Jabotinsky persisted in his calls for greater daring. He traveled to the United States, where he quarreled with Weizmann's chief supporter, Justice Louis Brandeis, whom he accused of "minimalism." Yet Jabotinsky's pluck soon turned to recklessness. At his own initiative, and without the approval of the rest of the WZO executive, Jabotinsky entered into secret negotiations with an official of Simon Petliura's anti-Semitic Ukrainian government-in-exile; Petliura was threatening to march into the Soviet Ukraine and reestablish White rule. Now, thousands of Jews had been murdered when Petliura's forces had ruled the Ukraine just after the Revolution, and Jabotinsky's gambit reminded Zionists old enough to remember of Herzl's imprudent effort to gain the support of Plehve —indeed, Jabotinsky claimed his negotiations were modeled after Herzl's. Jabotinsky insisted that he wanted to organize a Jewish self-defense force within the framework of some future Petliura regime. Of course, Petliura's planned march against the Red Army came to nothing, and the fact that Jabotinsky approached him in the first place not only seemed bad judgment but smacked of reaction. (Petliura was killed by a Jewish student in Paris a few years later.)

Jabotinsky resigned from the Zionist executive in January 1923. Later that year, he made a speaking tour of many European countries, including Latvia and Lithuania. Close to his native ground, he remonstrated with Jewish audiences to restore the tradition of Herzl and Nordau. Jabotinsky was an accomplished orator in many languages; Arthur Koestler claimed he once saw him keep an open-air audience of thousands spellbound for five solid hours in Vienna. Few of Jabotinsky's Polish-Jewish audiences knew Palestinian conditions firsthand. His message was Jewish self-defense, and his criticism of socialism in Palestine sounded right to Jews increasingly hounded by anti-Semitism at home and fearful of Soviet Marxism abroad. By the end of the year, Jabotinsky had stirred up a sufficient body of students and young activists to found a new youth movement, which he called Betar—an acronym for *Brit Trumpeldor*, the League of Trumpeldor.

Jabotinsky taught his youth movement that modern nations could, in the end, assimilate only two claims to political legitimacy, both of which were in effect authoritarian. The first was socialism, and its most detestable product was the Soviet Union; the second was nationalism, and its highest product, for Jews at any rate, was Zionism. Ironically, Betar was the place where Simon Bar-Kochba's rebel legions had made a last, futile stand against the Romans in the second century A.D. Jabotinsky knew this, and he seemed to want his followers to understand that making a stand can be as important as winning a victory. The primary tenet of Betar was the ideal of Jewish statehood, of political Zionism and mass emigration. The moral basis for Jabotinsky's statism was, however, not the ruthlessness of Gentiles, but rather allegiance to the integral Jewish nation. "Let us draw for ourselves the ideal type of an absolute nation," Jabotinsky wrote.

> It would have to possess a racial appearance of marked, unique character . . . It would have to occupy from time immemorial a continuous and clearly defined piece of land; it would be highly desirable if in that area there were no alien minorities who would weaken national unity. It would have to maintain an original national language, which is not derived from another nation.[19]

Members of Betar were not permitted to advocate any ideology other than nationalism, an implicit criticism of the Labor Zionists, who considered socialism and nationalism to be indivisible. Indeed, Jabotinsky would later invest the idea of nation with a kind of racialism:

> Every race possessing a definite uniqueness seeks to become a nation, that is, to create for itself an economic, political and intellectual environment in which every detail will derive from its specific thought and consequently will also relate to its specific taste. A specific race can establish such an environment only in its own country, where it is the master. For this reason every race seeks to become a state.[20]

Thus, the state apparatus or government-in-exile, not the Histadrut, should serve as the point of identity for the Jewish nation and, moreover, should seek to reconcile economic conflicts, not provoke them as class conflict.

In retrospect, it seems peculiar that Jabotinsky scarcely noticed how, in the absence of a state apparatus, the Histadrut pretty much conformed to his state ideal, not to the Marxist ideal of revolutionary socialists. Histadrut "conquered labor"—called strikes, provided services—for the sake of the Hebrew nation and its language, not for any internationalism or cosmopolitan class struggle. Indeed, it was to mitigate the divisive influence of the Marxist radicals that Ben-Gurion organized the Histadrut in the way he did.

Yet the Histadrut also opposed the interests of Palestine's private entrepreneurs, and in stifling the capitalist class, it suppressed, or so Jabotinsky thought, the individual's status in society. "The principles of liberty, equality, and fraternity," Jabotinsky wrote in 1927, "were the inventions of the bourgeoisie, not the classless intelligentsia." Moreover, he strongly believed that Polish Jews, who were mainly "bourgeois," would never go to a Histadrut-dominated Yishuv, though it was these people who needed the protection of Zionism most. Betar, in contrast with the Labor Zionist youth movements, was to exemplify how Polish Jews might be mobilized by martial ideals. Jabotinsky insinuated that traditional Jewish life bred youth who would not wait to be hunted to hide. Betar would train these young men and women, organize them, transform their consciousness with epic literature, and teach them military skills. Betar would prepare the Jewish nation as a whole for a spontaneous mass drive to Palestine.

According to Betar myth, recruits would be ready to fight to secure their independence; indeed, they were subject to be called up to a new Jewish Legion at any time, and they accepted Jabotinsky's absolute authority. They were also expected to devote their first two years in Palestine to national service. Nor did Jabotinsky discourage a cult of personality, or other analogies to the organization of Fascist movements in Central Europe and Italy. Jabotinsky was called *Rosh*, the "head" of the movement; his photograph was displayed prominently in Betar homes. "The highest achievement of a multitude of free human beings," he wrote, "is to be able to act together with the absolute precision of a machine."[21] (Some years later Jabotinsky published a romantic novel about Samson: in the spectacle of thousands of Philistines "obeying a single will," he wrote, Samson "glimpsed the great secret of the politically minded.")[22]

Betar members, finally, were expected to comport themselves with *hadar*, Jabotinsky's word for self-conscious grace—dignity, honor, chivalry—a testament to the exalting power of national sacrifice and ceremony. *Hadar* implied unflappable confidence, coolness in adversity, self-sufficiency, and *noblesse oblige*. ("*Hadar, hadar, lamut o lichbosh et ha'har*": "Pride, pride, conquer the mountain or die!") Jabotinsky, who was impressed by the manner of Poland's Marshal Pilsudski, thought that Jewish leaders must present themselves with similar grandeur and panache. It was *hadar*, not any instrumental calculation, which determined Betar's attitude toward territorial demands. When it came to Eretz Yisrael, it was not enough to have land for settlement; the Jews must rather claim their patrimony on both sides of the Jordan, if only to let the world know that they could not be pushed around.

Yet Jabotinsky's vision for Betar was not wholly reactionary. His attitude toward the use of Hebrew was particularly fascinating since, though all members of Betar were expected to learn and use the language, Jabotinsky boldly advocated the latinization of the Hebrew alphabet. He shared the modernizing impulse that had inspired Kemal Atatürk's ruthless secularization of postwar Turkey, and he hoped that latinization would open Hebrew up to greater literary invention and Western influences. Arthur Koestler put Jabotinsky's view this way:

> Hebrew has become totally unsuitable for the treatment of abstract subjects and for a precise expression of thought. This is not merely a matter of vocabulary; modern scientific terms can be borrowed from European languages . . . The difficulty lies in the archaic structure of the language . . . an inflexibility of style which causes translations of Hemingway to be practically indistinguishable from translations of Proust. The instrument on which the Hebrew novelist has to express the nuances of his twentieth century emotions has no half-tones or modulations of key and timbre. Hebrew is admirably suited for producing prophetic thunder; but you cannot play a scherzo on a ram's horn.[23]

Correspondingly, Jabotinsky railed against the influence of Jewish Orthodoxy, which, he thought, impeded scientific study, compromised the position of women, and interfered with everyday life in a modern society. He was distressed that Mizrachi, the Orthodox Zionists, seemed protected by the Labor Zionist umbrella. When, in 1921, Sir Herbert Samuel had appointed Haj-Amin Mufti of Jerusalem, Samuel had also appointed Rabbi Abraham Isaac Kook Chief Rabbi of Palestine, and Kook thereafter won jurisdiction over all Jewish marriages, divorces, burials, and inheritances. What Samuel had done, perhaps inadvertently, was to give Kook's religious courts official power over a Jewish population which was predominantly secular, and the Histadrut went along.

Jabotinsky thought this was a retrograde step. Betar's vision could not be said to be democratic. But Jabotinsky took for granted the evolution of a Hebrew civil society more liberal in substance and individualist in style than what the Labor Zionists were creating. Incidentally, Orthodox Polish youth, impressed by the élan of the Third Ascent, succeeded in founding Ha'Poel Ha'Mizrachi—the "Workers' Mizrachi"—in 1921, and organized branches in Jaffa, Petach Tiqvah, Jerusalem, and Rishon Le'Zion. Together with Mizrachi, they organized the Bnei Akiva youth movement the following year. In contrast, Jabotinsky thought, the Yishuv should be a place for high art, the expressions of the great soul, the maximization of private interest. The claims of the patriotism and the dynamism of leadership should hold people together, not the economic threats of a union or the moral blackmail of rabbis.

.

In 1925, Jabotinsky founded the Zionist Revisionist Organization, a larger movement to promote his ideals within the WZO. Revisionism appealed to middle-class Polish intellectuals; it never made much headway in the Yishuv. When, after the depression of 1927, entry permits grew more difficult to obtain, Jabotinsky railed the more fervently against the Histadrut's political economy, accusing it of discriminating against his people. Revisionists were not wholly opposed to some form of state intervention; they accepted some features of the welfare state. What they opposed was any form of planning or class struggle. The state must be paternal, corporatist. Wage disputes, Jabotinsky thought, should be adjudicated by a state-appointed arbitrator, as in Mussolini's Italy. Some years later, Jabotinsky clarified the point:

> The competitive order of the world's economy which causes one man to win and another to lose is here recognized as the normal and permanent foundation of all social activity. Society (or Law, or the State) shall only interfere from time to time as a sort of jobbing gardener who, on each of his periodic visits, uses his pruning knife to stop such exaggerated growth as might endanger the development of its neighbors. Liberalism means people triumph or fail . . . so long as no one is allowed to go hungry or homeless, and no one need submit to slavery for want of food or a home.[24]

Of course, it is hard to see how, except by "interference," Jabotinsky could have reconciled Arabs to the unifying power of Jewish "will." The liberal institutions attached to Jabotinsky's market ideal would have transformed Jewish settlers into a permanent minority, a colonialist one at that.

vi

The Revisionists' statist views put them in direct confrontation with the Histadrut and the leadership of the WZO. A showdown of sorts came at the Seventeenth Zionist Congress in 1931, and the growing rivalry between Ben-Gurion and Weizmann made it a highly complicated affair. Two years before, prior to the Sixteenth Zionist Congress, Weizmann had successfully founded the Jewish Agency for Palestine, with himself as chairman. This body had superseded the old Zionist Commission as the Jewish people's representative body to the British government and Mandatory administration, and Weizmann had negotiated more actual authority for it than the other constituent bodies of Zionism combined—including the Yishuv's National Council, which was dominated by Ben-Gurion's forces. Since Weizmann expected the Jewish Agency to be half composed of Western philanthropists who were friendly to him—men such as the American Justice Louis Marshall—he had expected to enhance his power. The labor parties supported the formation of the Agency.

However, Weizmann's position as president of the WZO became increasingly dependent on Ben-Gurion's backing. Marshall had died soon after the Jewish Agency was formed, and in any case, the influence of non-Zionists in the Jewish Agency was never as great as Weizmann had anticipated. In 1929, the Labor coalition that would become Mapai the following year gained 26 percent of the vote in the WZO—the first time since the Balfour Declaration that Weizmann's party, the General Zionists, lost an absolute majority. In 1931, a united Labor Zionist slate controlled by Ben-Gurion won 40 percent of the vote in elections for the Seventeenth Zionist Congress.

To be sure, Ben-Gurion did not go to the Seventeenth Congress expecting to displace Weizmann or defeat Jabotinsky. That the congress became a propitious moment to do both reflects the grave turn of events in Palestine and London between 1929 and 1931. During late August 1929, the Mufti had incited the Arab population in Jerusalem, Hebron, and Safad against the Jewish settlers: 133 Jews were killed and 339 wounded by Arab peasants;

about the same number of Arabs were killed and wounded by British policemen trying to quell the rioting.

The Arab leadership had always demanded an end to Jewish immigration and land purchase, while refusing to recognize the Mandatory government. In 1929, in speech after speech, Haj-Amin not only reiterated Arab demands but declared that Zionist settlers would eventually bring down the mosques of Jerusalem, just as they had brought down Arab tenant homes in the Jezreel Valley. (About 5,000 Arab peasant families had indeed been displaced after the JNF purchased much of the Jezreel Valley's land from Beirut's Sursok family in 1920. Most of those people relocated and became urban workers.) The Colonial Secretary of the new Labour government, Lord Passfield, formerly Sydney Webb, denounced the Arab attacks but issued a White Paper which cast doubt on the legitimacy of the Zionist executive and the terms of the Balfour Declaration. Passfield based his views on a report of John Hope Simpson, who had criticized the Histadrut's Hebrew-labor policies as the cause of Arab unemployment.

Passfield emphasized that the Balfour Declaration assumed "equality of obligation" to the Palestinian Arab community, and interpreted this to mean that a legislative council should now be formed based on proportional representation; obviously, the Arabs and British would command an overwhelming majority in it. (Passfield and his wife, Beatrice Webb, had always taken a dim view of Jewish nationalism.) Passfield's proposal was similar to the one Weizmann had agreed to in 1922. But now, in 1931, the Yishuv's labor institutions gave Jews the promise of political autonomy—at the very least, of bi-nationalism. Passfield's principles implied that, rather, Zionism should return to the mold of the Rothschild settlements; indeed, the report specifically called for capitalist farming in private enterprises.

The Passfield White Paper caused an outcry in liberal-minded circles in England. *The Manchester Guardian* denounced it, and many in the Labour Party—which had generally affected a greater sympathy for Zionism than the Tories—advocated withdrawing it. Weizmann appealed to Prime Minister Ramsay MacDonald, who finally decided to rescind the document. But the lesson for Palestinian Zionists seemed clear nevertheless: the British government might not be counted on to guarantee Jewish immigration or the right to purchase land. Could Weizmann's confidence in Britain have been misplaced all along? One need hardly add that the summer of 1931 had been Zionism's darkest hour so far. Poland's latently anti-Semitic Endecja movement was becoming steadily more influential; Hitler's electoral gains were ominous. In this atmosphere, Weizmann's pro-British reputation was bound to appear suspect. In any case, there could be no new capitulation to Britain.

．

At the opening of the Seventeenth Congress, Jabotinsky demanded, predictably, that the Zionist movement answer the Passfield White Paper with an explicit declaration that the "end goal" of Zionism was a Jewish state. Confident of Ben-Gurion's support, Weizmann roared back: "The walls of Jericho fell to the sounds of shouts and trumpets; I never heard of walls being raised by that means." Every year of cooperation with Britain had meant tens of thousands of new settlers. The Yishuv now numbered 175,000. There were scores of new Jewish farms and enterprises. Why jeopardize British support with fatuous declarations?

Yet Weizmann inadvertently forced Ben-Gurion to reconsider his support for Weizmann's leadership, in spite of his sympathy for Weizmann's line. It seems that after the congress began, Weizmann gave an unfortunate interview to the Jewish Telegraphic Agency, in which he dismissed Jabotinsky's statist slogans but added, remarkably, that he had no sympathy either for "a Jewish majority in Palestine." Weizmann later insisted that he was misquoted, that it was *sloganeering* about a Jewish majority that he opposed. ("It was the conflict," he wrote in his autobiography, "between those who believed that Palestine could be built only the hard way, by meticulous attention to every object; who believed that in this slow and difficult struggle with the marshes and the rocks of Palestine lies the great challenge to the creative forces of the Jewish people . . . and those who yielded to [Jewish] abnormalities, seeking to live by a sort of continuous miracle, snatching at occasions as they presented themselves, and believing that these accidental smiles of fortune constitute a real way of life."[25]) Still, Weizmann's published interview sent a shudder through the congress.

Labor Zionist delegates who had come to the congress prepared for no other president than Weizmann refused to support his re-election. In a dramatic reversal, Weizmann was defeated. Significantly, the repudiation of Weizmann's leadership was, however, no endorsement of Jabotinsky's statist line. Ben-Gurion had declared at the congress that Mapai remained open to any bi-national solution which would protect the integrity and growth of the socialist institutions of the Yishuv. What he would not concede was control over immigration and land purchase to a permanent Arab veto. Indeed, the following summer Ben-Gurion's chief diplomat, Chaim Arlozorov, wrote Weizmann secretly that, in the event of an emergency in Europe, Mapai might well contemplate an uprising against the Mandatory administration to wrest the levers of immigration from British hands. ("It may be impossible to attain a Jewish majority, or even numerical equality between the two peoples—or any other condition permitting the basis for the creation of a cultural centre by means of systematic immigration and colonization—without a transitional period of Jewish minority national rule."[26])

Ben-Gurion joined with Nachum Goldmann's Radical Party, a small group of German intellectuals, in electing Nahum Sokolow president. A more yielding man than his predecessor, Sokolow was identified with Weizmann's pre-congress line, but not his anglophilia. Then the Labor Zionists turned their guns on Jabotinsky, who for a fleeting moment had expected to make a run for the presidency himself. The debate was short. Jabotinsky's demand that Zionism declare for a Jewish state was defeated by a resounding majority. Goldmann later recalled a great cheer, and that Jabotinsky tore up his delegate's card.[27]

It cannot be said that Ben-Gurion was humbled by this turn of events, though it amounted to something of a Labor Zionist coup. After the Seventeenth Congress he wrote: "The party of the working-class . . . is responsible for the entire nation, and views itself as the nucleus of the future nation. The Labor movement, which fifteen years ago had hardly existed as a visible entity, has become the cornerstone of Zionism. Qualitatively and quantitatively, we have become the largest faction, directing and deciding Zionism's fate."[28] In 1933, Mapai got 44 percent of the vote to the Zionist congress, and Ben-Gurion himself controlled the Zionist executive. In 1935, Ben-Gurion became chairman of the Jewish Agency.

PART TWO

The Contradictions of

Self-determination

5 / Independence or Colonialism

When, in 1931, the Seventeenth Congress of the World Zionist Organization ended, Zionism had become, in David Ben-Gurion's words, a movement "directed and decided" by the Mapai leadership. Four years later, when Ben-Gurion became chairman of the Jewish Agency, most Zionist officials who were not affiliated with Revisionism had acquiesced in Mapai's victory and ceased putting forward competing versions of the national project either to British officials or in Diaspora Jewish communities. Chaim Weizmann was restored to the presidency of the WZO that same year. He now openly joined his diplomatic efforts and personal reputation to the larger prestige of the *chalutzin*—to the agricultural collectives, the Histadrut's self-help organizations, in other words, to the Labor Zionists' revolutionary culture.

Yet the timing of Labor Zionism's victory was sadly ironic, for this was the very moment when the animating principles of the Histadrut's revolution seemed, if not originally misguided, then at least superseded by the greater urgency of providing refuge for Central European Jews. There was little socialist fervor left among Jewish culturalists who had remained in the Soviet Union; what faith in internationalism the Yevsektzia (the infamous "Jewish section") could not destroy, Stalin's purges would. In any case, the ascendency of Hitler and the anti-Semitic atmosphere of Poland seemed to warrant the older, ruder, political Zionist assertion that the Jewish nation would have to engage in a ruthless struggle for existence. The idea of Hebrew national self-determination took on new force, not in Revisionist circles where Zionists had always upheld it, but among Labor Zionists who had repudiated Jabotinsky and the idea of a Jewish state in Basle. At the very least, Palestine seemed to all an increasingly likely place to which Jews might repair, and Ben-Gurion believed that he should have as much say as any British politician in determining its fate.

The concept of self-determination was not only the product of European developments, however. The outlines of an independent Jewish homeland had come into relief in Palestine, largely as a result of the Histadrut's success in organizing Hebrew workers during the twenties and thirties. There were many new Hebrew towns on the coastal plain, including such burgeoning commercial centers as Tel Aviv; while the Hula, Jezreel, and Beit She'an Valleys had all been brought under cultivation. Histadrut unions and corporations dominated the Jewish economy in these places, and its newspapers and political parties gave the promise of a national Hebrew politics. To the new generation born in Palestine, defending the socialist Yishuv seemed merely patriotic. And if Labor Zionists had lacked the ideology to justify self-determination in 1931, all Palestinian Jews would acquire sufficient enemies to justify it during the Arab revolt of 1936.

i

In the wake of the Seventeenth Congress, Jabotinsky founded a Revisionist labor organization in Palestine, the National Labor Federation, most of whose members had been affiliated with Betar. He made no effort to bring Palestinian Jews sympathetic to Revisionism into the Histadrut; indeed, he accused Ben-Gurion of engaging in class war at the very moment all Jews should unite. For the better part of 1932 and 1933, Betar activists in Palestine clashed, often violently, with the more highly organized workers of Mapai and the left-wing parties. During this period, there were 60,000 members in the Histadrut, 7,000 in the National Labor Federation.

Since Jabotinsky had not accepted the program adopted by the Seventeenth Congress, the two sides fought over the question of a

Jewish state. But they also fought over more tangible issues, such as the Histadrut's labor policy. The National Labor Federation challenged the propriety of Histadrut strikes against Jewish capitalists who failed to employ Hebrew workers exclusively. This policy, in Jabotinsky's view, had the effect of discouraging middle-class Polish Jews from identifying with the Yishuv. There was the related question of control over Jewish immigration to Palestine. The Mandatory administration had granted the Jewish Agency the right to issue a certain number of entry permits under what was called the "Laborers' Schedule." Betar charged, not without some justification, that Labor Zionist officials in the Jewish Agency discriminated in favor of members of Labor Zionist parties. As the crisis intensified, Jabotinsky suspended the Revisionist organization's elected bodies and established a provisional executive with himself as virtual dictator. He wrote:

> If the obese sarcoma called Histadrut which grows daily fatter and fatter on middle class gifts will be permitted to go on swelling it will stifle everything that is alive in Zionism . . . A stream of healthy blood, Betar, is fighting this malignant tumor . . . a handful of young people, for whom Zionism is everything . . . [They are fighting] the red banner —a rag, and alien at that—and are defending their right to serve the Jewish state ideal. For that they get beaten up . . . The Histadrut is not, and is not going to be, the only Jewish labor organization in Palestine.[1]

Relations between Revisionists and Labor Zionists deteriorated further when, in 1933, one of Ben-Gurion's closest collaborators, Chaim Arlozorov, was mysteriously assassinated. Abraham Stavsky, a Revisionist radical, was arrested for the crime, and although he was later exonerated, most Labor Zionists continued to believe that Betar was behind the murder. In 1934, Jabotinsky issued the crucial order that Betar members were not to apply for entry to Palestine through the Mapai-dominated Jewish Agency. Ben-Gurion's response was to deny all Betar members permits under the Laborers' Schedule. Jabotinsky escalated once again, founding a competing national fund, the "Keren Tel Chai." (Tel Chai, again, was where Trumpeldor had been killed by Arab attackers in 1920.)

In view of how acrimonious relations between Jabotinsky and Ben-Gurion had become, the executive of the WZO in Europe grew increasingly anxious that the Revisionists would secede or, worse, that there would be civil war in the Yishuv. Few held out hope that the two leaders could be reconciled. In the fall of 1934, the founder and director of the Palestine Electric Corporation, Pinchas Rutenberg, implored Jabotinsky and Ben-Gurion to meet together at his home in London. Remarkably enough, the two leaders agreed and much of their mutual animosity dissipated when, on October 11, they finally sat face to face. Ben-Gurion, who had recently called Jabotinsky "Vladimir Hitler," addressed his old commander in the Jewish Legion as "friend." Jabotinsky recipro-cated, recalling that Ben-Gurion had taken up arms to "liberate" the Yishuv in 1918. Within a few days, Jabotinsky and Ben-Gurion had worked out a draft agreement for cooperation, including a united labor federation and a "regime of national arbitration" of wage disputes. (The latter provision caused Jabotinsky to quip that, were he a socialist, he would have wanted Ben-Gurion shot.)

Yet in spite of their authority in their respective movements, the leaders' negotiations were in vain. Rank-and-file members on both sides could not quell animosities which Ben-Gurion and Jabotinsky had long inflamed and to which they had themselves become hostage. Though he did not have to do this, Jabotinsky decided to put the whole matter to a vote, and in February 1935 the Pales-tinian Revisionists joined world Betar in rejecting the proposal; in March, a referendum within the Histadrut defeated it in turn. From then on the schism within world Zionism was definitive. The execu-tive of the Revisionist movement seceded from the bodies of the WZO and the Jewish Agency in April 1935, and Jabotinsky an-nounced the founding of a New Zionist Organization, the NZO. Simultaneously, Jabotinsky called for elections to a First NZO Congress, to be held in Vienna in the fall of 1935, just after the WZO's Nineteenth Congress in Lucerne.

·

Lesser men might have satisfied themselves with symbolic ges-tures, but Jabotinsky was sincere when he expressed the ambition that one million people would participate in NZO elections. He set to work immediately to make the congress a success—writing, making public appearances, organizing details—driving himself to exhaustion. The results of the elections to the NZO did not quite match his expectations, but neither were they a disappointment:

713,000 voters in thirty-two countries participated, as compared with the 635,000 who had participated in the WZO.

Significantly, many of the NZO's electors voted in WZO elections as well. Jabotinsky had not demanded from any voter even a nominal fee for membership or a pledge to abstain from the WZO. A good many of the NZO's added votes came from non-Zionist Jews who were terrified by the ascendency of Fascism and had been impelled to consider emigrating to Palestine only after the United States and Canada, in the depths of economic depression, were closed to them. Voting in the NZO election was an act of defiance, however slight, against anti-Semitism. None of this can diminish the fact of Revisionism's growing popularity, especially in Poland. What could be doubted, in view of British authority over Palestine and Histadrut authority over the Yishuv, was that this popularity could readily be translated into political power.

Which brings us to the final test of strength between Jabotinsky and Ben-Gurion, the fight over British proposals that came in response to renewed Arab disturbances during 1936. Ever since the Seventeenth Zionist Congress, when he had expressed an interest in bi-nationalism, Ben-Gurion had hoped to negotiate directly with Arab leaders, without British mediation. In the early part of 1934, Ben-Gurion began to conduct discreet talks with Musa Alami, a prestigious member of the Palestinian intelligentsia who, like the Nashashibi clan, had accepted the authority of the Mandate. (Alami had helped found an Arab social democratic party and served in the Mandatory government as attorney general.) It should be stressed that Ben-Gurion had not expected any part of the Palestinian leadership to welcome Labor Zionism's minimal aims. But he hoped that Palestinian Arabs could be persuaded to accept a majority Jewish entity in Palestine if this were part of a larger, Arab-dominated, regional federation. Through Alami, Ben-Gurion endeavored to reach Arab moderates in Palestine, as well as leaders of surrounding states—Iraq, Transjordan, Saudi Arabia; he intended to propose just such a federation, without compromising on the prospect of a Jewish majority. ("If we are guaranteed unrestricted immigration and settlement rights west of the Jordan," he told Alami, "we will be prepared to discuss special arrangements —permanent or temporary—with Transjordan.")[2]

When Alami reported Ben-Gurion's proposals to the Mufti, Haj-

Amin neither accepted nor rejected them. In all probability, he assumed Ben-Gurion would bend further. While Haj-Amin stalled, Ben-Gurion traveled to Geneva to meet Ikhsan Bey al-Ja'abri and Shakib Arslan, the leaders of the radical Istaqlal, or Independence, Party. Unlike the Mufti, they rejected Ben-Gurion's overtures outright and leaked them to the Arab press; they were outraged, they said, and they implied that the time had come for violent resistance to the British. It should be reiterated here that nearly 150,000 Central European Jews had emigrated to Palestine between 1930 and 1934—i.e., with the Fifth Ascent. This large number of Jews, about 283,000 in all, gave pause to even such moderate Arab leaders as Alami; it seemed plausible that over 400,000 Jews would be residing in Palestine by the end of 1936.

At the same time, to be sure, tens of thousands of Arabs from neighboring lands were themselves emigrating to Mandate Palestine, attracted by an economic boom fueled by Zionist and British investments. Revisionists claimed that, since so many Palestinian Arabs were immigrants too, the Arab case against the British was no better than the Zionist one. Palestinian Arabs, so the argument continued, could not all be thought to merit the protection of their civil rights implied by the Balfour Declaration—indeed, but for Zionism there would have been no Palestinian nation at all. But most Arabs who moved to Palestine had never been much impressed by the artificial political borders imposed on them by British and French imperialism. Arabs who had lived in (or in the hinterlands of) Damascus, Amman, or Jerusalem under Ottoman governors were culturally indistinguishable and, in their own eyes, were doing no more than moving from one part of the Arab homeland to another.

Unlike the Revisionists, Ben-Gurion never quarreled with their view. He understood that no Arab would agree to be part of a minority in Palestine; that even moderate Arab leaders such as Alami had concluded that Britain's obligation to foster the Jewish National Home, if ever legitimate, was in any case long fulfilled. To the extent that Istaqlal's leaders *were* reconciled to the borders erected by the French and the British, they pointed to Iraq's having been granted its independence in 1930. Syria, Lebanon, and Egypt were to become independent by the end of 1936. Was it not understandable for Palestinian leaders to want independence as well?

"They cannot want the Jews to be a majority," Ben-Gurion lamented; "both we and they want to be the majority." The only serious question in Ben-Gurion's view was whether this tragic clash of rights, between Istaqlal's vision and Mapai's, could be played out without bloodshed.

In April 1936, the Mufti, who was now drawing closer to the Fascist powers, persuaded several of Palestine's most important clan leaders to establish a Higher Arab Committee under his leadership. All further contact with Ben-Gurion was curtailed. No sooner had the Higher Arab Committee come into being than it called for non-payment of taxes, to be followed by a nationwide strike of Arab workers and the closing of shops. In comparison with the Mufti's incitements during the disturbances of 1929, this may have seemed a rather moderate course. In fact, once it was under way, the strike inevitably led to bloody attacks on Jewish settlers.

To its credit, the Haganah held to a policy of *havlagah*, or "restraint," in the face of many armed provocations. The Mapai leadership determined to let British forces attempt to keep order—they could not, in any event, have kept order on their own—fearing that Haganah retaliations would lead to full-scale civil war. They organized to defend their settlements, as it were, in static lines: increasing the watches, surrounding common grounds with barbed wire. They submitted to British regulations, searches, and curfews. Jabotinsky, who was barred from Palestine by the British for his militant views, deeply resented the policy of *havlagah*, but he could do little to influence the Zionist side.

Not that the restraint of the Haganah diminished the fury of the Arab attacks. By midsummer, intense fighting had broken out between British forces and Arab irregulars in the hill country around Jerusalem. It finally dawned on the Mandatory authorities that they had a full-scale rebellion on their hands, and they began to refer to the disturbances as the "Arab revolt"; 20,000 British troops which had already been mobilized were reinforced by 10,000 more—an unprecedented show of force. Only in the fall did the Arab attacks begin to subside, though not, it seems, as a result of British military power alone. What had become increasingly clear to supporters of the Higher Arab Committee was that the Arab labor boycott only abetted the Histadrut's effort to force Jewish owners to employ only Hebrew workers. Indeed, the most burdensome economic effects of the strike were felt by poor Arab workers, and the disturbances cost Palestinian taxpayers, many of them peasants, about 6 million Palestinian pounds. By October, when the Higher Arab Committee called off the strike, all sides had suffered 1,351 casualties, including the deaths of 197 Arabs, 80 Jews, and 28 British personnel.

The British government, which before 1936 had been accustomed to putting up a brave front, immediately appointed a Royal Commission under Lord Robert Peel, charging it not only with the responsibility for looking into the sources of the disturbances but with making recommendations which might lead to a permanent political settlement. Peel did not delay; he arrived in Palestine with the other members of his commission in November 1936 and immediately summoned representatives from all sides to an unprecedented round of hearings—sixty-six meetings in all, of which thirty-one were public—which continued over several months in Palestine and later in England. In Jerusalem, Weizmann testified first for the Zionists, pressing Britain to live up to the terms of the Mandate. He pointed to the dire circumstances of European Jews, describing them as "pent up in places where they are not wanted, and for whom the world is divided into places where they cannot live, and places in which they cannot enter." He hailed the achievements of the pioneers. (The Labor Zionists generally echoed Weizmann's themes though they could hardly match Weizmann's performance.)

When—in London—Jabotinsky was finally allowed to address the commission in 1937, he eloquently repeated the Revisionist demand for a Jewish state in the *whole* territory of Palestine.

> The cause of our suffering [he told the commissioners] is the very fact of the Diaspora, that we are everywhere a minority. It is not the anti-Semitism of men; it is the anti-Semitism of things. When Oliver Twist came and asked for "more" he said "more" because he did not know how to express it; what he really meant was this: "Will you give me just that normal portion which is necessary for a boy of my age to live?" . . . What can be the concessions? We have got to save millions, many millions.[3]

Jabotinsky did not scoff at Arab national claims, which he considered natural, inferior to Jewish ones only as a claim of appetite is inferior to one of starvation. ("I am said to be an Arab-hater . . ." he had written in 1923; "that is not true. The Arabs cannot be driven from Eretz Yisrael . . . there should be rights for all nationalities living in the same country, equal rights.") Nor, it must be said, were Peel and his colleagues unmoved by Jabotinsky's entreaties. Still, they openly expressed a determination to find a compromise between the Arab and Jewish positions which might be based on demographic patterns of settlement already established in Palestine. It was out of the question that the whole of Palestine should be put under Zionist control. Jabotinsky's rhetoric notwithstanding, no such solution could result in equality of civil rights between Jews and Arabs, let alone equality of national rights.

Eventually the Peel Commission put forward a plan partitioning the country, making provision for a Jewish state, albeit a small one, in a territory roughly equal in area to that separating London and Oxford from Cambridge. According to Peel's plan, there would be 285,000 Jews in this state, a bare majority, though neither Jerusalem nor Haifa would be included in it. Some Arab residents would, in Peel's view, have to be transferred out of Jewish territory; the Higher Arab Committee emphasized this provision in rejecting partition out of hand. Yet Weizmann, for his part, accepted the plan in principle, in spite of its territorial limits—indeed, he did so enthusiastically. ("A Jewish state," Weizmann declared to one Labor Zionist skeptic, "the idea of Jewish independence in Palestine, even if only in a part of Palestine, is such a lofty thing that it ought to be treated like the ineffable Name, which is never pronounced in vain! By talking about it too much, by bringing it down to the level of the banal, you desecrate that which can only be approached with reverence.")[4] Ben-Gurion was more restrained, though he, too, defended the Peel Commission's plan to the Mapai executive. Interestingly enough, Berl Katznelson and Golda Meyerson expressed compunctions about the status of Jerusalem, and Yitzchak Tabenkin opposed partition or any plan which precluded his hope to continue transforming the Palestinian countryside with Hebrew collectives.

Most remarkable, however, was the response of Jabotinsky. More than any other Zionist leader, he had rested his case on the need for a state to mitigate the distress of world Jewry. Now, in the manner of the Mufti, Jabotinsky rejected Peel's partition plan without hesitation. Perhaps it was a matter of Jewish honor, perhaps a rapturous view of the ancient land. In any case, he wanted more. During 1937, while negotiations over partition proceeded, a small military organization, the Irgun Tvai Leumi—or "Organization of National Armies," the "Irgun"—broke with the Haganah and came under Revisionist influence. Delighted, Jabotinsky exhorted his men to retaliate for attacks against Jews with all the force at their disposal. He derided the Haganah's policy of restraint.

It must be said that Jabotinsky's chivalrous impulses were too strong for him ever to go along with what many in the Irgun were actually preparing, namely, a campaign of terror against British police and Arab towns. He told the Irgun to warn Arab settlements of impending attacks, so that women and children could be evacuated. (Irgun leaders insisted that this would be impractical.) But Jabotinsky's contradictory approach to terror only highlighted the difficulty he encountered when he tried to transmit his ambiguous liberalism to the militant young followers his strident nationalism attracted. In 1938, at a meeting in Warsaw, a number of Jabotinsky's most militant followers repudiated the Mandate and put forward a resolution calling for "liberating Palestine by force of arms." Some wanted to establish closer relations with what was left of Abba Achimeir's right-wing, terrorist underground, the Brit Ha'Biryonim, which had been active since the early thirties. Jabotinsky would have none of it. He chided one of his student critics, a leader of Polish Betar: "If you, Mr. Begin, have stopped believing in the conscience of the world, then my advice to you is to go and drown yourself in the Vistula River."[5] The resolution passed.

.

Jabotinsky's end was sadly inconspicuous. He spent the last years of his life in London and New York. His exhortations to Jewish settlers to take up arms against Jewish enemies earned him permanent exile from the Yishuv. His attempts to stifle the growing movement in Betar to carry out terrorist attacks on the British aroused new suspicions among young activists. When World War II began, he criticized the Jewish Agency for demanding only sufficient Jewish forces within the British Army to defend the Yishuv. He tried again to raise a Jewish army—but in vain. Isolated and depressed, as insensible as everybody else to the final depths of Nazi cruelty, Jabotinsky died at a Betar summer camp in New York, in 1940.

Reflecting on Jabotinsky's legacy, Shlomo Avineri justly observed that power politics could not have served the Jews whom Jabotinsky's power ideology was meant to reassure. "According to Jabotinsky's philosophy," Avineri wrote, "it was not morality but power that decides among the nations, and hence his moral claim, buttressed by unspeakable suffering but having no legions to support it, was doomed to failure according to Jabotinsky's own premise."[6]

ii

The Peel Commission's proposal of a Jewish state, and the sincerity with which so many Palestinian Zionists warmed to it, suggests how well the Histadrut had already developed Jewish political autonomy within the limits of the British occupation. To confirm the Yishuv's potential for autonomy, consider the nervous admiration of a contemporary Arab economist and social scientist, Professor Said B. Himadeh, of the American University of Beirut, whose invaluable book *The Economic Organization of Palestine* was published in 1938. What seemed obvious to Himadeh was that the Histadrut had become the source of Jewish *political* power, and that its principles now evolved as much out of frustration with the Arab population as out of socialist-Zionist idealism.

> The strong trade union movement of Jewish labor [Himadeh wrote] has been brought about partly by the desire to create a new social order based on collective lines, and partly to fight adverse natural and social conditions . . .
> The movement has been helped to a considerable extent by national funds and Jewish organizations interested in the settlement of Jews in Palestine. An important adverse economic factor was the presence of a cheap and unorganized or poorly organized native labor force. The problem of cheap native labor was attacked in part by attempts to organize Arab labor, but for various reasons, particularly because of the strong national feeling and the strained relations between the Arabs and the Jews, these attempts met with little success.[7]

Himadeh noted that the Histadrut arranged collective agreements regarding wages and conditions of work, and that it secured and distributed employment for its workers. The organization also arranged for the absorption of new immigrants through its central employment bureau, Mercaz Ha'Avodah, which ran labor exchanges in all the chief towns and in Jewish agricultural and industrial centers, assisted in the establishment of new cooperatives, and helped the unemployed. Histadrut carried out various economic, social, and cultural services. All of this, Himadeh explained, was directed toward building up the Jewish national home.

By 1937, Himadeh continued, the membership of the Histadrut was 73,944; with spouses and dependent juvenile workers, the figure was 98,636—or 80 percent of the Jewish urban and rural workers in Palestine. (Himadeh may actually have underestimated the total size of the Yishuv's labor force in that year, but he was right about the proportions constituting it.) About "17,200 members of the Histadrut were engaged in undertakings and cooperatives of the organization, 12,400 in cooperative agricultural settlements, 2,700 in transport and industrial cooperatives, and 2,000 in the contracting offices of the Histadrut itself." The remaining members were employed by private employers and agitated for the hiring of Jews—something Himadeh found distasteful, though he rightly observed that the practice was an instrument of cultural revolution, not bigotry.

Himadeh perceived as well as any Palestinian Jew that the power of the Histadrut lay not merely in its numbers but in having created institutions of Jewish national life, exclusive of the Arab and British economy so far as this was possible.

[These included] the Workers' Bank [Bank Ha'Poalim] . . . and the Nir Company, the Histadrut's financial organ for granting long-term loans to agricultural settlers; [also] the Tnuvah cooperative society, which markets the produce of all agricultural centres connected to the Histadrut; the Ha'Mashbir Ha'Merkazi, the center for the consumers' cooperatives . . . ; the Mercaz Ha'Cooperatzia, the center for transport [including the Egged bus cooperative] and industrial producers' cooperatives; the Shikun, through which workers' housing is planned and executed; the credit cooperatives, which take the form of workers' loan and savings funds; the Solel Boneh, which is the largest building contractor in the country; the Yachin, which undertakes the plantation and management of citrus groves [apart from kibbutzim and moshavim].

[And industrial concerns are augmented by service corporations] such as the *Kupat Holim*, the sick fund, which is the health insurance institution of the Histadrut; *Ha'Sneh*, which deals with various branches of insurance; and the Unemployment Fund. These economic and social institutions are centralized in one institution, the *Chevrat Ovdim*.

The cultural and educational activities of the Histadrut, Himadeh concluded, were undertaken by the Mercaz Lechinuch, which conducted the school system of the federation. The Mercaz Letarbut, which was the cultural organization of adult laborers, and Ha'Noar Ha'Oved organized the youth. *Davar*, the daily newspaper of the federation, and the Ha'Poel sports organization governed leisure time. Himadeh then added a lament: "Arab labor organization, as compared with the Jewish, is still at an early stage of development."

Himadeh's survey of Histadrut activities during the 1930s, our most comprehensive by an Arab scholar, is reliable testimony to the anti-colonialist ethos of the Labor Zionists' revolution. It comes in striking contrast to the more recent claims of those mentors of the Palestine Liberation Organization who have exhorted Palestinian fighters to prosecute what they've called an "anti-colonialist" campaign of armed struggle against the "Zionist entity," including terrorist strikes against Israeli civilians, civil aviation serving Israel, and even Jewish supporters of Israel abroad. The myth of Zionist colonialism has become a kind of touchstone of Palestinian national rhetoric, and to believe in it has become a test of faith for the PLO's radical factions. The myth of colonialism has engendered the hope that, like typical European interlopers, Israeli Jews could eventually be forced back to where they came from, that military shocks would shake the Jewish colonialists from Palestine as the FLN shook the *Pieds-Noirs* from Algiers—like "ripe olives from a tree." (As Yasir Arafat put it in his famous speech to the United Nations General Assembly in November 1974: "Zionism is a species of colonialism" whose aim is "the conquest of Palestinian land" by European immigrants "just as settlers colonized and indeed raided most of Africa.")

To the extent that this myth has been the tactical premise, if not the moral justification, for a campaign of terrorism against Israelis, it has brought disaster on the Palestinians. The implication of Himadeh's research, in any case, is that the myth never had any serious foundation. In cultivating a kind of socialist separatism, Histadrut institutions secured for Palestinian Jews their Hebrew national culture. The Labor Zionists did not "raid" or exploit or even rely on the labor of the emerging Arab proletariat. They did not merge with the Arab elites, neither with the urban notables connected to the Ottoman bureaucracy, the *ayan*, nor with the great landlord *effendis*. It is precisely because Zionists feared becoming a colonialist class that Israelis now have roots of their own. ("If we do not till the soil with our very own hands," Gordon warned, "the soil will not be ours.")

Moreover, given what Himadeh called the "early stage of development" of Arab workers, Labor Zionist institutions prevented the division of Jews and Arabs along class lines, which almost certainly would have precluded a democratic style of life evolving in the Yishuv or in any part of Palestine. True, every large estate appropriated by the JNF displaced a good number of *fellahin* and helped to encircle Arab towns; every new Jewish immigrant became a citizen of an encroaching Hebrew civilization. But in displacing Arab peasants from their land, Labor Zionists did not—at least, not in the thirties—displace Arab residents from their country. Again, Palestine was a net *importer* of Arab population between the wars, largely owing to the commercial activity generated by Jewish investment. The Arab population of Palestine rose by about 100 percent to 1,200,000, while between 1922 and 1947 it remained static in Transjordan. It rose even faster in areas that became part of Israel in 1948.[8]

Unfortunately, this bare fact could not make Zionism seem fairer to the Arabs, whose opinions were, after all, of critical importance. Their competition with Zionism was cultural, not just a matter of numbers. The *fellahin* feared losing the way of life implied by the land; the *effendis* feared losing their religious life and unchallenged social position. It is worth recalling in this context how, after 1921, some of the Arab elites inflamed peasants they were otherwise prepared to exploit. Jamal Husseini, who became chairman of the Higher Arab Committee after the Mufti was forced into exile, complained to the Peel Commission:

As to the Communist principles and ideals of the Jewish immigrants, most repugnant to the religion, customs, and ethical principles of this country, which are imported and disseminated, I need not dwell on them, as these are well known to have been imported by the Jewish Community.[9]

The area of land purchased by Jews grew rapidly from 1921 to 1940, and thousands of peasants suffered the shocks of dislocation and disenfranchisement. Reliable British estimates in 1938 put the total number of rural Arab families at 86,980, nearly 30 percent of whom were by then "landless." Yet this finding begs the question of why Arab landlords, families such as the Sursoks, were willing to sell in spite of the political embarrassment of doing so. Before 1920, the Jewish community held about 650,000 dunams. (One dunam equals a thousand square meters or a quarter of an acre.) Yet Jews were able to acquire another 514,000 dunams by 1930, and approximately another 150,000 dunams between 1930 and 1933.[10] Between June 1934 and August 1936, Jews purchased 122,000 dunams of land: over two thousand separate purchases of estates of less than 100 dunams, and forty-one purchases of estates greater than 500 dunams. From 1936 to 1940, Jews acquired title to an additional 100,000 dunams of registered land, and the JNF to another 60,000 dunams of unregistered land.

In fact, the economic underpinnings of traditional Palestinian Arab society were greatly undermined even before the time of the Zionist immigration; feudal relations and old Ottoman corruptions had made the peasant vulnerable to any offer, whether from an Arab or a Jew, to buy out his landlord's property. One major source of this vulnerability was the Ottoman Land Law of 1858, by which a great many urban notables had unscrupulously appropriated vast tracts in their own names. These people were absentee landlords from the start, looking to turn a quick profit; they were inhibited by few paternalistic obligations to their tenants. By 1932, fifty-nine important absentee landlords owned nearly 120,000 dunams of agricultural land in Palestine.[11] More traditional landlords were increasingly apprehensive about the insolvency of tenants. In 1930, for example, the average *fellah* owed Arab banks (often controlled by the same oligarchical families that owned the land) a sum roughly equal to an entire year's revenue. Usurious interest rates as high as 30 percent were not uncommon. In the final analysis, the average peasant worked a parcel of land which, given his level of technology, was too small to support his family. It is this indebtedness that explains how Zionist holdings grew faster after Arab opposition to Zionism surfaced than before. During the Arab revolt alone, the JNF was offered between 200,000 and 300,000 dunams by potential Arab sellers.

One cannot know just how many of the peasants were forced into the towns during the time of the Mandate, though the number must have been considerable, given that more than half the Arab population of Palestine was urban by 1948—a population that had been nearly all rural in 1917. The rate of displacement of peasants might well have been higher had the British and Zionists never come at all. Mandatory administrators, not Arab bankers, organized new sources of credit for the Arab peasants during the 1930s, through the Protection of Cultivators Ordinance. It was by this initiative alone that some peasants were able to maintain their patrimonies.

Incidentally, the modern technology imported by the British and the Jews gave those Arabs who managed to stay on the chance to improve their yields. Agricultural output of the Arab sector rose by 50 percent between 1922 and 1938. In pre-Zionist days, the hilly areas were considered inhospitable to fruit trees, yet Arab plantations there grew from 332,000 dunams in 1931 to 832,000 in 1942. Citrus production in the Arab sector grew from 22,000 dunams in 1922 to 144,000 dunams in 1937, roughly the same expansion as in the Jewish sector. Between 1922 and 1939, the annual consumption of principal commodities per head rose by 85 percent. Wages for skilled and unskilled labor were, respectively, seven and three times what they were in Syria or Iraq.[12] Nor did the progressive influences of the Mandate stop with the Palestinian economy. Between 1921 and 1939, the infant mortality rate in Transjordan declined by 7 percent, in Egypt by 9 percent. In Palestine, the Arab infant mortality rate declined by 27 percent, and varied directly with residency in areas of high Jewish concentration. Infant mortality for Arabs in Jaffa was less than half that of Ramallah, a mere thirty miles away. Expenditures on education in the Arab sector kept pace: they doubled between 1931 and 1939, as did the Arab rate of literacy. By the beginning of the Second World War, perhaps 25 percent of the population was literate, some 200,000 people.

Educational levels among the Arab population were still shockingly low, especially as compared with what Arthur Koestler called the "200 percent" literacy rate among the Jews (most of whom wrote Hebrew in addition to some European language). But the gain was high enough to demonstrate that, in contradistinction to patterns of colonialism, the Jews usually subjected the Arabs of Palestine to patterns of modernization. Naturally, the uncertainties of city life were disturbing to a peasant who had lost his land—no less than was debt to a greedy landlord. The openly condescending attitude of secularist Labor Zionists toward village life and Islam certainly did not endear the Jews to Palestinian Arabs. Neither did the exclusionary Hebrew labor policies of the Histadrut, which Arab workers understandably viewed as prejudicial to their livelihoods. But no nation evolves in a bell jar, without such external, formative influences. The Mandate and the Histadrut were critical for Palestinian Arabs to develop their national identity beyond what was possible in Greater Syria, much as the emancipationism of Alexander II and repressions of Alexander III were necessary for the Jews of the Pale.

More recently, a good number of Palestinian intellectuals have come to endorse dividing historic Palestine into two democratic states: one Jewish, one Palestinian. If Labor Zionist colonial strategy is to be faulted for the injury it caused to Arab parents and grandparents, must it not also be credited with creating the conditions for partitioning the land fairly, i.e., between the two nations which grew up in essentially distinct economic systems? Such a partition was never feasible between the propertied *Pieds-Noirs* and the Algerian Arabs who worked for them. How else but for the Histadrut's strategy could peaceful coexistence—i.e., coexistence between nations—have been contemplated by Lord Peel or by anyone else since?

iii

By 1938 the plight of Central European Jews had finally become something of an international issue. During the summer, the Western democracies convened an international conference at Evian to consider how some Jews might be given asylum. The conference made some headway—the Dominican Republic, for example, offered to take in 100,000 refugees—but to their everlasting discredit, the democracies failed to come up with any serious plan for Jewish refugees. Santo Domingo's offer was greater than those of all the other states combined. The nascent Hebrew democracy of Palestinian Jews, it must be said, did not do itself much credit at Evian. The Mapai leadership were dismayed by developments in Europe, but they were apprehensive that the conference might succeed so well as to preempt Peel's case for settling Jewish refugees in Palestine. Once Britain had the question of Palestine dropped from the agenda of the Evian Conference, Golda Meyerson, the Jewish Agency delegate to Evian, was content merely to observe the proceedings without uttering a word. "I didn't know then that not concentration-camps but death-camps awaited the refugees whom no one wanted," she wrote later in her memoirs. "If I had known that, I could not have gone on sitting there silently, hour after hour, being disciplined and polite."[13]

Ben-Gurion, for his part, had come to believe what had always been latent in his revolutionary ideology, and what had been made the more unyielding in the face of Jabotinsky's barrage of criticism. In his view, there could be no survival for the Jewish people apart from that which directly promoted the cause of the socialist Hebrew nation in Palestine. The Nazis, he said, had initiated a new type of persecution and seemed bent on "systematic extermination" of the Jews. But even rescue had merged in his mind with building the Yishuv. Several months after *Kristallnacht*, during the winter of 1939, Ben-Gurion told a closed meeting of the Jewish Agency: "If I knew that all the Jewish children of Europe could be saved by settlement in Britain and only half could be saved by settlement in Palestine, I should choose the latter!"—a chilling statement, almost certainly impulsive, but stark evidence of his fervor. (Also, no doubt, evidence of the difficulty of an honorable man grasping how unflinchingly the Nazi SS would inflict what must have seemed to him hypothetical cruelties.)[14]

In contrast, the Mapai leadership could not but view with mounting horror the growing power of the Arab states, which—in spite of Peel's rhetoric and Evian's concerns—more and more influenced British calculations. Since the Bludan Conference in Syria in 1937,

the whole Arab world had been mobilized behind the Mufti's extreme rejection of Zionism. In October 1938, just a month before
Kristallnacht, the Arab world convened an Inter-Parliamentary Congress in Cairo and in short order called for a halt—a *total* halt—to
Jewish emigration to Palestine. Haj-Amin openly solicited and received backing from Berlin and Rome. Nor did any of the Arab
states offer themselves as havens for Jewish refugees. The entire
question of Jewish persecution was dismissed as a European problem which, presumably, should not prejudice the status of Palestinian Arabs.

.

As if in response, the British government called all parties to a
conference on Palestine at St. James's Palace in March 1939. Soon
after it began, Britain informed the Zionist executive both that Zionist rights under the Balfour Declaration were abrogated and that
the offer of a Jewish state was rescinded. Nor was this all. A new
British White Paper conceived of a majority Arab state in an un-
divided Palestine and limited future Jewish immigration to 75,000
over five years. After this period, Arab consent would be required,
though none expected it would be forthcoming.

According to the White Paper, Jews already in Palestine would be
allowed to purchase land, but only under sharply restricted conditions. What lands the JNF had acquired would not be expropriated;
yet who, the Zionists wondered, would be permitted to live on
them? So soon after the Munich Conference, the White Paper
looked suspiciously to the Zionist executive like yet another effort
at appeasement. (In fact, the British government's new policy on
Palestine reflected a belated certainty that Neville Chamberlain had
failed to appease Hitler at Munich. The Third Reich was by this
time moving to occupy the whole of Bohemia; war in Europe was
inevitable. Since oil had been found in Arabia, it seemed of critical
importance that Britain secure Arab support for the coming confrontation with Fascism—whatever the consequences for European
Jews.)

Ben-Gurion was adamant. He warned the Palestinian delegation
to the St. James's Palace conference:

> The appeal to halt our work for some time resembles an appeal by
> happy families, blessed with many children and living in comfort, to

a woman who after many years of childlessness is about to give birth. When she is overtaken with birth pangs, the neighboring women rebuke her and shout: "Could you stop this noise so that we can sleep in peace?" The mother cannot stop. It is possible to kill the child or kill the mother; but it is impossible to expect her to cease giving birth.[15]

By June 1939 Ben-Gurion had authorized illegal immigration under the auspices of the Haganah. When the ship *Colorado*, with 380 refugees on board, approached Palestine, he instructed the Haganah to bring it to Tel Aviv and challenge the police. The British intercepted the ship at sea and brought it to Haifa. After the outbreak of war in September 1939, Ben-Gurion announced that Zionists should fight Nazis as if there were no White Paper and fight the White Paper as if there were no Nazis. But this was a formula that was hard to make good on. Indeed, the British had left Zionism in the impossible position of being entirely at odds with the Mandatory government at precisely the time Jews everywhere looked to the Western powers to scotch Hitler. In February 1940, Ben-Gurion organized a general strike of Jewish workers and a series of angry demonstrations. Yet the Yishuv soon fell in line behind the Mandatory regime, gloomily, without a clear sense of the future. Weizmann wrote to Chamberlain: "We would like our differences to give way before the greater and more pressing necessities of the time." Then, in the executive of the Jewish Agency, Weizmann defeated Ben-Gurion's proposal to try the hard line. All acts of Jewish resistance stopped. Even the illegal Haganah radio station was closed down.

iv

The promulgation of the White Paper and Ben-Gurion's temporary defeat in the Jewish Agency halted Jewish immigration to Palestine when it was most urgently needed. But these developments did not mean the end of opportunities for the Yishuv to come into its own. The war fostered unprecedented growth of the Yishuv's military power, for example. After Winston Churchill became Prime Minister in 1940, Weizmann solicited permission to develop a Jewish Army for the defense of Palestine. By September—the "Phony War" over

—Churchill assented, and the British government then ratified a plan for a Jewish Army of 10,000 men from the Near East, 4,000 from the Yishuv. The Jewish force did not actually see action until 1944, and then only under the restricted conditions imposed by Colonial Secretary Lord Moyne, who feared inflaming Arab leaders. Nevertheless, there were many opportunities for the development of an officer corps under the plan, and Palestinian Jews did not fail to take advantage of them. An even more important source of military training came from service in the regular British forces. Some 27,000 young men and women from the Yishuv volunteered, and about 1,000 more served in the Free French Brigade—of whom only 45 survived the defense of Bir Hacheim.

In the first month of the war, interestingly enough, the Vaad Ha'Leumi announced registration of volunteers for national service. Within five days, 136,000 men and women enlisted.[16] Meanwhile, surreptitiously, the Haganah mustered forces and evolved the potential for military offensives. In 1938, the eccentric British colonel Orde Wingate had organized a small group of Haganah youth into the Night Squads; abandoning the policy of restraint, commandos connected to the Night Squads retaliated for Arab strikes, ambushed Arab irregulars, and disrupted road and rail traffic between Arab villages. Among the squads' most valued NCOs was Yitzchak Sadeh, who subsequently commanded a 1,000-man strike force known as Fosh. (A burly and charismatic man, Sadeh had served in the Red Army and had never abandoned his socialist radicalism. Nor, apparently, had he forgotten how to spot potential military talent, discovering Yigal Allon and Moshe Dayan while they were still in their teens.) Fosh was disbanded after the White Paper, but the Haganah's commanders went underground. Still lacking in combat units, they set up a permanent mobile force known as Hish, disheartened that, with so many Jewish cadres serving in the British Army, further attempts to muster forces would not be worthwhile.

In May 1941, when Rommel's offensive reached the entrance to Egypt, Haganah leaders determined to establish combat units with whatever manpower was available. They revamped their national command once more, and founded the Plugot Machatz (or "Striking Troops")—the Palmach—under Sadeh's leadership. Palmach forces operated in the open at first, in an unofficial arrangement with the British; its first two companies of recruits took part in the Allied invasion of Syria and Lebanon in August, and many performed well as scouts and guides. (It was here that Moshe Dayan lost his eye.) Indeed, when Rommel was poised to attack Alexandria, Sadeh proposed a plan—the so-called Carmel Plan—by which the whole population of the Yishuv would repair to an enclave in the Carmel mountain range and would live out the Nazi siege supplied by the RAF and the Yishuv's own agricultural resources. After Montgomery's defeat of Rommel at El Alamein, however, formal British contact with the Palmach became impossible, and the new force was secretly absorbed into the shadowy command structure of the Haganah.[17] British police closed Palmach training bases in the autumn of 1942 and tried to disarm some Palmach units. But the force resisted dissolution and went underground, and the Haganah swelled to about 21,000 fighters by the end of 1943. (A great many Palmach units were hidden, in the manner of guerrilla fighters, in the kibbutzim and especially in Tabenkin's left-wing kibbutz, the Kibbutz Ha'Meuchad.)

The Yishuv's industrial base also grew during the war. Soil under tillage expanded by 70 percent. Some 63 percent of the Jewish labor force worked for the British defense network, making weapons, engines, light naval craft, machine tools, uniforms. The number of industrial workers doubled to 46,000. The economy diversified to accommodate the need for specialized scientific products—optical instruments, pharmaceuticals. In this atmosphere of growth, Histadrut corporations thrived. Solel Boneh grew to become the largest construction firm in the Middle East, contracting for British bases and transport infrastructure. By 1943, 400 Jewish factories were added to the 2,000 already in operation. Another 800 would be built by the end of the war. The Jewish population itself grew to over half a million, and more than fifty new villages were founded. The value of Jewish industrial production increased nearly fivefold, from 7.9 million Palestinian pounds to 37.5 million.

v

At the Biltmore Hotel Conference of 1942—just two years after Jabotinsky's death—Ben-Gurion endorsed what had been the Revisionists' program, a Jewish state in the whole of Palestine. In 1944 Ben-Gurion would announce to workers in Haifa:

The meaning of the Jewish revolution is contained in one word: Independence! Independence for the Jewish people in its homeland! Our independence will be shaped further by the conquest of labor, of the land, by broadening the range of our language and its culture, by perfecting the methods of self-government and self-defense, by creating conditions for national creativity, and—finally—by attaining political independence . . .[18]

There is some question here whether, in view of the European catastrophe, Jabotinsky's ideology of power, race, and capitalism superseded the revolutionary ideals of Labor Zionism in the minds of Mapai leaders. Such distinct critics of Zionism as Hannah Arendt and Noam Chomsky have charged as much, arguing that Ben-Gurion and his colleagues took a turn toward Revisionism at Biltmore, at least insofar as they abandoned any hint of favor for bi-nationalism, or even for partitioning the country. The inference to be drawn from such criticism is that the subsequent establishment of a Jewish state, more precisely the war by which the state arose, were unnecessary: presumably it was Ben-Gurion's submission to Jabotinsky's ideology that doomed any further efforts to seek a peaceful compromise.[19]

Arendt and Chomsky have seriously misunderstood the slow conversion of Labor Zionism to the state ideal, and perhaps also the way ideas influence events: men are not said to drown, after all, merely because they are possessed of the idea of gravity. By May 1942, it had begun to dawn on the Allies that victory was only a matter of time. It was to consider the consequences of victory that American Zionists convened the Biltmore Conference in New York. At the meeting were representatives from the Zionist executive, including Ben-Gurion and Weizmann, and they were joined by leaders of nearly all the major American Jewish organizations. (Only the American Jewish Committee did not participate.) Could such a group really hand Jabotinsky a posthumous triumph?

In fact, the consequences of Biltmore were not clearly anticipated by anyone on the Jewish Agency executive. Four months earlier, Weizmann had written an article in *Foreign Affairs* in which he called for a state, albeit in general terms. Weizmann was still open to partition, but through 1940 and 1941 he had negotiated secretly with the Anglo-Arab diplomat St. John Abdullah Philby in the hope

of reviving the plan for a federation with ibn-Saud. Though negotiations had failed to this point, they still seemed promising to him.
Once Weizmann and the rest of the WZO leadership convened at
Biltmore, however, they were faced with a resolution which had
been hastily framed by Ben-Gurion, a much more strident call for
a state than anything Weizmann had envisioned. It stated that "the
gates of Palestine be opened and that the Jewish Agency be vested
with the control of immigration into Palestine, and with the necessary authority for building up the country, including the development of its unoccupied and uncultivated lands." Then came the
crucial phrase: Palestine—the whole of Palestine—"should be
established as a Jewish Commonwealth, to be integrated into the
structure of the new democratic world."

Obviously Ben-Gurion was motivated by Arab opposition to and
British repression of minimum Zionist aims—immigration and the
right to purchase land—not any maximalist ideology. Most important, in May 1942, was that Ben-Gurion still expected millions of
Jews to need resettlement after the war; that the Jews would become an overwhelming majority in Palestine when Polish Jewry
was liberated.

Some months before, Ben-Gurion had circulated a document in
the Jewish Agency executive in which he wrote of "immigration
and settlement of Jews on a grand scale" when the war was over,
"the transfer of millions of Jews and their settlement as a self-
governing people"—the immediate transfer of "at least two million."
Then, as if anticipating how his words could be mistaken for Revisionist rhetoric, Ben-Gurion added: "We are not the ones to have
created this reality, but we must adjust to it."[20]

The Biltmore Conference passed Ben-Gurion's resolution without
a dissenting vote; Weizmann could hardly repudiate its principle,
since he had seemed to endorse it just four months before. But the
spurious charge of Revisionism against Ben-Gurion only obscures
the real, emerging tensions underneath the apparent consensus.
Weizmann still considered British patronage to be indispensable,
and he viewed Biltmore's resolution as nothing more than a "demand," a negotiating position from which to work out with Britain
the transfer of immigration and settlement authority to the Jewish
Agency. In Ben-Gurion's view, however, the resolution carried the
force of national policy. Ben-Gurion was deeply impressed by

America, and by the growing power of its 5 million Jews. He was hoping a Jewish state would be tied to the United States and would come about by Anglo-American fiat.

The military power of the Haganah was also beginning to shape Ben-Gurion's thinking. Youth must be ready for "armed struggle," Ben-Gurion told the Jewish Agency executive in the spring of 1941: "They must be prepared to do everything possible when the right moment comes." Incidentally, all the delegates to Biltmore, including Weizmann, debated the fate of postwar Palestine as if millions of European Jews would soon be in need of refuge. Weizmann was tormented by the fear that Hitler might kill as many as a million people. He assumed the rest would be attended to by Zionism. It did not really seem possible to anyone that the Nazis would attempt systematically to murder the entire Jewish population of Europe.

vi

The first confirmed reports of Nazi massacres of Jews in Poland and the Ukraine filtered through to the Allies early in the summer of 1942. Thomas Mann had broadcast warnings over the BBC in December 1941 and throughout the winter, but civilized people were still not inclined to take them seriously. By the summer of 1942, there was no more doubt about the facts, though scarcely more comprehension. Returning to a dreary Palestine in October 1942, just when the full story of the "final solution" got out, Ben-Gurion tried to rally the Yishuv, calling an unprecedented number of demonstrations. But what thing of substance could be demanded? Ben-Gurion asserted the right of the Jewish Agency to make national policy in defiance, if necessary, of British designs; the Arab world remained steadfast, even cavalier. He also insisted that Zionism break not only with Britain but with the kind of moderation symbolized by the anglophile Weizmann. He pressed his case in the Jewish Agency executive and won a decisive majority. Only Ha'Shomer Ha'Tzair, still committed to the remote chance for binationalism, stood with Weizmann.

In April 1943 the German Army annihilated the Warsaw ghetto against unanticipated Jewish resistance. With the ghetto, the main part of the Eastern Jewish heartland not under Soviet domination was murdered. Three and a half million Polish, Russian, and Ukrainian Jews were eventually put to death, including over a million infants, tots, and children. By the summer of 1944, the death camps would take in 2.5 million Jews from Germany, Austria, France, Belgium, Holland, and Czechoslovakia; also from Yugoslavia, Rumania, and Greece. Over half the Jews of Hungary had been deported as well.

The mass killings put the executive of the Jewish Agency, like all Jews, in a state of shocked mourning. Zionist efforts were endowed with a new sense of radicalism: whatever the pioneers had wanted they now wanted more intensely. Golda Meyerson recalled Bialik's epic poem of the Kishinev pogrom and the phrase "the senseless living and the senseless dying" of the Jews in the Diaspora. Yet Meyerson's recollection of Bialik is instructive, as well as poignant, for it helps to account for the poise with which Zionist leaders faced the European catastrophe. Not that Ben-Gurion's Zionism had anticipated the final solution all along; apparently the leaders of the Nazi SS themselves had not conceived of such a thing until after occupying Poland. But unlike most Western Jews (and many non-Jews, for that matter), Zionists had a ready ideological framework in which to fit their rage. So many European revolutions had degenerated into barbarism; this fact did not dampen the Zionists' enthusiasm for revolutionary politics but reinforced it.

There had always been a sense of doubt in Labor Zionism about the way Jews behaved and would be treated in Europe—not the abstract sense of doom implied by Jabotinsky, not a theory of antagonistic nations and racial struggle—but skepticism regarding Jews in their classes, shops, synagogues, unions. In 1914, Brenner had asked: "A 'living' people? Whose members have no power but for moaning and hiding a while until the storm blows over, turning away from their poor brethren to pile up their pennies in secret, scratching around among the *goyim*, making a living from them and complaining about their ill will?" Brenner had answered: "Our urge for life whispers hopefully in our ear: 'Workers' settlements, workers' settlements,' this is our revolution, the only one."[21]

If Brenner's (hence Ben-Gurion's) equation of Jewish survival with the building of the Yishuv was too one-sided, it was nevertheless ratified for most Palestinian Jews by the actions of the British and the other Allied powers. The White Paper had called for the absorption of 75,000 Jewish immigrants over five years and 25,000 immediately. In fact, the number of immigrants dropped from

27,500 in 1939 to 8,000 in 1940; it dropped further to 6,000 in 1941 and 3,700 in 1942. In May 1940 the Jewish Agency pleaded that an exception be made for children. The Mandatory government took two years to make up its mind. Nor did the British government relax its control over the Palestinian coastline. In November 1940 the refugee passengers of the steamer *Patria* headed toward the beaches. The British tried to put them out to sea. The day before, 1,880 refugees from Danzig—passengers on the ship *Atlantic*— had already been dispatched by the Mandatory government to Mauritius. Rather than allow the *Patria's* wretched cargo to be sent to internment camps as well, Haganah agents secretly boarded the ship at Haifa, hoping to disable its engines with an explosive charge. But they badly miscalculated. Two hundred and sixty people were blown to bits or drowned. Thousands watching from the slopes of Mount Carmel saw the ship go down.

In March 1942 the *Struma Danube* anchored off the coast of Turkey. A cattle boat, the *Struma* carried 769 Jewish passengers, some on the verge of insanity. When finally it lurched into Istanbul's harbor, Jewish Agency officials there implored Turkish authorities to let it land. The British government would not allow it to proceed to Palestine. The Turks tried to put the ship out to sea, but it sank, with the loss of nearly all on board, a mile off the Turkish coast. Weizmann would reflect:

> It was not merely a tragedy of physical suffering and destruction, so common throughout the world though nowhere so intensively visited as upon the Jews. It was a tragedy of humiliation and betrayal. Much of the calamity was unavoidable; but a great part of it could have been mitigated, many thousands of lives could have been saved, both in the period preceding the war and during the war itself, had the democratic countries and their governments been sufficiently concerned.[22]

Weizmann's claims against all the Western democracies seem the more warranted in light of subsequent research into documents Weizmann could not have seen. After the grim revelations of the summer of 1942, British and American groups began to agitate publicly for action on behalf of European Jewry. In mid-April 1943, just as the Nazis mounted their assault on the Warsaw ghetto, the Allies finally met in Bermuda to consider the fate of war refugees, and specifically Nazi atrocities against European Jews. Yet the

United States government appointed a rather low-ranking delegation to this conference—Supreme Court Justice Owen Roberts declined to serve—and the only American Jewish representative to the conference, Congressman Sol Bloom of New York (the chairman of the House Foreign Relations Committee), had hardly raised the plight of European Jews in public.

Significantly, President Roosevelt had not distinguished himself on the Jewish question either, though his prestige might have made saving the Jews a top priority. The State Department's memorandum to the U.S. delegation included instructions not to limit the discussion to Jewish refugees, not to raise questions of religious faith or race in appealing for public support or promising U.S. funds, not to make commitments regarding shipping space for refugees, not to expect naval escort or safe conduct for refugees, not to delay the wartime shipping program by offering that homeward-bound, empty transports might pick up refugees en route, not to bring refugees across the ocean if any space for them could not be found in Europe, not to pledge funds. The delegation should not even expect any changes in the U.S. immigration laws.

For Britain's part, there would be no direct appeal to the Germans, no exchange of prisoners for refugees or a relaxation of the blockade to send relief supplies. The chief of the British delegation, Richard Kitson Law, cited the danger of "dumping" large numbers of refugees on the Allies, some of whom might be Nazi sympathizers. When Congressman Bloom, sensing now the conference's historic task, argued to permit large numbers of refugees to enter the Western countries—questioning Britain's closed door in Palestine—the head of the American delegation, Princeton University President Harold Willis Dodds, silenced him.

The upshot of the Bermuda Conference was stagnation. Once again pressure mounted in America, fueled largely by that extraordinary firebrand Hillel Kook (or as he called himself in America, Peter Bergson), whose roots were in the Revisionist movement. Kook spearheaded a campaign to call an Emergency Conference to Save the Jewish People of Europe, which took place during the summer of 1943 at Madison Square Garden. Finally, in the wake of the conference and in consequence of congressional lobbying, high officials in Roosevelt's Departments of State and Treasury began to develop a plan for the formation of a War Refugees Board.

But President Roosevelt still did not actively campaign for its establishment. Not until December 1943 was the WRB given serious attention, when State Department officials were defied by people in Treasury. (A secret proposal that American and British aircraft bomb the Auschwitz death camp was mooted but never made much headway.)

The record of the Jewish Agency leadership with regard to the rescue of European Jewry was not unblemished either—precisely because of the intensity with which people like Ben-Gurion and Weizmann had come to associate rescue with the Yishuv's national aims. Certainly the Jewish Agency executive did not always exploit to the full what opportunities they had. At the beginning of the war, a nonsectarian rescue committee was set up in Istanbul, mainly at the initiative of Palestinian Jewish volunteers connected with the Mosad L'Aliyah Bet—the illegal immigration organization of the Haganah. (The Revisionist liaison to the committee was Jabotinsky's own son.) Astonishing in their selflessness, some thirty-two of the rescue committee's Palestinian volunteers, including Enzo Sereni and the poet Hanah Senesh, parachuted behind enemy lines to organize resistance and escape. They were eventually captured and sent to the death camps. For its part, however, the Mapai leadership gave the rescue committee little material support. In late August 1943, the Istanbul committee wrote a critical letter to Ben-Gurion accusing him of indifference to their efforts. Typically, perhaps, Ben-Gurion wrote back that he was opposed to giving the committee support either from the JNF or from any other Zionist fund needed for building up the Yishuv. (Golda Meyerson [Meir] wrote in her memoir that Sereni "symbolized the basic helplessness of our situation.")

The most controversial case against the Mapai leadership comes from Hillel Kook himself, who charged that Ben-Gurion's chief supporter in the United States, Rabbi Stephen Wise, in effect delayed the formation of the War Refugees Board in a futile effort to capitalize on the drama created by the Biltmore Conference. Nobody could deny that Wise had been among those who pressured Treasury officials to take action. But in addition to wanting legislation funding the WRB, Kook alleged, Wise wanted a resolution from Congress endorsing the settlement of Jewish refugees in Palestine. (In congressional hearings conducted after the war,

Wise did not deny that he had supported a resolution to the effect that "the gates of Palestine be kept open to the refugees of Hitler's Europe, and that as many enter into Palestine as can possibly enter it"—a contentious resolution, given British sensitivities, and one which almost certainly held up passage of the main legislation to some extent.)[23] The WRB finally did get its mandate in January of 1944—by President Roosevelt's executive order, largely as a result of the intervention of Secretary of the Treasury Henry Morgenthau. But without a hired staff and clear line of authority, it could not start its work immediately. Nearly a year had passed since the Bermuda Conference, and it was now too late for any action on behalf of Polish Jews. Yet some 700,000 Jews remained alive in Hungary, and as many as 200,000 in Budapest even after the deportations of May through July. What might have been done for them had the WRB been operating effectively only several months earlier than it was?

In May 1944, a man claiming to be Adolf Eichmann's emissary, Joel Brand, arrived in Istanbul with the infamous offer to exchange Allied trucks for Hungarian Jewish lives. The Allies balked and the plan came to nothing. But in July of that year, the Swedish diplomat Raoul Wallenberg arrived in Budapest with the modest financial backing of the WRB—a mere $100,000—and, improvising heroically, saved as many as 100,000 Jews. Could thousands more people have escaped death had Wallenberg arrived earlier, had he been on the scene to explore Eichmann's alleged offer? (Wallenberg was arrested by the Soviets after the Red Army marched into Budapest. Officially, he was never heard from again.)

vii

Ben-Gurion's tough-minded Biltmore policy was, at first, reinforced by knowledge of the final solution. Inevitably, however, it was undermined by the murderous actions of the Nazi SS. Biltmore's governing premise had been, after all, that at least 2 million Jews would immediately have to be settled in Palestine after the war. Even before the war's end, all knew this was, horribly, an exaggerrated figure. In consequence, Ben-Gurion began to distance himself from his former, maximalist aims. He certainly swung away from Jabotinsky's ideological heirs, and nothing proved this so well as his decision to help the British hunt down the Irgun.

Since its split with the Haganah, the Irgun had had only one outstanding leader, Yair Stern, a man of poetry and fire—and such extreme anti-British views that the Mandatory government finally arrested him in August 1939. Stern was released the following summer, and he founded the Lehi—the "Israel Freedom Fighters" —which carried out many terrorist attacks in association with the Irgun. But Stern promoted a vaguely anti-imperialist line—some in his group even mooted the idea of an alliance with the Soviet Union—and eventually this rankled with the major part of Betar's fighters, some 3,000 young men and women who were the majority of the Irgun. Stern was finally gunned down by the British in February 1942. The right-wing underground's crisis of leadership ended —and its rivalry with the Haganah began in earnest—only with the arrival of Menachem Begin in the Yishuv in 1943.

.

Born in Brest-Litovsk in 1913, Begin had been a political Zionist literally from birth. His father, though an observant Jew, had been open to secular knowledge; when Herzl died in 1904, the older Begin had broken down the door of the synagogue to hold a memorial service. The young Menachem was given an Orthodox education at a Mizrachi school and was taught modern Hebrew. He later explained that he had observed the law as much to make a display of national pride as out of conviction: curiously, he attended the Polish high school on the Sabbath, but he would not write!

There had also been lessons in Jewish honor:

> One day, my father was walking with a rabbi when a Polish sergeant tried to cut off the rabbi's beard, a popular sport among anti-Semites. My father carried a cane topped by a silver knob, fashioned in the shape of Emile Zola's head, and inscribed with a text from *J'Accuse*. My father did not hesitate. He hit the sergeant on the hand with his cane. In those days, hitting a sergeant was a signal for a pogrom. Both my father and the rabbi were arrested. They were taken to the River Bug and their captors threatened to throw them in. They were beaten until they bled. But my father was happy. He said he had defended the honour of the Jewish people and the honour of the rabbi.[24]

The Begins might have come to the Yishuv in the mid-twenties, but they did not. Instead, Menachem joined the Ha'Shomer

Ha'Tzair, and then left the movement when, in his words, it "turned from scouting to Communism." In 1929, at the age of fifteen, Begin joined Betar. (A year later, he heard Jabotinsky speak for the first time: "I was won over by his ideas: the willingness to fight for the liberation of the homeland, and the logical analysis of facts in political matters.") Begin went on to study law at Warsaw University, and he endured the anti-Semitic barbs of his professors with the kind of grace he imagined Jabotinsky (and Pilsudski) would admire. In 1936 he had been appointed commander of Betar in Czechoslovakia, though, it should be stressed, Begin's relations with Jabotinsky were never entirely without strain. After 1936, Begin was one of the Young Turks in Betar who had begun to promote greater contacts with Abba Achimeir's Palestinian terrorist group, whose tactics Jabotinsky had denounced.

In 1938, Begin represented Polish Betar at the World Congress of the New Zionist Organization in Warsaw. It was here that Begin had led the Betar congress in amending the Betar oath to include a vow to "conquer the Jewish homeland by force of arms"—and Jabotinsky told him to go drown himself in the Vistula. As it happened, Begin was more prescient than Jabotinsky about the "conscience of the world." That oath, however, was sadly inconsistent with the political world that soon closed in on him. He was appointed commander of Betar in Poland in 1939, but was arrested by Polish security forces for leading an anti-British demonstration. He fled to Vilna just as Poland collapsed before the Nazi onslaught, but the Soviet authorities arrested him in late 1940. Separated from his wife, Begin could only speculate on the miserable fate of his family.

Never without a stiff backbone, Begin began an eight-year sentence with stoic contempt for his Soviet wardens—and for the Stalinist Marxism of his interrogators. Begin wrote that he had told one of them: "To you, my having been a Zionist, a Betar member, is my guilt. To me that was service to my people."[25] At the end of 1941, Begin was transported to the Gulag, where he struggled to maintain his civility and learned to live with his "companions," the fleas. He did not languish in prison for nearly as long as he feared, however. After Hitler attacked the Soviet Union, Begin was released under the terms of the Soviet-Polish treaty, enlisting in the Free Polish Army in 1942. He then got to Palestine in the uniform

of a Polish soldier, just when the Betar underground had suc-
cumbed to general demoralization. Begin assumed command of
the Irgun at the end of 1943, and immediately went into hiding.
(Punctilious to a fault, he had first secured a "temporary" discharge from the Polish Army.)

From 1944 on, the Irgun undertook to consolidate all Jewish
forces in Palestine for an armed revolt against the British. The
Haganah would not go along, of course, but Begin's forces struck
out on their own nevertheless: in February there were attacks on
the immigration offices in Jerusalem, Tel Aviv, and Haifa. In
November a Sternist squad assassinated Lord Moyne. (One of the
assassins, Elyahu Ben-Hakim, had seen the *Patria* go down from
Haifa's Panorama Road. He was hanged.) It was after Moyne's
assassination, which greatly soured Winston Churchill on Zionist
demands, that Ben-Gurion began to cooperate with the British in
searching for Jewish terrorists and bringing them to justice. "There
are two choices facing us," Ben-Gurion proclaimed, "terrorism or a
Zionist political struggle; terrorist organizations or an organized
Jewish community. If we want a Zionist political struggle we
must rise and take action against terrorism and terrorist organizations. It is necessary to act, not just talk."[26]

Thus began the *Saison*, in which some 279 Irgun followers (and
Sternists) were rounded up. The whole number of underground
supporters delivered to the police for interrogation may have totaled
as many as 1,000. By this time, Begin had been apprised of the
fact that virtually his entire family had been wiped out in the death
camps. The actions of the Haganah against the Irgun—which
seemed to him all the worse in view of Mapai's left-wing rhetoric—
inflamed him against Labor Zionism as never before.

In later years, incidentally, Begin would assert that the Holocaust
itself would have been impossible if Zionism had founded the Jewish state before the war, that the Mapai leadership's pusillanimity
was at least in part to blame. Besides, had not the Nazis vindicated
Jabotinsky's position? Had not the Holocaust justified precisely
what the Revisionists had wanted all along, a Jewish state? "Out of
the blood and tears and ashes," Begin would write in his brilliant
chronicle of the Irgun, "a new specimen of Jew was born, a specimen completely unknown to the world for over eighteen hundred

years: 'the FIGHTING JEW' . . ."[27] Of course, it was Jabotinsky who had opposed Peel's offer of a state, and much good it did Weizmann and Ben-Gurion to endorse it! States, like honor, are won with physical courage, but they are not so easily won. Nor would "fighting Jews" on their own have secured the survival of the Jewish people without a British victory at El Alamein and a Russian victory at Stalingrad. Ironically, Begin's notion that a revolt against the British in Palestine should have been Zionism's response to Hitler, indeed, to all anti-Semitism, greatly overestimated Zionism's power to influence events during World War II—at the same time as it underestimated the Histadrut's work before it.

What Begin's statement failed to convey, perhaps the most important point, was that the Nazis did not so much vindicate Revisionism as murder the people who were the reserves of the Labor Zionist revolution. Begin was right to imply that the Holocaust had changed the terms by which the Yishuv would be judged by the Great Powers and speeded up the coming of sovereignty. But as the late Jacob Talmon has cautioned, one ought not to lose sight of the gradual process by which the Hebrew nation had been and was still being made, mainly by Polish and Eastern European immigrants. More and more highly motivated Hebrew-speaking Jews would surely have come, perhaps 2 million more from Poland alone. Without the Holocaust, Israel might not have arisen in 1948. But with those people it would have arisen all the more inevitably.

viii

As the war was ending, Ben-Gurion began to doubt the prospects for the Biltmore Plan, though his contempt for the legacy of the White Paper had not lessened. He prepared the Haganah for the worst, intensifying efforts to organize *Bricha*, the mass flight of illegal immigrants. By this time, Haganah was working closely with the Joint Distribution Committee; with the additional help of some sympathetic French bureaucrats, Haganah arranged the escape from Europe of some 70,000 Jewish refugees. Yet the fate of those refugees revealed how ugly the impasse with Britain had become.

Palestinian Arabs were hardly more disposed to any compromise acceptable to the Zionist movement than they had been before the war. They wanted the British to keep to the policy of the White

Paper of 1939 and saw no reason to deviate from it. The British government, for its part, was now pulled in contradictory directions. The British public were, in view of the Holocaust, much more sympathetic to Zionism than before. Yet the Mandatory government continued to rule the country and increasingly came into conflict with Zionist leaders. Certainly it did not waver in its restrictions of Jewish immigration. In the immediate postwar period, the British Navy captured some 51,500 Jewish refugees and interned them. The American government also figured in Britain's calculations, since it seemed more and more determined to pressure Britain to act in a way disposed to Zionist claims. Back in 1944, Secretary of State Henry L. Stimson had blocked a congressional resolution favoring the Biltmore Plan. Just such a resolution passed the Congress in December 1945.

In temperament and philosophy, President Truman was bound to Zionism in a way Roosevelt had not been. Ben-Gurion did not fail to play on the latent tensions between Britain and the United States. In October 1945 he traveled to occupied Europe to meet with General Dwight D. Eisenhower and proposed a plan to give Zionism even more leverage against the Mandatory authorities. Ben-Gurion requested that all European Jews who survived the war and had come to Eisenhower's zone, some 98,000 people, should be concentrated in displaced persons' camps, where the Jewish Agency would have special privileges—including the right to give the DPs agricultural and vocational training preparatory to their emigration to the Yishuv. The Allied command could not accommodate all of Ben-Gurion's requests, but Eisenhower did permit the housing of Jews in his zone and allowed the Jewish Agency to post representatives. Meanwhile, Ben-Gurion authorized cooperation with the Irgun, a temporary expediency but one he justified so long as Britain refused to rescind the White Paper. Immediately there was a raid on the detention center at Atlit, which resulted in the release of 200 illegal immigrants. On November 1, Haganah and Irgun people together sabotaged British railway lines and blew up British coast-guard vessels.

Still, time was running out on him, and Ben-Gurion was shrewd enough to see this. Delay would bring increasing sentiment among Jewish DPs in Eisenhower's zone to emigrate to America. The new Labour government of Clement Attlee, meanwhile, began a series of stalling tactics. It hinted at a willingness to raise the quota on Jewish immigration but dismissed out of hand any discussion of new political arrangements. Indeed, Attlee saw as his main problem the appeasement of the American Congress, which was then voting Britain financial aid; presumably the British Army could handle any challenges by Jewish forces in Palestine.

Attlee's Foreign Minister, Ernest Bevin, sponsored the Grady-Morrison Plan, which offered permission for 100,000 Jewish immigrants to land. In Bevin's view, the plan answered America's most pressing demand—that the DPs should be allowed to find homes in Palestine—though the concession was in reality nothing but an amendment to the White Paper. "The Jews," Bevin said, "want to get too much at the head of the queue." They will thus face "the danger of another anti-Semitic reaction." The Jewish Agency rejected the Grady-Morrison proposal in early 1946 with a righteousness appropriate to Bevin's tactlessness. Britain responded with the big stick.

On June 29, 1946—which came to be known as "Black Saturday" —the British police in Palestine turned on the Haganah and the Palmach. The Mandatory government jailed the leaders of the Jewish Agency in Palestine and rounded up thousands from the kibbutzim. British troops scoured Jewish settlements for weapons, and the entire Yishuv was placed under curfew; many Jews were beaten, some were tortured, three were killed. At the height of the British crackdown, the Haganah commander, Moshe Sneh, tried to organize resistance. Weizmann forced him to resign. Ben-Gurion was in Paris at the time and so escaped detention. Two weeks later —in retaliation for the arrests, but without Haganah approval—the Irgun blew up the King David Hotel, British Mandate headquarters, killing 91 people.

.

Ben-Gurion might well have done what other national leaders have done in similar situations, reject compromise for the sake of national unity and exhort his forces to general resistance. A working relationship of sorts with the Irgun had already been established, before the bombing of the King David Hotel. In what was perhaps his finest hour, however, Ben-Gurion recoiled from general violence. In view of Arab hostility and Nazi atrocity, Ben-Gurion was by no means prepared to compromise on the principle of self-determination. But a Jewish state did not have to conform to the Biltmore Plan. Ben-Gurion called a meeting of the main part of the WZO executive in Paris. Nachum Goldmann proposed that a Jewish state be constituted in only "a sufficient portion of the land of Israel" to be "viable," refraining from laying claim even to Jerusalem. This was a far cry from the ideal of a Jewish commonwealth in the whole of Palestine with which Ben-Gurion had rallied his people over four harrowing years. Nevertheless, Ben-Gurion endorsed Goldmann's plan and made it public. In effect, Ben-Gurion had again broken with the maximalists and renewed the Yishuv's offer of partition.

It should be stressed that Ben-Gurion's shift to this more moderate course did not mean he believed a war with the Arabs would be avoided or that Zionists should be unwilling to count on the use of military force. The Arab states continued to reject even minimum Zionist demands, including Britain's proposal that a mere 100,000 Jews be resettled in Palestine. Would Palestinian national groups ever acquiesce in Jewish political rights not won by force? (When the Zionist Congress met in Basle that fall, Weizmann passionately addressed it: "I warn you against shortcuts, against following false prophets and will-o'-the-wisp generalizations. I do not believe in violence . . . Zion will be redeemed through righteousness and not by any other means." The speech got a standing ovation, but Ben-Gurion saw to it that Weizmann was not reelected president of the WZO. In marked contrast to Weizmann, Ben-Gurion praised the Haganah's growing resistance movement, "a new event in the chronicles of Israel."[28])

What Ben-Gurion's offer of partition had meant, rather, was that he had committed Labor Zionism, once and for all, to the only democratic solution possible under the circumstances: one to inspire his own forces, gain the sympathy of the Western democracies, and eventually, perhaps, be accepted by fair-minded Arab leaders. Partition meant that the Jewish state's political borders would conform to the Hebrew nation's cultural borders, and that Hebrew self-determination would not lock Jews and Palestinians into a permanent conflict. Ben-Gurion, to be sure, was bracing for war. It would be, he thought, a just war.

6 / State and Revolution

When Ben-Gurion accepted partition in 1947, he did so not only to provide refuge for Jews still in European displaced-person camps but to consolidate the strong institutions Labor Zionism had established in Palestine. The Mapai leadership had created a fighting force united by ideology; it had become a legitimate and democratic quasi-government, and had gained international recognition. The Histadrut had given the Yishuv a public chain of command, unions, and services, along with self-sustaining fields and factories. Ben-Gurion's intention was to defend Labor Zionist principles: Hebrew labor, autonomy, science, secularism, refuge—these had been at the heart of Mapai's revolution. The main point of partition was to finish what had been started, with moral reasoning if possible, but also with diplomacy and industry, with men and women at arms.

Yet the consolidation of Ben-Gurion's revolution set the stage for the demise of his revolutionary ideas. Within seven years after the founding of the state of Israel, Labor Zionist veterans found themselves presiding over a population at least twice that of their compact socialist and mainly European Yishuv. This added population was increasingly composed of young people—their own children included—who were never Zionists in any profound sense. More important, perhaps, there were hundreds of thousands of Jews from Arab countries, most of whom had never had to come to terms with the ways of a secular democracy; only a few from Cairo or Baghdad had ever grappled with the rather esoteric principles of Labor Zionism. Given the new challenges, Ben-Gurion began to rely on a kind of state cult to mobilize the population. Economic sacrifices were necessary to absorb the new immigrants, and military sacrifices to defend the state's borders. In consequence, Ben-Gurion determined to attract foreign investors and gain Western, and Western Jewish, backing—even if this meant surrendering the socialist economy to market expansion. Mapai leaders, to be sure, remained in control. But if power corrupts, then control, too, exacted a price.

i

Ben-Gurion's drive to get the Yishuv's claim of self-determination recognized by the Great Powers—what was left of them—finally achieved its goal during the spring of 1947. Even the Soviets backed a Jewish state, their rhetorical assaults on Zionism silenced temporarily by the death camps, but also by a certain *Realpolitik*. During the summer of 1947, there were 100,000 British troops in Palestine. Although these forces were barely able to keep the peace between Arab irregulars and Haganah forces, they were available to buttress British clients in Iraq, Aden, Transjordan, and the smaller oil sheikdoms of the Gulf. Needless to say, the Soviets were eager for the British to withdraw from the Middle East, particularly from Palestine. Nor could Attlee's government, straining under the burden of postwar reconstruction, afford to keep so many troops there much longer—not at an annual cost of between £30 and £40 million. There was direct American aid, which Britain increasingly relied upon. But this only made the British government more subject to American pressures.

The United States government, for its part, was not much happier about the British presence in Palestine than was Stalin. Unlike most State Department officials, the President and Congress were inclined to view Zionism with profound sympathy. At the same time, the State Department openly argued that there were no risks from Soviet machinations in the Persian Gulf to compare with the gains to be made by American oil firms there. The Arab states of the Gulf certainly did not require a British patron in addition to an American one. The question was how long Attlee would defy the combined will of the United States and the Soviet Union over Palestine? If Britain could withdraw from India, could she not from Palestine? Once the Grady-Morrison plan was rejected by all sides, Bevin took no further unilateral action. On April 2, 1947, the British delegate to the United Nations asked for a special session on Palestine, and a month later the entire problem was thrown to the General Assembly.

Representatives to the United Nations Special Committee on Palestine (UNSCOP) arrived in Palestine in June to gather evidence for a recommendation. That same month—fittingly, perhaps —4,500 Jewish refugees crammed aboard the now legendary ship *Exodus 1947* and made for the Palestinian coast. UNSCOP representatives were deeply shocked when the British off-loaded the refugees onto British vessels and returned them to France; Jewish Agency spokesmen did not fail to point out that the refugees finally wound up in, of all places, Hamburg, Germany. The Higher Arab Committee, meanwhile, still dominated by the Mufti's men, boycotted UNSCOP deliberations altogether. Sentiment was widespread in the Arab world that Arab armies should achieve with military force what the British had not achieved with the White Paper. Begin, too, rebuffed all talk of compromise. Under his leadership, Irgun forces had grown to about 5,000 men and women—roughly the same size as the Palmach—and carried out operations resulting in the deaths of some 300 British personnel. (In July 1947 Begin hanged two captured British sergeants, in apparent retaliation for the execution of three of his own men. Thousands of pained and disgusted British mothers, many of whom now hated all Zionists, appealed to Bevin to bring the boys home.)

UNSCOP made far-reaching recommendations on September 1, calling for the partition of the country into a Jewish state and an Arab one, much along the lines of the proposal of the Zionist executive in 1946. According to the UNSCOP plan, Jerusalem would be "internationalized." Most of northern Galilee would be part of a Palestinian Arab state, as would the town of Acre and all of what has come to be known as the West Bank. Jaffa and the whole of the Negev would be Jewish, in addition to the coastal plain and other territories included in the Peel plan. This new partition was no less difficult to envision than Peel's, what with the projected border between the two states weaving in and out. Yet the Jewish Agency executive was well satisfied. Not only had the international community recognized Jewish self-determination, it had also recognized the implicit political border established by the Zionist Yishuv.

Satisfaction turned to jubilation on November 29, when UNSCOP won over the General Assembly—though the Assembly reduced the Jewish zone by some five hundred square miles, lopping off the town of Beersheba. France cast the deciding vote in favor. Perhaps the most eloquent defense of partition was offered by the young Soviet ambassador, Andrei Gromyko:

> The Jews as a people have suffered more than any other people . . . You know there was not a single country in Western Europe which succeeded in adequately protecting the interests of the Jewish people against the arbitrary acts and violence of the Hitlerites . . . [Partition] will meet the legitimate demands of the Jewish people, hundreds of thousands of whom, you know, are still without a country, without homes, having found temporary shelter only in special camps . . .

The Jewish Agency promptly accepted the amended partition plan. Predictably, the Arab states voted against it *en bloc*. Begin, too, rejected partition and dug in for a "war of liberation."

.

Ben-Gurion's endorsement of the UNSCOP plan, like his offer of partition in 1946, ought not to obscure his own growing apprehension that the Jewish state would have to rise by force of arms—though not from Begin's basements and attics. Ben-Gurion began to devote himself to organizing Labor Zionist settlements according to the Haganah's military strategy, embodied in its detailed "Plan D," to drive out the Palestinian Arab forces that had been operating there since the Second World War. Weizmann by now was telling friends that Ben-Gurion was a "hothead." In fact, Ben-Gurion knew that the Jews could win. Behind the scenes Jewish Agency representatives began negotiating a critical arms deal for the Haganah with Czechoslovakia. Golda Meyerson was dispatched to the United States to raise funds. By the end of 1948, the United Jewish Appeal would deliver some $75 million.

After some fussing, Bevin set May 15, 1948, as the date for withdrawing the Mandatory regime. In anticipation, the Haganah expanded its force to roughly 35,000 fighters. Arab forces included the Syrian-backed Arab Liberation Army headed by the Fawzi al-Kaukji (who had seen action in Palestine during the Arab Revolt); also the Mufti's forces, with whom, significantly, Kaukji feuded. (Even then, the Syrian government regarded Palestine as nothing but a portion of Greater Syria.) Yet Kaukji and the Mufti did not represent the only armies arrayed against the Yishuv. Abdullah had designs on the territories west of the Jordan, especially Jerusalem; it was just a matter of time, Ben-Gurion knew, until the Haganah would have to cope with Sir John Glubb's ("Glubb Pasha") highly trained Transjordanian Arab Legion. Other Arab states threatened invasion: Iraq, Syria, even Egypt. With winter came civil anarchy. Haganah ran more and more British blockades to land new Jewish refugees, and over 30,000 Jews were in British detention camps, on Cyprus and elsewhere. Meanwhile, as Jews arrived, thousands of Arab residents were in frantic flight; over a quarter million would be gone by May.

Paradoxically, Ben-Gurion was not at all reassured by the flight of so many Arabs—not yet, at any rate.[1] Naturally, he wanted a large Jewish majority, but he feared that manifest public disorder would discredit the UNSCOP partition plan before it could be implemented. In particular, Ben-Gurion was anxious that the U.S. State Department, which he knew to be influenced by the oil lobby, would find in the general panic a pretext to renege on the U.S. government's implicit commitment to recognize the Jewish state when sovereignty was declared in May. The State Department had all along been trying to persuade President Truman to stall, or at least to let it be known that, however much he approved of the UNSCOP plan in principle, his Administration might have to withhold recognition of a Jewish state beyond the date of British evacuation. In February, Chaim Weizmann met privately with President Truman and seemed to secure a promise of recognition. ("He talked," Truman wrote, "about the possibilities of development in Palestine, about the scientific work that he and his assistants had done that would someday be translated into industrial activity in the Jewish state that he envisaged. He spoke of the need for land if future immigrants were to be cared for. He impressed on me the importance for any Jewish state of the Negev area in the south . . .")[2] Yet, on March 19, the American ambassador to the UN dramatically announced that his government wanted the General Assembly recalled, to develop a *new* plan based on a temporary UN "trustee-ship"—implying that the UNSCOP plan might be shelved. This turn of events deeply disturbed Ben-Gurion and seemed to vindicate his dismay over the Arab panic. Ben-Gurion had no way of knowing then that Truman had never authorized the reversal of policy, and that he would override his own State Department, if need be, to make good on his "promise to Dr. Weizmann."

Nor did Irgun actions help matters. Most of the Arabs who had left the country during the fall and winter knew that a war was coming and, understandably, hoped to return in the wake of victorious Arab armies. There had been atrocities on both sides. Yet, as if to exacerbate the State Department's reservations, the Irgun massacred an estimated 110 Arab civilians at Dir Yassin in April. (That horrible act is still shrouded in mystery; the Irgun claimed there was a battle; Arab survivors claimed as many as 254 dead.)[3] Reports of the massacre started something of a stampede out of Arab Jerusalem; Arab radio dwelt relentlessly on tales of Jewish cruelty, while Jewish radio exaggerated Jewish strength. A few days after Dir Yassin, 77 Jewish doctors, nurses, and students were murdered on the road to Mt. Scopus's Hadassah Hospital. Interestingly enough, nearly as many Arabs fled Palestine after the Mt. Scopus massacre as left after Dir Yassin.

Irgun terror thus continued to have an effect on political events which was generally the opposite of what the Irgun aimed to achieve. Whatever its impact on the morale of the British public, the Irgun's attack on the King David Hotel had actually split Zionism, not Zionism's opponents. The civil anarchy to which Irgun contributed during the winter of 1948 nearly cost Zionism its most important source of potential power, the backing of the U.S. government. In contrast, the Mapai leadership tried to reassure Arab city dwellers, in the hope that a sign of fellowship would help them regain their composure. Later in April, when Haganah forces captured Haifa, Golda Meyerson joined the city's liberal mayor Shabbetai Levi at an open forum to remonstrate with the city's 40,000 Arab residents to stay. "Do not fear," read the leaflet from the Jewish Workers' Council; "by moving out you will bring poverty and humiliation upon yourselves; remain in the city which is both yours and ours!"[4] Haganah vans with loudspeakers urged calm. But the

vans and the noise of the loudspeakers were apparently more impressive than anything the Haganah people were announcing.
Nearly the whole Arab population of the city fled.

ii

On May 14, 1948, Ben-Gurion announced the founding of the state
of Israel. The United States competed with the Soviet Union to be
the first to extend *de facto* recognition (though *de jure* recognition
was not granted by Washington until the following February).
With great emotion, Ben-Gurion read Israel's Declaration of Independence at the Tel Aviv Museum.

> Eretz Yisrael was the birthplace of the Jewish people [he read].
> Here, their spiritual, religious, and political identity was shaped.
> Here, they first attained to statehood, created cultural values of a
> national and a universal significance, and gave the world the eternal
> book of books . . .
> The catastrophe which recently befell the Jewish people—the
> massacre of millions of Jews in Europe—was another clear demon-
> stration of the urgency of solving the problems of its homelessness by
> establishing the Jewish state in Eretz Yisrael, which would open wide
> the gates of the homeland to every Jew and confer upon the Jewish
> people the status of a fully privileged member of the comity of na-
> tions . . . This right is the natural right of the Jewish people to be
> master of its own fate, like all other nations, in its own sovereign
> state . . .
> The state of Israel will be open for Jewish immigration and for the
> Ingathering of the Exiles; it will foster the development of the country
> for all its inhabitants; it will be founded on freedom, justice and peace
> as envisaged by the prophets of Israel; it will ensure the complete
> equality of social and political rights to all its inhabitants, irrespective
> of religion, race or sex; it will guarantee freedom of religion, conscience,
> language, education, and culture; it will safeguard the Holy Places of
> all religions; it will be faithful to the principles of the Charter of the
> United Nations.

After reading the declaration, Ben-Gurion announced the formation of a Provisional Council of State, actually a transformed Jewish
Agency executive, with himself as Prime Minister. Weizmann would
be President of the Council—though Ben-Gurion was careful to
make of the presidency a distinctly ceremonial position. The pro-

visional government would hold elections "no later than October 1948" for a constituent assembly to draw up a formal constitution. Most important, all British legislation prohibiting Jewish immigration was annulled.

Understandably, Ben-Gurion's words touched off elation in the Yishuv which can be compared in intensity only with the sorrow caused by the news of the death camps. When Ben-Gurion finished, street celebrations broke out and continued through the night. But Ben-Gurion knew as he spoke that the euphoria would not last long. Between the beginning of April and mid-May, guerrilla actions had become pitched battles. A Haganah offensive already had cost the lives of some 1,250 Jewish fighters. King Abdullah's Transjordanian Arab Legion had attacked on May 12. The Jewish state soon would be fighting for its life.

Five Arab expeditionary forces invaded over the next five days. Jews who had been celebrating on the night of May 14 were mustered into militia units the following morning. Newly landed immigrants were taken directly from their ships to military bases hastily constructed from corrugated tin and barbed wire. Only after war had raged for several weeks did it gradually become clear that Jewish forces were gaining the upper hand. By the beginning of June, Palmach units were poised to capture the Negev in the south and the whole upper Galilee in the north, including the Arab town of Nazareth. Around Jerusalem, the Palmach and the Arab Legion fought to a standoff, dividing the city between them. The Jewish residents of the Old City had to be evacuated.

The UN finally arranged a truce in early June, and Ben-Gurion used the time to organize the nascent Israel Defense Forces (or IDF) into three frontal divisions, eliminating the independent Palmach brigades (though not the Palmach itself). He organized the General Staff under civilian control and appointed his first chief. There was an obvious point to these actions, though not all in the Palmach welcomed them: some 75,000 Israeli men and women were now under arms (and recruitment from new immigration would bring the number up to 90,000 by mid-October); this was too great a force to be accommodated within the voluntaristic structure of the Haganah and Palmach. Israeli forces scored victories, Ben-Gurion knew, when their commanders succeeded in organizing numerical superiority for them in individual actions. (Jewish forces outnumbered the combined strength of the Arab forces and Palestinian irregulars 2 to 1—a fact which should dispel misty notions about how courage alone vanquished the Arab Goliath—and examples of outstanding defense against high odds in the enemy's favor—by kibbutz fighters at Yad Mordechai, say, or by Arab Legion troops at the Latrun Police Station—were few and far between.)

It was precisely to organize command of all Israeli forces, moreover, that Ben-Gurion chose the lull created by the UN truce to strike at the Irgun. Up to that point, half Begin's underground was under the joint command of the Israeli Army, and the other half was operating independently around Jerusalem. Golda Meyerson, now Meir, had secretly conferred with Abdullah in May, and Ben-Gurion supposed it would eventually be possible to reach a territorial compromise with him. Though Ben-Gurion was disheartened about Jewish residents having had to flee the Old City, he was anxious about becoming further embroiled with the only Arab army, the Transjordanian Arab Legion, that could pin Israeli forces down. Begin, for his part, had never fully resigned himself to Ben-Gurion's authority. Nor had the Irgun renounced its independent right to procure arms. Haganah leaders feared that Irgun units would try to retake the Old City and then make a grab for the West Bank.

Apparently heedless of Ben-Gurion's political difficulties—perhaps because of them—Irgun operatives commissioned a French cargo ship in early June and filled it with 900 volunteers and dozens of cases of automatic weapons. The ship, renamed *Altalena*—in honor of Jabotinsky's pen name—sailed from the port of Marseilles on June 11, the day the UN-sponsored cease-fire went into effect. Now, the state's patched-together army had been apprised of the arrival of the *Altalena* by the Irgun. Haganah leaders had entered into negotiations with Irgun representatives regarding the dispersal of the arms. But negotiations failed because the Irgun demanded that 20 percent of the weapons go to its forces around Jerusalem and 40 percent to other Irgun units. Palmach commanders weighed in, expressing alarm to Ben-Gurion that Begin might try to overthrow the Provisional Council. (This fear now seems rather hysterical in view of the Palmach's now superior forces, and yet the mere threat of civil war was a terrible prospect.)

Ben-Gurion decided to defend the Provisional Council's authority with decisive action. Haganah commanders informed the Irgun that the Haganah would not participate in joint operations to unload the ship. When the *Altalena* finally arrived on June 20, at the beach off moshav Kfar Vitkin—some twenty miles north of Tel Aviv—Irgun people ignored the deadlock and began to unload the ship by themselves. During the evening, the ship's 900 volunteers came ashore and were welcomed by the residents of the moshav, a Mapai stronghold; about a quarter of the cargo was brought ashore. But the warmth of welcome belied what was to follow. In what may be called his first important act of statecraft, Ben-Gurion ordered Haganah units affiliated with the IDF to lay siege to the ship and demand unconditional surrender. There were altercations. (Some at Kfar Vitkin still maintain that the Irgun immediately began to set up independent bases.)

Begin boarded the ship and made for the shallows off Tel Aviv. Old animosities boiled over: the *Altalena*'s captain had once been jailed by the British during the *Saison*—with Haganah connivance, he thought. The ship dropped anchor off the Tel Aviv beaches; thousands gathered to watch. Ben-Gurion again gave Begin an ultimatum, which had now been approved by the Israeli Cabinet. There was no response. Finally, at 4 p.m., Haganah artillery opened fire, and the *Altalena* was sunk right in front of the UN observation post at the Kaete Dan Hotel.

Sixteen Irgunists were killed by the fire, including Abraham Stavsky, the man who had once been accused of murdering Chaim Arlozorov. The vessel's cargo was lost. Begin was among the last to abandon ship, swimming ashore under machine-gun fire. Still dripping, he made his way to the Irgun's underground radio station and delivered a bitter speech denouncing the government's alleged double-dealing. Begin cursed Ben-Gurion as "that fool, that idiot," who had plotted to murder him. He boasted that he could have eliminated the Prime Minister with a "wave of the finger."[5] He threatened to rescind his order to Irgun troops to join the Israeli Army in the areas outside Jerusalem. But he also declared that Irgun people should not fire on the Haganah or on IDF forces. Thus, in effect, he capitulated.

That night the government arrested some 250 Irgun men, and about 100 soldiers who had refused to open fire on Irgun fighters.

From that moment on, the Irgun ceased to play an independent role in the war, though its units would not be totally absorbed into the IDF until the fall. (Showing unexpected resilience, Begin then moved quickly, and gingerly, to convert his armed movement to a political party, the Herut or "Freedom" Party, preparing for elections to the constituent assembly.) Ben-Gurion reported to the State Council: "Blessed is the gun that set fire to the ship—it will have its place in Israel's War Museum!"

.

The UN truce expired and the war resumed on July 9, increasingly reshaping the attitudes of the Israeli citizenry. By the time the Israeli Army finally established the borders of the state during the summer of 1949, some 300,000 Jewish refugees had landed in the country—from Czechoslovakia, Bulgaria, Yugoslavia, Turkey, Morocco, Yemen. As the battles intensified, everyone was touched by the killing; people witnessed battles, mourned relatives, comforted friends. The pristine libertarianism that figured so prominently in the Declaration of May 14 was a kind of casualty, too, eclipsed by the logic of fire and cease-fire, of fifth columns and armed camps. In the end, over 6,000 Jewish fighters and civilians died, fully 1 percent of the Jewish population.

The Palestinian Arab civilian population suffered not so much from the fighting as from the war's most lasting consequence—exile. Beginning on July 12, an IDF force (commanded by Moshe Dayan) virtually expelled the entire populations of Ramle and Lod. Thousands of others followed. Only in Nazareth, where Arab municipal leaders refused to be intimidated, did Arab residents stay put, though it must be said that no harm came to Nazareth Arabs who defied Israeli forces. Of course, no Jew doubted that the Arabs would have expelled the Jews had they had the chance. The merciless logic of the war had certainly superseded any of the compunctions Ben-Gurion had expressed about Arab flight between the time of the partition vote at the UN and the founding of the state. ("War is war," Ben-Gurion declared; "we did not want war. Tel Aviv did not attack Jaffa. Jaffa attacked Tel Aviv and this must not occur again. Jaffa will be a Jewish town.") By the summer of 1949, some 750,000 Palestinian Arabs were living in squalid refugee camps, set up virtually overnight in territories adjacent to Israel's borders.

About 300,000 lived in the Gaza Strip, which was occupied by the Egyptian Army. Another 450,000 became rather unwelcome residents of the West Bank of the Jordan, recently occupied by the Transjordanian Legion. What had been a competition with Zionism for control of Palestine had suddenly turned into a struggle to regain the homeland.

The war changed the priorities of Israeli leaders as well. That it transformed Israel into a country under an indeterminate siege encouraged Ben-Gurion further to consolidate the power of the Provisional Council; indeed, the shelling of the *Altalena* proved only the opening salvo of his intense campaign to make the jurisdiction of the Jewish state apparatus paramount with respect to all factions of Zionism. Back in September 1948, after a group of recalcitrant Sternists assassinated UN mediator Count Folke Bernadotte, Ben-Gurion had forcibly integrated the Irgun into the IDF. Immediately thereafter, he startled the Labor Zionist left by hinting that he intended to dissolve the Palmach as well. By then the Palmach included three brigades and it was commanded by 64 of the young state's most seasoned officers—about 90 percent of whom were part of a kibbutz-based, left-wing splinter party now calling itself, pointedly, Achdut Ha'Avodah, the original name of Ben-Gurion's Mapai.

Under Tabenkin's leadership, members of Achdut Ha'Avodah had split from Mapai in 1944, over what they considered Ben-Gurion's drift away from socialist principles and his commitment to the Biltmore program. Palmach leaders now doubted Mapai's abiding commitment to a radical Histadrut. They wanted to remain a militia in the service of Zionist socialism, on the model of the Red Army, and many wanted a kind of "dictatorship of the proletariat." They were determined to keep their force independent of the Israeli Army. At bottom, they expected the kibbutz movement, not the state, to play the leading role in settling new immigrants. (Some still suggested that the disbanding of the Labor movement's army would open the way for a *coup d'état* by Begin.)

Ben-Gurion would have none of it. The army, he believed, should be strong and unified, a leading institution of the new state. He did not equate the moral standing of the Palmach with that of the Irgun, but he was firm about ending factionalism among Israel's soldiers.

By October 7 he had dissolved the Palmach and incorporated its units into the army. Some of the force's most able officers, including Sadeh and Allon, retired in protest.

iii

While a viable democratic Jewish state might have arisen in a climate of peace, without Palestinian refugees, the war did underline the latent contradiction between the national Jewish majority envisioned by Zionism and Israel's secular democratic goals. How could a Jewish state at war with the Arab world—a state which aimed to "ingather exiles" and exert the "natural right" of the Jewish people to be "master of its fate" in Eretz Yisrael—also guarantee the "complete equality of social and political rights" to all of its citizens, including hundreds of thousands of Arab residents who bitterly opposed its creation? There can be no doubt that democracy—at least what Labor Zionists understood by democracy: majority rule, elections, property rights, such freedom of speech as was consistent with their physical security—was as heartfelt among the framers of the Declaration of Independence as was the Hebrēw national project. They had proved this in accepting partition. But was it not inevitable that Ben-Gurion would have to put aside the strictly democratic ideals of his revolution whenever these were at odds with the expediencies he deemed necessary to consolidate state power?

No doubt, the extraordinary status accorded in the Declaration to Jewish nationalism would, two generations later, be of little consequence to the rights of Israeli citizens—including Arab citizens—had Ben-Gurion followed through on the next constitutional step he promised, which was to convene a constitutional congress as soon as practicable. In that case, Zionism would have been enshrined as Israel's heroic prelude, identified with a gallery of personalities—Herzl, Achad Haam, Gordon—and would now be remembered for its revolutionary sentiments and slogans. Zionism's principles of action, however, would have been rightly judged as having had a historically limited purpose; having been realized, Zionism would have been superseded by Israeli law. What was so tragic about Ben-Gurion's actions at this crucial time was that, as the war dragged on through October, he worked to establish a firm hold on state power without any further concessions to constitu-

tional principles. He invested his growing prestige in efforts to consolidate the military, and presided over a state of emergency under
which ninety-eight ordinances were enacted. He did not work
seriously to develop a climate conducive to enacting the promised
constitution, and in fact, many of the emergency ordinances of the
Provisional Council of State were still in force twenty years later.

On January 6, 1949, Egypt agreed to enter into armistice negotiations with Israel at the headquarters of acting UN mediator
Ralph J. Bunche, on the island of Rhodes. With military victory at
hand, the citizens of Israel went to the polls for the first time, to
elect a constituent assembly which would draw up the state's constitution. Mapai entered the race expecting to prevail, and it did
so, but with a plurality far short of a majority, about 36 percent of
the vote, or 46 seats in the 120-person assembly. Next came the
Mapam, or United Workers' Party, made up of Ha'Shomer Ha'Tzair
and Achdut Ha'Avodah, with 19 seats. The Mizrachi-dominated
religious parties trailed with 16, then Herut with 14, and the
General Zionists (Weizmann's people) with 7. What kind of constitution would the assembly adopt?

The debate was not conducted along party lines and it raised
extraordinary passions. A draft had been prepared by Dr. Yehuda
Leo Kohn, an expert on constitutional affairs (and the political
secretary of the Jewish Agency), but it seemed to satisfy none of
the participants. Dr. Kohn had said: "The state of Israel is being
rebuilt under modern conditions. It cannot but adopt the institutional forms and civic conceptions by which alone the mass life
of a modern political community can be organized. But if these
forms and conceptions are to have more than a transient meaning,
they must strike in the deeper recesses of the soul of the people . . .
by infusion of the Hebrew spiritual tradition into their functional
framework."[6]

Accordingly, the preamble to Kohn's draft constitution gave
thanks "to Almighty God for having delivered us from the burden
of exile and brought us back to our ancient land." It expressed
the resolve to rebuild the Jewish commonwealth "in accordance
with the ideals of peace and righteousness of the prophets of Israel."
The first chapter dealt with the name of the state—and its design
as "the National Home of the Jewish people with the right of all
Jews to immigrate"; the second chapter dealt with fundamental

rights and had provisions to safeguard freedom of conscience and religious worship, while the Jewish Sabbath and the festival days were to be "days of rest and spiritual elevation." In the fifth chapter, the judicial system was outlined; the eighth chapter authorized adopting the Mandatory regime's legal code, but stipulated that future legislation in Israel would be guided by "the basic principles of Jewish Law."

Mapam members, who should have been Mapai's most natural allies in the debate, were put off by the religious cast of Kohn's draft. They argued for a stricter separation of religion and state, a bill of rights, and greater impartiality by the state apparatus with regard to matters of personal status, especially as concerned the right of Jews, Christians, and Moslems to obtain a civil marriage. (They had no objection, understandably, to ordaining Jewish festivals as national holidays.) Ironically, though not surprisingly, Mapam's most vociferous support for secularization of the draft came not from Mapai but from Jabotinsky's disciples in Herut. Mizrachi, in contrast, argued that Hebrew should be the only official language and that the President should be a Jew.

Members of the Mapai mainstream were divided on many of these questions. But less lofty political considerations intruded in any case. The Ha'Shomer Ha'Tzair faction of Mapam had opposed Ben-Gurion on partition, wanting the Jewish Agency to propose a bi-national state to the Arabs. After May 14, Ha'Shomer Ha'Tzair cadres had no more illusions about Arab attitudes toward such a proposal, but they remained far more conciliatory than Ben-Gurion on the question of the Arab refugees and hewed to a pro-Soviet line at odds with Ben-Gurion's pro-American stance. For its part, the Achdut Ha'Avodah faction was still smarting over Ben-Gurion's dismantling of the Palmach and his threat to extend the jurisdiction of the state into education, welfare, and medical services—where the kibbutzim and Histadrut had acted on their own. Mapam as a whole had an understandable aversion to Ben-Gurion's plan to scrap the WZO's proportional representation system in favor of a constituency system, which would have greatly diminished the influence of the kibbutzim.

The religious parties were agnostic on military, welfare, and diplomatic questions, but were more amenable to Ben-Gurion's effort to make the state bureaucracy more powerful than any of the

Labor Zionist institutions. They certainly would not have minded dismantling the Histadrut, though they resented the prospect of electoral reform as much as the kibbutz-based groups. What rankled most with the religious parties was the prospect of a secular, democratic slant to the constitution. Should the state adopt one, they reasoned, it would dash their hopes, which they had nurtured since the time of Rabbi Kook, to establish the Orthodox law as the governing culture of the state. A secularist constitution would eventually strip the rabbinate of their acquired jurisdiction in civil law— marriage, divorce, burial, etc.—and open the way for violations of the Sabbath. (During the debate, the ultra-Orthodox Agudat Yisrael Party argued that it would be enough to declare: "Israel's Torah is her constitution." Mizrachi's Rabbi Fishman, then the Minister of Religious Affairs in Ben-Gurion's provisional cabinet, told Arthur Koestler: "Israel will live according to the law of Moses, which needs not the slightest reform.")[7]

Faced with the choice of making common cause with the revolutionary Zionist left or the compliant, Torah-bound rabbinate—the idea of governing with Herut never entered his mind!—Ben-Gurion chose the rabbis. It meant giving up the chance to promulgate a constitution, but it gave Mapai the undreamed-of chance to form a Cabinet without any real partners. Naturally, an even more bitter debate ensued in the constituent assembly, but Ben-Gurion got his way. Instead of proceeding to the constitutional issue, Ben-Gurion mustered a majority of the members to convert the constituent assembly into Israel's first Knesset, or parliament, which declared itself sovereign on February 16. Ben-Gurion formed the first Cabinet together with the religious parties; shortly thereafter, he took in some of the smaller, liberal factions.

.

Mapai's first Knesset immediately initiated a series of "basic" laws, which, piecemeal, were meant to take on the force of a constitution governing electoral and parliamentary procedures—what Mapai people called a "small constitution." Whatever the small constitution left out, Ben-Gurion thought, could be made up for by modifying and absorbing into the state apparatus the institutions and conventions of the Zionist Yishuv: the political structure of the Jewish Agency, the common law of the Mandatory government, the religious authority of the Vaad Leumi. Eventually four "basic laws" would be ratified by the Knesset: the Law of the Knesset, modified from the proportional representation system of WZO elections, and the related Law of the Presidency—conceived to keep Weizmann powerless; there was also the Law of the Executive Branch, which was derived from the authority of the Jewish Agency and Vaad Leumi, and, finally, the Law of Lands of Israel, adapted from the regulations of the Jewish National Fund. The judicial system remained independent, more or less according to the precedents of the Mandatory government, though, again, laws meant to keep out Jewish immigrants had been abolished by the Provisional Council of State. There was no comprehensive bill of rights and no secular state authority in many civil areas, including marriage and divorce.

Interestingly enough, the state did not now expunge from the judicial code the "emergency regulations" which the Mandatory government had enacted in 1946 to imprison the leadership of the Jewish Agency and disarm the Haganah. These regulations included preventive detention, censorship, search and seizure, and other potential violations of civil liberty which a formal constitution should have precluded. Insofar as the Law of Lands of Israel took over the estates of the JNF and adopted its regulations, it provided a permanent basis for discrimination against the Arab community. Since Ruppin's day, the JNF leased lands to pioneers in perpetuity, on condition that the land would not be alienated to non-Jews. This was once a defensible principle of Zionist revolutionary struggle. In practice, now, it became the basis to deny about 200,000 Israeli citizens (and their descendants) access to 95 percent of Israel's land.

In defense of Ben-Gurion's decision to put off a constitution, it should be noted that the strict separation of religion and state would have been intolerable to the 10 percent of the population that had voted for the religious parties and had never adjusted to a secular national life.[8] Many of those who did not vote for the religious parties, and most of the immigrants, were at least sentimentally devoted to Orthodox law. Had Ben-Gurion—himself a radical secularist—faced the challenge of building a state apparatus only, he might have undertaken the *Kulturkampf* then and there. But he was also trying to find lines of cultural unity among veterans and immigrants. Divisions over a constitution would have undermined the unifying social role that a majority of Israelis, especially the newcomers, looked to the state apparatus to provide at a time of war. Which is why Ben-Gurion, to his credit, was even prepared to keep on those residual Zionist institutions which undermined his personal power as Prime Minister. He had wanted, for example, to abolish the Jewish Agency as soon as the state was declared, reasoning that any Jew who wanted to come to the Jewish home could now do so, and that the agency's functions could be absorbed by the state's Immigration Ministry. But we shall see that Ben-Gurion relented when he grasped that the fund-raising bureaucracy already established in America needed the framework of the Jewish Agency to continue its operations. (It was only by virtue of the Jewish Agency that American Jews could get a tax deduction for contributions to Israel.) Besides, hundreds of thousands of Jewish immigrants would still need mortgages, loans, lands; these advantages would have to be granted them in preference over Israel citizens per se, among whom were a considerable number of Arabs.

A constitution would also have interfered with the first Knesset's enacting other legislation that was thought to be urgent—the Law of Return, for example, which the Knesset passed in July 1950 and which gave legally designated Jewish immigrants (many of whom were stateless) citizenship in the state of Israel immediately upon landing. Just as important, correspondingly, was the law confiscating property abandoned (or allegedly abandoned) by Arab refugees during the war. Neither of these laws should have long survived the era of emergency immigration, and almost certainly would not have done so had a bill of rights been enacted by the Israeli state in 1949. However, they resulted in the housing of hundreds of thousands of Jewish refugees. Israelis asked themselves to what bill of rights could 120,000 expropriated Iraqi Jews appeal?

None of this is to suggest that Israel failed to become a democracy in essential respects. It enjoyed parliamentary rule, and Arab citizens voted—though, from the first, the Arab community as a whole was governed by the military and Arab nationalist political parties were banned. Ben-Gurion did manage to push through laws ensuring a secular and national system of education and permitting Arabs a separate curriculum and autonomous religious institutions. British common law guaranteed the basic freedoms of speech, assembly, the press, worship, and so on, and the state established an independent judiciary. Besides, democratic life cannot be reduced to this or that network of law, but depends on widespread support among a country's citizens for liberal values and tolerant attitudes. Most veterans of the Yishuv were consciously democratic. Still, Israel did not become the resilient, secular democracy Labor Zionists had taken for granted it would. The basic laws were not, as Ben-Gurion maintained, a "small constitution." They were a testament to the obstacles in the way of the Mapai leadership to propose any constitution. The old was dead, the new was not yet born.

iv

In putting Israel at odds with the entire Arab world, the 1949 victory provoked the first large-scale immigration of Middle Eastern Jews, most of whom had landed by the end of 1951. There were about 300,000 in the first wave, mainly from Iraq, Egypt, and Yemen. For the Sephardi immigrants, 600,000 Jewish refugees had replaced as many Arab refugees, and they believed that a Zionist ought to defend the equation without shame. How was the state to house, clothe, and feed so many people? The socialist veterans submitted to a strictly rationed diet of eggplant, an egg, and a weekly portion of fish. But something more was needed than altruism. At least 50 percent of Israel's GNP was produced directly by the Histadrut; whole markets were dominated by Chevrat Ovdim corporations. New immigrants with a little capital asked if the Israeli economy should continue to be so dominated by planned, socialist enterprise. Would the Histadrut corporations allow sufficient flexibility for the economy to expand quickly?

For Ben-Gurion, the war seemed a kind of crucible in which the old political economy had melted away. To be sure, workers' settlements had made the Jewish nation, and had carried on the business of that nation in the absence of a Jewish state. Ben-Gurion continued to hope that *chalutziyut*, the spirit of pioneering, could be held up to the younger generation, whom he counted on to develop the Negev and the South. But there was a new national agenda, after all, superseding Labor Zionism's socialist ethos: the need to fight a war, to take sides in the Cold War, to find capital to house and feed new immigrants who were more numerous than the veteran Zionists themselves. Before the state, the Yishuv's major sources of investment capital had been the personal assets of immigrants.

After World War II began, the Allied war economy boosted exports, and Histadrut enterprises played a leading role in the boom. But exports were negligible during the years after the 1948 war, owing to war damage to the citrus plantations, and there were virtually no earnings in foreign exchange. What was to be done?

Ben-Gurion perceived that the growing trade deficit could be defrayed only by importing capital from abroad on an unprecedented scale, though this could well subvert the Histadrut's planned economy.[9] At the end of 1951, Ben-Gurion personally launched the Israel Bonds campaign and urged foreign Jews to invest in or start up private companies. Public-sector corporations in Israel were able to generate many times the investment capital of Israel's puny private economy. But their potential was, Ben-Gurion knew, nothing to compare with the capital of Western Jewish entrepreneurs. Between 1950 and 1954, some $1,317 million was raised abroad: $277 million from private sources, $1,040 million from public sources. About $859 million represented unilateral transfers. As to labor relations, the public corporations of Chevrat Ovdim presented little problem, since workers and management remained on an equal social footing now as in the thirties. Chevrat Ovdim employed thousands of workers; they now employed thousands of the new immigrants.

The monopoly advantages of Chevrat Ovdim corporations could not remain Ben-Gurion's only target. Eventually he was forced to take aim at the voluntaristic socialism of the kibbutzim as well. Interestingly enough, many of the agricultural collectives had housed immigrants and taught them Hebrew during the first stages of their absorption. Yet most of those people wound up in transit camps, the *maabarot*, and were anxious to find gainful employment without having to join any collective. They didn't care a jot about the "classless society"; indeed, they understood Zionism mainly in terms of religious messianism unalloyed by any of the secular, socialist categories of the Labor Zionist revolution. They were people of families, markets, sexual modesty, and religion. Kibbutz members were none of the above, but the kibbutzim not only farmed most of the arable land, they also had strict rules against employing wage labor. The specter arose of the whole agricultural sector being closed to the immigrants. Ben-Gurion stepped in and demanded that the rules on the kibbutzim be relaxed, that the collectives set up enterprises which could employ outside workers. Not all complied at first, certainly not the kibbutzim of Ha'Shomer Ha'Tzair. Gradually, most came around.

v

Ben-Gurion's expediencies in organizing the Jewish state gave way to a new and zealous Israeli nationalism. The diplomatic stalemate and the tightening circle of Arab hostility seemed to awaken his strident side, most evidently in his attitude toward the use of military force. He moved the capital to Jerusalem in 1950. When the Israeli delegation to the United Nations informed him by cable that they alone would vote to ratify the move, Ben-Gurion told the press: "That is the only vote that counts." As if to underscore the brave new era ushered in by the state—also by the economic emergency—he authorized Nachum Goldmann to negotiate reparations from the West German government. The following January, a multimillion-dollar pact was signed. "Let not the murderers of our people also be the beneficiaries of its property," he declared to a stunned Knesset, though outside, unappeased, Begin led a rock-throwing riot in which ninety-two policemen and thirty-six civilians were injured.

The linchpin of Ben-Gurion's militancy on behalf of the state was the Israel Defense Forces, its symbols, its leaders, its style of organization. In Ben-Gurion's view, IDF leaders personified sacrifice, efficiency, glamour, service; their virtue was that they were utterly free of political sectarianism. They had defended the state with vigor in 1949; they would defend the new status quo with ruthless efficiency. Ben-Gurion proposed that service in the IDF was to be the preeminent experience of every new immigrant, that which would galvanize a nation out of "exiles." The officer corps, not kibbutz members, would embody the new era, and Ben-Gurion celebrated their periodic exploits against border terrorism to impress the Jews as much as the Arabs.

> Look at these Jews. They came from Iraq, from Kurdistan, from North Africa. They come from countries where their blood was unavenged . . . Here we have to show them that the Jewish people has a state and an army that will no longer permit them to be abused. We must straighten their backs . . . and demonstrate that those who attack them will not get away unpunished; that they are citizens of a sovereign state which is responsible for their lives and their safety.[10]

During the war, and following it, Ben-Gurion did not invite President Weizmann to a single Cabinet meeting, as much because of the moderation Weizmann continued to symbolize as out of vindictiveness. Increasingly infirm, Weizmann rarely left his residence in Rehovot. (When once a visiting orchestra played for him privately, Weizmann quipped sardonically about his own diminished role in government: "They refer to me as a symbol, so here I am cymbaling away.") Weizmann shared his bitterness only with friends. He died in November 1952, survived by his older son, Benjy; the younger, Michael, had been killed flying for the RAF in 1942. Ben-Gurion's Mapai colleague Yitzchak Ben-Tzvi became the new President of Israel.

Ben-Gurion began to argue that the spirit of the corporate state, citizenship—what he would call *mamlachtiyut*, literally, "statism" —should be treated as an end in itself. The new patriotism, he reasoned, should transcend any "particularistic" version of the national ideal. He did not give up on the word "Zionism." Yet he made it clear that the culmination of Labor Zionism was his point of departure. Zionism's revolutionary war created new opportunities for working out national priorities—building the national army and establishing the authority of the government. The land had been settled, as had the old debates about how to make the Jews a nation. The revolution against the Jewish condition was over. Ben-Gurion wrote:

> The revival of Jewish sovereignty brought the Jewish people face to face with its destiny, without an intervening barrier. Immediately on the proclamation of its independence, the young state had to face the attack of five of its neighbours—and gained a victory . . . [But] the supreme test of Israel in our generation lies not in its struggle against hostile forces from without, but in its success in gaining domination, through science and pioneering, over the wastelands of its country.[11]

To people who now called themselves Zionists, this statement did not seem particularly contentious. But its blandness is what made it interesting. Labor Zionist ideals had been complex, formal, demanding. Ben-Gurion was now content to leave most of them aside and concentrate on the Negev. Ben-Gurion had increasingly little patience for the old guard of Mapai, the veterans who spoke in terms of proletarian virtue and were anxious about the Histadrut losing power to the state bureaucracy. Ben-Gurion had even less patience for Mapam, which failed to put the principles of state building above the interests of the Histadrut and, for that matter, stubbornly refused to see that the Arab world would not make peace according to any reasonable offer of partition.

.

After the war, in February 1950, the Israeli government had discreetly negotiated a draft treaty with King Abdullah of Transjordan, including a five-year non-aggression pact, open borders, and free access to the port of Haifa. The Egyptian and other Arab governments firmly opposed the plan, as they had refused to accept Israel's terms to expand the UN-sponsored talks at Rhodes into peace negotiations. In April, Abdullah contented himself with annexing the West Bank and East Jerusalem, thus creating the united Hashemite Kingdom of Jordan. Ben-Gurion acquiesced, since he thought this would mean an end to the prospect of an independent Palestinian state with irredentist claims on Israeli territory and material claims on confiscated Arab property. (Israel had signed an armistice with Egypt in February 1950, with Lebanon in March, and with Syria in July.) In fact, the new arrangements meant the start of a succession of Palestinian commando raids from the West Bank and Gaza, and in response, Ben-Gurion authorized devastating retaliatory attacks. In 1951, Abdullah was assassinated in Jerusalem, the last Arab leader of his day who would even consider making peace without demanding a return to the conditions existing before November 1947. To Ben-Gurion it seemed that, since 1922, Arab leaders had always been prepared to base compromise on that state of affairs just superseded by the consequences of their own former rejectionism.

One may look back on Ben-Gurion's record during these years and wish, as did Ha'Shomer Ha'Tzair, for more diplomatic initiatives toward the Palestinian Arabs, for a greater emphasis on diplomacy where there was retaliation. But one cannot fail to be impressed by the fundamental pragmatism of Ben-Gurion's approach. More supple-minded than his colleagues on the left, Ben-Gurion realized that the Israeli nation would have to be tirelessly sustained in the face of enemies, and that this was a cultural matter in addition to requiring a defense strategy. In the thirties, Ben-Gurion assumed that the conquest of labor had formed the myths and purposes of the future Hebrew nation once and for all. "Statism" implied that this had not been the case, that—at least in Ben-Gurion's view—victory in the 1948–49 war was every bit as much a formative event for the Hebrew nation as the triumph of the Histadrut. What is more, Ben-Gurion saw that the new generation of Israelis, including many new immigrants, would have an easier affinity for a new nationalism than for the old Zionism. After the demoralizations of the Holocaust, "the revival of Jewish sovereignty" could not be treated as—say, what Achad Haam had wished—some mere instrument to preserve pristine cultural Zionist ideology. For Israeli Jews—indeed, for Jews around the world—the War of Independence had redeemed what could only be called "Jewish honor."

Not that Israeli leaders could consciously cut themselves away from Labor Zionist roots. Ben-Gurion's point was that Zionists should now redefine in a more abstractly classical way just what those roots were for. Instead of looking back to the class conflicts of Eastern Europe, Ben-Gurion enjoined the new generation to look further back, to the glories of ancient times. Ostentatiously he scanned the Scriptures to find the Negev's hidden sources of water. He conjured a more biblical, hence more inclusive version of the national identity. Ben-Gurion gave the public new heroes: army officers, such as Yigael Yadin—in effect, Ben-Gurion's first Chief of Staff—whose archaeological digs at Masada, like Ben-Gurion's own hydrological studies, blended scientific method with ancient myth, and both with military bearing. Added to the roster were Moshe Dayan and Shimon Peres: Dayan, the military hero *par excellence*, from Moshav Nahalal; Peres, the model technocrat, born in Poland, educated at Mapai's Ben-Shemen youth village.

Nor was Ben-Gurion alone in proposing the lines of a new civil religion. Many of the intellectuals among the coming generations went further. The novelist Yizhar Smilansky and former Labor-laureate Natan Alterman agreed that Israelis should not lament the passing of what many saw as a golden age in Zionism. Smilansky was a peace activist where Alterman was increasingly hard-line; yet both began to probe deeply into the Histadrut's little hypocrisies. Palmach writers such as Moshe Shamir and Natan Shacham tended to think Ben-Gurion's statism yet another betrayal. But they, too, had inadvertently accepted his cultural premise. Born in the Yishuv, the Palmach generation had been educated to a rather automatic cynicism regarding European life. They were all fascinated by what they took to be the ruthless, backward, enviably "authentic" Arab. One could detect the sensibility of Jabotinsky in their style, at least insofar as they all seemed to feel that the various theories of Zionism were vaguely absorbed together into some greater Zionist saga. In 1948, young Israelis thought, all the theories had won. Indeed, the prestige of Zionism now attached to concrete things, not to ideas. The past was recast in a vocabulary of mobilization.

Indeed, the triumph of Zionism, so it seemed, had been to strip the younger generation of an excess of historical consciousness, that typically "Diaspora" frame of mind which, presumably, weakened the power of will. In contrast, the new statist Zionism suggested the value of common sense, spontaneity against alienation, action against resignation, love against death. The folk songs of postwar Israel eulogized the night, the coffeepot, the road to Eilat. There was praise for the battalion, for the soldier, for the lover who put lover aside for the heroic deed. (*"Tzeina, Tzeina,"* went the folk song of the thirties, popularized during the 1948 war: "Please come out and see, daughters, soldiers in the settlement; do not hide from our young men-at-arms!") Even the modern Hebrew language had become, as it were, second nature. Just how the language came into being seemed beside the point.

vi

Ben-Gurion wanted Mapai to dominate the state apparatus, and he wanted the state, not the Histadrut, to be the major force for social integration. His statism called for technocracy, merit, capitalist incentives, foreign investment—toughness. He advocated a kind of government activism, what he called "*bitzuism,*" to replace the equivocal gradualism of the old Jewish Agency. "It matters not what *goyim* say," he announced after a bloody retaliation against Palestinian commandos on the border; "it matters what Jews do." His more moderate Foreign Minister, Moshe Sharett, retorted wryly that it also matters what *goyim do.* Ben-Gurion gave him short shrift. (It was Sharett who had pushed for an agreement with Abdullah in 1950, over the objections of many skeptics in the Cabinet; now he wanted an initiative to settle the Palestinian refugee question through the UN.)

That Sharett had the impulse to dissent at all raises an interesting question, however. Ben-Gurion's statism challenged some of the most profound ideals and threatened the positions of many Mapai leaders. Just how far were these people prepared to be pushed by Ben-Gurion on defense and other issues? Sharett, Levi Eshkol, Golda Meir, Zalman Aranne, and Pinchas Lavon had all been appointed to the Cabinet and readily acknowledged Ben-Gurion's authority; most felt genuine deference before the "Old Man." Yet some—not only Sharett, but Eshkol as well—had reservations about Ben-Gurion's growing militarism, and they had no loyalty at all to Ben-Gurion's young warriors, especially not to Dayan, whom they considered an upstart. Others—Lavon and Meir, for example— went along with Ben-Gurion's hard line but resented such young technocrats as Peres. Histadrut leaders and managers had developed what can only be called vested interests: jobs, prestige, the habits of patronage.

The Mapai old guard, like the parties of the left, were much more strongly represented in the Histadrut General Council than they were in the Knesset. They were seriously committed to the ideal of a workers' state based on the agricultural collectives, public corporations, trade-union organizations, health-care facilities, and social and athletic clubs—in short, the full range of activities organized by the party apparatus which they ran. Statism not only implied the cultural diminution of Labor Zionism, it meant that the hard-core Labor Zionist cadres might be assigned a marginal role. Would there be no more vanguard organization in which the union bosses and kibbutz aristocracy could make their influence felt? Even with Mapam out of the government, a clash of vision and vanity between Ben-Gurion and the other Histadrut leaders was unlikely to be averted.

In the spring of 1953, Ben-Gurion visited Kibbutz Sde Boker, a new kibbutz in the Negev where a young group of settlers had just started to raise cattle. The idea took shape in Ben-Gurion's mind that he should temporarily retire to this place. He was emotionally exhausted after years of service, and he sensed the drama of leading the country's youth southward by means of a personal example. Of course, "retirement" was also good politics. In making his appealing gesture, Ben-Gurion thought he could steal a march on the Mapai old guard, establish himself as the truly indispensable leader called to a higher vocation than power—and just when Sharett had begun to imply that Ben-Gurion's feelings for the army issued from a kind of megalomania! Reassuringly, Ben-Gurion's most adamant supporters responded on cue. "We begged him not to go," wrote Golda Meir. "It was far too soon; the state was only five years old; the ingathering of the exiles was far from completed; Israel's neighbors were still at war with her. It was no time for Ben-Gurion to desert the country that had looked to him for guidance and inspiration for so many years—or us."[12] But to no avail. Ben-Gurion tendered his resignation on November 2, 1953. He would be gone, he said, for two years. Moshe Sharett, the senior colleague of the Cabinet, would form the next government.

Or would he? Ben-Gurion had first secured Pinchas Lavon's appointment to the Defense Ministry, and Lavon tended to side with Ben-Gurion against Sharett on the need for an "activist" military posture. Ben-Gurion had also secured Moshe Dayan's appointment as Chief of the General Staff. Was this not just enough rope for Sharett to hang himself? (Sharett wrote in his diary on October 11, 1953: "Moshe Dayan is only a soldier at war time, but during peace time he is a man of politics. He has no interest in running the army's business. His nomination [as Chief of Staff] means 'politicization' of the headquarters.")[13] Sharett certainly could not exert the authority of a prime minister when the preeminent institution of the new state was out of his hands and in those of Ben-Gurion's protégés—not only Lavon, but Dayan and Peres as well.

Just a few weeks before Sharett took office, incidentally, Dayan had launched a reprisal attack on the Jordanian town of Kibya. The town had suffered more than sixty killed. Sharett knew that Lavon had approved of the raid and was "utterly depressed" by this, but also by the sarcastic and insubordinate way Lavon comported himself in Sharett's presence. Sharett's only consolation, if consolation it was, was that Lavon quickly alienated Dayan and Peres as well. A stalwart of the Histadrut, Lavon was not favorably disposed to the young men who embodied criticism of it. Again, Ben-Gurion may have realized that he might profit from this tangle of ambition and political disagreement. What he could not have known was that tensions would bring scandal, and scandal would bring the whole Labor Zionist establishment to the brink of moral collapse and public disrepute. Lavon authorized intelligence chief Benjamin Gibly to unleash Israeli spy rings in Cairo and Alexandria. Lavon hoped that Gibly could cause disorder with a few well-placed bombs and, if possible, so embarrass the new strongman, President Gamal Abdul Nasser, that the British would reconsider withdrawing from the Suez Canal Zone. (Typically, Prime Minister Sharett was not properly informed in advance of the operation.) Gibly's plan was immediately botched, however, and Israeli agents were arrested on July 25, 1954. In public, the Israeli government denounced the Egyptian arrests and Sharett personally protested Nasser's subsequent show trials. When the agents were executed, Israelis were perplexed and outraged; rumors swept the country. In secret, however, Sharett determined to win control of his own defense establishment—only to find that Lavon had never put his authorization to Gibly in writing and was now disclaiming responsibility for the mess.

Of course, Sharett would have been glad to be rid of Lavon, but he knew that any government from which the Old Man was missing would not easily stand up to public dismay over any lapse in security. He wanted things hushed up. At Lavon's insistence, Sharett agreed to set up a secret commission of inquiry under Yitzchak Olshan, a Supreme Court Justice, and Yaacov Dori, a former Chief of Staff. But Lavon's confidence in the procedures promised by the Olshan-Dori Commission proved to be misplaced. The IDF's top leadership, including Dayan and Peres, campaigned in private against him. Seeking to help Gibly and protect their own position, other intelligence officers tampered with documents which might have incriminated Gibly—and some even committed perjury to place the whole responsibility on Lavon. For his part, Lavon committed perjury to preempt Gibly's lie. In the final analysis, the commission's investigation boiled down to a test of prestige between the young military establishment—including Dayan and Peres—and the Mapai old guard, whose support Lavon now solicited.

On January 13, 1955, the Olshan-Dori Commission finally came to a decision. It pronounced that it was not "convinced beyond all reasonable doubt that the Chief of Military Intelligence had not received orders from the Defense Minister." What more clear-cut decision was possible in view of so much duplicity? Lavon was outraged and refused to resign unless the entire Cabinet followed suit. He threatened suicide. He also said that he would demand an *open* parliamentary commission of inquiry, which Sharett instantly took to be the more ominous warning. Significantly, the Mapai old guard had never closed ranks behind Lavon. Most had condemned his threats and, like Sharett, feared a showdown. But after the Olshan-Dori decision, they determined that they must support their Mapai colleague. Finance Minister Levi Eshkol, who was also a mainstay of the Tel Aviv machine, the *Gush*, opposed the Defense Minister's dismissal in spite of the Olshan-Dori report. He insisted that the government should "reduce the damage." It was necessary to consult with Ben-Gurion.

At Sde Boker, Ben-Gurion reviewed the findings of the commission and determined that Lavon should resign, if only to accept ministerial responsibility. But this merely added fuel to the fire. The careers of Ben-Gurion's own young men were also at stake; his views hardly seemed impartial to Lavon. The latter railed on, demanding that Gibly and Peres be sacked. Dayan stood by Peres and tried to convince the waffling Sharett to face the inevitable. "Five Jews have concluded that Lavon has to go," Dayan expostulated. "You, Dori, Olshan, Shaul [i.e., Shaul Avigur, an intelligence chief and Sharett's brother-in-law], and Ben-Gurion."[14] The Prime Minister procrastinated further, losing the respect of his Cabinet in the process. Finally Lavon resigned, furious over his treatment at the hands of Ben-Gurion and his young men. The Israeli Cabinet then bowed to the inevitable and prevailed upon Ben-Gurion to return to the Defense Ministry in February 1955.

Had anything of importance been settled? On the one side stood the old guard: loyal to Ben-Gurion's pre-state line, in awe of his magnetic bearing, but resentful of his army elite, of technocratic rhetoric and military adventurism—not to mention the diminution of Histadrut ideals in the new cultural life. On the other side stood Dayan, Peres, and the other Young Turks. Ben-Gurion fancied them the authentic Israeli type, unencumbered by ghetto breeding, and forgave them their suspicions of socialism. Had not socialist rhetoric itself become the cover under which Histadrut bosses exercised vast networks of patronage to the detriment of the rising classes and new immigrants?

The "mishap"—or *esek bish*, as Gibly's gambit had come to be known—was itself kept under wraps; but the ideological divisions it engendered soon spilled over into public debate, engaging the attention of the other political parties. The bourgeois-liberal parties out of power—the Liberals and Herut—lined up behind statism. The parties to the left of Mapai—Mapam and Achdut Ha'Avodah (which had split off from pro-Soviet Mapam during the Slansky trials of 1952)—inclined toward the old-guard defenders of Histadrut's golden age. These sides were evenly matched at first: if Mapam lost ground supporting the Soviet Union, Begin's style made few friends for Herut: in those years, Begin campaigned like an old-world "Duce," riding around Tel Aviv in motorcades, escorted by motorcyclists sporting black leather jackets. On the whole, however, the right-wing parties were going to do rather better than their left-wing rivals, especially among members of the new generation of Sephardi immigrants.

vii

When Ben-Gurion returned to the Defense Ministry in February 1955, he no longer had much of an opponent in Prime Minister Sharett; indeed, the Cabinet gave the Old Man a free hand. Since the IDF's punitive raid on Kibya, there had been no more Palestinian actions from the West Bank. But the cease-fire on the border with Gaza was deteriorating daily and Ben-Gurion was eager to take action. Later that winter he got his opening, when an Israeli cyclist was murdered by Egyptian intelligence agents who had infiltrated from the Strip. Ben-Gurion and Dayan sent a force under Ariel Sharon to attack the Egyptian Army in Gaza. (Sharon, who had participated in the raid against the Jordanian town of Kibya, routed the Egyptian garrison, but at a terrible price: thirty-eight Egyptian soldiers were killed and thirty wounded. Eight Israeli paratroopers lost their lives.) Sharett was horrified; he was convinced that this raid would lead to further bloodletting. But had Sharett's own more moderate attitudes led to reciprocal moderation on the other side?

After the raid, though not merely because of it, Ben-Gurion was restored to the leadership of the Mapai government. He now expressed apprehension about the developing *rapprochement* between the pan-Arab nationalists and the Communist bloc; indeed, it was partly because he wanted to prove that Israel could be an

202 / THE TRAGEDY OF ZIONISM

important client for Western interests that he had directed Dayan to attack in Gaza. By the way, even before Israel's big reprisal, Nasser had opposed the British-sponsored Baghdad Pact, obviously out of deference to Soviet interests.

During the summer, Nasser organized more and more aggressive Palestinian *fedayeen,* or guerrilla, raids from Gaza and Khan Yunis. In August, he publicly acclaimed the Palestinian raiders as national heroes. By October 1955 he had signed an agreement to buy arms on a large scale from the Soviet Union and Czechoslovakia. In December Ben-Gurion launched a punishing reprisal raid on Syria, the "Kinneret incident," which mainly confounded efforts by the Israeli Foreign Ministry to buy arms from the United States. Ben-Gurion was increasingly shaken by the pace of Soviet-Egyptian cooperation, especially while Israel remained without Great Power backing. Incidentally, the Soviets still affected normal relations with Israel, but Nasser was by no means willing to talk peace with the "Zionist entity," and he had continued the blockade of Israeli shipping through the Straits of Tiran, on the Gulf of Aqaba. For his part, Ben-Gurion determined that Egypt would never deploy the new Soviet weapons.

During the summer of 1955, while Nasser regaled the *fedayeen,* Ben-Gurion had led the Mapai government into new elections. Mapai won 40 seats, but Herut doubled its seats to 15. What was this result if not an endorsement of tough diplomacy? During the following year, Ben-Gurion began an unprecedented effort to gain direct support from France. With support from Washington blocked, Peres negotiated Israel's first major arms deal in Paris, which included the delivery of Mystère jet fighters. Meanwhile, Nasser continued to pursue a course antagonistic to Western interests. He extended diplomatic recognition to the People's Republic of China, and in July 1956—after the U.S. government withdrew its offer to build the high dam at Aswan—Nasser nationalized the Suez Canal. That summer, Ben-Gurion pushed Sharett from the government and presented a secret plan to launch a preemptive war on Egypt. He entered into talks with the French government regarding the possibility of an attack. According to the plan, Israel would strike at the Sinai, France and Britain at the Suez Canal, ostensibly to protect Western shipping from the combat. France, meanwhile, would help provide Israeli cities with air cover.

In late October 1956, Israel struck. The IDF routed the Egyptian Army at Gaza and, after a week, pushed to the Gidi and Mitla Passes. On November 5 French and British forces moved to retake the Suez Canal. But Soviet threats intimidated British Prime Minister Anthony Eden, and after a few hours of desultory action in Port Said, the European powers acceded to an Egyptian demand for a cease-fire. The attack might not have turned into such a diplomatic debacle for France and Britain had they gained American backing. But in a rare show of common purpose, American and Soviet diplomats at the United Nations called for the creation of a UN emergency force to take up the positions occupied by the Israeli Army, cutting the ground out from under the French-British pretext for interventions. John Foster Dulles, the American Secretary of State, seems to have taken Soviet threats seriously. The Red Army had just crushed the Hungarian revolt. Dulles was also afraid that Israel had designs on Jordan. He was sure he could counter Soviet influence in Egypt without having to resort to European colonialism.

In March 1957, Israeli troops were forced to withdraw. Israel had nearly 180 dead. Still, for most Israelis, the war was a tremendous success. The raids from Gaza ceased. UN forces separated Israelis from their most implacable enemies. Peres now began to develop an elaborate network of cooperation with the French, eventually leading to even more arms sales and the building of a nuclear reactor. The Straits of Tiran, hence the ports of Africa, were opened to Israeli shipping. Most important, perhaps, the army's near-flawless performance had given all Israelis a profound sense of relief—one with obvious political consequences. The principles of statism had evolved out of circumstances of Israel's first war; a second victory could not but reinforce their appeal. In the words of Noah Lucas, the sense of normalization ushered in by the Sinai War proved an "epitaph for socialist-Zionism."[15] Within two years, Dayan was in the Cabinet as Minister of Agriculture, a hero not of Zionism but of Israel.

7 / The End of Zionism?

After the Sinai campaign, the political world for which Histadrut had been evolved seemed to evaporate. The Jews were an overwhelming majority in the Hebrew homeland; discrimination against the Arab minority did not imply any danger of Hebrew colonials dominating a larger class of Arab workers and peasants. With the Mandatory government gone, the world beyond the organized Hebrew working class was increasingly Hebrew, too, though composed of strange immigrants, rabbis, generals, rival "bourgeois" parties, American Zionists—all of whom accepted the legitimacy of the Jewish state apparatus and made claims on it. The Jewish economy had become the national economy, and it had been transformed by reliance on foreign investment, market incentives, and the new freedom accorded domestic entrepreneurs. "Security, immigration, and education!"—these were the new priorities Ben-Gurion announced. They were clearly the state's responsibilities, the basics of statism. Was the Histadrut still necessary at all?

Moshe Dayan seemed to believe it was not. After leaving the army in 1958, he put the statist case starkly, attacking the Mapai bosses, the Histadrut monopolies, the kibbutz culture, the economic leadership of the party functionaries, even the voluntarist Nachal units of the army, which established new settlements. Dayan's brush with Lavon seemed to whet his appetite for confrontation. "The men of the last generation," Dayan said, "have reached an age when they can no longer carry out revolutions. Every source of energy ultimately spends itself. These men look back proudly on their achievements of 1902. But we are interested in what will be in 1962."[1]

Dayan's cavalier talk implied that responsibility for the consolidation of the Jewish nation should be completely given over to the state—the army, the civil service, the universities. It was time, he thought, to retire Histadrut leaders for the sake of growth, efficiency, youth. Histadrut seemed to him the source of national disunity, a remnant of class struggle, which was anachronistic but also too much for Israel to allow in the face of Arab threats to its existence. Histadrut also implied a kind of sectarian ideology when something more inclusive was instinctively wanted—land, power, Bible—not only by new immigrants, but also by American Jewish philanthropists. Histadrut, in contrast, smacked of smugness, control, connections.

Ben-Gurion, for his part, found some of Dayan's criticism unsettling. He could not imagine simply banishing Histadrut to the margins of national life. It was a fact of life for him, indistinguishable from Zionism's prestige. Histadrut was the common achievement of his closest and most valued associates since his youth, a kind of living tribute to Berl Katznelson's memory. Thus, Ben-Gurion continued to see Histadrut as Israel's One Big Union, its central instrument for economic expansion, if not any longer for socialist planning. The Ha'Poel athletic and cultural clubs no longer seemed as important as the army in providing for the cultural assimilation of new immigrants. Nevertheless, they were dear to his heart. Besides, Dayan's extreme animus toward the Histadrut was not shared even among those new immigrants—from the Arab states or from Soviet-dominated Eastern Europe—who were naturally inclined to view socialist ideals with suspicion, and Histadrut leaders as the establishment. There are times—the first few years in a new country are surely among them—when one finds security in the paternalism of the men and women who were there before, when there is solace in another's smug confidence.

If nothing else, a kind of social inertia guaranteed that the Labor leadership would have a preeminent position in the state.

Golda Meir, who had been Minister of Labor in the early 1950s, probably expressed this burden of feelings better than most:

> Whenever the majority of the Labor community wanted something, they knew how to attain it. When, as our Sabras say, "they really, really wanted," they succeeded. We wanted to bring in immigrants by every method. Did everyone want this? No. But when our youth and our workers realized that this was the essence of Zionism and the meaning of their lives, they brought in the immigrants. Of course, we made sacrifices and endured hardships. But what was ever easy? Did the employers in this country want a Histadrut? . . . The workers' movement, the wonderfully strong and visionary organization of the Histadrut, will revert to its beginnings, and so we will undertake afresh our present duty: to implement the goal of proper immigrant absorption.[2]

Yet inertia alone could not settle the matter of Histadrut's task in the state. After 1957, when the IDF withdrew to what seemed comparatively safe and permanent borders, debate over the Histadrut's prerogatives became the basis for new political divisions— between proponents of state capitalism and laissez-faire, haves and have-nots, Europeans and Orientals, young and old, prominent and anonymous, reactionary and dissident. Statism, to be sure, had begun to win what intellectual contest there was. But Dayan's logic did not vitiate Mrs. Meir's power. (Her affectionate—and plainly condescending—allusion to "our Sabras'" lack of patience was a portent of growing and mutual disenchantment; certainly she expected to be around in 1962.) The emerging conflict between statist ideas and Histadrut power would have been easier on all concerned—and on the young state of Israel—if it had been resolved quickly in favor of one side or the other. But given the balance of political forces in the government, and also Ben-Gurion's own equivocal feelings, nothing could be hurried.

For most of the late fifties and early sixties, Dayan's logic and Meir's power were forced into a syncretistic arrangement, so that statist policies freed up the Israeli economy while Histadrut monopoly went on functioning more or less as before. This produced worse consequences than either side had anticipated, including the windfall enrichment of Yishuv veterans as compared with the new immigrants—what Mrs. Meir referred to euphemistically as the "social gap," *ha'paar ha'sotziali.* (The gap was only made worse when many European refugees received reparations from Germany.) Indeed, in the market climate generated by statism, Histadrut veterans shed some of their egalitarian impulses. They had little in the way of a common language with the immigrants their collectives and public corporations employed. The government bureaucracy and the Histadrut's social and political institutions were natural networks of privilege and patronage, since Histadrut had been built up as an integrated economic monopoly with a self-perpetuating leadership.

Things might have been much worse for the new immigrants had it not been for the social services maintained by the Histadrut, including comprehensive health care and the protection of Histadrut unions. But this was rather hard to explain to the majority of the new immigrants, who were more naturally inclined toward market ethics, and with whom the Histadrut competed on unequal terms. Histadrut was certainly the first to profit from any influx of capital or stimulation of market growth. Its "public sector" corporations were positioned to cash in, much like the landed English nobility during Manchester's free-trade expansion a century before. Paradoxically, the same revolutionary institutions which were meant to preempt Zionist colonialism in an Arab country became the instruments of a protected labor aristocracy in a Jewish state.

i

Between 1948 and 1952, some 300,000 Sephardi immigrants came to Israel. The 120,000 from Iraq were, on the whole, a highly educated and cosmopolitan community that had had many Zionist clubs and associations. Another 10,000 Jews, from Egypt, were of an equally cosmopolitan background. (The remaining 65,000 Egyptian Jews held on for better times, though a substantial minority made for Europe.) The case of the 55,000 Turkish Jews was quite different, however. Most of them had come from the poorer strata, like the nearly 40,000 wretched immigrants from Tehran's forgotten neighborhoods. Tens of thousands more had poured in from Jewish enclaves in Afghanistan, the Caucasus, and Cochin. As many as 55,000 impoverished and backward (though not illiterate) refugees were air-lifted by the Jewish Agency out of Yemen. Golda Meir wrote of the settlement camps:

> There were 200,000 people living (if that's the word) in tents, more often than not, two families to a tent—and not necessarily families from the same country or even the same continent . . . The man who had lived through years of Nazi slave labor, survived the DP camp and braved the trip to Israel and who was at best in poor health . . . and was entitled to the best possible conditions found himself and his family (if he still had one) living in unbearable proximity to people with whom he didn't even have a common language. Nine times out of ten he even regarded his neighbors as primitive because they had never seen a flush toilet . . . Or consider the illiterate woman from Libya or Yemen or the caves of the Atlas Mountains, who was stuck with her children in a drafty, leaky tent with Polish or Czech Jews who prepared food differently, ate things that made her feel sick, and, by her standards, weren't even Jews at all because they weren't ob-servant . . .[3]

The immigrants brought with them diseases like tuberculosis, trachoma, ringworm, malaria, typhoid, dysentery, measles, and pellagra, which the Yishuv's doctors worked tirelessly to eradicate. Just where could these people be housed and could a veteran family be expected to share their food with two or three other families? "Old-timers," Mrs. Meir added pointedly, "who had just emerged from months of terrible war might have been forgiven for rebelling against the new demands made on them. But no one rebelled." It was now that Mapai leaders put the whole veteran community on strict rationing. Mrs. Meir was proud of the fact that she had never even used up her own coupon books, which would have permitted her to queue up for a feast of fish and potatoes. "I relied on three things," she concluded, "the dedication of the old-timers; the growing desire of the new immigrants (most of whom had no skills applicable to the circumstances of the new state) to earn an honest day's wage and not become permanent wards of the state or the Jewish Agency; and the understanding and generosity of world Jewry."

As things turned out, this first rush of immigration was just the beginning. The aftermath of the Sinai war left the entire Arab world in frenzied opposition to the Jewish state. Israel had been in open conflict with Egypt on their common border since the summer of 1955; the Palestinian question, once a remote ideal of pan-Arab nationalists, led to armed clashes with Jordan and Syria. In Nasser's mind, Israel's attack in 1956 transformed the "Zionist entity" into a central symbol of pan-Arab frustration and impotence. So did Israel's growing cooperation with France, then fighting in Algeria against the forces of Arab self-determination. Understandably, if wrongly, Nasser charged that Israel was a conscious tool—not just the vestige—of European imperialism, and anti-Jewish feeling swept the Arab world. There were repressions, insults, and threats; the major cities of North Africa became sites for anti-Zionist riots.

The repressions brought on a new flood of mainly undereducated Jews from Morocco, Algeria, Tunisia, and Egypt. Estimates range to about 400,000 Sephardi immigrants between 1955 and 1963, but this is an underestimate of the North African immigration's cumulative impact, since many immediately expanded their families in their new homes and transit camps. The total addition to Israel's population during the first twelve years was about 1,200,000, and at least two thirds of the newcomers were of Sephardi extraction. By 1961, the Sephardi population of the Jewish state was about 45 percent, approximately 800,000 people, most of whom were, as Mrs. Meir lamented, ill equipped for Labor Zionist methods of work and politics. Nearly all the women from the countries of North Africa were illiterate; a good part of the men had learned to read the Torah and little else.

•

So great an influx of immigrants raises the question of just who "absorbed" whom. There was no doubt about who took charge. In the manner of the Yishuv's doctors, who selflessly treated the immigrants' diseases, the leaders of Mapai determined to minister to what they took to be the immigrants' cultural deprivations. Ben-Gurion declared that Israel would be not a melting pot but a "pressure cooker."

> We must break down the barriers of geography and culture, of society and speech, which keep the sections apart. We must endow them with a single language, a single culture, a single citizenship, with new legislation and new laws. We must give them a new spirit, a culture and literature, science and art.[4]

Veterans such as Ben-Gurion had subjected themselves to a highly personal cultural transformation for most of their adult lives. Triumphantly they had wrapped their tongues around Hebrew words, abjured the pleasures of faith, strained their bodies for the sake of proletarian and modernizing virtues. Correspondingly, the Zionist veterans had taken a kind of mandatory pleasure in the works of high culture, best symbolized perhaps by Ben-Gurion's reading of the Declaration of Independence at the Tel Aviv Museum while the Palestine Philharmonic played "*Ha'Tiqva*" (after all, a melody by Smetana). Not surprisingly, the veterans tended to see in the new mélange of Sephardi families and Eastern European refugees a distant mirror of their own origins. One kibbutz secretary put it this way: "You know, we never asked of these people what we had not once asked of ourselves."[5]

In retrospect, however, Ben-Gurion's statement seems obviously vain and a formula for mutual disappointment. The immigrants were not just raw material for a Zionist education. Much as the European immigrants—the Poles, Germans, Hungarians, Bulgarians, Rumanians—were impressed by the fact of the Jewish state, few were now receptive to Ben-Gurion's Labor Zionist folk culture. In fact, most had been consciously aloof from the Zionist clubs of their youth and found in Israel's confrontation with the Arabs a near-maddening continuation of their struggle against anti-Semitism. It was not the promise of Jewish modernism that moved them to the Jewish state but an all too vivid understanding of the modern world's tribal and dark side. Indeed, many now felt like outcasts of Western civilization. They wanted private space. They were certainly estranged from the social utopianism which still inspired much of the Histadrut and kibbutz intellectuals.

The Sephardi immigrants had lived mainly on the margins of North African city commerce—in Algiers, Casablanca, Tunis. What they had had of a liberal intelligentsia never went to Israel but stayed put, or went to Paris, New York, and Montreal. Nor did Sephardi immigrants have any ready sympathy for socialist political economy, even when this seemed in what others called their "class interest." They dreamed of a more perfect freedom of enterprise, of securing the family and father's respect by buying a little business. The writer Amos Oz has observed that, like so many of the

Polish immigrants of the Fourth Ascent—the people to whom Jabotinsky had particularly appealed—the Sephardi immigrants were, if only half-consciously, the products of ideals and notions of property belonging to the French bourgeoisie. To the educated among the Sephardi immigrants, certainly, the bourgeoisie belonged to Flaubert's world, not Marx's. Thus, wage labor brought with it a certain shame, which was the more annoying if the manager spoke in socialist platitudes. To Sephardi immigrants, democracy—*democratia*—implied that their children could answer them with impudence.

Israel was their chance to be strong against the Arabs—the only *goyim* Sephardi immigrants had ever experienced. They had lived in countries dominated by Islam and had themselves nurtured a rather Orthodox approach to Judaism. They had no feel for secular categories and expected messianic symbols to fire the Jewish nation, which was to them indistinguishable from the Jewish people. (Israel's most famous, if apocryphal, story from the period of mass immigration recounts how the refugees from Yemen, who had never seen aircraft before the Jewish Agency sent planes to collect them, thought the planes the wings of the Messiah sent to take them to the Promised Land.) Nevertheless, Islamic society had kept Sephardi immigrants strongly inclined toward sexual modesty and the inequality of women. They could not accept the collectivism of Histadrut and kibbutz as a moral ideal and responded to emancipated Zionist women not unlike the Arab workers who rioted against Hebrew Communists in 1921. (The writer Shulamith Hareven recalls that she had once good-naturedly shortened the skirt of a young Moroccan immigrant, to help her be in style— only to hear later how the girl was beaten by her father: "She was black and blue, and her father called her a whore!")

Of course, government efforts to improve the immigrants were not all skewed by Labor Zionist hubris. The government worked admirably to set up a national system of education, though, revealingly, only about 10 percent of the state's teachers were recruited from the Sephardi community during the fifties. This small number may have reflected the levels of illiteracy among Sephardi women. Still, a want of science is not also a want of art or guile. Sephardi immigrants came with a rich folk art, which they were challenged to cast away. Ben-Gurion's policy of "pressure cooker" —reinforced by the theses of Hebrew University sociologists—was inadvertently, perhaps, a warrant for European snobbishness regarding Sephardi dress, diet, poetry, and music.

ii

The spurning of the kibbutzim by European and Sephardi immigrants came as an especially serious blow to the Mapai leadership. It was also the prelude to deep social tensions. Though the two left-wing kibbutz movements, Kibbutz Ha'Meuchad and Kibbutz Ha'Artzi, had resisted hiring people to work in their fields and factories after the Sinai campaign, Ben-Gurion prevailed upon the movement leaders to hire new immigrants who refused to become members. In 1950 only fifty factories were located on the kibbutzim; by 1965 over 134 were set up there. (By 1979 the number was 332.) Yet there were negative social consequences to the new economic policy in the countryside, whatever the good faith with which it had been undertaken. Every day Sephardi workers came to kibbutz factories from nearby "development towns"—ersatz villages such as Dimona, Yoqne'am, Beit She'an—only to take orders from European veterans whose children, cloistered in kibbutz schools, shunned their children.

In the new capitalist environment, the kibbutzim were unwilling to discipline their spending as before; by 1960 they were largely consuming their surpluses. They made funds available for investments in new plants, or for sister kibbutzim that were just getting started. But funds were found also for handsome dining halls and Olympic-size swimming pools. Needless to say, Sephardi immigrants thought those expenditures inconsiderate, or at least at odds with the socialist rhetoric one heard at the lunch table. Even by 1960, tens of thousands of the newcomers were still in transit camps.

The new, more liberal economic climate which the kibbutzim exploited had, ironically, developed to absorb new immigrants; it was just what the vast majority of immigrants wanted in their bones. "Besides," one kibbutz veteran recalled, "there comes a point when people want to stop trying so hard, when one wants to do something for one's own." Yet that notion—"one's own"—betrayed something no kibbutz veteran was prepared to concede as yet, though

Sephardi immigrants who lived on a kibbutz for a while quickly grasped it: changes had occurred in the collective life and they went further than the reach of any ideology.

The collective had begun to resemble an extended family more than a revolutionary community. Palmach legends and stately old water towers had become something of a false front. Not that all ideological issues had been fought out; after the Prague trials, for example, some pro-Stalinist members of various kibbutzim suddenly found themselves out on the road, gathering up their belongings. Achdut Ha'Avodah and Ha'Shomer Ha'Tzair split in 1954. But if the kibbutz had been a fragment of a classless Zionist society in the 1930s, it was, by 1960, a little scar on a map full of cliques, gossip, rivalries, and infidelities. Its high morality and anarchist ideals provided vast opportunities for conformist reproach and hurt feelings. Loving kibbutz life in principle—and who could not, in principle?—did not spare new candidates from having to adjust to the lives of fellow members, to their reticent children, and to endless stories of how it all began in rock and sweat. Ironically, collective child-rearing only intensified the cliquishness of the kibbutz. The fellow feeling of parents, so reassuring during the Yishuv's siege, was now an invisible barrier to any newcomer. Immigrants felt, literally, as if they were moving into somebody else's house; they felt that they could never insinuate themselves into that circle of old affections—or old resentments, for that matter—which the veterans took for granted. Were the moral sentiments of their own families to be suppressed for so domestic a form of socialism? Collective child-rearing must have seemed weird to Sephardi parents, and the more so, since anyone who got close to kibbutzim discovered that—for all the indoctrination—truly ambitious kibbutz children were leaving to take dominant positions in the urban economy.

In the thirties, the kibbutz had prided itself on the comparative richness of its cultural life, the élan of its revolutionary politics, the standards of its schools. By 1960, Israel's politics and university were in Jerusalem, and its vanguard culture was being created in Tel Aviv. Meanwhile, the kibbutz population remained steady—about 4 percent of the population at large. In fact, no more than half the kibbutz children ever stayed on, which caused even more friction. As the founding generation grew steadily older, the successor generation that remained in the kibbutz found itself caring for and supporting many of the parents of people who had left.

iii

The new immigration served to justify the expropriation of Arab lands for the development of agricultural collectives, including the kibbutzim. The major part of the increment accruing to Israel from the War of Independence was about a million acres of fertile land in the northern and central regions, which were, arguably, abandoned by their Arab owners in headlong flight. Another 400,000 acres of marginal land in the northern Negev, to which Arab title was considered uncertain, were taken. In 1950 the Knesset enacted the Absentee Property Law, to legalize the major expropriations; only a small proportion of Arabs recovered lands thereafter. In 1951, 25 percent of the Israeli population was housed on abandoned Arab property; the acreage of Jewish farmland, largely cultivated by the kibbutzim and moshavim, jumped from 400,000 in 1949 to 890,000 in 1953. After 1956, new moshavim (such as those in the Lachish salient in the northern Negev) proved more attractive to the Sephardi population than to the kibbutzim.

All through the 1950s, the Mapai leadership consolidated the state's territory, making ruins of abandoned Arab towns. Dayan insisted that expropriations of this sort had always been a fact of Zionism. His father's cohorts had, after all, built the first moshav, Nahalal, on lands in the Jezreel Valley bought from Arab peasants. But were the times the same, and were Zionist purposes ever so mechanical? In fact, the survival of Hebrew culture was no longer at stake, nor was the Zionist idea intrinsically expansionist. The stronger argument in favor of expropriating the Arab lands is simply that new Jewish refugees were now desperate for homes and took their own plight to be a warrant for the further displacement of Palestinian Arabs. As the historian Howard Sachar put it: "Two hundred thousand Jewish immigrants preempted 80,000 Arab rooms."[6] Arab regimes had confiscated the property of many Jewish refugees before 1956; Arab speculators throughout North Africa made handsome profits buying out Jews who were in a state of panic after the Sinai war. True, Palestinian Arabs were not the beneficiaries of either misfortune. But who is to say what misfortunes Palestinian fighters had in mind for Jews had they won the war? Palestinian leaders certainly made no effort to restore property to Jews displaced from East Jerusalem or Hebron. Golda Meir put the Zionist case bluntly: "We used the houses of those Arabs who ran away from the country whenever we could for new immigrant housing . . . We did not keep our refugees in camps."[7]

During the late fifties, moreover, a combination of state planning and Histadrut corporate power brought off the construction of ambitious infrastructural projects: army encampments, a national water carrier, the Dead Sea works, hundreds of miles of roads, and many new neighborhoods and towns which depleted the *maabarot*, or tent villages. (*Maabarot* were almost entirely gone by 1967.) Between 1948 and 1967, an impressive 650,000 dwellings were put up. The Mapai-dominated state apparatus imported as loans, bonds, grants, and business investment some $6,000 per immigrant from 1949 to 1967, and personal graft was almost entirely absent in the administration of the funds. By 1960 foreign investment quadrupled; domestic savings grew to half the total available for investment. Industry's contribution to exports grew from $18 million in 1949 to $375 million by 1965. From 1955 to 1964, real consumption in the country grew at an annual rate of 5 percent a year. By 1960, after the full effects of the German reparations had been felt, there was not much left of the planned economy. The private sector grew to about three fifths of the total output by 1960, with the Histadrut and the state splitting the remaining two fifths. Which is not to say the public corporations were suffering. Indeed, the Histadrut and state cartels usually retained commanding positions in various markets, using interlocking Mapai connections and control of banking and public resources. The Histadrut ran businesses now; it did not run them as proletarian associations.

·

In spite of these public projects—in some cases, because of them —the social gap between the Sephardi immigrant population, the so-called Second Israel, and the European labor community tended to grow, not lessen. More and more, the Mapai old guard—as distinct from Ben-Gurion's statist forces—seemed notorious as the source of apartments, favors, promotions. It was the neighborhood Mapai official who got you a government job or a Kupat Holim clinic sinecure, who made you a teller in Bank Leumi or got your son to coach a Ha'Poel football team. Everyone, including the newest of new immigrants, knew enough to carry the red coupon booklet of the Histadrut union when applying for a mortgage, a scholarship, or a bank account. Granted, few would have wanted to do without the Histadrut's welfare services—an education for one's children, jobs, and housing. Yet the sense of a gap was exacerbated by the old guard's paternalistic attitude toward Sephardi cultural traditions. By clinging to patriarchal families and styles of religious piety, Sephardi Jews came to feel naked in the country. They were half the population; yet they were dominated by European wit, heroes, and politicians—by what seemed to them a closed shop of a privileged caste. (One of the canniest satiric statements of the time, the film *Salah Shabbati*, depicts a wily Moroccan patriarch as he is taken through a maze of government bureaucrats and Mapai *apparatchiks*. His burgeoning family finally obtains a tidy apartment, but not before we get a rather cutting view of his alienation. He is set upon by party officials who try to teach him how to vote; he is badgered by a naïve young social worker who tries to teach him—and, predictably, learns from him—about family responsibility.)

Of course, the alienation of the Second Israel derived from an inevitable clash of worlds. Yet what may have seemed merely poignant to individuals entailed larger economic and social grievances. By the end of the first decade, about four fifths of the Sephardi population lived in the large towns and cities, where they became workers in an economy dominated by Europeans; the Sephardi immigrants became waitresses and cashiers, petty clerks. The most ambitious were retailers, car mechanics, taxi drivers, and vegetable peddlers—the *sans-culottes* of Tel Aviv, Haifa, and Jerusalem. About 80 percent were wage-earners, workers. Labor exchanges guaranteed equal pay for all in particular fields of work, and income distribution was the most egalitarian in the free world, but menial jobs were being abandoned by the sons and daughters of the veterans. Sephardi Jews were 75 percent of workers in forestation work, drainage, and clearing, where wages were very low.[8] They were doing a disproportionate share of the work of construction, even when Solel Boneh was the employer.

The veterans did not directly profit from the public corporations; all members of the Histadrut, including the new immigrants, were equal shareholders. But dividends were never paid out as such; they were reinvested in new enterprises, and it was the veterans who became their managers, as well as the teachers and the technicians. Even the unions' shop stewards were chosen from slates presented to the workers as in Mandate times. Most of these people were Ashkenazi, who were better connected within the major labor parties. Between 1956 and 1958, over 60 percent of the Sephardi immigrants had been percolated through the decrepit *maabarot* to development towns; only 30 percent of the European immigrants had ever endured either. Then there was the matter of the inequalities introduced by German reparations, though the Mapai government had negotiated for these funds precisely to house the new immigrants. Some reparations were paid to Israelis as individuals, to Polish and German immigrants, the same people who were refugees after the war and who had once lived alongside the Sephardim. Thus, a Sephardi's European neighbor might come into wealth overnight, which made for hurt feelings, social jealousies, even a hint of resentment for the solemnity with which the government commemorated the Holocaust. By 1959 the bottom 10 percent of Israeli households were receiving 1.6 percent of the national income, and these were mainly Sephardi Moroccans. The top 10 percent, mainly European, received about 24 percent. Of 100,000 students registering to begin high school, only 4,000 were Sephardim.

It is true that, by 1965, 45,000 of these children, some 63 percent of the Sephardi group, were attending high school; the Ministry of Education was spending some 12 percent of the government budget. But Sephardi Jews accounted for no more than 16 percent of college students. Sephardi Jews had become powerful in municipal affairs; 44 percent of municipal councils were made up of Sephardi Jews by 1965. Yet by 1965 no more than 16 percent were represented on the national level, in the Knesset. The Mapai coalition had yet to produce a single minister from the Second Israel. Of the 120,000 families who lived in substandard housing—in Tel Aviv's Shechunat Ha'Tiqvah or Jerusalem's Katamon Tet—fully 83 percent were Sephardi, usually Moroccan. As late as 1970, Orientals accounted for no more than 3 percent of upper-level management jobs in the public corporations of the state bureaucracy, 16 percent of the nation's professionals, and 19 percent of the white-collar workers.

"Shall we ever be able to raise these immigrants to a suitable level of civilization?" Golda Meir asked.

iv

The transformation of the Histadrut and the collective life associated with it was bound to have an impact on the country's political style. Not surprisingly, the debates of old Zionist movements were overtaken by the campaigns of political parties searching for more votes. Curiously, the old rhetoric did not quite dissipate; Begin still dredged up charges from the forties, Mapam from the thirties. Yet, as Noah Lucas wryly noted, though the language of political life remained fixed on "architecture," actual political life now turned on the "furnishings."

> Mapai talked the language of social democracy while promoting the capitalist economy; the religious parties deployed the imagery of theocracy while indulging in petty clerical politics; the parties of the left elaborated socialist doctrine while protecting the market interests of their kibbutzim; the middle class parties expressed themselves in the language of classical liberalism while pressing for government protection and largesse; and the right-wing cultivated the rhetoric of chauvinist hysteria while nurturing the populism of the dispossessed.[9]

Throughout the fifties, the Sephardi population remained largely under Ben-Gurion's sway. His government provided a panoply of trusted faces. After the Sinai campaign, the Old Man established himself as a world leader—a friend to Black Africa, newly opened to Israel by shipping lanes through the Gulf of Aqaba; a friend to such Third World leaders as Burma's U Nu. Ben-Gurion corresponded with Nehru; he was magnanimous to West Germany's Konrad Adenauer. His prestige reached a peak in May 1960, when he announced to a stunned Knesset that Israeli forces had captured Adolf Eichmann in Argentina and that the war criminal would be tried in Jerusalem according to Israeli law.

Yet the first sign of trouble for Mapai had already come, in 1959, when riots broke out in the Wadi Salib section of Haifa. Then, and throughout the early sixties, the disaffection of the Second Israel from the Mapai establishment became palpable—in expressions of black humor and outbreaks of crime. Herut began to win a steadily increasing proportion of the Sephardi vote, 17 seats by 1961—not from those who were well educated, comparatively wealthy, or in the country for a long time, but from the poor, the badly educated, the North African newcomers.[10] Somewhat shaken, Mapai leaders promised reforms. The Minister of Education, Zalman Aranne, began to speak of Israeli culture as no longer monolithic; indeed, he began to evolve a curriculum (which was finally introduced in 1965) which taught students that Israel was to be a collection of subcultures and that various folk cultures of the Sephardi community would enjoy complete equality. But was this the point? In fact, the children of the Sephardi immigrants were now more devoted to rock stars than to the Moroccan-Jewish *Mamouna* festival. All could agree that equality was perfect in the army's boot camps—i.e., where it meant social acceptance, honor, making a date without suffering the sting of prejudice. What was wanting was social prestige, cash, political power. These could not be legislated as could a nod to Sephardi folk culture.

Nor did Menachem Begin fail to play on the Second Israel's frustrations. He invited them to imagine how much better off they would have been had Histadrut not existed; had the newcomers been able to make their way into a fully capitalist economy, family by family, in cities and in a national economy unencumbered by tax breaks for kibbutzim. Begin vaguely insinuated that the whole Labor Zionist tradition was Communist, and promised to line up behind Western interests without equivocation. He railed against the "bureaucratic-socialist despots" of the Histadrut, against their *proteksia*, and he embellished his dismay over Mapai's high-handedness with retrospective criticism of the elitist, exclusive pioneering of the Second Ascent. Had not the Mapai clique always discouraged middle-class idealists from coming into their own in the Promised Land? Begin touched sympathetic nerves in the North African community, as his notions of family, religion, and commerce sincerely conformed to their own. And who could say that Begin's middle-class ideal would have been out of place in France or Canada, where so many relatives of the Sephardi immigrants had gone? Perhaps the only place in the free world such middle-class values *were* out of place was in the Valley of Jezreel.

At the same time, the old divisions still plagued Mapai, at least since the time of Pinchas Lavon's resignation. Levi Eshkol coordinated the new economic policy and the Mapai machine. Golda

Meir was Foreign Minister in Sharett's place, but Shimon Peres was still in the defense establishment, presiding over Israel's special, largely secret relations with France. After the Sinai campaign, all sides had agreed that Lavon should be rehabilitated; in 1958, Ben-Gurion appointed him to the prestigious secretary-general's chair at the Histadrut, and from his new position, Lavon began fervently to preach the old values of Labor Zionism, as much out of spite for Ben-Gurion's young men as out of conviction. But for his part, Dayan (the Agriculture Minister) aimed sharp barbs at the Histadrut in party forums, as well as in the press. He condemned Histadrut's methods of collective bargaining, its protection of inefficient workers and "tenured" union bosses. He called for an end to the ideals of "pioneering"—of personal, revolutionary transformation in collective institutions—and hailed the efficiency which he felt was personified by the army.

Dayan called for retiring "voluntarist" institutions in favor of state agencies. Palmach had been surrendered to the army; labor-movement schools (outside the kibbutzim) had been surrendered to a unified, secular system of education. He demanded that the bus cooperatives, too, be nationalized. He even suggested that it was time to dismantle Kupat Holim, the sick fund, though he knew that this was the main benefit for which all workers, even those in the expanding private sector, joined the Histadrut. Giving as good as they got, Eshkol and Meir pointed out that Lavon had already decentralized Solel Boneh, the huge construction firm, and moderated Histadrut wage demands. Lavon professionalized the Histadrut staff and reformed the Egged and Dan transport cooperatives. (When the veteran head of Solel Boneh, Hillel Dan, overstepped his power—Dan had bought a Swiss bank without consulting the Histadrut or Mapai—it was Lavon who dismembered Dan's empire, splitting it up into leaner, more competitive firms.) Could Lavon now abandon the Histadrut's essential prerogatives to organize workers, heal them, protect them—employ them? Lavon charged that Dayan sounded like a proponent of Jabotinsky's old plans for the Yishuv.

To be sure, nobody in Ben-Gurion's camp, not even Dayan, ever implied that Jabotinsky had been right in his strategy for building the Yishuv or promoting Zionism's claims against Britain's. Yet the new statism was indeed a kind of rehabilitation of Revisionist rhetoric. To the extent that the state was considered superior to all other moral values, it was hard not to go along with Jabotinsky's correlative views regarding political economy—i.e., that wage disputes should be subject to national arbitration, that Histadrut property should be nationalized. The Sinai war had proven the value of national power; so had the Eichmann trial. And why not a diminution of "proletarian" influence, why not militarist models of social organization? Since Labor Zionist goals had been fulfilled, the Revisionist ideal of the state was the only coherent Zionism left standing. Nor did the forces for that kind of Zionism lack a national majority. If one added the power of the Dayan-Peres faction of Mapai to the Liberals who catered to the growing Tel Aviv bourgeoisie, to the Herut populists who plied the slums of the Second Israel, and then added also the religious groups who tended to be dovish but sympathized with statism, it was clear that the Histadrut was representing a declining national minority. These numbers did not yet translate into an electoral defeat for Mapai. But no one impartially surveying the political map in 1960 could seriously doubt that a new Israel was emerging.

.

If by 1960 there were divisions within Mapai that weakened the party, these did not discredit the reputations of Mapai's key leaders like the scandal which was about to break, the concluding chapter of Lavon's "mishap" of 1954. In April 1960, Lavon was informed by Israeli intelligence that inconsistencies had been established in the testimony of his erstwhile intelligence chief, Colonel Benjamin Gibly; one document, which had swayed the Olshan-Dori commission against Lavon, was now proven to be a forgery. A few months later Lavon was informed that crucial testimony against him had been coached perjury, that the conspiracy may have reached as high as Gibly and beyond to Peres and Dayan. Of course for Lavon the revelations were a godsend. He wanted to avoid an open split with Ben-Gurion, and he hoped the Old Man would promise to curb Dayan and Peres. Still, he took for granted that he would be exonerated. (His own prevarications before the Olshan-Dori investigation had not yet been discovered.) Ben-Gurion, for his part, received the news with tact, though he immediately hinted that he would not allow the good name of the IDF to be the victim of a political vendetta. He agreed to Lavon's demand for a series of secret hearings before a select committee of investigation, headed by Justice Chaim Cohen.

As Lavon was testifying, some of his dramatic accusations against the IDF command were leaked to the press, apparently with his connivance. The Defense Ministry struck back, leaking documents of their own, which were far more damaging to Lavon than his leaks had been to it. This is not the place to go into the charges; suffice it to say the political atmosphere became volatile. In October, the Cohen Committee issued its own report: perjury had indeed prejudiced the Olshan-Dori Commission, whose findings were now invalid. What should now be done? Ben-Gurion unhesitatingly took the part of the army and implied that an open Judicial Commission of Inquiry should be empowered. Eshkol, hoping once again to spread oil on the waters, extracted a statement from Moshe Sharett to the effect that the new findings would have substantially vindicated Lavon. (This was not just sourness on Sharett's part, since he had harbored his own deep suspicions about foul play in the Defense Ministry back in 1954.)[11] At the same time, Sharett bent over backward to be evenhanded; he declared that he would *not* have asked for Peres's resignation in 1955, even on the basis of the new evidence.

Sharett's statement was just what Eshkol wanted, but Ben-Gurion would not leave it there. "He went on demanding legal procedures," Golda Meir complained, "while Eshkol, [Pinchas] Sapir, and I tried to resolve the conflict on the Cabinet level—decently and discreetly."[12] In fact, Ben-Gurion considered the Sharett statement a slander of the IDF and reaffirmed his call for a commission of inquiry. Since so many charges had leaked out, he said, there was no point pretending the public could be spared anxiety; only a legally constituted commission could settle the dispute. Interestingly enough, Ben-Gurion's call for a judicial commission independent of the Mapai leadership inadvertently exposed the basic contradiction between the old guard's way of doing things and Israel's constitutional drift. Was not Mrs. Meir's notion of government by Mapai fiat, albeit "decent and discreet," one of the issues Ben-Gurion's young men had been raising against Lavon's Histadrut all along? Yitzchak Navon, who was Ben-Gurion's private secretary then, put it this way:

Israel had become a plural, fractious, and urban society. It needed a new social contract, new institutions to manage the unanticipated difficulties of national life. Not that Ben-Gurion wished only to create constitutional precedents. He behaved badly. He wanted to protect his protégés. Yet to shove the Lavon case—a clear challenge to procedures in the IDF—into the secretive, informal councils of Mapai leaders, to make it a matter for internal political bargaining, was to miss an important opportunity.[13]

Nevertheless, Eshkol prevailed upon the Cabinet to set up a ministerial committee under the chairmanship of Justice Minister Pinchas Rosen—not a judicial commission of inquiry but a sort of blue-ribbon panel. Ben-Gurion made clear his opposition and launched a bitter public assault on Lavon's integrity. Indeed, Ben-Gurion grouchily denounced most of the Mapai old guard, speaking with far less restraint than befitted one who aimed to establish new rules for civil procedure. Incidentally, this was the very time Shimon Peres was in France conducting secret and highly delicate negotiations concerning construction of the Dimona nuclear reactor. Ben-Gurion assumed the deal with France would result in Israel acquiring a potential to make nuclear weapons—another reason, if any more were needed, for putting up a ferocious defense of Peres's standing in the Defense Ministry. Peres returned early in November and appeared before the Knesset Foreign Affairs and Security Committee to refute Lavon's own increasingly bitter accusations. Neither he nor Ben-Gurion could prevent Eshkol's panel from beginning its work.

Eshkol's Committee of Seven Ministers deliberated intensely between November 3 and December 20. They did not follow strict rules of evidence, and they did not call witnesses or allow for cross-examination of those who submitted documents. Ben-Gurion wrapped himself in the mantle of impartial justice and vilified the man for whom justice would presumably be done. On December 20 the Committee of Seven announced the verdict Ben-Gurion most feared: "Lavon did *not* give the order cited by the 'senior officer,' the 'mishap' happened without the Minister's knowledge." Ben-Gurion refused to take part in the Cabinet vote on the report, Dayan abstained, and it passed 8–0. Then Ben-Gurion addressed the Justice Minister: "You have made your decisions. There are findings. There is a Cabinet decision approving these findings. The Cabinet has a law of collective responsibility. I am no partner to this responsibility . . . I am no longer a member of this Cabinet." He presented his resignation to President Ben-Tzvi on January 31, 1961.[14]

To say the least, Ben-Gurion's resignation left Mapai in a severe quandary. Eshkol was still determined to avoid a split, but Ben-Gurion was now forcing a choice between loyalty to him and the integrity of the old guard, and neither choice was politic. To go along with Ben-Gurion was to submit to a man who was by now widely perceived to be ruthless—perhaps unstable—in the pursuit of questionable political vengeance; sadly, the good constitutional principle for which the Prime Minister had begun his fight was completely eclipsed by the feud. To oppose Ben-Gurion, however, was to appear to be opposed to his statist views and the army's élan, both of which had brought Mapai victories at the polls. Eventually Eshkol capitulated to the Old Man's will. On February 4 the party's Central Committee convened and voted to dismiss Lavon.

There was a considerable price to pay for this expedient course. Achdut Ha'Avodah, with whom Eshkol had been discussing entry into the coalition, now refused to join. Achdut Ha'Avodah's leaders, especially Yigal Allon, derided Ben-Gurion's young men. Allon had never forgiven Dayan for inheriting command of the IDF after he, Allon, had retired when the Palmach was disbanded. And Mapai now lost many of its Hebrew University intellectuals as well: the philosopher Natan Rotenstreich joined with Lavon to form an influential socialist group called Min Hayesod, or "From the Foundation," which openly criticized Ben-Gurion's statist deviations and argued for reviving the Histadrut. In August 1961 new elections were held. Mapai lost five seats, and it was clear that its reputation had been severely tarnished. Eshkol patched together a new government for Ben-Gurion, but it was questionable how long it could last.

·

As the rift between the young guard and the old would not subside, Ben-Gurion resigned again in June 1963. This time no delegation went to implore him to return. Eshkol assumed the Prime Minister's job himself; Dayan, Peres, and others close to Ben-Gurion were systematically excluded from the centers of power. More and more, political loyalties shifted. With Ben-Gurion out of office, Israel's right-wing political parties realigned, sensing the chance to take over the mantle of statism, or at least to make significant gains. Begin, the leader of Herut, met with the heads of the Liberal Party and entered into negotiations for the creation of a single, market-oriented, nationalist party. The result was Gahal, the Herut-Liberal bloc, which hammered out a common platform in time for the elections of 1965. (Significantly, though the charismatic Begin became leader, it was the platform of the Liberals that mainly carried the day. Herut even dropped its long-standing commitment to unify the West Bank with Israel.) Eshkol, meanwhile, tried to deny the Israeli right its chance to take the initiative away from him. Having alienated Ben-Gurion's young men, he drew much closer to the Achdut Ha'Avodah. Eshkol wrote Min Hayesod, welcoming Lavon back into the fold. Then, in 1965, the Mapai-Histadrut old guard sealed their break with Ben-Gurion by creating the Labor Alignment, along with Achdut Ha'Avodah—though the latter party forced Eshkol's Mapai to drop electoral reform from the Alignment's platform. Finally came the turn of Ben-Gurion's men. Peres snatched away Dayan, Yosef Almogi, and several other young disciples from Mapai for a final test of the Old Man's prestige. They formed the Rafi Party, the "List of Israeli Workers," with Ben-Gurion at the head of the list.

Predictably, the 1965 elections were the longest, angriest, dirtiest, and most expensive in the country's history. Eshkol's Labor Alignment came out on top, but it was a Pyrrhic victory. Gahal returned 26 members, and Rafi 10. The Labor Alignment won only 9 seats more than the combined strength of its statist rivals, 45 seats. This was enough to dispatch Ben-Gurion to political oblivion, and indeed, much of the campaign seemed a national referendum on whether the Old Man was really an old man. Still, with or without him, Ben-Gurion's statism was clearly on the ascendency. Eshkol could hardly ignore that, without the religious parties supporting it, Mapai no longer controlled a majority of the Knesset. For all the egalitarian rhetoric which Allon imported to the Cabinet from the kibbutzim, moreover, the post-1965 period intensified the estrangement of the Histadrut from the Second Israel. The old proportional representation entrenched the party machines that made up the candidate lists. Unlike the kibbutz members of Achdut Ha'Avodah,

Sephardi voters justifiably viewed constituency-based elections as the only way to clear away dead wood to make room for new, more representative forces in the national life.

Incidentally, out of 212 Jewish members of the Knesset who served between 1949 and 1964, 73 percent were from Eastern Europe, many from the Second Ascent. It became common parlance to refer to the Tel Aviv headquarters of the Histadrut as "the Kremlin." What made matters worse, even nasty, was that after 1965 the country felt the full effects of economic recession. By 1965, 85 percent of Israeli households boasted refrigerators. But the following year tens of thousands—perhaps 100,000—were unemployed, and 400,000 were officially living below the poverty line; GNP growth dwindled to 1 percent. Mapai leaders and the members of kibbutzim continued to argue in terms of revolutionary Zionism. Yet more people were leaving the country than were coming to it— for the first time since the 1920s.

v

Recession was probably inevitable in view of the diminished demand for housing which attended the drop in immigration from the countries of North Africa. Still, the precipitousness of that drop raised the question of what had become of Zionist arguments that once drew Jews from around the world to Palestine. American Jews, some 6 million, had not come; and even the Jews of Western Europe would not leave countries whose governments had surrendered Jews to Eichmann only twenty years before. The politicians who headed the dominant parties still called themselves leaders of Zionist movements. Yet what did they mean by this other than to declare an intention to rest on their laurels and take funds from the Jewish Agency to run political campaigns? Israeli youngsters grasped that, in particular, the labor establishment's Zionism was largely casuistry and began to use the word "Zionism"—"*Tzyonut*" —as a kind of epithet, suggesting people who are showy about their patriotism or naïve about politics. "Zionism" became a word one expected from editorials but not from friends. Labor Alignment supporters who sincerely identified with the tradition of Katznelson risked an hour's lecture on the selfishness of Egged bus drivers or the rudeness of nurses in Kupat Holim clinics. Worse, they might be accused of identifying overmuch with the lives of Jews outside

the state, whose moral fecklessness was implicitly repudiated by the
state's very existence.

Again, the dilution of Zionist principles had begun more than a
decade before, though at first Ben-Gurion had tried to preempt this
with plain talk. When the state was declared, Ben-Gurion had announced to Western Zionists that he was himself no longer a Zionist but a Jew and an Israeli. He had insisted that Zionist executives
in the United States and Europe immediately commit themselves to
emigrate to Israel, and he even scoffed at their Zionist organizations:
"The pseudo-Zionism of today *helps* Jews to be naturalized and
more deeply rooted in a non-Jewish environment and in the pro-
cesses of assimilation which endanger the future of Jewry in the
Diaspora."[15] Such bluntness had caused a good deal of consternation among American and Canadian Zionist leaders, but Ben-Gurion
did not relent. He was obviously right that a movement is unnecessary where a plane ticket will do.

Ben-Gurion backed off somewhat as it dawned on him how
difficult it would be to organize the state. Certainly the fund-raising
activities of the United Jewish Appeal and Israel Bonds, both working through the Jewish Agency, had become indispensable to the
state's economic development. In November 1952, the Knesset enacted the World Zionist Organization–Jewish Agency (Status) Law,
which confirmed the continued existence of the Jewish Agency and
the Zionist organizations abroad, while abolishing their jurisdictions within the state. Nor did the evolving statist line by which
Ben-Gurion justified this and other expediencies fail to impress the
Zionists of Brooklyn and Montreal, and for much the same reasons
it had made sense to new immigrants of Tel Aviv's Shechunat
Ha'Tiqvah quarter; Western Jews were certainly more receptive to
a Zionism of defiance, technocracy, and Bible than they had been to
the Zionism of the kibbutzim. Ben-Gurion could never accept that
a New Yorker's money could be as Zionist as an immigrant's muscle.
Yet he declared in a 1957 Independence Day speech:

> The unity of the Jewish people, its sense of a common responsibility
> for its fate, its attachments to its spiritual heritage, and its love for the
> nation's ancient homeland, have become more and more intense as a
> result of the rise of the Third Commonwealth. The ingathering of
> Israel's exiled and scattered sons is the common task of the Jewish

people *wherever they may live.* Everything that has been created in this country is the common possession of the Jews of all lands. [emphasis added][16]

American Jews did not lack rejoinders to the classic Zionist claims. To the extent that Zionist arguments harked back to political Zionism, they invited American Jews to consider only their vulnerability. The Holocaust provided world Jewry with a kind of miserable proof that Herzl had been, if not right, then at least prophetic. There was a certain military heroism in Israel with which to identify. But many more American Jews had died defending America during the Second World War than Israelis had died in the War of Independence and the Sinai campaign. American Jews had entered their own national life in force during the war against Hitler—in the U.S. armed forces, as part of anti-Fascist movements, and, ironically, in pro-Zionist groups. Anti-Semitism still festered in parts of the Old World, in Poland and the Soviet Union. But not, surely, in America. On the contrary, the persecuted Jews of Eastern Europe were still going to America as readily as they were going to Israel. Besides, the main virtue of political Zionism was that it had analyzed the fate of Jews in the context of the risks of modernization. Herzl, Syrkin, and Jabotinsky—a liberal, a socialist, and a romantic authoritarian—had all expressed apprehension about the fate of Jews in societies emerging from feudalism, backwardness, orthodox Christianity. But where, of all places, had the Jewish national home been planted? Right in the middle of fragmented, pre-modern Arab peoples, possessed by Islam and confounded by urbanization, the new technologies, the Cold War, and the stain of a colonial past.

For Israelis themselves the old political Zionist claims had something of a hollow ring. Israeli youth were defending disputed borders while American cousins were defending Ph.D. theses. A well-known Israeli journalist of the time, Baruch Nadel, wryly defined Zionism as "the movement of Western Jews to save the Eastern Jews that built a home for Oriental Jews." (A Sternist in his youth, Nadel is rumored to have been among those who assassinated Count Bernadotte. In 1979 he was reported living in Brooklyn.) Political Zionism worked insofar as it was synonymous with statism. There was an army, a bureaucracy, a diplomatic apparatus. Israelis were un-

willing to trade pride in these for—how did Achad Haam put it?
—"all the civil rights in the world," and they were anxious to welcome more Western Jews to their ranks. The children of the old
Zionist left certainly liked to think that they presided over a more
progressive society than any in the West, that demonstrations of
more social idealism would draw American Jews away from their
"fleshpots." Yet beneath the cloak of Zionist debate, new generations of Israelis actually voiced not elaborated Zionist theories so
much as vaguely conceived dogmas. "Zionism," which once implied
a national solution to the chronic difficulties of the Diaspora, now
seemed to mean that Diaspora Jews should want to participate in
solving the chronic problems of the national center. The Diaspora
Jew who could not see that his own best possibilities were linked
to the Jewish state's struggle was said to betray a kind of false
consciousness, like the workingman who won't see that he is also a
proletarian. Curiously, this blindness suggested a double recrimi-
nation: if only Israelis were better, it was thought, American Jews
would be attracted to their country; if only American Jews were
more worthy, they wouldn't need so much seduction.

As for cultural Zionism, American Jews were no better candidates in 1966 than French and German Jews had been in 1893.
For Bellow-reading, Wheaties-eating, Gershwin-humming, world-
hopping American Jews, Israel offered merely the chance of being
of value to others—arguably, good potential consumers of Israelis'
Hebrew culture, but not potential producers. Significantly, many
Israelis of European origin hoped more American and Western
Jews would come, not for their likely contributions to Hebrew
poetry, but to teach Israelis of Moroccan origin how to queue for a
bus. This was hardly what Borochov had meant by a material force.
Israel was, to be sure, the only Jewish public realm left in the
world. But as far as American Jews were concerned, that realm was
a place that turned one's children into strangers, much as American
Jews had alienated themselves from their Yiddish-speaking parents
in New York. Besides, for most American Jews, Judaism now implied
a tradition to help them adjust to a public realm of English liberal
democracy, a tradition of historical disquisition, ethics, and texts—
not the aesthetic, legal, and linguistic norms of the Hebrew nation.

There were several hundred thousand American Jews, the products of Hebrew education, who seriously considered joining the

Jewish national project. Some 35,000 eventually found a home in the Israeli mainstream. But even such highly motivated American Jews could not be assumed to have found in Israel what the Zionist revolutionaries had called "self-realization." Too many Israeli "selves" had already been realized. A part of what inhibited immigration from the Western democracies was the very sophistication of Israel's Hebrew culture. It is worth noting here that Israel's first generation of novelists and writers reflected seriously on the exhaustion of Zionist terms. Growing up in the shadow of the Palmach generation, they viewed Zionism as a gray burden of received authority, the legacy of a lapsed revolution that issued inflexible and obsolete demands. A. B. Yehoshua, Amos Oz, Yoram Kaniuk, along with journalists such as Amos Elon, raised new moral voices in the 1960s, exploring the dark, private side of the revolution.

Ironically, their willingness to consider what was private and unique to Israelis marked the beginning of a serious national literature. Yehoshua, for example, addressed the Arab problem squarely, as a deforming national obsession. In his moving, perverse story *Mul Ha'Yearot*—"Facing the Forests"—Yehoshua's young protagonist becomes the passive accomplice of an Arab worker who torches a JNF forest, now standing over the ruins of an Arab town. Yehoshua's generation noticed how revolutionary Zionist obligations, like old *halachic* norms, repressed individual life, also equivocation, sexuality, shame. Zionism—the war, the clear boundaries of Hebrew identity; what Yehoshua called, cryptically, the "center"—seemed a source of suffocation to these writers. More strident journalists and politicians such as Uri Avnery and Amos Kenan joined the "Canaanite" movement, which had boldly demanded an end to all ties to Western Jews, and to their now presumptuous, now obsequious Zionist institutions. How, the Canaanites asked, could Israelis come into their own if their main measure of success was whether or not Western Jews wanted to live with them?

Of course, most of the young people who admired the New Wave writers could not support such frankly post-Zionist doctrine without ambivalence. The word "Zionism" still conjured cherished associations and nuances derived from many different theories and bureaucratic interests. However, the problem with such Zionism was in its very eclecticism, its inability to inspire people other than Israelis. The word came to mean something precious, non-ideological, as much embedded in the Israeli political culture as, say, the word *"fraternité"* was embedded in the French.

Zionist rhetoric implied something like this: that Israelis should be strong and united against the outside world; that religious splits and class conflicts must be suppressed for the sake of unity. Correspondingly, Zionism implied that the Jewish state was every Jew's patrimony; that, for example, the Law of Return was not merely an immigration law promulgated for refugees but the highest expression of the centrality of Israel to Diaspora Jews. Jews everywhere, presumably, constituted a political, corporate interest which the Jewish state most perfectly represented. Zionism entailed sacrifice for the national good, *hagshama*, "self-realization," the most noble example of which was settling remote outposts of the ancient land. Zionist settlement yielded security and inspiration, the spirit of the pioneers.

The soil of Eretz Yisrael was the new, actual center of Jewish spiritual life, which seemed automatically to banish alienation. Zionism was the main link to the past, a mine of interior life, a force that mediated between the Bible, Jewish historical scholarship, and archaeology. Zionism meant that Jews would never again go like "sheep to the slaughter." Public discipline, as in the army, was the only way to reenter history, so the saying went, "as actors and not merely as victims." Zionism alone gave Jews the promise of normalcy and peace.

This was what was left of revolutionary Zionism on the eve of the Six-Day War. If all of its parts did not fit together neatly, there was comfort in the fact that—given the recession, the peaceful borders, the routines of middle-class life—it was not to be taken all that seriously.

PART THREE

New Zionism and the

Trial of Israeli Democracy

8 / A New Zionism for

Greater Israel

It has often been asserted, since Amos Elon first dared to raise the point in the fall of 1967, that Israel's victory in the Six-Day War was too smashing by half: Israeli society was not ready to absorb the war's diplomatic, economic, and demographic consequences, and —so the argument goes—a great many Israelis were simply carried away. There is a good deal of truth in this view, though nobody who went through those difficult days before the war, or the exhilarating days afterward—Elon included—would want to concede that historical events should be judged solely by such practical criteria as diplomacy and demography. What seems less arguable is that Israeli attitudes toward their conflict with the Arab states— more precisely, toward the value of any peace settlement—took on a new slant soon after the war's end. Gradually the Israeli government's willingness to withdraw from the West Bank, Gaza, the Golan Heights, and the Sinai in exchange for new diplomatic arrangements, or even peace treaties, could less and less be taken for granted.

Part of the change in the government's attitude may be explained by the traumatic nature of both the prewar crisis and the war itself. Yet it may be a mistake to concentrate only on the spontaneous feelings and strategic conclusions these evoked. The crisis and war catalyzed sentiments they alone could not have created but which became evident very soon after the guns fell silent; sentiments favoring those barely digested but deeply felt statist myths which had been evolving in the guise of Zionism for a generation—among the young, among newcomers, not to mention military figures impatient with Labor Zionist ideas. A mere two weeks after the war, the Israeli government, reflecting public consensus, announced that the whole of Jerusalem had been annexed. Within six months, it was widely thought that Golan was inseparable from Galilee, and that a great part of the West Bank could never be, in Moshe Dayan's word, "abandoned." By year's end, Jewish settlers sought to establish permanent control over all these territories, and the Israeli government acquiesced in or—as in the case of Golan— actively encouraged the efforts of squatters.

What the new Israel had already acquired before 1967 was a vaguely spiritual ideal of a holy land—blended with the nostalgic Labor Zionist notion of Jewish revolution through settlement. Ben-Gurion had intended this blend for the Negev; the war gave Israelis other ideas. Moreover, a part of Ben-Gurion's statist logic had been the principle, now thrice tested, that in the face of Arab threats, the Israeli Defense Forces need not await the approval of Western opinion. There was the anti-myth of Holocaust and the heroic ideal of the Third Jewish Commonwealth. A generation of compromise between the secular government and the rabbinate, in the absence of a liberal-democratic constitution, had produced a rhetoric that frankly justified Israeli national rights in the terms of Orthodox claims. The clearer reasons for the Zionist revolution having faded, a new Zionism emerged.

i

On April 6, 1967, Israeli jet fighters shot down six Syrian planes over the Golan Heights, and later that day other Israeli jets buzzed Damascus. This was the culmination of many months of tension. Three years before, in 1964, Israel's National Water Carrier had been completed, diverting the headwaters of the Jordan River from the Sea of Galilee to Israel's southlands. The source of this water was on the Golan Heights, runoff from Mt. Hermon and the springs at Banias. In response to the Israeli project, Syria had begun to build its own diverting facilities, which the IDF had attacked again and again.

Another source of tension was in the new rivalry among Arab leaders. Syrian Ba'athists had come to power in Damascus in February 1966, seceding from the Iraqi Ba'athist regime in Baghdad (which in 1963 had overthrown the Soviet-backed dictator Abdul Karim Kassem). In the flush of its revolutionary coup, the new Syrian regime remained keen to participate in a front of "progressive" Arab regimes against Israel and "imperialism"—a front to be armed by the Soviet Union and organized by President Gamal Abdul Nasser of Egypt. Iraqi Ba'athists, for their part, remained dissatisfied with both Soviet patronage and Nasser's leadership. Though they could hardly oppose common action against Israel, they retained deeply anti-Communist views and (if only in this, like Kassem) considered Iraq the natural center of the Arab nation.

Nasser, to be sure, was willing to cooperate in some new offensive against the "Zionist entity" and thus hold off Iraq's challenge to his leadership. Since 1957 the Soviets had armed Egypt beyond his expectations and had even supplied advanced MiG-21 jet fighters. Nasser certainly had no reason to pacify the American government by this time, in spite of U.S. government support for Egypt after the Sinai campaign. Egyptian relations with the Johnson Administration had deteriorated badly over Nasser's war in Yemen against Saudi Arabian forces. In 1964, Nasser had orchestrated the founding of the Palestine Liberation Organization in Gaza, though this remained a rather weak group led by an extremist lawyer from Acre, Ahmed Shukeri. (It was Shukeri who first bragged that Israelis would be "thrown into the sea.")

Matters came to a head between Syria and Israel in the spring of 1967. Damascus and the PLO openly plotted a campaign of sabotage inside the Jewish state; there were dogfights in the air— for Syria, the worst came on April 6—and Israeli and Syrian artillery exchanged rounds on a weekly basis. The Soviets were not eager to have their unexpected (and hence, all the more precious) Syrian client take on the Israelis, but after the debacle in Iraq, Soviet leaders were anxious that the pro-Soviet regime in Damascus be neither undermined nor discredited. They were deeply dismayed that Israeli warplanes could appear in the skies over the Syrian capital. Soviet intelligence reported to Nasser again and again that Israeli troops were massing for a strike against Syria, and Soviet leaders implored the Egyptian President to help preempt them. Nasser blustered and did nothing; the rest of the Arab world waited and watched. Finally, on May 13, the Soviets warned of an impending large-scale invasion of Syria.

On the face of it, this was an absurd charge. The Israeli government had not even mobilized reserves. Yet Nasser determined that he could not fail to respond again; as one keen observer put it, he "chose to believe" the Soviet report.[1] Egypt had any number of diplomatic options at the United Nations and might have reinforced the PLO, but having committed himself to action, Nasser chose to act rather more grandly than anyone expected. On May 14, he put the Egyptian Army on maximum alert and, in a well-publicized show, marched troops across the Suez Canal into the Sinai. On May 16, 1967, Nasser demanded the evacuation of the United Nations peacekeeping force from observation posts on the Egyptian side of the Sinai frontier. Just two days later, he notified the UN that Egypt had "terminated the existence" of the emergency force on its own soil and in the Gaza Strip.

Remarkably, United Nations Secretary-General U Thant—a colleague of Ben-Gurion's old friend U Nu—capitulated to Nasser's demands immediately, though the emergency force, the UNEF, had separated Israeli and Egyptian armies since 1957 and, by its very presence, imposed a measure of tranquillity. This was an important diplomatic gain for Nasser, who seemed genuinely surprised by the speed of UN compliance. But he was not yet done. On May 22 Nasser began to mass troops in the Sinai, and announced that Egypt would reimpose a blockade on Israeli shipping through the Straits of Tiran. Inevitably, he began to feel he could unite the Arab world and enlisted Syria in a pact of war against the Jewish state. Throngs danced in Cairo, chanting: "Haifa, Jaffa, Acco." On May 26 the Egyptian President addressed Arab trade-union leaders:

> The battle will be a general one and our basic objective will be to destroy Israel. I probably could not have said such things five or even three years ago. If I had said such things and had been unable to carry them out my words would have been empty and valueless. Today, some eleven years after 1956, I say such things because I am confident. I know what we have here in Egypt and what Syria has. I know that other states—Iraq, for instance, has sent its troops to Syria; Algeria will send troops; Kuwait will send troops . . . This is Arab power.[2]

In actuality, Iraq did not commit forces to Syria until the third of June. But the mere fact that Nasser could announce the impending reconciliation of the two Ba'athist rivals, Iraq and Syria, seemed to imply that general war was imminent. By May 30, after the Straits of Tiran were closed to Israeli shipping, Jordan had joined them as well—a sure sign that the whole Arab world was smelling, if not victory, then an honorable bloody standoff. Israeli columnists, meanwhile, had begun to ask how long it would be before Israel undertook some preemptive action; if Hussein, weak as he was, could not stay out of the Arab alliance, why should anyone doubt that a battle was coming? The blockade of the Gulf of Aqaba was, after all, an act of war. Israeli reserves were gradually mobilized to full force.

Israeli Foreign Minister Abba Eban frantically canvassed diplomats in Western Europe and the United States to pressure Nasser into a reversal of course. French President Charles de Gaulle chose this very moment to threaten a cutoff of arms to the country that fired the first shot—an especially bitter blow, since France supplied Israel in particular and the IDF would almost certainly have to strike first. Nasser began to savor what seemed to him, at the very least, a diplomatic windfall. Were the superpowers in any position to reimpose the agreements of 1957? President Johnson reassured Eban privately that the United States fully backed Israel's position. A plan emerged in the American Department of State to get up an international "flotilla" to test, or pierce, the Egyptian blockade. But there was a serious question in Washington whether America could guarantee Israeli shipping in the Gulf of Aqaba. The U.S. military could not take on what some U.S. officials feared might turn into "a second Vietnam."[3] Analysts in the American Department of Defense secretly expressed confidence that the IDF would win a decisive victory in any event, that Israel ought to be "unleashed" against Nasser's Soviet-supplied arsenal. Eban got official sympathy and encouragement, but he got no maritime convoy. The Israelis were told to be patient.

．

Most Israelis had long ago adjusted to their country's encirclement; even to the endless cycle of strike and counterstrike on their borders. Yet the Israeli public was both surprised and chagrined by Nasser's newest gambit. A whole generation had grown up accustomed to a quiet border in the south, and to taking for granted Israel's port in Eilat and the network of relations Eilat afforded, not only trade and cultural exchanges with Black Africa, but also oil shipments from Iran. Going back to conditions prior to the Sinai campaign was unthinkable. And although few Israelis doubted that the IDF would prevail in any military combat—the IDF had obtained the latest French Mirage jets and some American and British armaments—it was not at all clear how great a price would have to be paid in the lives of Israeli soldiers or how decisive the victory would be. Veteran Israelis wondered if the allegedly less highly motivated children of the new immigrants could be counted on to fight as bravely and efficiently as their own Sabras had done in the Sinai campaign. The Sheraton and Hilton Hotels on the beaches of Tel Aviv were quietly converted to emergency hospitals; a rumor spread that the government anticipated as many as 50,000 casualties from Egyptian aerial bombing and Jordanian shelling. To the man and woman on the street it seemed that, just five years after trying Eichmann, Jews were again being abandoned to the wolves.

Nor did Levi Eshkol's self-mocking Yiddish wit reassure the public at this difficult moment. It has been said of Eshkol that, given the choice between tea and coffee, he'd reply, "Half and half." Israelis asked themselves if Eshkol, who held the Defense portfolio in addition to the premiership, had David Ben-Gurion's stomach for combat; could he be decisive, this man of higgling and bargaining? "The ledger is open and the pen is writing," Eshkol announced solemnly over the radio on May 28, as if to ward off the Arab leaders with threats of eventual retaliation. But Eshkol muffed some lines of his speech and even dropped the text on the floor; for what seemed endless seconds the airwaves were dead, except for the sounds of the Prime Minister fumbling to pick up his papers. Miserable as that radio performance was, it only seemed to match the lackluster showing of the Histadrut-dominated economy during the preceding year, for which Eshkol was thought to be mainly responsible. For a growing Israeli minority—disproportionately young, disproportionately Oriental, the coming Israel—Eshkol's manner implied that a corrupt clique of Histadrut old-timers had brought national disaster this time, not, as with the Lavon Affair, merely political disgrace.

Eshkol's speech belied the vigor with which he and his Chief of Staff, General Yitzchak Rabin, had readied the IDF, in particular the air force under General Ezer Weizman. Israeli intelligence had prepared plans for a preemptive assault on the Egyptian airbases with exquisite care: the plans noted the patterns by which Egyptian pilots scrambled, the time it took them to eat breakfast, the decoys on Egyptian runways. The Southern Command's tank force under General Israel Tal was correspondingly poised to move on Gaza. Still, the public's perception of vacillation and moral uncertainty at the top was not without foundation. Anxiety plagued some of the very people who had planned for the crisis; indeed, on May 23, in secret, Rabin had suffered a temporary nervous collapse. (He later confided that he believed he would be responsible for the "destruction of the Third Temple.")

Menachem Begin now demanded that Ben-Gurion—of all people, the murderer of the *Altalena!*—be brought back to head a government of national unity. Eshkol and the other old Mapai leaders of the governing Labor Alignment rejected this demand out of hand, though they could not deny the mounting feeling that a "wall-to-wall" coalition was the only way to rally the nation. Curiously, Ben-Gurion was by now rather wary of provoking military hostilities with Egypt in any case, and counseled patience, much in the manner of President Johnson; he was eighty years old, much of his former militancy was exhausted and he was scarcely the right choice to prepare the country for war. Ben-Gurion did suggest bringing into the government as Defense Minister his favorite Chief of Staff, Yigael Yadin, and the idea of stripping Eshkol of the Defense portfolio immediately began to gain momentum. For his part, Yadin still shunned political life and suggested that Moshe Dayan be appointed—to which Golda Meir objected strenuously. She put forward the name of Yigal Allon.

Before long all the parties in the Knesset save Mapai and Achdut Ha'Avodah had come to believe that Dayan was the best choice. Dayan had brought victory in the Sinai in 1956, they argued— though beneath the surface it was understood that only a man not associated with the old guard would satisfy the youthful, changing Israeli public. Even the National Religious Party began lobbying on behalf of Dayan—a bitter moment of truth for the people of the old Labor Zionist era. On June 1 Eshkol capitulated. Dayan moved into the Defense Ministry; Begin's Gahal joined the government, as did Rafi.

ii

As Israel's politicians made peace, its youth prepared for war. The entire reserves, which constituted about four fifths of the IDF, were in place for an attack by June 1; nearly every factory in the country was forced to shut down or run at reduced capacity. It was as if the whole country were standing still; one waited for the inevitable and prayed to be delivered from it. Israel had never fought a war on more than one front before; studies showed that any war which lasted more than a week, which involved more than 100,000 troops, would do irreparable damage to the country's economy. People asked how long the government could wait for Great Power initiatives. Yet Dayan exuded an infectious cockiness and the public mood began to change. In a huge bluffing operation, Dayan furloughed a large part of the reservists and declared that Israel would wait a number of weeks for international pressure on Nasser to build. In fact, the decision to attack was already taken. Would the Egyptians use missiles in the case of a war, reporters asked. Dayan replied, "Let them try." Then he brilliantly addressed the troops, calling them as if to a moral crusade, reminding Israeli soldiers of what would be expected of them in victory. ("We are the defense force of Israel," he announced, "not the slaughterers of Egyptians.")

The pace of events quickened. Iraq sent its troops to the front on June 3, and the Israeli Cabinet went ahead with plans for a preemptive strike. This came on June 5. On the morning of June 6, Radio Cairo provided some anxious moments (and comic relief) when it proclaimed in stiff Hebrew that Egyptian forces were advancing "bechol ha'chaziot"—they meant to say, Israelis knew, "bechol ha'chazitot," "on all fronts," though what they actually said was "in all brassieres." By the evening of that second day, Israelis were whispering to each other that Egypt's air force had been destroyed; in fact, 320 of Nasser's 340 combat aircraft had been reduced to flaming ruins the day before. At the start of the fighting, Eshkol secretly cabled Hussein that if Jordanian forces stayed out of the hostilities, the Israeli Army would leave the eastern front in peace. But Nasser lied to Hussein about Egyptian losses, and the Hashemite King precipitously authorized Jordanian artillery to fire rounds on Jerusalem. By June 8 Israeli soldiers had captured the Old City of Jerusalem. On June 13 Israeli forces stood at the Suez Canal and on Mt. Hermon overlooking the Golan Heights. They also stood at the Jordan River in Jericho.

Ironically, Dayan had originally determined that Israeli advances should stop well short of these goals. Since he had expected Israel to annex much of the Sinai this time, he had not wanted to close the Suez Canal, which he shrewdly surmised would provide Egypt an ongoing *casus belli*. Moreover, Dayan had been skeptical of Jordanian military intentions. He had certainly not been eager to take the casualties entailed by an offensive for Jerusalem, and he reckoned that Jordanian guns would cease firing as soon as Egypt's defeat in the Sinai became known. Besides, he asked his generals, how could Jerusalem be taken without capturing its West Bank hinterland as well? Dayan expressed similar reservations about attacking the Golan Heights, even after Syrian gunners opened up on the Hula Valley from Tel Azazyat and other fortifications. After all, Syrian forces on the Golan posed no threat comparable to Egypt's in the Sinai, and he was justifiably cautious regarding potential Israeli losses in any two-front war. Dayan explicitly forbade the Israeli Army to engage the Syrians and insisted that assaults on Jordan and Syria were political decisions he was not yet prepared to authorize; they were not military decisions *per se*.

Yet the ease with which the Egyptians had been defeated infused government leaders—including Dayan—with an intoxicating feeling that this was precisely the political moment to be seized. Even such Mapai bosses as Eshkol and Finance Minister Pinchas Sapir—people who had tended to follow Sharett's cooler approach to military action—swept aside former reservations. By the evening of June 7, Begin had made an unlikely partnership with Yigal Allon to convince Dayan of the need for an assault on Jerusalem. As things turned out, the Defense Minister was hardly in need of persuasion. Once Jerusalem had been conquered, representatives of the labor settlements in the north, long suffering under Syrian guns, prevailed upon Eshkol to force Dayan's hand on the Golan. Dayan continued to balk. But then, on June 9, word reached Dayan that Egypt was suing for peace at the United Nations. It was suddenly clear to him that the IDF could move on the Syrian front without further challenges from Egyptian forces in the Sinai. Without consulting the Cabinet, Dayan ordered General David Elazar to attack. That decision—or so Dayan's father, Shmuel Dayan, noted with obvious pride—marked the moment at which Moshe finally redefined the war: "from a defensive operation to a war to regain the land of Israel's forefathers."[4]

The nation's deliverance was singularly caught—in a way, consecrated—in popular songs of thanksgiving. A few weeks before the war, a new song, a paean to ancient Jerusalem entitled "Jerusalem of Gold," had been introduced at the annual folk festival. After the Old City was taken, the song's writer, Naomi Shemer, penned a new verse suggesting how the battle had been a kind of spiritual deed: "We have returned to the springs, to the marketplace; the trumpet sounds on the Templemount . . . Again, we shall descend to the Sea of Salt by way of Jericho!" When an uncharacteristically brash Levi Eshkol entered the Old City, he declared: "I see myself as a representative of an entire nation and of many past generations whose souls yearn for Jerusalem and its holiness."

"Jerusalem of Gold" was, to be sure, a song of mourning as well. Many paratroopers fell storming Lion's Gate, and in all, 769 young men had been killed in the battles, a quarter of them lost in the battle for Jerusalem. But necessary as it was to mourn, it was hard to walk the streets of Jerusalem lugubriously. Who could say those soldiers had died in vain? The ancient city seemed to fit the Zionist saga like the last piece of a puzzle. On June 12, the government announced to the Knesset that Israel would never "return to the conditions that existed a week ago."[5] The nation sang: "Oh, Sharm-el-Sheikh, we have returned to you the second time, you are in our hearts forever." Rabin addressed the nation on the radio: "No one in the world understands how it was done and foreigners seek technological explanations or secret weapons." The streets chirped back the jingoistic song they had sung before the war: "Nasser is waiting for Rabin, ay-yey-yey: let him wait and not move, for he'll come, one hundred percent!" It was on June 28 that the government jubilantly announced the annexation of Arab East Jerusalem. The radio played Shemer's ballad over and over; it was by now an anthem.

The politician whom the war had made indispensable was Dayan. He had prepared none of the IDF's battle plans and had at first suggested pursuing modest aims, but few in the Israeli public were privy to the government's deliberations and fewer now wanted to bother with the details. Dayan was a continuing symbol of intense spirit and action: his virility and reticence, his youthful petulance, his patched eye, his pedigree in the Valley of Jezreel— all of these contributed to his legend. Crowds formed wherever Dayan's car stopped; poll after poll showed him the majority's choice for Prime Minister, and by a wide margin. Young Israelis increasingly asked themselves how long it would be before the Mapai clique stepped aside. Not that Dayan needed the Prime Minister's job to shape defense and security policy, which was actually what he cared about. Several weeks after the war, he told reporters with an air of perfect nonchalance that the Israeli government was "waiting for a phone call" from King Hussein. The inference to be drawn was that Israel could not dream of a better strategic position; if the Jordanian monarch wanted to talk, then *he* should call.

But precisely what was there to talk about? As he entered ancient Jerusalem, Dayan had said: "We have returned to all that is holy in our land. We have returned never to be parted from it again." On August 3, Dayan spoke on the Mount of Olives, at a reinterment ceremony for soldiers killed in Jerusalem in 1948:

> Our brothers who fought in the War of Independence: We have not abandoned your dream, nor forgotten the lesson you taught us . . . We have returned to the mount, to the cradle of the nation's history, to the land of our forefathers, to the land of the Judges, and to the fortress of David's dynasty. We have returned to Hebron, to Shechem, to Bethlehem, and Anatoth, to Jericho and the ford over the Jordan.
>
> Our brothers, we bear your lessons with us . . . we know that to give life to Jerusalem we must station the soldiers and armor of the IDF on the Shechem mountains, and on the bridges over the Jordan.[6]

It must be said that Dayan's growing reluctance to consider a return of territory was only one side of an emerging deadlock. Later in August the Arab states met in Khartoum. Hussein argued for recognition of the Jewish state, in the hope that a peace settlement would lead to full Israeli withdrawal from the occupied territory, including Jerusalem, which had been the jewel of his united kingdom. But the leading Arab regimes were less drastically dismembered than Jordan and more sensitive to appearing soft on the Palestinian issue, the principal symbol of pan-Arabism. The PLO rejected any possible compromise that would return what they still defined as Palestine to Jordanian control. Arab states had been humiliated; most were in no mood for compromise. On September 1 the Arab leaders jointly announced a rejectionist policy, what came to be called the "three no's" of Khartoum: no peace, no recognition, no negotiation.

The Israeli government immediately declared in response that it would be willing to negotiate—"everything," according to Abba Eban—but only for a *full* peace, which is to say, for a peace that would be achieved by direct talks "without preconditions." These would lead to a formal treaty, free passage through the Suez Canal and the Straits of Tiran, and a solution to the "refugee problem" in the context of regional cooperation—fair terms, in retrospect—and there can be little doubt that, despite Begin's opposition, Eshkol was himself still open to major concessions, perhaps total withdrawal. Yet the mood of the government and the public began to shift during the fall after the Khartoum rebuff. Israeli government demands for peace became more absolute and more hollow. On September 24, Eshkol announced plans for the resettlement of the Old City of Jerusalem, of the Etzion bloc— kibbutzim on the Bethlehem-Hebron road wiped out by Palestinian gangs during the 1948 war—and for kibbutzim in the northern sector of the Golan Heights. Plans were unveiled also for new neighborhoods around Jerusalem, near the old buildings of Hebrew University and Hadassah Hospital on Mt. Scopus. An Arab village along the Latrun highway was leveled, and plans went forward for an expressway to join Jerusalem and Tel Aviv. By the end of October, a prominent rabbinic authority in an official position had stipulated that Jewish law prohibited ceding an inch of the West Bank.

That rabbi was not dictating foreign policy, of course, and as late as November Israeli representatives to the United Nations discreetly helped to frame Security Council Resolution 242, which called for the return of "territories occupied in the recent conflict" in exchange for peace and recognition. In December the Israeli Cabinet agreed, albeit without enthusiasm, to receive U Thant's appointed mediator, Dr. Gunnar Jarring of Sweden. However, in view of Israel's annexation of Jerusalem and its development plans for various parts of the West Bank, the question that began to plague any effort to mediate the dispute was, again, just which territories would the Israeli government be willing to return in the context of any negotiated settlement? (That Israeli representatives to the UN negotiations over Resolution 242 had insisted on the deletion of the article "the" from the original phrase "*the* territories occupied, etc." suggested that nothing could budge Israel from the Old City of Jerusalem and other places.) True, Israel still faced the absolute refusal of the Arab governments to enter into any kind of negotiations, to recognize Israel or learn to live with it. Yet not even Hussein, who was open to recognition, would have dreamed of making peace with Israel without getting back sovereignty over Arab Jerusalem and the Old City's holy mosques.

In Dayan's view, moreover, the principle that Israel should control occupied territory in perpetuity amounted to a new and exciting strategic conception of deterrence. The new borders were of such disadvantage to Israel's neighbors that even good armies would hesitate to attack from them. How could demonstrably inept armies cope with them? The Arab governments had brought about the new state of affairs by their own intransigent actions; they had again and again closed the door to peace. Dayan invited Israelis to enjoy a condition of "no war" instead; this presumably permitted the Jewish state to retain the fruits of victory—land, armistice, retribution—without formal peace, but also without fear of attack. The new borders, what Dayan began to call "security borders," or *gevulot betachon,* implied a certain faith in the future; that Jews, for once, could control the future whatever the Arab governments did. As if to underline how Israeli policy could determine events with or without Arab acquiescence, Dayan boldly removed all barriers in the formerly divided Jerusalem and reopened the bridges over the Jordan River; quietly, systematically, he laid the foundations for military government. The phone call from Hussein never came. Yet the nation sang: "The bounties of peace are not a dream, they will come as surely as the light at noon; all this will come tomorrow if not today, and if not tomorrow then the day after."

iii

If Israeli perceptions of peace hardened with Dayan's arguments for "security borders," then perceptions of Zionism were transformed by the heroic quality of victory, the rush of American Jewish support, and the sheer pleasure of claiming proprietary rights in the ancient land. What had seemed an increasingly disingenuous, even archaic Zionist debate before the Six-Day War now seemed to have a focus, even an agenda: the potential unity of Eretz Yisrael. This was hardly planned, though the war had gained what can only be called a kind of Zionist momentum. For Menachem Begin, certainly, the war had had two stages: a two-day defensive operation against Egypt and a four-day offensive against Jordan and Syria to unify the land of Israel. Dayan's views had not been this clear-cut, and Eshkol's even less so, but like most Israelis, both had been caught in the grip of an irresistible opportunity to materialize—and in the most perfect possible way—the ideals of the new generation: power, Bible, defiance, settlement, economic growth; in short, Ben-Gurion's post-Zionist matrix.

This is not to say that Israeli leaders provoked the war or welcomed it. Had the 1967 war not been forced upon the Jewish state, the strident national myths of statist ideology might have receded, and the more liberal side of statism might have come to the fore— sentiments implying the need to dismantle the Histadrut and challenge the virtually authoritarian power of the Mapai leadership itself. (Significantly, the Rafi platform of 1965 had called for meritocracy, scientific advance, electoral and constitutional reform; also, greater economic liberty, greater individualism and pluralism, more respect for the cultures of Jews from Middle Eastern society.) As it was, however, the 1967 war seemed to confirm statism's darker visions. Had not U Thant's capitulation proved that international guarantees were phony; had not Khartoum proved that Arabs considered Jewish national existence itself to be a kind of fatal provocation? True, President Johnson was now willing to sell Israel advanced weaponry. But did this not prove once and for all—

what political Zionists had insisted from the start—that Gentiles respect only power?

Dayan proposed the construction of new settlements in North Sinai. "Better Sharm-el-Sheikh without peace," he said, "than peace without Sharm-el-Sheikh." For Dayan, Zionism itself became a way of acknowledging that, for Jews, peace was merely a respite from combat, the product of force, an incidental reprieve from the permanent threat of destruction. This is the way he put the case three years later:

> Death in combat is not the end of the fight but its *peak*; and since combat is a part, and at times the *sum total* of life, death, which is the peak of combat, is not the *destruction* of life, but its fullest, most powerful *expression* . . . Man goes to his death in battle not to bring *salvation to others*, not in order to sacrifice himself to the future; man goes to battle because he, personally, is unwilling to surrender, to be defeated; he does not wish to fight for his *survival*, but for him the content of his life and death is merely the supreme expression of the ferocity of his struggle . . . it is a personal dynamic death, intrinsic in the *struggle*, the combat, not the war . . .
>
> Most of my years have been spent in one way or another in the company of fighters. These men lived in the shadow of death yet this did not darken their lives or brand them with the stamp of grief. The opposite was true. These men were driven by an immense *life force*, and it is this life force that makes them fighters.[7]

Old-guard leaders of Mapai who were immune to Dayan's macabre reflections increasingly became hostage to his influence. They were unsure of their right to pronounce about military affairs and were, in any case, no longer in control where they seemed to preside. Dayan had redeemed their political careers and made all Israeli leaders international heroes overnight. After the Six-Day War, Israel became the darling of a Vietnam-stricken America; a poster of an Orthodox Jew, resembling Eshkol, changing to Superman in a New York phone booth became the rage of college dormitories across the United States. Nor was celebration confined to America. Czech students defiantly sewed Israeli flags onto the backs of their jackets; Poles marched spontaneously to share in the defeat Israelis inflicted upon Soviet clients. Even Soviet Jews boldly began clamoring for exit visas. Old Labor Zionists began to ask themselves if Zionist history made sense only in the secular categories of their youth. There was Jerusalem, prosperity, unity. If the victory could not, strictly speaking, be called a miracle, was there not something mysterious and wonderful about Jewish history that they had missed?

Many Diaspora Jews obviously thought so, or seemed to by the way they demonstrated solidarity with Greater Israel as they had never done for the Labor Zionist revolution. Fifty thousand volunteers from the United States and Canada had streamed into the country during the summer of 1967, to work in orchards and on assembly lines while the reserves were at the front; UJA contributions quadrupled. Such manifest demonstrations of American Jewish support constituted something of a false dawn for active Zionism in America and Europe; no mass immigration of Jews was forthcoming. Yet Israeli journalists, some who had flirted with Canaanism in the early sixties, were deeply impressed by the worldwide expressions of loyalty. Many Israelis wondered if immigration would match what had come in the wake of the War of Independence. Some seriously asked themselves if more territory—and what territory!—would be needed to accommodate the influx.

The hardening of Israeli attitudes toward territorial compromise brought with it a new Zionist vocabulary of double-think names for occupied territory: Yehuda V'Shomron ("Judea and Samaria") for the West Bank, Shechem for the Arab town of Nablus. The Education Ministry quickly issued new national maps of Eretz Yisrael to public-school classrooms, maps without clear borders, or even the "green line," which had previously divided Israel and the West Bank. What such maps implied was that young people could sacrifice for the new Jewish commonwealth in the manner of their grandparents; they could rehearse pioneering exploits next to which their own middle-class lives had come to seem sadly inconspicuous.

Moreover, the Six-Day War had been the first national event in which soldiers from the Sephardi community distinguished themselves in large numbers. Sephardi families instinctively took to the Promised Land, which they saw in terms of displays of religiosity and revenge against former oppressors. The new Zionism was a kind of invitation to the Second Israel as a whole to participate more fully in the national life. It promised a kind of social breakthrough, including economic expansion and a pool of willing Arab laborers. Many young Sephardi Jews were quick to grasp that they could climb out of poverty to a rung above.

Arthur Koestler once quipped that the Zionist pioneers of the Yishuv suffered from a kind of "claustrophilia." The opposite was true of their children, who, for twenty years since 1948, had been raised bounded by hostile neighbors and the sea; dozens of teen-agers had risked everything—indeed, some had lost their lives—crossing the Jordanian border to see Petra. After June 1967, all Israelis, but particularly the young, seemed to break their fetters. People who had never entered a synagogue in their lives now lined up to join a prayer quorum at the Wailing Wall or the Tomb of Rachel, on the road outside Bethlehem. Israelis toured the Sinai, camped on the Gulf, and dove to view the coral along the Red Sea coast. They visited Jericho and Hebron like privileged tourists, developing tastes for quaint old restaurants and Persian antiques—also for the *souk*, the glitter, the bargain.

> Jews streamed to Jerusalem [Golda Meir wrote], but we went also to Bethlehem, Jericho, Hebron, and Gaza, and Sharm-el-Sheikh . . . Offices, factories, kibbutzim and schools—all participated in the end-less excursions . . . Cars, buses, trucks, and even taxis, packed to the brim, criss-crossed the country for months en route to Mt. Hebron in the north or Mt. Sinai in the south . . .
>
> Everywhere we went during that elated, almost carefree summer, we met the Arabs of the territories that we now administered, smiled at them, bought their produce . . . sharing a vision of peace that sud-denly seemed to become a reality . . . But we were not prepared to go back where we had been on June 4, 1967. That accommodating we couldn't be, not even to save Nasser's face or to make the Syrians feel better about not having destroyed us.[8]

To Mrs. Meir, but also to the great majority of her fellow citizens, it seemed the best, most Zionist thing to do was nothing.

iv

Over the two or three years following the 1967 war, new Zionist ideas found more and more champions in and out of government. Eshkol's National Unity government was dominated by a coalition of Dayan, the National Religious Party, Begin, and also by the

increasingly hawkish ministers from Achdut Ha'Avodah, most notable among them, Israel Galili. Accordingly, Dayan told the mayors
of West Bank villages that they had better get used to a long-term
Israeli occupation, and that his "open bridge" policy might well be
the Israeli government's final policy. He continued to reassure the
public that the *status quo* was superior to any conceivable negotiation; and consciously in the manner of the Labor Zionists of the
1930s, he argued that a final settlement might be left to the next
generation to work out, that Israel should meanwhile "establish
facts." The leaders of the NRP, themselves increasingly pressured
by young scripture hawks in Bnei Akiva yeshivas, demanded
that a national referendum precede any negotiations over the
sacred patrimony. Begin, for his part, called for outright annexation and threatened to quit the coalition if UN Resolution 242 was
allowed to apply to "Judea and Samaria." His nationalism began
to seem prophetic, familiar, even avuncular. It grew more intense
when Nasser initiated the War of Attrition on the Suez Canal in
1969.

Yigal Allon suggested a plan by which Jerusalem and the Gush
Etzion salient near Hebron would be annexed to the Jewish state,
with Israel's coastal plain protected by a string of settlements
running along the ridges of the Judean Hills and along the Jordan
River. Jordan, by this plan, would get back most of the heavily
populated areas of the West Bank, including the towns of Nablus,
Jenin, Ramallah, and Hebron, and would be expected to help set
up a Palestinian "entity" in the Hashemite state. Allon's plan was
by no means satisfactory to the Jordanian government. Yet it came
to be regarded as the Israeli government's most moderate policy.
Meanwhile, West Bank squatters were tolerated, partly because
they consciously presented themselves as the new incarnation of
pioneering Zionism.

Perhaps no Israeli more clearly confirmed the passing of the
mantle of Zionism to statists of Dayan's stripe—and thence to
Revisionists and NRP messianists—than Natan Alterman, the laureate of the Labor Zionist Yishuv. During the Lavon Affair, Alterman had drifted into anti-Lavon circles; he joined the Rafi Party in
1965. In the two years after the 1967 war, Alterman broke with the
Labor Alignment completely and joined the front ranks of Ha'Tnua
Le'Maan Eretz Yisrael Ha'Shlemah, the "Whole Land of Israel

Movement," which had been founded by an old leader of the kibbutz movement, Eliezer Livneh. (Alterman was joined by the Palmach writer Moshe Shamir, and by Ben-Gurion's old leftist nemesis from Achdut Ha'Avodah, Yitzchak Tabenkin.) Alterman advocated outright annexation of conquered lands, for the sake of "completing" Zionism. One Land of Israel Movement spokesman, the Revisionist writer Israel Eldad, chided the ambivalence of the old Labor establishment:

> Precisely those people who from the point of faith and ideals were furthest from the concept of a "great-State Zionism," and in the past derided those who wanted a state . . . it was precisely those individuals who reached sovereignty—state budgets, flags, ceremonies, international and national receptions. They never dreamt of this in their little Zionism of "furrow after furrow." But they became intoxicated with statehood . . . and its satisfactions blinded them, making "Israel" the essence and the Land of Israel "foreign territory" . . . For years one had to fight to make Zionism state-oriented. Today . . . one has to fight that the state should be—Zionist![9]

In Eldad's blunt, cryptic lexicon, Zionism assumed that Jews were only an instrument to liberate the land. "The existence of the partition of the country is a function of the division of the existential soul of Zionism . . ." And as if to console the nation that its "guilt feelings toward the cosmopolitan ideals of socialism and liberalism" were misplaced, Eldad revealed what he supposed to be the new Zionism's secret:

> Had it only been possible to implement "utopian Zionism" in peace, to convince the Arabs that we bring blessings to them too, and socialists —liberation and progress. But in vain! What is left is the feeling that, perhaps, Zionism is after all only a reactionary movement.

The corollary inferred by Livneh, Alterman, Eldad, and the rest was that Diaspora Jews would not be "ingathered" unless it was to redeem the unified land, that the twin goals of the new Zionism —more land and more immigrants—were inextricably bound together. To give up the land would be to betray Zionism itself. "There is no alternative of going back to the old boundaries," said a Movement spokesman; "we are condemned to be strong."

The cadres of the Land of Israel Movement never attracted a mass following. Yet the inertia of the occupation itself was on their side. In contrast with the heady dreams of the new Zionists, old Mapai bosses such as Pinchas Sapir had rather drab arguments, warnings about the "demographic problem," implying that annexation would mean the end of the Jewish majority, hence the Jewish state. In fairness to Sapir, he had been part of Eshkol's pre-1967 government, which had made an honorable effort to boost libertarian forces in the country by lifting military rule of Israeli Arabs in 1966. Sapir's logic in and of itself testified to his belief in majority rule. Yet Sapir's demographic argument only reinforced the notion that an integralist Jewish state without Arabs was Zionism's basic goal, and that the major problem of the occupation was that it might force more Arabs into the Jews' midst; his view only exacerbated the alienation of Israeli Arab citizens, who now made up about a sixth of the population. Worse, Sapir's demographic criteria made the values of secularism and democracy seem a failure of nerve. They evoked memories of the ghetto Jew who could not make up his mind whether adopting the Gentile's freedoms was worth having to live with Gentile neighbors; they evoked images of Histadrut bosses looking for facile compromises.

.

The one important leader who would not appropriate the new Zionist logic was Ben-Gurion himself, though, again, it was widely perceived to be the completion of his own statist ideal. Ben-Gurion had not lacked expansionist plans of his own; Sharett's diaries reveal that as early as February 1954 Ben-Gurion had proposed an attack upon Lebanon, to set up a pro-Israeli, Maronite regime there. But for Ben-Gurion, this old plan had nothing to do with his Zionism. Statism seemed to him a guide to culture, not diplomacy. It was certainly not an invitation to take the whole of ancient Eretz Yisrael, where one million Arabs lived. How could Israel rule one million Arabs and remain a democracy? Indeed, statism had been Ben-Gurion's way of saying that Zionism was dead, that a militant defense strategy superseded national construction. The Negev was Ben-Gurion's idea of the new frontier. Though he had publicly embraced Begin after the 1967 war, Ben-Gurion remained uncharacteristically ambiguous even about East Jerusalem, which he once referred to as so much "real estate." Correspondingly, and with increasing vehemence, Ben-Gurion insisted that the West Bank and the Sinai be kept only as bargaining chips.

Yet ironically, Ben-Gurion was increasingly isolated during his final years, just as Weizmann had been. Dayan mused:

> When I look out of the window and see the sun setting, I understand it to mean that the sun is setting and that evening is coming on . . .
>
> [Ben Gurion] sees the stars move and the cosmos turn on its axis, and the entire world in flux . . . [He] is incapable of considering a single detail as a separate entity.[10]

Dayan's words now read like self-reproach; in fact, they were meant as a kind of self-congratulation. Dayan proudly took a narrow and mechanistic view of his mentor's heroism and ideology—this, alas, is what disciples often do—and fancied himself on the verge of fulfilling Zionist dreams more completely than the Old Man had dared to. Yet Ben-Gurion only specified what common sense failed to grasp: that occupied territory—and why not all of it?—could be exchanged for peace treaties, free access to the Suez Canal, security guarantees; also demilitarized zones, diplomatic exchanges, joint commercial ventures. So long as the Arab states resisted peace and recognition, and the guarantees these implied, then there would be no return of territory. If the Arabs agreed only to a partial peace, to begin the process of normalization, then there might be return of only a part of the territory. But what was the point of Israel annexing the West Bank and starting the construction of suburbs and settlements?

Until his death, during the disturbing gray days just following the Yom Kippur War in 1973, Ben-Gurion reiterated these points in interviews and periodic public appearances at Sde Boker. Few took them seriously; one heard grumblings about his senility.

v

In 1968 the Labor Alignment had been expanded to include both Rafi and Mapam. Levi Eshkol died in February 1969, just as Nasser was escalating the skirmishes along the Suez border into a full-scale war of attrition. When the newly reconciled factions of the party could not decide between Dayan and Allon as Eshkol's successor, they coaxed Golda Meir out of the party secretariat and offered to put her at the head of the government. "I couldn't make up my mind," Mrs. Meir recalled. Polls showed that she was the preferred candidate of some 3 percent of the public, "not exactly a landslide," and a "seventy-year-old grandmother was hardly the perfect candidate . . ."

> On the one hand, I realized that unless I agreed there would be a tremendous tug-of-war between Dayan and Allon, which is the one thing Israel did not need then. It was enough that we had a war with the Arabs on our hands; we could wait for that to end before we could embark upon a war of the Jews. On the other hand, I honestly didn't want the responsibility, the awful stress, the strain of being Prime Minister.[11]

In the end, Mrs. Meir agreed to abide by din ha'tnuah, the "verdict of the movement." With dispatch, she formed a government quite similar in composition to Eshkol's, except that her disarming blend of sarcasm, blunt patriotism, and righteousness— so apparent in this and other quoted passages—quickly won for her much more popularity than Eshkol had ever enjoyed. She was a grand and charming woman, tough as leather, sentimental, affectionate, and clever; in a way, the perfect leader to preside over the novel unity that the Six-Day War had ushered in. In the fall, the Labor Alignment won a resounding victory at the polls, 56 seats to Gahal's 26.

Had Golda Meir underestimated her ability to cope with the burdens of office? This seems doubtful. Four pivotal questions remained to be settled when she assumed office. They were, in order of importance, the fate of the occupied territories and the question of Jewish settlements, the style and structure of the economy, the related identity of the disaffected Second Israel, and, finally, the lingering question of whether Zionist institutions—those which impinged on matters of religion and state, say, or on the status of Israeli Arabs—ought to be retired. Mrs. Meir continued to command a great personal following, but few Israelis would say in retrospect that she gave moral leadership on any of the great issues. Where she did act, it was largely to keep her fractious coalition together.

Mrs. Meir proved wanting in vision, incapable of speaking about

any national problem except in terms of an anachronistic Labor
Zionist rhetoric which sounded hypocritical even to diehard Labor
supporters—and all but guaranteed the accession to power of her
old Revisionist rivals. She even failed to keep the Labor Alignment *apparat* free from the ordinary corruptions which would sink
any party and particularly one that had reached ideological exhaustion. When backbenchers opposed her, she fired them. (The list
included such brilliant people—all doves—as Arie Eliav, "Lova,"
the secretary of the Alignment; Yitzchak Ben-Aharon, the secretary-
general of Histadrut; Shulamith Aloni, the civil-rights activist.)

On the question of the occupied territories, Mrs. Meir's impulses
proved particularly disastrous. She would not endorse annexation,
but she never clarified the reasons for her opposition. At first she
seemed to subscribe to the Allon plan, which called for an eventual
territorial compromise with Jordan and the Palestinians. At the
same time, she insisted that *she* was, or had been, "a Palestinian,"
too, as if to imply that the Palestinian claim to national identity
of any kind was fraudulent, if not outpaced by events. Mrs. Meir's
attitude was not the critical one; claiming incompetence, she all
but ceded responsibility for security issues to Dayan and the other
hard-liner in her "kitchen cabinet," Israel Galili. Yet when illegal
Jewish settlements sprang up on the West Bank, modesty did not
inhibit her.

> After 1948, the Jordanians would not let Jews visit the holy Cave
> of Machpelah or pray at the tomb of the Patriarchs. But Hebron
> remained holy to the Jews, and on Passover eve, 1968, after it had
> come under Israeli administration, a group of young and militant
> Orthodox Jews, defying the military ban on settlement in the West
> Bank, moved into the Hebron Police compound and remained there
> without permission . . .
>
> The Arabs immediately set up a great hue and cry about the Jewish
> "annexation" of Hebron, and Israeli opinion was very divided about it.
> On the one hand, the would-be settlers were obviously trying to create
> a *fait accompli* and force the Israeli government to make up its mind
> prematurely about the future of the West Bank and Jewish settlement
> there. On the other hand . . . was it logical for the world (including
> our own superpious doves) to demand of a Jewish government that it
> pass legislation expressly forbidding Jews to settle anywhere on earth?[12]

To be fair, the War of Attrition made any peace seem far away; Soviet advisors had begun to intervene directly in battle. Every day pictures of soldiers killed in the Canal Zone appeared in the newspapers; casualties eventually came to some 3,000, and deaths exceeded the number killed during the Six-Day War. Moreover, Palestinian terrorism was a day-to-day crisis, from both the West Bank and Gaza. Yet, in retrospect, can any statement seem a greater invitation to catastrophe than Mrs. Meir's glib reference to Jewish settlements? The settlers were not, as Mrs. Meir implied, out to win the right to own a home in some Arab neighborhood. Rather, they explicitly sought to establish a bridgehead of Hebrew sovereignty in Hebron and elsewhere. By the time Mrs. Meir left office, several thousand settlers had built homes all over the West Bank, the Golan Heights, and North Sinai.

As to the larger issue of Israel's defense strategy, Mrs. Meir's record was equally questionable. She viewed the Arabs as implacably hostile. Yet she refused to plan, as Dayan was at least willing to do, for a generation of deadlock and conflict. During the latter part of the War of Attrition, Mrs. Meir approved deep-penetration raids against Cairo. (She had been encouraged in this course, ironically, by Allon and the other moderates in the Cabinet, who remained determined to reimpose the *status quo ante* and thus recreate conditions for peace talks like those that had been created after June 1967; the Khartoum spirit, Allon reasoned, would not last forever.) Significantly, this was the one important time Mrs. Meir opposed Dayan, who was cool to the raids and had proposed a unilateral Israeli pullback from the Canal Zone instead. More than ever, Dayan wanted Nasser to reopen the waterway, precisely because Israeli plans for settlements in the North Sinai Rafah salient were already being put into effect. But the air raids only provoked the Egyptian government to acquire from the Soviets one of the most elaborate antiaircraft missile defenses in the world, and increased Egyptian dependence on Soviet advisors. Mrs. Meir asked newly elected President Nixon to supply Israel with Phantom jets, which were eventually delivered. The Phantoms became increasingly vulnerable to Egyptian ground-to-air missiles; seven were shot down in June and July of 1970.

Later in the summer, American Secretary of State William Rogers mediated a cease-fire along the Suez Canal, demanding that Israel formally accept UN Resolution 242—if it wanted more advanced weapons from America. Mrs. Meir accepted Rogers's stipulation, and she brought her government around over Begin's vociferous objections—among them that the United States had no choice but to back Israel in a war against a Soviet client. Mrs. Meir did insist that Egypt undertake to bring no new antiaircraft missiles into the Canal Zone; Begin openly doubted that Nasser could be trusted. Then Rogers's cease-fire negotiations gave way to their logical complement, a more ambitious plan for a comprehensive political settlement—the so-called Rogers Plan—which envisioned Israeli withdrawal to the 1967 borders beginning with the Sinai, in exchange for peace and recognition from Egypt. Curiously, this proved too much for Mrs. Meir. Having defied Begin, she adopted his negotiating position, demanding "direct negotiations without preconditions"; she made it plain that Israel would never withdraw from Jerusalem and other territories.

As a result, the Israeli government had neither peace talks nor the ability to take any unilateral military action. Once the cease-fire was in place and the Rogers Plan rebuffed, Nasser predictably ignored his promise not to bring new missiles up to the Canal Zone. In anticipation, Menachem Begin and his Gahal bloc had resigned from the Cabinet, accusing Mrs. Meir of appeasement and warning of a military catastrophe. Critics on Mrs. Meir's left simultaneously distanced themselves from her, observing that this was hardly the time or the way to confront Begin on the question of UN Resolution 242. Had she not made the principle of partition seem like nothing more than unwillingness to stand up to the American administration? Certainly, Begin's annexationism pertained to a vision of the Jewish state, not to the trustworthiness of any Arab leader.

In any case, Dayan and the ministers of the NRP now hardened the government's line, becoming virtual allies of Mrs. Meir's opposition. Embarrassed and pressured, she solemnly promised the NRP not to negotiate over the West Bank without first calling an election. That promise not only proved to be the *coup de grâce* for the Rogers Plan but it preempted subsequent diplomatic initiatives, such as President Anwar Sadat's efforts to renew United States mediation after the Egyptian government expelled all Soviet advisors in 1972. Most important, perhaps, her undertaking preempted King Hussein's offer of a federal plan for the West Bank during

1972 and 1973. None of these plans would necessarily have produced peace, but pursuit of any one of them might have prevented another war.

On economic matters, Mrs. Meir continued to refer to herself as a socialist and spoke with enormous apparent conviction of her desire to close what she called the "social gap" in Israel. Yet from 1968 on, Pinchas Sapir deliberately set out to industrialize and develop Israel's economy by subsidizing private investments even more than Ben-Gurion had done, claiming that Israel must rationalize production by encouraging market forces. At first this was intended to lure foreign Jewish investors. (Sapir, Mrs. Meir wrote, began every conversation with an American Jew with the question: "How much money do you have?" To her surprise, most of them told him!) But Sapir also decided to attract capital with matching, low-interest government loans to assure a profitable return. He soon extended this practice to domestic investors.

Thus, Sapir's policy rapidly degenerated into the "system"—ha'shitah—in which the Finance Minister, putatively acting in the name of a workers' state, acquired unprecedented economic power. Sapir bestowed bundles of money and wry jokes on the big-shot entrepreneurs of Tel Aviv, London, and New York, and on the Histadrut enterprises as well. Accordingly, the economy prospered; by 1971, Israeli GNP was growing at a rate of 7 percent a year, largely owing to the tremendous rise in investment from abroad, and to Israel's domination of labor and patterns of consumption in the West Bank and Gaza Strip. But as always it was the kibbutzim, moshavim, and Chevrat Ovdim enterprises which did especially well in this new economic boom, as did private defense and housing contractors with connections to the Labor machine. Sapir even poured money into a crony's automobile plant, which finally failed. Worst of all (as it was later revealed), high Labor officials such as Asher Yadlin, the former head of the Histadrut Sick Fund, initiated kickback schemes to profit the party.

Some in the Second Israel adjusted nicely to the boom, especially those family businesses which could expand in the rapidly developing service sector. The Carraso brothers sold cars; the Shirazi family sold television sets. Small contractors made good livelihoods building the Bar-Lev defense line along the Suez Canal.

Yet instead of creating the streamlined mixed economy which Ben-Gurion had hoped to develop, Sapir's market approach only created an oligarchy of people with connections in both the public and private sectors. It also generated uneven growth and the obvious enrichment of Israel's bourgeoisie—all behind the mask of the traditional Labor movement. Under Sapir, government spending went out of control, which became apparent after the 1973 war dampened Israel's post-1970 boom. His resignation (and subsequent death in the fall of 1975) left his economic program in a shambles; without him there was nobody left to manage the flow of money from abroad and to coax investors into some of the government's economically important but less profitable projects, such as the textile mills in the Second Israel's development towns.

For most in the Second Israel, the gap only grew wider. By the end of the seventies, 15 percent of the people in the top two deciles of income were Orientals; nearly 50 percent in the bottom two deciles.[13] Protest movements, like the Black Panthers, started up in the slums of Jerusalem. Mrs. Meir responded sanctimoniously that it was more important to put a roof "over a Phantom than a Panther." She reminded the Moroccan youth of the ration cards of the fifties, of her eggplant dinners. She challenged them to be grateful. (They demonstrated in front of her residence instead. Some placards read: GOLDA, TEACH US YIDDISH.) Nor were her deteriorating relations with the Second Israel irrelevant to her Zionism, since Mrs. Meir's government's approach to immigrant absorption only exacerbated hard feelings among poorer Israelis. New immigrant housing was luxurious as compared with the Shechunat, the North African neighborhoods from the fifties. Immigrants could import all consumer durables tax free for three years—cars, washing machines, furniture—while young couples who had served in the armed forces could not afford to move out of their parents' flats.

If we judge by the superficial identification of Diaspora Jews with the Jewish state, Mrs. Meir's tenure can certainly be counted a success; few other Israeli leaders have so captured the imaginations of Western Jewish audiences. Moreover, this was a time when nearly 100,000 Jews from the Soviet Union were settled in the country. To Israelis Mrs. Meir flatly declared that if the choice ever came down to social fairness or *aliyah*, she would certainly choose the latter. Yet by the time she left office, more Soviet Jews were emigrating to the United States than to Israel. Zionism had necessarily become little more than a catchword for Mrs. Meir, an emblem of patriotic unity. She used the word to defend whatever would hold her coalition together, even if this meant pandering to the Orthodox forces in the country, whom she ought to have confronted.

Consider, for example, her behavior in the wake of the infamous "Shalit case." In January 1970, the Israeli Supreme Court handed down a landmark judgment which might have greatly furthered Israeli civil liberties. Benjamin Shalit and his wife, Ann, who was of Scottish origin and had never converted to Judaism, had petitioned the Interior Ministry to have their children accorded the legal status of "Jew." (The Shalits were professed atheists, but Jewish status was an important legal designation, especially in view of the social and economic benefits accruing to Jews by extragovernmental agencies such as the Jewish Agency; the Shalits pointed to their strong participation in the "national-historical" community of Jews.) After eighteen months of deliberation, a divided court backed up the Shalits' petition. Of course, the National Religious Party was outraged. The decision implied, in effect, that Jewish nationality could be claimed by anyone born in Israel, including atheists who were not of Arab origin—a clear departure from the norms of Orthodox law. NRP ministers threatened to resign from the government if the Knesset did not pass legislation amending the Law of Registration of Inhabitants to overturn the court's interpretation; in the absence of a broader constitutional framework, the Knesset was sovereign. Mrs. Meir expressed personal sympathy for the Shalits, yet her government rushed through the legislation in a matter of days. (Answering for this decision two years later, before a group of Jewish students in New York, Mrs. Meir rather impatiently explained that Israel could not have a written constitution until it "ingathered *all* the exiles." Presumably the fault lay with the students, not with her.)

Incidentally, Mrs. Meir did nothing to integrate Israeli Arabs into the national life. The one time a decision about Israeli Arabs was forced upon her, she only increased tensions. During the War of Independence, the army had ordered that the residents of the northeastern, mainly Christian Arab towns of Biram and Ikrit be evacuated for "security reasons." The residents were promised the right to return when it was safe. Remarkably, the matter dragged on for over twenty years, when, finally, Mrs. Meir's government was petitioned by the residents' priest to permit the townspeople to return. Many of Israel's writers and academics supported the petition; indeed, it became something of a *cause célèbre*, a symbol of the country's commitment to civil rights and simple equity. Mrs. Meir's own advisor on Arab affairs, Shmuel Toledano, supported the petition. The Prime Minister turned it down.

vi

The final downfall of Labor Zionism was brought on by the Yom Kippur War. On October 6, 1973, Syria and Egypt jointly attacked; in one day, Syrian forces reached the outer perimeter of the Golan Heights overlooking the Hula Valley and the Egyptian Third Army crossed the Suez Canal to the East Bank, making nonsense of the famed Bar-Lev line. Israeli counterattacks failed at first, and the IDF had many casualties. Nearly 150 Israeli planes were shot down before Israeli pilots mastered the means to overcome Soviet missiles. Moreover, the IDF proved critically short on ordnance; long wars no longer fit in with Defense Ministry plans. Panicked, the Meir government requested that the Nixon Administration airlift support. Meanwhile, Jordan sent a force to Syria, though it scrupulously maintained a cease-fire along the Jordan River. The West Bank, fortunately, remained calm. It was ten days more until the IDF, having regained its composure, pushed the Syrians back to the outskirts of Damascus. Not until three weeks later did a paratroop force led by Ariel Sharon encircle the Egyptian Third Army, after having itself crossed the Suez Canal to its West Bank. The United States and the Soviet Union demanded a cease-fire before the Third Army could be attacked. Israeli casualties numbered over 10,000.

For most Israelis, the October War confirmed the value of the territories and the shortsightedness of people in the Labor Alignment who had argued for giving them up. It made little sense now to recall Dayan's assertions that the borders were going to make Arab attacks a thing of the past; after the war, few doubted that, because of Greater Israel, the battles had been kept far away from civilian areas. Coming as it did on Yom Kippur, the Arab surprise attack provided yet another demonstration of the Arab world's enmity, much as the apparent helplessness of Arab armies up to that time had seemed to provide a demonstration of the borders' deterrent power. Some Israeli officers drew conclusions from the war quite different from what the new Zionists maintained. Generals Mattityahu Peled and Meir Pa'il charged that the very concept of security borders had become a serious liability to peace. President Sadat had spoken of peace in 1972. If this was a bluff, should it not have been called? Were not the building of settlements and the hardening of lines bound to discourage similar feelers? Other Israeli peace activists noted the strategic disadvantages of holding the territories, the attenuated lines of supply they imposed on the IDF, the need to go to a style of static defense which made hostages of front-line troops. Was not the occupation an invitation to limited war? Could Dayan speak sensibly about security borders when the lives of 2,500 young men, and the limbs of 8,000 others, were not factored into the equation? When war documents were released, they tended to confirm the view of Israel's doves. The Arab attacks had manifestly not been planned to invade the Jewish state, though no one doubted an invasion force would have gone farther had the IDF collapsed. In fact, the Syrian advance was initially halted not because of Israeli defenses but because Syrian plans simply did not call for supplying Syrian troops once they reached the edges of the Golan Heights; the Syrian Army literally had run out of gas. Moreover, far from preventing a Syrian attack, the Jewish settlements on the Golan Heights only hampered the IDF attempt to counterattack, since they had to evacuate under the worst possible conditions. For his part, Sadat had called for a cease-fire as soon as the Third Army had crossed the Suez Canal. His point was political, not military; it cost the lives of 500 Israeli soldiers on the first day. Still, a majority of Israelis were turning to the logic of annexation.

·

The war had preempted the national elections, which had been scheduled for October. After the war, it was clear that Mrs. Meir's government had lost support from both the left and the right. Dayan's return to the Labor Alignment had given the party something of a reprieve in 1969, but now even Dayan was widely perceived to be a failure: the IDF had clearly not been ready for combat. Nor had Mrs. Meir persuaded many uncommitted voters of her competence to lead. Word leaked out that she had rejected her Chief of Staff's proposal for a preemptive strike on the morning of October 6, so as not to appear to have initiated hostilities. Given the public's state of shock, the full force of the disaffection with Mrs. Meir could not surface right away. Promising wholesale reforms, she appointed a Judicial Commission of Inquiry; she implored the voters for forbearance, pointing to an impending meeting of Israeli diplomats with representatives of Arab states scheduled for Geneva in the winter. Was this the time to change horses, she asked.

When the election was finally held in December, the Labor Alignment lost five critical seats, down to 51 from 56, which gave the NRP the balance of power. Begin's new Likud bloc, the brainchild of war hero General Ariel Sharon, climbed to 38 Knesset seats, and for the first time seemed a plausible alternative to the Labor Alignment. Significantly, the Likud brought together not only Herut and the Liberals but a host of splinter parties of the right and center, including the "State List," which had originated in Dayan's Rafi. During the election campaign, Sharon had visited the troops saying, "*Al tazdiah, tazbiah!*" ("Don't salute me, vote for me!"). A majority of the army voted for the Likud opposition.[14] (This was the first time the army had not gone for Mapai and its successors.)

This shift in Israel's domestic political climate could not have been more at odds with the warming trend in the Sinai. Relations between Israeli and Egyptian troops along the Suez Canal became reciprocal; the troops attended each other's campfires and exchanged addresses. Under the pressure of political events, there were also exchanges of shells. Yet at Kilometer 101, where Israeli and Egyptian lines met, Israeli General Yariv and Egyptian General Gamsi greeted each other with genuine cordiality. Nobody was surprised when, in March 1974, the Israeli government concluded a disengagement-of-forces agreement with Egypt which permitted the eventual reopening of the Suez Canal—the first product of Secretary of State Henry Kissinger's shuttle diplomacy. Significantly, however, the Meir government flatly refused to consider any similar agreement with Jordan. The National Religious Party, increasingly associated with a new extremist settlers' organization, Gush Emunim, "Bloc of the Faithful," demanded, as the price for joining any new coalition, that Mrs. Meir put in writing what she had promised before, that her government would not negotiate return of the West Bank without first calling an election.

The Judicial Commission under Chief Justice Shmuel Agranat—

which had been appointed to determine just why the army had
been so ill prepared for the Arab assault—began its hearings before the elections. Its report was not available when the country
went to the polls in December, but it broke, with devastating
results, later that winter. Agranat reported major failures in the
IDF's General Staff and Intelligence Department: the Chief of
Staff, David Elazar, was immediately forced to resign. But the
government had refused to authorize the commission to look into
the failures of the Cabinet. Consequently, though Elazar was re-
proached, Dayan was exonerated—a relief to Mrs. Meir, since
Dayan had insisted that ministerial responsibility should be collective. Many were outraged. After the report was released to the
public, one civic-minded war hero—an officer by the name of Motti
Ashkenazi, whose bunker on the Bar-Lev line was the only one not
to fall to the Egyptian onslaught—stood vigil alone outside the
Knesset demanding Dayan's resignation, a small act that set off
what came to be known as the "earthquake." By the time another
week went by, thousands had joined him. (Revealingly, when
Ashkenazi addressed the swelling crowd, his first demand was for a
written constitution; the crowd burst into wild cheers. To all, the
performance of the army was but a symptom of something deeper.)

Ashkenazi's protest movement succeeded better than anyone expected. Fed up with the houndings of the press, also with Dayan's
repeated threats to quit if the entire government did not back him
up, Mrs. Meir announced her own resignation in early April. In June,
having concluded a disengagement agreement with Syria, she
brusquely left the stage.[15] Her government was succeeded by a new
one, headed by Yitzchak Rabin, whose main claim to the leadership
—or so said Pinchas Sapir, the person who engineered Rabin's
majority in the Labor Alignment's central committee—was that,
having been ambassador to Washington during the war, he had
been far away from the *mechdal* (literally, the "debacle") which
had ruined every other minister's reputation.

．

Rabin's was, to be sure, not an auspicious beginning. But he came
into power with a measure of public goodwill, if only because he
was the first of the "younger" generation to hold the Prime Minister's
job. Nor did Rabin seem unwilling to consider some diplomatic
departures at first. Before winning the post, he had declared that it

would be no hardship "if Israelis had to get a visa to visit Rachel's Tomb," a statement to rally the dovish forces Mrs. Meir had estranged. Rabin also gained support from the larger secular center when, after he took office, he responded to the NRP's demand that the criteria of Jewish law apply to the Law of Return by forming a minority government without any religious party. (Secretly, the Prime Minister even met with King Hussein to discuss the possibility of a disengagement-of-forces agreement.)

Yet in view of the persistence of Palestinian terrorism—during the summer of 1974 there were attacks in Kiryat Shemona, Ma'alot, and Jerusalem—would the public be willing to support a Jordanian initiative regarding the West Bank? Rabin could not say. The Israeli public had proven fickle regarding the fate of all negotiations and generally responded to government leadership; polls showed widespread opposition to both disengagement agreements during the time they were negotiated and overwhelming support for them after they were signed. Yet the country's two major dailies, *Ma'ariv* and *Yediot Achronot*, warned Rabin not to include Arab members of the Knesset in the count of his narrow parliamentary majority. "Reliance on the Arabs would not be a violation of democratic principles," *Ma'ariv* stated, "but it would surely violate *Zionist* principles." In the end, Rabin proved too timid to follow through on any new course. Instead of calling a new election, to pursue a new initiative with Jordan or just to get a mandate of his own, Rabin virtually capitulated to the National Religious Party and the Labor right wing, then led by Dayan's friend and protégé Defense Minister Shimon Peres. (Peres coveted Rabin's job and steadily undermined him.) Rabin took the NRP back into the government and put an end to any peace initiatives. Significantly, later in the summer of 1974 the Arab states met in Rabat and stripped Hussein of the right to represent the Palestinians, awarding it instead to the PLO.

The rest of Rabin's term may be briefly noted, for it left no lasting mark on what was to follow. Rabin concluded an "interim settlement" with Egypt in September 1975; Henry Kissinger had threatened to suspend some American aid when, in March, the Israeli government had turned down a first draft agreement; by the fall, Rabin gave up trying to win a statement of non-belligerency from Sadat. Israel pulled back beyond the passes, left the oil fields at Abu Rodes, and obtained the right of navigation through the

Suez Canal. Rabin called this a piece of land for a piece of peace. He presented the pact to his increasingly demoralized followers as an effort to buy time. Yet when in late 1976 strong feelers went out to Rabin from the Egyptian President through the Rumanian government, Rabin ignored them. He thought, or so one close advisor later confided, that it would be impolitic to visit Communist Rumania before an election. (A similar feeler to Menachem Begin helped bring Sadat to Jerusalem in November 1977.)

In his government's settlement policies, Rabin tacitly acquiesced in the Zionist logic of his opposition. He did little to remove West Bank squatters from such settlements as Elon Moreh, near Nablus, in the heart of Arab population centers. Rather than build a constituency for more territorial concessions in exchange for peace treaties, Rabin sought to work with his NRP coalition partners. He also shunned any philosophical debate, which caused Lova Eliav to quip bitterly that Rabin was "a Sphinx with no secrets."[16] The Entebbe raid improved his standing, but also the logic of staking Israel's security on military power. In any case, perceptions of Rabin's diplomatic artlessness increasingly merged with accumulated resentments for suspected Labor corruption. Asher Yadlin and the director general of the Finance Ministry, a protégé of Sapir, Michael Tzur, were caught in various extortion schemes. The Housing Minister, Avraham Ofer, was suspected of shady deals. In the winter of 1977, Rabin was himself forced to resign when it was discovered that he and his wife, Leah, had kept a small illegal bank account in the United States.

Rabin's government could not even point to economic gains. For the three years before the 1974 election, inflation continued to run at between 40 to 50 percent. As a result, real wages fell sharply, while labor unrest (including wildcat strikes) and white-collar crime increased dramatically. Much of this inflation was attributable to a rise in the world price of oil and food staples and, more significantly, to Israel's huge defense budget comprising about 40 percent of total expenditures and 35 percent of GNP. But tax evasion was rampant. Sapir's undistinguished heir, Yehoshua Rabinowitz (who was rewarded with the Finance Ministry after being defeated by a Likud candidate for reelection as mayor of Tel Aviv), did little to salvage the situation. The Israeli government was still stuck with outstanding low-interest loans amounting to billions of

Israeli pounds and had to borrow at interest rates fully 25 percent higher than those at which it had been lending. Almost 26 percent of Israel's budget was now gobbled up by new subsidies for capital investment and by servicing the debts on old ones; literally, socialism for the rich. To make matters worse, state welfare programs had to be cut correspondingly. By 1977 they accounted for only about 18 percent of the national budget.

vii

If political revolutions can be compared to kicking through rotting doors, Israel's Labor Alignment provided just such a barrier to Likud's stunning victory on May 17, 1977.[17] Yadlin and Tzur had been jailed. Avraham Ofer committed suicide before he could be thoroughly investigated. Shimon Peres had succeeded Rabin, but Labor's campaign under Peres was uninspired and was pursued without genuine enthusiasm. The Friday before election day the party took a full-page advertisement in *Ha'Aretz* in which a number of prominent academics grudgingly and circuitously explained why voting for the Labor Alignment was the least depressing of available choices.

When times were better, Labor highhandedness was overlooked; but times were not good in Israel in the spring of 1977. Conservative estimates put the amount of unreported or "black money" income in Israel's economy at around I£15 billion, then worth about $2.5 billion. This money was spent quickly, mainly on luxury housing or imported commodities, and traded on the black market for export to Switzerland. Merchants grew accustomed to 50 percent profit margins on durable consumer goods. Clearly, the Labor Party had created a crippled, incompetent, highly inflationary capitalism which was hard on the workers and middle-class wage earners who had once been Labor's natural constituency outside the workers' agricultural settlements. It was hardest on the Second Israel. Yet it also offended the sensibilities of the same intellectuals and businessmen who most benefited from it. The Israeli middle class wanted to see the ethics of a market society honestly declared and enforced, and their vote reflected the view that the country had in fact become a market society of profit-seeking enterprises that ought to be administered by those who recognized this fact and were not cynical about it. Many of those middle-class voters supported Yigael

Yadin's new centrist list, the Democratic Movement for Change, or DMC, which won 15 seats.

Yet the real source of the anomie which seized so many voters in the weeks before the election was in the feeling that the very survival of the country was at stake, that the machinery of daily life was out of control. Some of this feeling, generated by the failing economy, was sublimated into the language of Zionism: how, it was asked, could Israel survive the Arabs if people did not want to live there? The question was whether the time of Labor Zionism finally was over. During the election, young voters from all backgrounds turned to the Likud and to the National Religious Party in overwhelming numbers; for these parties consistently promoted a rhetoric which frankly justified the West Bank settlements, while Rabin's government was often equivocal about them in principle and helpful to them in practice. Unfortunately for Labor, in this election young Israelis tended to vote to get their parents to live up to what they perceived were the latter's ideological pretensions. Yitzchak Navon explains his party's defeat this way:

> By 1977, the Israelis were not a people of movements anymore. Israelis less and less liked to think hard about national problems. They needed their government to provide security and protect their salaries; they wanted leaders they could trust. By 1977, Labor had obviously failed to do what was needed or be what was wanted. The party was split since the Lavon Affair. Tabenkin was with the Whole Land of Israel group. Rabin knew only the party hierarchy. Inflation was high. There had been a surprise attack which Israel repulsed only at great cost.
>
> There was no majority for Begin in foreign affairs. But people trusted him to know what to want. They were supporters of strong leadership, and were willing to give a chance to people who seemed to speak for unity and strength. Oppositions do not win elections, governments lose them.

Yet Navon's analysis omits something that helps to explain Likud's growing power. While Yadin split the Labor vote, the two parties still comprised only a parliamentary minority. Likud, by itself, won a solid 45 seats; and it had put together an impressive political coalition which, even then, seemed likely to endure and even expand considerably: the young, the Sephardi groups, the old underground right, the petit bourgeois entrepreneurs. Added to these were 150,000 immigrants from the Soviet Union whose hatred for things socialist exceeded that of even the most extreme Sephardi Jews.

There is an analogy to be drawn here between the Likud of 1977 and the American Democratic Party of the 1930s. The Likud, too, consolidated the forces of the young, the new immigrants, the less-well-educated, the ethnic have-nots, who wished to participate in national life. While American Republicans spoke grandly of free enterprise during the 1920s, the immigrant Irish, Italians, and Jews, and the blacks interpreted this—quite rightly—to mean freedom for the big corporations, for Wall Street, and for the men who frequented restricted country clubs. The Israeli Labor Party, similarly, spoke grandly of socialist ideals in 1977. But the young Israelis and the Sephardi immigrant communities took this to mean the extension of Histadrut patronage—and also protection for kibbutzim, moshavim, and public corporations. European-descended managers and union bosses rarely exposed themselves to votes from the rank and file, most of whom were Sephardi.

Some young Sephardi voters turned to Begin in 1977, though they may have been indifferent to his West Bank policies. Most certainly did not want a state with as many Arabs as Jews. Begin's free-market economic policies did not promise to allay the distress of the Second Israel. But again, diplomacy, economics, and demographics are not always the point. Sometimes one stakes a claim on what can only be called the national identity. For the Second Israel, there was pleasure in a kind of political retaliation, what the French call *ressentiment*. Besides, when the bread runs out, there are always circuses.

9 / The West Bank Tragedy

Though new Zionists such as Moshe Dayan had planned Israel's national agenda since the 1967 war, the election of Menachem Begin in 1977 did not necessarily mean that a majority of Israelis had come to perceive annexation of the occupied territories as a foregone conclusion. Yitzchak Rabin's interim agreement with Egypt suggested that American diplomacy might yield another breakthrough; revealingly, Dayan himself would not agree to join Begin's first government as Foreign Minister unless Begin promised in writing not to extend the reach of Israeli law to the West Bank and Gaza. Polls showed support for a policy of restraint.

Yet for most Israelis, especially young people, Greater Israel had become something of an answer to the military failure of 1973, and West Bank settlers seemed to provide a clear national purpose where the tradition of Labor Zionism did not. What the new Zionists could not do was solve Labor's demographic question: how to incorporate the territories into Israel and yet keep the state democratic and Jewish. But, then, Labor had itself annexed Jerusalem, and this seemed enough to make moot Labor's hope for a territorial compromise with Jordan; in the absence of compromise, why not extend the logic of annexation to Jerusalem's hinterland?

By 1981, the year Begin won a second term, some 20,000 Jewish settlers had begun to live in the territories, and the most serious peace initiative in Israel's history had failed. Even more important, perhaps, a whole generation of Israelis had grown up in Greater Israel and could not remember what it felt like to be bounded by the old green line. The West Bank and Gaza were still not part of Israel. Even so, Labor had cut the road to annexation—and Begin paved it.

i

During the June 1967 war, some 1.1 million Palestinian Arabs living in the West Bank and Gaza came under Israeli rule. Most of the 750,000 people on the West Bank had become citizens of the Hashemite Kingdom of Jordan, although some had long-standing grievances against the regime. As early as 1949, West Bank lawyers tried to petition the UN peace conference at Rhodes to found a Palestinian state, as was authorized by the Partition Resolution of 1947. The Jordanians shunted them aside. In occupying the West Bank, Israel took over an area roughly equal to that of Israel itself without the Negev Desert—some 2,270 square miles. Its six small cities—East Jerusalem, Hebron, Ramallah, Nablus, Jenin, and Bethlehem—had not been doing well under Jordan; King Hussein preferred to develop the East Bank. Between 1952 and 1961, the size of East Jerusalem's population of 60,000 people stayed the same, while Amman grew from 108,000 residents to a quarter of a million. Eighty percent of the population of the West Bank lived in 396 villages, and 40 percent of the labor force worked in agriculture. They fared no better than the Palestinians in the cities. When the occupation began, officials counted only sixty-seven tractors in the area. Of the 200,000 people in UN refugee camps, half had fled across the Jordan to the East Bank during the six days of fighting in 1967.

Most of the West Bank's leading urban families and virtually all of its rural clans had cooperated with Hussein. Two of the most prominent East Jerusalem Palestinians, Anwar el-Khatib and Anwar Nusseibah, had been ministers in the Jordanian government. Sheik Ali Ja'abri, the influential mayor of the more rural, and more pious, town of Hebron, had allied himself and his considerable following with Hussein. Only in Nablus, the largest city outside greater Jerusalem, had serious anti-Jordanian feeling emerged. A few months before the June 1967 war, Hussein's forces put down anti-government protests in the city, killing twenty young demonstrators. The mayor, Hamdi Kenan, was quick to grasp that feelings of Palestinian nationalism might intensify once Israeli tanks moved into the town.

On the Gaza Strip, on the other side of Israel, the 350,000 Palestinian residents, with the highest density of population in the world, had been ruled by an Egyptian administration much worse than Jordan's. Denied Egyptian citizenship, Gaza's Palestinian residents were stateless. They needed little encouragement to hate the Israelis from Nasser's officials, who either fomented, or turned a blind eye to, raids by *fedayeen*—Palestinian terrorists—on southern Israeli settlements. It was in this atmosphere that, in 1964, Nasser had helped to set up the Palestine Liberation Organization. The 150,000 refugees Israeli troops found in Gaza were much poorer than those on the West Bank and were treated with contempt by the permanent residents of Gaza City and Khan Yunis. The prominent Gaza families were not inclined to provide political leadership under Nasser's regime and left to the UN the work of housing and educating the refugees. Fewer than 20 percent of the Palestinians in Gaza could make a living from the land.

Conditions were far better under Hussein on the West Bank, where 50,000 agricultural families farmed about half a million acres. Hussein's police sharply restricted liberties but judiciously created a civil service for West Bank teachers, postmen, clerks, etc. No doubt the more prosperous West Bank residents resented Hussein's discrimination: in 1965 the West Bank contributed to Jordan 2.4 million more dinars toward indirect taxes and public services than it got back. But these families nevertheless owned enterprises accounting for 40 percent of Jordanian GNP in industry, banking, and trade. In contrast, Gaza's industry was as feeble as its agriculture. Twenty percent of family incomes came from UN welfare payments.[1] With UN schooling, the rate of literacy among all refugees was high. It is not surprising, therefore, that after the Israelis took over the West Bank, Palestinians tended to be peaceful, while Gaza was seething with violence. Indeed, Hamdi Kenan and Sheik Ja'abri seemed to take the occupation in stride, in spite of Kenan's submerged Palestinian nationalism and Ja'abri's Jordanian connections. Both mayors and most of the Jerusalem notables assumed Israeli rule would be temporary until some new arrangements, favorable to their autonomy, could be worked out with Hussein. Encouraging them in their view was the fact that Moshe Dayan permitted the bridge across the Jordan to remain open.

There were immediate and frightening problems engendered by the threat of terrorism and the counterthreat of Israeli retaliation. In 1967 alone, Israeli officials conducted some 1,100 trials for various security offenses on the West Bank, and in Gaza there was frequent, bloody violence. In 1970, 106 Gaza residents were killed, 94 by terrorists and 12 by Israeli forces. Of some 1,200 young people arrested during the disturbances, half confessed to guerrilla activities.² Under General Sharon, then commander of the southern front, Israeli forces finally regained control of Gaza by cracking down harshly. (Only in 1972 did Rashad a-Shawa, a member of Gaza's most prestigious family, agree to become mayor, and he subsequently used his nonpartisan relations with Jordan, Egypt, and the PLO to provide the competent leadership that was previously lacking.) Between June 1967 and September 1970, Israeli authorities had to deal with more than 5,000 attacks and bombings of one kind or another in the occupied territory.

Yet perhaps the most lasting effect of terrorism was the extent to which it helped preclude serious diplomacy. For Dayan, terrorism was a clear reason never to return the West Bank or to allow Palestinians to organize politically. As one looks back through the history of West Bank occupation, Dayan appears as something like a modern pharaoh who, facing a plague of terror, inflicted hardships on his alien subjects, inflamed their desire for freedom, and increased the prestige of the radicals among them. (It should be noted that, in 1968, Yasir Arafat was still an unlikely guerrilla, crisscrossing the West Bank on a motorcycle while trying to build an underground network of young nationalists.) Immediately after the Israeli Knesset annexed East Jerusalem, the army destroyed several Arab villages, claiming that their location made them potential threats to the Latrun highway to Jerusalem. The government built new Jewish neighborhoods in Jerusalem, displacing Arab residents. Protests from the West Bank leaders and intellectuals were turned aside. When Palestinian leaders requested Dayan to allow them to organize their own political parties independent of hostile Arab states, he replied, "Not under the Israeli flag"; under Dayan's rules, local leaders were expected to help keep order but were severely restricted as a political group, not allowed to travel freely or hold open political meetings. Dayan, moreover, set up the policy of collective punishment by which the security forces routinely destroyed the homes of relatives and neighbors of convicted terrorists. No doubt, such punishment intimidated many of the other people, but it only stiffened the resistance of those young men who were drawn to radical politics. By 1968, Hamdi Kenan was saying openly that were he a young man, he would join Fatah, and Fatah denounced the other mayors and leaders for their ties to the old feudal order.

By 1973, about a third of Gaza's laborers—including many children—were employed on Israel's farms, factories, and construction sites, earning better money than they had ever known. About 50,000 workers were commuting from the West Bank by this time, most under the auspices of labor exchanges set up by the Labor government. This pattern of employment contributed to calm, but it also led, as A. D. Gordon might have predicted, to new kinds of resentment. Significantly, Dayan's policy also undermined the traditional urban leaders and landlords. He promoted quick economic development as a way of quieting Palestinian restlessness. The gross product grew by 14.5 percent annually between 1968 and 1973 in the West Bank, and 19.4 percent in Gaza. Agriculture was rapidly being mechanized: Meron Benvenisti points out that many West Bank Palestinians who profited from Israel's economic boom used the money to purchase land.[3] (The number of tractors rose to well over a thousand by 1972.)

Thus, the typical peasant became less isolated and more dependent on urban mechanics and merchants. The landscape of his town was dotted with television antennas; his children were seeing doctors—infant mortality was reduced by half—and more of them were attending school. Most interesting, between 1967 and 1980 the number of classrooms in the West Bank almost doubled, from 6,167 to 11,187. The student population rose from 250,000 to 400,000, a change that no doubt had the effect of reinforcing radical politics. Yet as the social gap closed between Arab notable and Arab peasant, the Arab middle class did not much prosper. In 1967 Arab banks were closed and merchant classes began to face Israeli competition. High per capita growth stimulated the integration of the occupied territory into Israel's economy. Even under Labor governments, by 1977 the West Bank was exporting 91 percent of its commodities to Israel. There was little capital investment in the West Bank economy itself, and Israeli banks were unwilling to extend credit.

Would it not have been much better for local manufacturing to have been encouraged? Then the old Jerusalem and Nablus middle class might have evolved into an industrial leadership independent of the largesse of the Gulf countries and more able to deal on nearly equal terms with Israel's new entrepreneurs—which might have yielded mutual political confidence as well. As it was, the West Bank became almost totally dependent on the Israeli economy. Between 1974 and 1978, when the Israeli economy went into recession following the costly war with Egypt and Syria, the West Bank's rate of growth sharply declined to 5.1 percent and Gaza's to 4.5 percent. Subsequent recessions in the Israeli economy hit Arab workers first.

.

The difficulties of their economic and social position undermined Kenan and Ja'abri, el-Khatib and Nusseibah; but so did Israeli diplomacy, which, though justified by officials as a response to terrorism and PLO rejectionism, seemed to be more the product of Israeli military and political complacency, at least until the October War in 1973. After the "black" September of 1970, when Hussein killed many Palestinians and drove PLO leaders and thousands of refugees to South Lebanon, the West Bank remained relatively calm. Soon thereafter, in the fall of 1972, the Jordanian regime proposed a federal plan for the territory which Israel turned down, mainly because Hussein insisted that East Jerusalem and the mosques come under his sovereignty. During the October War, the West Bank again did not become violent, but by now Hussein was losing his prestige in the territories. He tried once more to initiate negotiations, hoping for an agreement on disengagement of forces similar to the ones that Israel concluded with Egypt and Syria during the spring of 1974. The new Rabin government showed some interest during the summer; again, Rabin secretly met with Hussein to discuss the question of a withdrawal from Jericho. However, Rabin could not summon up the courage to defy his National Religious Party coalition partners or face an election. Peres was still in league with Dayan, and Dayan's heart had been hardened by terrorist attacks such as the one at Ma'alot—also by the accusations that he had failed to prepare for the 1973 war.

When Rabin floated the possibility of a disengagement-of-forces agreement with Hussein, Gush Emunim, which had been founded in 1973, circulated a petition among public officials ruling out all negotiations for "Judea and Samaria." Dayan, along with a majority of members of the Knesset, signed it. Rabin then turned Hussein down, for want of a mandate to negotiate any new arrangement for Jerusalem or to return any part of the West Bank, a decision he would come to regret. In the fall of 1974, the Arab states, meeting at Rabat, stripped Hussein of the right to negotiate for the territory and endorsed the PLO instead as the sole legitimate representative of the Palestinian people. Arafat triumphantly addressed the UN General Assembly in November; West Bank and Gaza Arabs were deeply impressed.

Significantly, Gush Emunim quickly thereafter established itself as the essential voice of the new Zionist program. Its founders had come out of the strident young guard of the Mizrachi movement, the Bnei Akiva organization—e.g., Hanan Porat and Chaim Druckman. For them—young men with gleaming eyes—the Promised Land was united and the Messiah was at hand. One leader expostulated: "Amos was here, David was here, he tended his sheep here, everything that makes us a nation happened here." The group even attracted some Labor Party hawks, not only the people of the Whole Land of Israel Movement, but tough army *moshavniks* who frequented the ultra-nationalist Ein Vered circle (which Amos Elon had dubbed the "agrarian reaction"). These people were impressed by Gush's commitment to what looked like the kind of settlement they, the pioneers, had performed in their youth. One often heard the point that the Gush Emunin were the only Israelis in the country "with civic idealism."

Gush Emunim influence grew also in the middle classes, their cadres' knitted yarmulkes becoming the symbol of the postwar Zionist sacrifice. During the Kissinger initiatives of 1974, Gush Emunim organized street demonstrations of 100,000 people or more. (On one of the American Secretary of State's shuttles to Jerusalem, Gush demonstrators shouted, "Jew-boy, Jew-boy!" at him, as if to suggest that any Diaspora Jew was sly and grasping and willing to forsake the Jewish nation for private gain.) Yet did anybody else's interpretation of the Zionist past make sense? The Labor Zionist mainstream was in disrepute, except for the historic accomplishment of *hityashvut*, or "pioneering settlement," which Gush Emunim people seemed to be emulating. It was hard not to see in the Gush's enthusiasm the reassurances of religion, unity, continuity. Besides, the men of the *yeshivot* had fought with extraordinary bravery in the October War. For many, Gush settlements seemed a reincarnation of halcyon days, of more noble historical efforts than the styles of Tel Aviv seemed to promise. In fact, Gush Emunim settlements not only helped to bring about a PLO victory over Hussein; they also became the main impediment to improving relations with the new, more nationalist politicians who emerged on the West Bank once the old guard of pro-Jordanian leaders like Sheik Ja'abri had been made somewhat obsolete by the decision at Rabat.

By the time Mrs. Meir left office in 1974, many Gush settlements had sprung up, with and without the government's consent. By 1976, more than thirty settlements had been implanted on the West Bank, ramshackle affairs to be sure, but led by religious zealots, like Rabbi Moshe Levinger, who illegally moved his followers to Hebron in 1968 and then established the Kiryat Arba quarter outside the city. Then there were more settlements, such as Elon Moreh, which were founded by the Gush Emunim in the spaces between the West Bank's most populous cities. (It is curious that Gush Emunim successfully promoted its devotion to settlement in, of all times, the years following the October War. Israelis knew that the counterattack on the Golan Heights had been delayed in desperate efforts to evacuate the settlers there, including hundreds of women and children. It was obvious folly to hold the Heights in order to prevent attack on civilians in the Hula Valley and then put civilians directly in the line of fire of 1,200 Syrian tanks and 2,000 artillery pieces. Surely, Gush Emunim settlements were not aiming to secure the kind of advantage that Labor settlements had secured in 1948. The Gush meant to secure the whole territory of Eretz Yisrael, where "security" had taken on a kind of absolute meaning for them, more fit for religious rhetoric than military judgment.)

.

In the spring of 1976, Shimon Peres, the Israeli Defense Minister, decided to hold on the West Bank the municipal elections that had previously been scheduled under Jordanian law. Since the October War, resistance to occupation among Palestinian youth had been rising. In 1974, soon after Bir Zeit College was set up near Ramallah, Peres expelled its president, Hana Nasir, along with some other younger West Bank nationalists. He also stepped up repression of the increasingly influential Palestinian nationalist newspaper *al-Fajr*. Now Peres wanted to reassert the authority of the Palestinian old guard, the pro-Jordanians, and he assumed that the PLO would boycott the elections as they had all other Israeli initiatives in the past. At the same time, Yigal Allon, who had become Rabin's Foreign Minister, stepped forward once more with his own plan for the West Bank.

Both badly miscalculated. Pro-PLO candidates ran for mayor in every major town, and all but one—in Bethlehem, where the pro-Jordanian Elias Freij was reelected—were swept into office. Even Ja'abri was replaced by an old Nasserite rival, Fahed Kawasmeh. The mayor elected in Nablus was Bassam Shaka, a former Syrian Ba'athist, whose views were close to those of the Palestinian rejectionists calling for the liquidation of Israel in favor of a "democratic secular state." This was the position of the Popular Front for the Liberation of Palestine (PFLP) terrorists who carried out the Entebbe hijacking just after the elections. Moreover, Hussein had already refused to be a party to any deal that did not include Jerusalem; the more his prestige declined, the more he needed manifest demonstrations of diplomatic victory.

Taken as a group, the mayors nevertheless represented a new opportunity for Israeli diplomacy. Peres would not acknowledge this, but some in the Labor Party, including Knesset member Yossi Sarid, began to argue for a dialogue with them. Kawasmeh was known for his humane attitudes, shrewdness, and moderation. (When Levinger's group had originally moved to Hebron in 1968, Kawasmeh allowed them to stay in his family's hotel as an act of good faith.) Moreover, Kawasmeh remained pro-Egyptian even after Nasser died, and subsequently drew close to the Saudis and Jordanians. Except for Shaka, all the new mayors—Mohammed Milhem in Halhul, Karim Halaf in Ramallah, Ibrahim Tawil in El-Bireh, and Kawasmeh himself—were close to Fatah, and joined Freij and a-Shawa in Gaza in endorsing a Palestinian state at peace with Israel. Indeed, the mayors took a liberal view of the Rabat decision in favor of a possible two-state solution, the "Palestinian state in whatever part of the homeland would be liberated." They saw the organization representing Palestinian national aspirations, but they also believed in federal links to Jordan. The mayors were, in short, loyal to the PLO but not simply its tools. They were the closest thing to being the authoritative voices of the modernizing Arab society Israeli policy had inadvertently produced.

ii

The election of the West Bank mayors was intrinsically important, but it took on an even greater weight in view of the evolution of Egyptian diplomacy. During the year after the interim settlement of 1975, President Sadat began to speak openly of general peace, in return for Israeli withdrawal and cooperation on the Palestinian question. Over 1976 and 1977, he sent secret feelers to Israeli leaders indicating the possibility of direct negotiations. Since similar discussions with the PLO seemed a vain hope, the fact that the West Bank mayors constituted a Palestinian leadership—connected to the PLO, also independent of it—held out hope for the establishment of Palestinian autonomy, if only on a temporary basis. Autonomy might then give Jordan a chance to reestablish its prestige or prepare the ground for a settlement with a part of the PLO itself.

When President Sadat came to Jerusalem in November 1977, he certainly stole a march on Arab rejectionists—not only Syria, Iraq, and Libya, but all the important factions of the PLO: the Syrian-backed Saika, the Iraqi-backed Arab Liberation Front (ALF), Naif Hawatme's Popular Democratic Front for the Liberation of Palestine (PDFLP), and George Habash's PFLP. Most of these factions, and their backers, were bitterly feuding with one another then. The Syrian and Iraqi Ba'athists were competing to dominate the region north of the Persian Gulf. Arafat's Fatah and Syria (hence Saika) were at odds over President Assad's strong-armed intervention in Lebanon, particularly the Syrian Army's participation in the murderous crushing of Fatah at the Tel-a-Zaatar refugee camp during the summer of 1976. Fatah, for its part, was feuding both with the Libyan-financed PFLP over Arafat's apparent readiness to negotiate with the United States, and with the Iraqi ALF, which had long resented Arafat's prior involvements with the Syrians. The Syrians had accepted UN Resolution 242 when they negotiated a disengagement agreement with Israel in 1974; Assad had recently met with President Carter and was apparently eager to go to a peace conference in Geneva.

Surrounded by such ideological antagonism and ambition, Arafat's position was diminished in comparison with that of the mayors, even if they could not concede this. His only patron was King Khalid of Saudi Arabia, who cautiously preferred Fatah's non-Marxist, pan-Islamic line to that of the PLO radicals, and was hedging against Syria's growing power. But Khalid was closely tied to the U.S. government. Indeed, when Sadat went to Israel, he had the tacit—albeit tenuous and temporary—support of both Khalid (whom, all knew, the Egyptian Army would protect in a crisis) and Hussein, who had substantial allies in the West Bank and Gaza, and was still anxious to rule the mosques of Jerusalem. Few West Bankers could deny that Sadat's initiative seemed superbly pragmatic. It offered a chance to secure the return of Arab lands captured in 1967 and to pressure the Americans into forcing Israel to change its position on Jerusalem and the Palestinian question—and to do so without a risky Geneva conference, which would give Syria and the Soviets a kind of veto power over the progress of negotiations.

The Palestinian Arabs in the West Bank and Gaza were, then as now, mainly supporters of the PLO, the only visible symbol of Palestinian self-determination. But this was vague support, since the PLO's leadership was disorganized and exhausted. That peace seemed a real alternative to occupation was dramatized by the way Arafat sat shocked and helpless in the Egyptian parliament as Sadat announced his determination to address the Knesset. Sadat seemed to promise a more plausible first step to political independence from Israel than Arafat. Nor was Sadat wrong to expect how impressed West Bank and Gaza Palestinians would be by the huge popular success of his trip, in both Jerusalem and Cairo—by the breaking of what he called the "psychological barriers." A delegation, mainly from Gaza, went to Cairo to greet the "hero of peace" just three weeks after his historic visit.

·

Had the Israeli and Egyptian governments worked out some peace settlement soon after Sadat's visit to Jerusalem, the PLO leaders, like the rest of the Arab world, would have had to continue to respond to events which outflanked their policies and

exacerbated their old divisions. And any reasonable political settlement would have been reinforced by the enthusiasm of tens of
millions of Egyptians, who had been prepared by Sadat's regime
to view peace as the beginning of domestic development: the
population would move from the Nile Valley to the Canal Zone,
conditions for foreign investment would improve, funds would
shift from the army to public utilities, to economic integration
with Sudan, and so on. There was little cynicism evident in Egypt
during those days, and Sadat's growing prestige might have been
a decisive American and Israeli asset in the search for a comprehensive settlement with the other Arab nations.

According to Ezer Weizman, then the Israeli Defense Minister,
peace might well have been concluded quickly had Israel agreed
to evacuate the whole of the Sinai, including the Rafah settlements,
and promised merely *to search* for a way to return the West Bank
and Gaza to Arab rule, making all provisions for Israeli security.
Political organizing of the West Bank might have been permitted,
along with an increase, by surreptitious stages, of Jordanian administrators and police. Sadat told the Knesset that he offered
Israel "borders secure against aggression" and whatever form of
international guarantees Israel desired. In return, Sadat insisted
on complete Israeli withdrawal from Arab territories occupied by
force, "including *Arab* Jerusalem," and reiterated that the city
should be "a free and open city for all believers." He identified
the Palestinian problem as the "core and essence of the conflict";
he pointedly omitted mention of the PLO as the Palestinians' sole
legitimate representative. Such ideas were consistent not only with
the priorities of the Egyptian elite but also with the principles of
a good part of the Labor Alignment. Sadat's views reflected established American policy, and the American ambassador to Israel,
Samuel Lewis, said as much. Indeed, after meeting Sadat in person,
Weizman made it clear that he largely sympathized with Sadat's
approach as well. Even Foreign Minister Moshe Dayan, who was
more skeptical, stood by his secret diplomacy, including a promise
to Sadat that the Sinai would be returned; obviously Dayan wanted
to redeem his place in Israeli history by bringing peace.

Yet Prime Minister Menachem Begin was the last person open to
compromise when Sadat came to Jerusalem; he was not ready
either to suspend Jewish settlements on the West Bank or to keep

silent about the future status of Arab Jerusalem. Who could forget how Begin answered Sadat's moving speech to the Knesset—"I tell you sincerely: We welcome you!"—with a rehearsal of Jewish catastrophes, including Revisionist clichés regarding the historic rights of Jews to Jerusalem; how Begin referred to Palestinian Arabs as the "Arabs of Eretz Yisrael"! The "generation of annihilation," Begin said, would never put the Jewish people in danger again. A month later, after his meeting with Begin at Ismailia failed to produce the breakthrough, a dejected Sadat met with President Carter at Aswan. The two leaders issued a joint communiqué calling on Israel only to recognize the right of Palestinians "to participate in the determination of their future." Begin rejected this principle as well (though he would later be forced to endorse it—and more—at the Camp David conference).

Early in 1978, the West Bank mayors nevertheless formed a National Guidance Committee, which could have had a useful part in carrying out the transitional plans that were mooted immediately after Sadat's visit. Since transition could be only to some independent Palestinian entity acceptable to both Israel and Jordan, the mayors seemed a likely group to preside over that transition, with or without proxy from Arafat; they constituted an alternative to Fatah leaders, with whom it appeared premature, if not impossible, to negotiate. But not only were the mayors not consulted during this period, they were hamstrung. Begin announced in January that he rejected UN Resolution 242 as applying to the West Bank. Late in the winter he announced an "autonomy" plan of his own which envisaged not transition but Israeli control of Eretz Yisrael in perpetuity. During the spring of 1978, after a particularly bloody terrorist raid on the Haifa road, the IDF invaded South Lebanon as part of the so-called Litani Operation. Agreement on the West Bank question seemed more unlikely than ever.

·

Weizman and Dayan were anxious to salvage the Sadat initiative, and the public seemed increasingly behind them. A group of more than thirty reserve IDF officers wrote Begin a public letter, demanding that he not squander this unprecedented chance for peace; they formed a new movement, "Peace Now," and called for a public demonstration, which tens of thousands attended. President Carter had begun to identify U.S. interests with Sadat's success, since any hope of a Geneva conference had been dashed. Dayan, Secretary of State Cyrus Vance, and Egyptian representatives met in England. Finally, Carter suggested bilateral negotiations between Begin and Sadat in the United States, with himself acting as mediator; he was clearly prepared to apply some pressure and expected Begin's leading ministers to help bring the Israeli Prime Minister around.

In September, at Camp David, Begin did indeed capitulate on most major points having to do with Egypt, including complete withdrawal from the Sinai and destruction of the North Sinai settlements. The autonomy plan to which Begin agreed at Camp David was one he really should have abhorred, since it called for full Palestinian autonomy, an elected council, an end to the military government, a "strong indigenous Palestinian police force," and the retreat of the Israel Defense Forces to specified enclaves. It also called for a "transitional" autonomy, leading to Palestinians enjoying their "legitimate rights." Yet Begin worked to undermine this plan, even before he returned to Israel. Carter had extracted the promise from him that there would be no new Israeli settlements "for the period of the negotiations," and Carter plausibly interpreted this to mean for the entire period in which the fate of the West Bank was to be negotiated, i.e., five years. Immediately Begin publicly contradicted Carter, claiming he had meant to suspend settlement only for the three months of anticipated negotiations with Egypt. Jordan took Begin's demurrer to be sufficient cause to join opponents of the Camp David accords in Baghdad.

Whoever was the more truthful about the time limit implied by Begin's promise, Carter was right to see settlements as political events—an obstacle to peace—and not merely as abstract numbers of Jews to be compared with numbers of Arabs. Ultra-nationalist settlers such as those at Elon Moreh seemed determined to show that Israel would annex the West Bank just at the time Sadat and Carter were asking Palestinians to live through a five-year period of transition. The aim of the Camp David accords was to make security depend not simply on land but on reciprocal acts that would build trust over a considerable period of time. Yet the settlements, and the religious and historical rhetoric of the movements responsible for them, raised bitter, reasonable suspicions that Israel would use the time to grab the land, i.e., would destroy the Palestinian claims to sovereignty over the West Bank by putting Jewish extremists in every corner of it.

When Begin returned to Israel, the great majority of Knesset members voted in favor of the Camp David accords, though not a good many of his colleagues in Herut, who chastised him for laying the groundwork for a Palestinian state. One particularly dramatic exchange took place in November, when he met the Herut plenum. Begin reminded the restive audience that autonomy had been his idea. His old comrade-in-arms Yochanan Baader replied, "A tiger is also a 'cat,' but what a difference!" Begin became impatient. The only autonomy provision which really mattered, he said, was the one that gave the Israeli government a veto on the progress of any negotiations. "Don't teach me Jabotinsky's doctrine," he chided them, "and don't teach me love for the land of Israel." The following month, Sadat refused to appear with Begin in Oslo to accept the Nobel Peace Prize.

.

Begin eventually put his signature to an Israeli-Egyptian peace agreement in April 1978. But only after a further six months of wrangling, which gave Sadat's opponents the opportunity to isolate him—after renewed Jewish settlement of the West Bank, which embarrassed Sadat and implied that, after all, Egypt would abandon the Palestinian cause and opt for a separate agreement with Greater Israel. Under such conditions, the importance of the Israeli-Egyptian treaty quickly diminished. More and more it was perceived as a kind of further interim settlement, such as the one Rabin had worked out with Sadat in 1975. There would be no more wars, as Sadat had vowed in 1975. Egypt got the Sinai; Israel got demilitarized zones and an embassy in Cairo. Yet the rest of the agreement was mere paper even as it was signed. Extensive trade and cultural exchanges would be impossible.

On April 22, 1979, after the signing of the treaty, Begin's government approved two new settlements between Ramallah and Nablus. The military government established civilian regional councils for the Jewish settlements, an evident prelude to some Israeli claim of sovereignty over at least part of the territory. Most provocative and discouraging of all, the director-general of the Prime Minister's office, Eliyahu Ben-Elissar, prepared plans for autonomy under which Israel would keep exclusive control of the West Bank's water table, its "state" lands—i.e., common lands farmed by Arab peasants, which, before 1967, had been registered in the name of Jordan's King, its communications and roads, and public order. Israel would also control immigration into the West Bank and Gaza. Palestinian Arab residents, according to this plan, would have "autonomy over their persons but not over their resources." (One thoughtful Israeli observer, *Davar's* West Bank correspondent, Danny Rubinstein, noted that this much autonomy was substantially less than what Arabs had under the military government.)

Significantly, President Sadat never repudiated the peace treaty, though it was hard to know if he continued to regard the Camp David provisions as fair or whether he simply did not want to put at risk Egypt's chance to regain the whole of the Sinai. Was his Jerusalem initiative doomed from the start? Since Sadat's assassination, certainly, it has become fashionable to regard the Camp David process as impetuous, individual. His death, so the argument goes, suggested that the Arab world was by no means as ready for peace as he was and that the Israeli government may have been shrewd to move so grudgingly. There is obviously a measure of truth to this view, but it greatly obscures how imposing Sadat's prestige was in the Arab world after the 1973 war and how divided his opposition was until Begin's procrastinations and Gush Emunim's settlements united it. In fact, Zionism's greatest tragedy was that the disciples of mainstream Labor Zionism, for all their faults, had been thrown out of power just months before; that in the name of *his* Zionism, which had become indistinguishable from the new Zionism of Greater Israel after 1967, Begin refused to take seriously any solution to the Palestinian question based on partition.

Sadat claimed that he could have made peace with Golda Meir in an hour. Perhaps not; Mrs. Meir, for her part, suggested that Begin and Sadat deserved not the Nobel Prize but an Oscar. Still, Sadat was certainly right to hope that, once the principle of partition was agreed to, his diplomacy might capture the imagination of the Palestinians on the West Bank and give Jordan the opening it had been waiting for since Rabat. It was, in part, Begin's apparent strength of leadership that encouraged Sadat's gambit, and to be sure, Begin was now speaking for the Israelis who elected him, not just a little Revisionist sect. The resentments inspired by Labor

Zionist institutions were chronic and understandable. None of this changes the fact that the hold of the new Zionism was temporarily relaxed by Sadat's dramatic move, and that Labor politicians might well have gained widespread support for territorial compromise. While he was in Jerusalem, polls showed that 90 percent of respondents now believed in peace, that Sadat had indeed taken down the psychological barrier which the wars of 1956, 1967, and 1973 had erected. For a while, Sephardi groups openly bragged of their Arab roots; there was a feeling that all must look to the future, not dwell on the ideological claims of the past. An overwhelming majority now believed the West Bank could be swapped for peace, not because they gained a language to renounce "Judea and Samaria," but because the prospect of peace seemed so real and compelling. Even ten months later, after the Camp David accords were signed, 85 percent of respondents endorsed the provisions, though fully 50 percent thought they might lead to a Palestinian state.[4]

The collapse of the Sadat initiative was not only Begin's fault. The PLO as a whole remained a militant and authoritarian organization, obviously intent on seizing power as a group, its chain of command intact. It was wary of transitional democracy breaking its ranks. Moreover, the PLO leadership had turned down Sadat's invitation to participate in a Cairo conference during the winter of 1978. They rejected all subsequent overtures of the "peace process," though some of their own important intellectuals—Professor Hisham Sharabi, for instance—later acknowledged that Camp David's version of autonomy might have led to a Palestinian state.[5] Again, in early 1978, the PLO countered with terrorist attacks, such as the Haifa road massacre, in which nearly forty were killed. After Israel withdrew from Lebanon, the PLO established a repressive and plunderous regime in areas of the south. As long as the PLO was united, Arafat never seemed capable of more than defiance; he would not seize the rich historical opportunities that West Bank leaders seemed to lay at his feet.

Still, it is difficult to blame the PLO for having tried to sink the Sadat initiative, since he presupposed such opposition. In a way, Sadat undertook his trip to Jerusalem precisely to circumvent Arafat, or even defeat him. The idea was to create a kind of momentum for peace, so that a Jordanian solution could look plausible again; a momentum which would force Arafat's putatively more moderate wing of the PLO, Fatah, to join in the process with Hussein or make Arafat himself superfluous to the residents of the West Bank and Gaza. Sadat's initiative was thus the Israeli government's to win or lose, not the PLO's. The unwillingness of the Begin government to work with moderates who had been sympathetic to King Hussein before 1974, or with the middle-class mayors after the Sadat initiative, was all the more difficult to justify precisely because of PLO rejectionism. Israel might well have helped Sadat create an alternative to the Fatah veto.

Significantly, Mayors a-Shawa and Kawasmeh were openly willing to be a bridge between Fatah and King Hussein after Camp David, to discuss compromise, transitional arrangements—if only the Israeli government was willing to state that autonomy gave the promise of an eventual West Bank Palestinian entity, perhaps linked to Jordan—but independent of Israel. They agreed that, implicit in any transitional arrangements, would be all necessary guarantees for Israel's security, including, most importantly, a democratic process which would undermine PLO militarism. "After Rabat," said the Palestinian journalist Jamil Hamad, "every Palestinian had become a PLO supporter. But not all had become a PLO member."

iii

Nothing so clearly reflects this pattern of lost opportunity than the response of the Jordanian government to the Camp David accords. After "black" September, from the 1974 Rabat conference (at which the PLO gained the right from the Arab League to represent the Palestinians), the PLO's claim to be waging armed struggle from the north, and its threats against the lives of pro-Hashemite people on the West Bank, undermined the prestige of the former Jordanian administration. Even Labor-led coalitions refused to negotiate the status of Jerusalem. Still, King Hussein did not immediately reject the Camp David principles and, according to President Carter, expressed some interest in helping to "implement the agreement" as President Sadat understood it. He had told Carter in Tehran just after Sadat's Jerusalem initiative that Jordan would consider some "minor modifications of the 1967 border." In 1978, Hussein consulted with Sadat about the Camp David talks and, some insist, was willing to join them himself.[6]

Once it became clear that the Begin government would not relent on its program of annexation, that Sadat's initiative had failed to procure the elements of an overall settlement, Hussein attended the Arab League's various conferences in Baghdad and elsewhere, and declared Sadat anathema. He drew much closer to the Saudis— the blood enemies of his family since ibn-Saud threw the Hashemite clan out of Mecca in 1925—and closer also to Iraq. At the urging of his brother, Crown Prince Hassan, Hussein decided to become a model of cooperation within the Arab League consensus. He even moved to coordinate military policy with the Syrians, though President Assad's predecessor had sent tanks to try to bring Hussein down in September 1970. This new spirit of accommodation brought the Hashemite regime immediate gains, which helped confound prospects for peace. ("His neighbors had oil, and he had a natural resource that was nearly as good," a former American diplomat to Jordan put it, "and this was his long border with Israel.")[7] By turns, the Saudis and the Iraqis began to support Hussein with enormous grants-in-aid, well over a billion dollars a year, which the American government was never in a position to match. By degrees, Hussein was being drawn away from the peace process, though his participation in the transitional arrangements envisioned by the Camp David accords was deemed crucial by anyone who took them seriously.

Most direct aid went into the Jordanian military. But even larger sums accrued to educated Jordanian citizens, as many as 400,000 people, who began to work in the Gulf countries as technicians, engineers, accountants, clerks, contractors. Their remittances fueled an economic expansion in which Jordanians and Palestinians both shared. After 1978, Amman grew to a city of over a million people, though it had been no bigger than a quarter of that size in the sixties. Between 1978 and 1981, the Jordanian gross national product doubled, from 793 million dinars to 1,466 (1 dinar = $3.35). But the word "product" in that economic measure dignifies the growth too much. In fact, Jordan's economy became a commercial bubble, highly susceptible to political ruin. Only 10 percent of the national income came from manufacturing; only about 34 percent from agriculture, which declined during this period. Tourism expanded, and the country developed some natural resources; yet by the winter of 1982 Jordan was exporting a great deal more labor power than any other commodity (such as potash or phosphate).

The Begin government's settlement program after 1978 kept bringing to Jordan people with intense national feelings, people Hussein could keep at bay only with what Crown Prince Hassan has called "the politics of economic legitimacy." Between 250,000 and 300,000 Palestinians moved to Amman between 1972 and 1982, largely owing to Israeli repression of Palestinian nationalism or to the military government's economic constraints. Jordan's economic expansion helped to reduce tensions considerably between the Jordanian population and the Palestinians, i.e., the hundreds of thousands of people who had taken up residence on the East Bank since 1948, but especially those more radically embittered people who had fled the West Bank since 1967. In all, self-defined Palestinians began to make up about 60–65 percent of Jordan's population in the late seventies. The Jordanian regime could not now override Palestinian feeling on the West Bank, as before 1967, without risking its legitimacy on the East Bank.

It might be said in justification of Israeli settlements that the flow of Palestinians to the East Bank only forced the Jordanian regime to seek an end to the state of war with a greater sense of urgency than before. Certainly the presence of so many Palestinians in Amman has caused Hussein to feel that he must actively try to shape Palestinian nationalism in the long run, since any independent Palestinian state or fully independent national movement on the West Bank would inevitably create tensions between Jordanians and Palestinians on the East. In a way, the movement of so many Palestinians to Amman has made the prospect of a Palestinian state more remote than ever, since, in consequence of it, the Hashemite regime has come to view an independent PLO as deeply threatening to its own internal cohesion. The more important point is that, nevertheless, the Palestinian emigration to Amman undermined the independence of Jordan's King. Hussein's economic relations with the Gulf countries after Camp David diminished his freedom of action, since Amman would be swamped with unemployed people if the Gulf countries ever had reason to retaliate against Hussein. Israeli Labor Party officials who—without conceding Hashemite claims in Jerusalem—continued to call on Hussein to break ranks as Sadat did seemed to miss this completely. Egypt, Sadat declared when Arab sanctions were imposed on him, *was* "the Arab world." Considering how Jordan's political economy and social peace depend on Gulf oil and Gulf jobs, Hussein could only envy Sadat's pretensions.

iv

However frustrating was the aftermath of the Israeli-Egyptian peace treaty, it was a much better time than the one it prefigured. Autonomy negotiations dragged on inconclusively. Labor called for a Jordanian option; Jordan had apparently joined the ranks of the rejectionists. Moshe Dayan resigned in frustration, Ezer Weizman resigned in disgust. In June 1981, the electorate went to the polls once again, and Begin was reelected by a wider margin than in 1977. After the election Ariel Sharon became Defense Minister.

This proved a turning point. In November 1981, Sharon installed a civilian administration in the West Bank, headed by Professor Menachem Milson. A month later, the Israeli government formally annexed the Golan Heights. Then, during the winter, Professor Milson deposed the pro-PLO mayors of Nablus, Ramallah, and El-Bireh (Shaka, Halaf, and Tawil), and dissolved the mayors' National Guidance Committee, which still included moderates such as Freij and a-Shawa, who stayed apart from the PLO. In consequence, West Bank and Gaza politicians, intellectuals, students, and merchants mobilized as never before. Milson closed down two Arab newspapers and Bir Zeit University, a center of Palestinian national sentiment. Thousands of Palestinian demonstrators took to the streets, erupting in anger. In April, a Jewish fanatic connected to Meir Kahane's Kach group attacked the Mosque of Omar. The West Bank and Gaza Palestinians organized the most effective general strike since 1936.

In all, seventeen Palestinians were killed during the winter, some of them while attempting to assault Israeli soldiers or settlers. Eighty were seriously wounded. Palestinian youths at rallies defiantly showed the PLO flag, although it had long been banned. The Israelis sent paratroops to break up these rallies and to arrest organized gangs of rock throwers. Jewish vigilantes from Gush Emunim settlements, armed by the government, fired on Arab students in el-Bireh, and some warned farmers against building on their own land. A group of students at Bir Zeit University attacked one of Milson's officials and publicly burned his knitted yarmulke. Indeed, the pro-PLO sentiment that brought the mayors to power only grew as Milson transformed the incoherent policies of the Labor government into one of outright repression.

By now, incidentally, the Israeli government had brought the number of Jewish settlers to 25,000, perhaps more. Begin's regime built huge new military bases, and along with them extensive roads and electricity and water lines that provided services for civilian settlements and could easily be turned over to civilian administration. Sharon announced plans for 120,000 settlers by the end of 1985. Young Israeli couples were offered low-interest mortgages to live in new West Bank projects, or, indeed, to build private villas. Rabbi Levinger occupied the heart of the Hebron casbah. Some 175,000 acres of land had been expropriated by the government as "state" land, but more was acquired for "security reasons" or by agents acting on behalf of Israeli developers, especially around Jerusalem. (By 1982, 75 percent of undeveloped land was in Israeli hands.)

In this climate, the Jewish settlers, armed as reservists, went out on patrol. Two Palestinian youths who died during the winter revolt were shot by Jewish settlers, not by soldiers. Many settlers were organized by Elyakim Ha'Etzni, a lawyer from Kiryat Arba, a Jewish settlement near Hebron, into vigilante groups. It later came out that some of the vigilantes connected to Gush Emunim engaged in terrorist activity themselves, placing bombs that maimed Mayor Shaka and Mayor Halaf in June 1980, a month after PLO terrorists killed six Jewish settlers in Hebron. Others attacked an Arab school, and though Israeli police arrested them before they could consummate the plan, some conspired to blow up Arab buses filled with passengers. Begin's government used much harsher collective punishment against incidents of Arab terror than did Dayan. After the attack on Jewish settlers in Hebron in May 1980, Mayor Kawasmeh was finally deported, the whole town was placed under curfew for a month, travel was banned, telephones were cut off for forty-five days; all the men were interrogated, and many house-to-house searches led to beatings. Some 1,100 books were banned, including works on Islam by the French Jewish leftist Maxime Rodinson, although most contained anti-Semitic material. Chief of

Staff Rafael Eitan, who was deeply sympathetic to Gush Emunim, issued orders to Israeli soldiers to rough up students and demonstrators, to "deter" further disturbances.

Thus, a ghastly cycle of retribution set in. Reservists noted a sharp rise in aggressiveness among Palestinians. Israeli patrols were increasingly the targets of Molotov cocktails thrown by cocky gangs of children. And Arab death squads were active against dissident Arabs. Two men who had opposed the PLO and supported President Sadat—Hamdi el-Kadi of Ramallah and Hashem Khuzandar of Gaza—were murdered. Professor Milson claimed to be acting against the mayors to prevent just this rise of PLO power and violence. And certainly the PLO's attacks on other Arabs portended a militant and authoritarian style of politics which any thoughtful Israeli despised. But Milson's claims seemed disingenuous, for they ignored Israeli politics that undermined moderate West Bank leaders, including some of the mayors. (Kawasmeh was assassinated in Amman in December 1984, apparently by agents of the Syrian-backed Saika.)

The expansion of Jewish settlements certainly soured any opportunities for compromise after the Camp David accords. Milson announced his intention to "root out the PLO from its bases on the West Bank." Having attempted to discredit the mayors, he tried to enlist the rural village people, whose leaders once seemed more inclined to a Jordanian solution than to a separate state. Milson evidently believed that the people in the rural villages were less radical and more susceptible to control than the more sophisticated and militant urban Palestinians. From November 1981 on, Milson began to organize an association of village leagues, led by the clan patriarch Mustafa Dudin, who served in the Jordanian government and openly broke with the pro-PLO mayors.

Clearly Milson would have liked to reinvent a leadership composed of men like Sheik Ja'abri (whom he once described as "willing to work within the necessities and constraints of reality").[8] He cut off the municipalities from the Saudi funds paid out by a joint Jordanian-PLO committee created after Rabat. He gave the village leagues some funds from the defense budget. Milson even distributed small arms to Dudin and his followers. (The PLO assassinated Yusuf al-Katib, the head of the much less influential Ramallah Village League in November, and in March it attacked

Kamal al-Fataftah of the Tarquimiya League. Dudin then took the offensive himself, roughing up opponents, such as a dean of Bethlehem University, who tried to prevent his men from entering the campus.) Milson was counting on Jordan's interest in regaining the West Bank, with or without an inter-Arab consensus, and to be sure, Hussein remained interested in regaining some authority to negotiate with the Israelis as a proxy for the PLO, so that his regime could control the depth and range of PLO influence in the Palestinian homeland. Besides, about 70 percent of West Bank Palestinians remained in rural villages. A poll taken by the Political Science Department of Al-Najah University in Nablus in April 1982 revealed that about a quarter of the West Bank population conceded that King Hussein was a legitimate representative of the Palestinians, and 60 percent preferred a Jordanian connection, even though some 90 percent expressed pro-PLO loyalty. Behind this group was a good part of the old oligarchy, and some mayors, such as Elias Freij of Bethlehem.

But Milson's power within the Israeli government was slight and his timing was sadly wrong. He was boxed in between the demands of his Defense Minister to prepare the ground for annexation and the extremism of the West Bank streets. Even if Sharon had permitted Milson to encourage a pro-Jordanian leadership—and Sharon did not—Milson more easily found candidates for the army's patronage and power than reinvented the world in which Ja'abri wielded his. Nor were the Jordanians willing to lend support to any breaking of ranks just now, not when the village leagues seemed no more than a tool of permanent Israeli rule. The Jordanian Prime Minister, Mudar Badran, denounced Dudin and declared that all the leaders who participated in the leagues would be subject to a charge of treason should they fall into the hands of the Jordanian authorities.

Besides, the changes in culture and demographic structure brought about by Israel's economic policy worked against anyone who wanted to diminish enthusiasm for the PLO as an ideal if not, properly, a government-in-exile. About as many villagers now had jobs in Israel proper as farmed their land. Israeli expropriations of land for Jewish settlement had their most adverse effects on the villagers—the lands from Rujeib (near Nablus) were used, for example, to build Elon Moreh, those from Tarquimiya (near Hebron) to build Kiryat Arba. The villagers might not be of the modern world, but they knew they were in it when they saw Jewish settlements enjoying the modern roads, electrification, and water mains they were themselves denied. They were not searching for new *effendis*.

•

What was perfectly obvious about Israeli policy under General Sharon was that repression of West Bank leaders—the house arrest of mayors, the deportation of security offenders, the economic constraints, and the land expropriations—was meant to create a situation which forced educated Palestinians to leave and seek their fortunes in the Gulf or in the West. Moreover, the policy of Begin's government suggested an annexationist view of Israeli borders shared—if the 1981 election results were to be taken seriously—by something more than half the Israeli population. "If not Hebron, then not Tel Aviv." Begin spoke this formula with the reverence reserved for a law of nature. But how to consolidate Eretz Yisrael? General Sharon convinced him that Israel could not reduce the influence of the PLO on the West Bank and Gaza without trying to inflict a crushing blow on the PLO leadership and bases in Lebanon. He urged Begin to undertake a war, assuring him that he had enlisted the support of the Gemayel family and the whole Maronite Phalange. There was talk of a grand design, of expelling both the PLO and Syria from Lebanon, and then setting up a pro-Israeli government. Would Jordan be next?[9]

After months of preparation—and a few days of mutual provocation—the Begin government launched an all-out invasion of southern Lebanon on June 5, 1982. The IDF quickly overran PLO forces that had been shelling the Galilee, and then laid siege to Beirut. By the end of August, the PLO leaders were scattered among the Arab states, their military organization of Lebanon's 400,000 refugees in ruins. At least 2,000 Lebanese civilians—the Red Cross claimed three times that number—had been killed, and over 500 Israeli soldiers. Once again relations between Arabs and Jews were dominated by Palestinians who believed that time worked against Israel, and Israelis who believed they could make time work against Palestinians. Both were right.

10 / Democracy or Zionism?

One may learn a good deal about the evolution of Israeli politics merely by noting the artwork on Israeli money over the years. During the 1950s and 1960s, until the Six-Day War, Israeli lira notes depicted farmers, scientists, and industrial workers in fields, laboratories, and factories. By the early 1970s, there were portraits of Zionist luminaries—Herzl, Weizmann (even Albert Einstein on the five-lira note)—framed by state buildings. Around the time of the October War, scenes of the Old City began to appear on the currency, until, under Menachem Begin, all the state buildings were replaced by pictures of Jerusalem's gates. (Galloping inflation provided the excuse to drop Einstein in 1979; Vladimir Jabotinsky was added in 1980.)

This lagging transformation in official aesthetics—from Histadrut to statism, from statism to the new Zionism—corresponds to the sea change that has come over Israeli voters since 1967, especially since the time of Golda Meir's incumbency. Between 1969 and 1981, more than half a million new Jewish voters entered the rolls of the Israeli electorate. Of these, more than two-thirds, including a narrow majority of young people from old Zionist, European homes, swung to the parties of the right and the religious parties. Young people voted this way for reasons of identity, to shake off the world of the Histadrut. To the extent that the occupation allowed for

298 / THE TRAGEDY OF ZIONISM

economic expansion and the employment of low-wage Arab workers, Greater Israel seemed to help the Second Israel out of its economic morass. Yet there was more to this trend than either identity or money. The unity of Eretz Yisrael also became vaguely identified with the very prestige of the Zionist past.

Through Begin, this Zionism of Greater Israel has had a plain impact on Israeli diplomacy. Its consequences for Israeli civil society, in particular, for the deeper democratic standards of Israeli youth, have been less clear. After Moshe Dayan died in the fall of 1981, the new Zionism found an even more vociferous champion in Ariel Sharon, who not only defined the Jewish state as a continuing, militant cause but, unlike Dayan, was willing to trivialize other civic values standing in its way. When the Israeli Supreme Court decided one case against Jewish squatters in favor of West Bank Arab plaintiffs, Sharon demanded that the government ignore their decision entirely. In the Knesset, he denounced his opponents as "traitors." Before the Lebanon debacle, Sharon implied that the Arabs of Greater Israel might ultimately have to be expelled, warning darkly that they "not forget the lesson of 1948"; during the war, he relied on military force not only to fight the PLO but to deceive the Israeli Cabinet and, worse, rally the great part of Israeli youth to his leadership.

i

A healthy society, Plato observed, needs laws no more than a healthy man needs medicine. But Israel is not the mobilized little commune the Biluim had in mind. Before 1984, poll after poll disclosed that about 90 percent of Israeli youth called themselves democratic, and to be sure, the majority have been greatly influenced by the styles of the Western industrial democracies— Yale T-shirts, Sony ghetto blasters. The question remained, however, whether Israeli youth have had any profound understanding of what living in a democratic country entails; what are the arguments to justify democracy, what are the laws to ensure civility and tolerance? A poll in 1984 revealed that some 60 percent of Israeli youth would have curtailed the rights of Israeli Arabs and that 57 percent thought Arabs in the occupied territories who refused Israeli citizenship ought to be expelled. Not surprisingly, among those who expressed such stridently anti-democratic views, most favored annexing the West Bank over any territorial compromise.[1] Insofar as the new Zionist program called for annexing the West Bank and Gaza, it alienated Israeli adolescents from the Palestinian community as a whole and deeply estranged them from nearly 18 percent of Israel's enfranchised population, who are themselves of Palestinian Arab origin. Meanwhile, the leaders of the Likud all but repudiated Revisionism's traditional commitment to secular liberty and, under the banner of Eretz Yisrael, made common cause with Israel's messianic religious parties. In contrast, Israeli liberal groups did not succeed in persuading young people to examine the need for reforming the state's political institutions.

The social tensions entailed by occupation would have taken their toll on any democracy, but they have had a peculiar and unfortunate impact on Israel—inasmuch as Israeli democracy was improvised in 1948 and has subsequently been made to coexist with a number of residual, genuinely Zionist institutions which had always excluded non-Jews. Under Levi Eshkol, the Israeli government made some strides toward reforming the state's judicial institutions: military rule of the Arab community was ended, and various cases were brought to court challenging the old Zionist framework. Yet electoral reform was buried for the sake of the Labor Alignment's gaining a narrow political advantage, and constitutional reform, perhaps the most important, was never seriously raised—largely as a result of the disingenuous arguments made on its behalf by Lavon's critics.

After the 1967 war and the initiation of occupation, moreover, all such movement toward reform halted. By 1984, in fact, Israel had no formal constitution, no developed tradition of parliamentary courtesy and ministerial responsibility, no effective checks on the executive, no checks at all on parliamentary authority, no regular or routine contact between electors and elected. The state still had Eight Basic Laws, four of which have been added since 1950. (The Basic Law for Economy pertains to the collection of taxes, and the Law of the Army mandates conscription. In 1967 the Law of Jerusalem extended Israeli law to the eastern, largely Arab city. The Law of the Judiciary took care of some technical matters pertaining to the appointment and tenure of judges. It passed the Knesset during the winter of 1984.) Significantly, the Justice Minister who prepared passage of the most recent Basic Law, Likud's Moshe

Nissim, promised a civil-rights bill by the end of 1985. An election intervened and Nissim could not carry through. Yet it should be noted that the bill of rights he had had in mind would not, in Nissim's words, "give comfort to those who believe they can make a revolution in Israel through the law."

During Begin's first term, Nissim's predecessor, Likud's Shmuel Tamir, steered a law through the Knesset authorizing judges to find precedents for "residual" law—cases of law for which there are no specific Knesset statutes or common-law cases—in Orthodox teaching. To be sure, normative, rabbinic Judaism does have many provisions which might be thought compatible with minority rights and democratic norms. The Torah enjoins Jews to deal justly with strangers because Jews, too, were "strangers in Egypt." There have even been times when normative Judaism filled up gaps created by the constitutional vacuum, as when the Kahan Commission, which investigated the Sabra and Shatila massacres, charged General Sharon with "indirect responsibility" for the murders by quoting a lovely passage from the Talmud. ("A basis for 'indirect responsibility' may be found in the outlook of our ancestors . . . 'It is said in Deuteronomy [21:6:7] that the elders of the city, who were near a slain victim who had been found [when it was not known who had struck him down], would wash their hands over the [victim] and state: "Our hands did not shed this blood and our eyes did not see" . . .' ")[2] Still, Arabs are not "strangers" in historic Palestine and they plausibly demand the privileges of citizenship in Israel, not greater magnanimity regarding their property.

Jews, too, may need legal recourse when the political majority fails them. As a matter of fact, judicial commissions are themselves constituted only by majority government decision, and Begin and Sharon nearly succeeded in heading off Kahan's. Four hundred thousand people—i.e., 10 percent of the population—took to the streets to demand one and President Navon had to threaten resignation. During Begin's tenure, the residents of Biram and Ikrit were again denied permission to return home. Television reporters critical of government policy were muzzled. Who marched for them? Nor is Jewish "spirit" as valuable as a bill of rights when it comes to cultural and social freedoms. The Israeli public is not inclined to stifle people; Amos Oz has insisted that, in any case, a kind of anarchism governs the country's artists. Nevertheless, Israeli censors *have* tangled with artists, not only over matters of obscenity, but over religious and political questions as well. Israeli censors banned the showing of *Jesus Christ Superstar* and the film *M*A*S*H*—the former on grounds of religious tact, the latter for its wry look at war. More recently, the censors imposed changes on Chanoch Levin's bitterly comic play *The Patriot*, which accused Israeli parents of profiteering from their children's wars—harsh stuff to be sure, but hardly a question divorced from political debate. The television program *Nikui Rosh* ("Brainwashing") was a blend of zany comedy and biting political satire that caused a sensation in the mid-seventies. Under Begin it was removed from the schedule once and for all, largely owing to the pressure of the National Religious Party.

.

The question of civil rights impinges most directly on the relations between religious institutions and the state. Since the time of the Mandatory government, rabbinical courts and councils have jealously guarded their acquired jurisdictions in marriage, divorce, burial. The NRP has used its influence not only on the television industry but to shut down public transportation on the Sabbath, also the cinema and the El Al international carrier. The Orthodox have sought to extend Orthodox criteria to the Law of Return, and to the legal privileges of Jews in semiofficial state institutions. Before 1967, rabbinic interference had been considered mild, even pleasurable. Many secular Jews secretly cherished the ambience of the Sabbath, even when they resented the suspension of public transportation. Most Israelis have since gained access to private cars and cabs; they've been able to get to Arab shops or restaurants that ignore the law. But if the commerce of secular Jews can ruin the ambience of the Sabbath, what has been the compounding effect of religious law on the ambience of Israeli democracy?

In fact, the encroachments of Orthodox Jews on secular life have only got worse in the wake of the new Zionism. The Begin coalition passed a law greatly restricting a hospital's right to perform autopsies. Orthodox yeshivas have been subsidized by the state much more than before, while the daughters of Orthodox families have been exempted from military service. Since 1980, religious fanatics in Ramot, a Jerusalem suburb, have regularly stoned cars that pass on public roads near their apartments, and rabbis have refused to marry two people who cannot prove they are Jewish according to Orthodox *halacha*. Once, the Burial Society even refused to bury a child whose mother was a Japanese immigrant. True, Jews may marry non-Jews by flying off to Cyprus. But this is hardly satisfactory public policy. Israel today has a broad middle class of secularist and cosmopolitan people whose sexual mores and notions of family have become increasingly liberal. For most, private life is grasped in terms of psychology, not any religious precept. Nor is rabbinic control of divorce courts widely appreciated in a country whose divorce rate is climbing to Western levels. The proceedings of rabbinical divorce courts put women at a particular disadvantage during custody hearings. Orthodox influence has been most pernicious, perhaps, in the Orthodox school system, now a virtual breeding ground for annexationist sentiment among some 30 percent of the student population.

ii

There is also the matter of politics and the Hebrew language. Isaiah Berlin distinguishes between liberty in the "positive" sense and in the "negative" sense, where positive liberty is our liberty *to become* good, fully human; it means doing what comes naturally, exerting our innate capacities to the full. (According to advocates of positive liberty, i.e., philosophers like Jean-Jacques Rousseau, we attain liberty in a way that is common and spontaneous—say, by making ourselves subject to the inspiration of charismatic leadership or a revolutionary vanguard, much as children come to maturity in consequence of the discipline of their parents.) In contrast, liberty in the negative sense is the individual's freedom *from* the invasions of others, especially the conformist majority or the government. Negative liberty is the right to do whatever we please so long as we do not encroach on the corresponding rights of others. (It is, for example, John Stuart Mill's demand that government provide for the toleration of minority views.)

Berlin concedes that these two concepts of liberty may not always be remote one from the another: any socialist will insist that our negative legal protections against the invasions of others (or the state) are not worth a great deal if we are lacking in the positive freedoms of food, education, and shelter to make the most of our rights; moreover, the political institutions of negative liberty are rarely established without the force of a vanguard movement, though the principle of non-violence is just what negative libertarians seek to enshrine. Still, Berlin argues forcefully, it is only liberty in the negative sense that is consistent with liberal-democratic institutions. Revolutionary proponents of positive liberty may create heroic, transformative moments. But revolutionary vanguards that are not superseded by the institutions of negative liberty usually degenerate into a kind of tyranny, not the least of which is the tyranny of the majority.

Berlin's nice distinction has an obvious relevance to Israel's predicament and the difficulties of grasping that predicament in Hebrew. Since the reading of the Declaration of Independence, positive and negative versions of liberty have implicitly struggled to define Israeli constitutional priorities, with revolutionary Zionism governing the positive side, and notions of civil liberty, imported from Europe and the Mandatory government, the negative. Moreover, young Israelis who are not highly educated may have trouble appreciating Berlin's refinement altogether. Israel has been under siege for so long that public discourse seems naturally to imply that the individual's conscience should attend to public distress before any private interest. In a way, the use of modern Hebrew may itself be confining the imaginations of young Israelis, though not—as Koestler had it—because of its syntax or absence of subtle adjectives. (Israeli poets and writers have more than made up for a want of adjectives with inventive metaphor and the generation of new words.) Rather, Hebrew is so ancient that, to anyone raised in it to the exclusion of other languages, it cannot fail to convey archaic ways of thinking about politics.

George Orwell once noted that the word "freedom" in English immediately suggests freedom in the individual sense of private rights and property. In classical Hebrew, the word for freedom is *"cherut,"* the nuances of which have been evolving since records were made of the exodus from Egypt, when the people of Israel passed from slavery to freedom, *"me'avdut le'cherut."* The point of that freedom was an implicit *common* desire, what Rousseau would have called the "general will"; to strive after the sacred, to worship God—hence, keep His law—and to build the Promised Land. (Moses, in this view, was the indispensable legislator of "freedom," the charismatic intermediary who made what was implicit explicit;

those Israelites who were too slavish to will the conditions of *cherut*, Moses forced to be free, or, as after the episode of the golden calf, put to death.)

Significantly, there was never a word for democracy in the Hebrew tradition, except for the borrowed word *"democratia."* *"Cherut"* directly implied national freedom in the positive sense; freedom from oppression, from foreign rule, from slavery—also from idol worship. During the time of the dispersion, *cherut* took on messianic connotations; it promised freedom for the Jewish people to practice Judaism, to have some autonomy, to have peace under rabbinic supervision—ultimately, to live in harmony with the Almighty's historical plan. If we judge by Achad Haam's view of normative Judaism, *cherut* might also have implied a considerable measure of personal, or negative, liberty. He thought that the ways of tolerance were imbedded in Judaism (though too deeply imbedded if you asked a *shtetl* Jew who had had the misfortune to cross the kehillah); to worship the ineffable Name was to worship an enigma; this required scope, doubt, reason. The Mosaic law demanded equal justice for strangers, and (as Heine observed) it outlawed perpetual servitude. Yet whatever personal freedom Achad Haam found in Judaism, his Zionism, too, was imbued with the notion of collective freedom. For Achad Haam, Zionism was necessary to redeem the Jewish spirit, consolidate the Hebrew language, nurture the "instinct for national self-preservation."

•

Many practical and Labor Zionists reasoned that when the Zionist revolution superseded the "repressive legalism" of Orthodoxy, a fully democratic and secular Hebrew society would emerge. The Palestinian Hebrew Labor movement stressed the need for workers' "self-realization" in collectives, for industrial democracy, and for economic self-sufficiency, so that Jews would not become colonialist settlers living off the work of disenfranchised Arabs. Labor Zionists emphasized the need for majority rule. And there is a modern Hebrew word for personal freedom, *"chofesh,"* as in *"chofesh ha'prat,"* literally, the license we are due for the sake of privacy. (Usually the term pertains to the family, the household.) Yet the underlying meanings of *"democratia"* and *"chofesh"* were learned in Europe, not in Palestine. Revolutionary Zionists had absorbed the words from a life that included reading Tolstoy and Plekhanov.

Today, students at Hebrew University may take their meanings for granted, but not the Rumanian-born dock worker in Haifa or the Yemenite cobbler in Jerusalem's Machane Yehuda market. Indeed, a young Israeli whose parents are from North Africa may have learned the word *"cherut"* directly from the Bible, the word *"democratia"* from resented Labor *apparatchiks*, and the word *"chofesh"* from the Zionist anthem *"Ha'Tiqva"*: "It is the hope of two thousand years to be a free people (*"am chofshi"*) in our land, the land of Zion, Jerusalem!"

In the absence of a bill of rights, certainly, only civil libertarians have carefully defined *"chofesh ha'prat"* as entailing liberal freedom in the American or British sense. Israeli courts are bound by various laws, some conforming to the libertarian's notion of liberty, some—the prerogatives of the Orthodox rabbinate, say—contradicting it. When asked if the Arabs of Judea, Samaria, and Gaza should be given the right to vote in the event of annexation, only 31.5 percent of high-school students said yes. Can this be unrelated to the fact that there is no legal apparatus for an Arab to marry a Jew in Israel? *"Democratia"* has always struck the Israeli ear the way other terms of Western social science sound during ordinary conversation, i.e., *"methodologia"* or *"ideologia,"* words of a higher order than common sense, yet alien to it, even affected. Since Israeli schools have taught children much more about the tribes of Israel than about the Enlightenment, the Hebrew language presents democracy as a mere technique of social organization—the best technique to be sure, the most advanced and civilized, but, like other advanced commodities from abroad, perhaps more than Israelis can afford. Thus democracy has seemed an added luxury free people enjoy, not a synonym for freedom. (The individualism implied by negative liberty certainly has an air of self-indulgence about it. The word for individual self-regard in modern Hebrew, *"enochiyut,"* is often used to denote selfishness.)

It should be noted that even left-wing Israeli secularists and civil libertarians, most of whom are stepchildren of revolutionary Labor Zionism, regard democracy largely in terms of majority rule, elections, privacy, where the corporate values are not really subject to question: a Jewish majority, the eminence of Hebrew culture, *aliyah*, national rehabilitation in a more or less self-sufficient Jewish economy. Such radical libertarians as Shulamith Aloni and Lova

Eliav have never advocated a secular-democratic or bi-national state to resolve the dilemmas of Greater Israel. Rather, they've defended partition and the vision of Israeli democracy in the rhetoric of old Labor Zionist principles, the building of a "higher form" of society— what Aloni used to call in her speeches *chevra metukenet*, "a perfected society," "not like all the others."

There may be excellent grounds for wanting a separate state with a Jewish majority; they can be found in Chapter 2 of this book. But Aloni's old slogan implies that Israelis should want democracy as a complement to some utopian pioneering experiment; that Israel should have more perfect democratic rights *in spite* of the risks, betrayals, and vanities of the political world, not—as Berlin would have it—because of them. At its worst, Aloni's defense of democracy carries with it an unearned sense of superiority, and it perpetuates a weird debate—which new Zionists win—about whether Jews should try to be better than everybody else. Lova Eliav's book *Land of the Hart* speaks movingly, and anachronistically, of a "normal pyramid" of manual and intellectual labor, in a technological economy of scale.[3] The children of the Second Israel regard this version of the secular Hebrew democracy—a society "based on justice, equality, and human freedom"—as a euphemism for economic planning, shame in one's origins, the loss of family pride.

The poet laureate of Gush Emunim, veteran songwriter Naomi Shemer (who wrote "Jerusalem of Gold"), stated that if the choice must be between peace and Eretz Yisrael she would choose the latter. Since 1967, young Israelis drawn to Gush Emunim have dismissed democratic arguments as warmed-over pleadings of ghetto Jews intent on showing Gentiles that the Jewish nation is still "elect." To be sure, the choice Shemer presents is a false one. That Hebrew democracy has not yet come fully into being is Zionism's tragedy, not its requirement. In any case, revolutionary Zionism completed its work long ago, as evidenced by Shemer's charming songs, if not by her new political alliances. It must be conceded, however, that Shemer is instinctively right to suggest that her new Zionist commitment to Greater Israel is deeply at odds with Israel's potential to become a democratic state.

There are hardships entailed by continued occupation; West Bank

Arabs may revolt again, or incite Israel's neighbors to attack, as in 1973. In a generation, Greater Israel may have an Arab majority; Israelis cannot retain the West Bank and also have peace with the Palestinian people. But so long as the Israeli Army promises to defeat Israel's enemies, Israelis may have no good reason to put an end to the occupation of their own accord, except to cherish *"democratia"*—that is, for the sake of a Hebrew word which seems to Shemer vaguely foreign, unfairly demanding, at odds with her past.

iii

A. B. Yehoshua has compared the West Bank to a tar baby; the more the Israeli government strives to subdue Arabs, the more it sacrifices its own moral independence. Most Israeli Jews have indeed become accustomed to living in what Meron Benvenisti, the former deputy mayor of Jerusalem, has called *Herrenvolk* democracy, with first-class citizenship for Jews and second-class citizenship for Arabs.[4] If the former are pushed to an even more extreme situation—a violent rising in the West Bank, say, or a bloody stalemate with Syria—there is bound to be a collapse of faith in the slow, centrifugal workings of parliament. Would more wars not create a yearning for *achdut leumit*, the national solidarity and transcendent power which tolerance only obstructs? Since 1967, there has been polarization, a coarsening of political rhetoric, the stirrings of racism; one poll in *Ha'Aretz* during 1984 revealed that 32 percent of Israelis felt violence toward Arabs, even terrorism, was either "totally" justified or had "some justification." Over 60 percent of young Israelis believe Arabs should not be accorded full rights in the state.[5] (The last student essay of "Peace Now" activist Emile Greensweig was an analysis of just this trend, about how political violence could subvert the spirit of Israeli democracy; he submitted it a few days before he was murdered by a grenade thrower during a demonstration against General Sharon.)

Significantly, the West Bank is ruled under British emergency regulations from 1946, which one former Israeli Justice Minister, Yaacov Shimshon Shapiro, has called Fascist; preventive detention is common. Amnesty International reported that, from January to June 1979 alone, some 1,500 youths were taken into custody. Tens of thousands more were interrogated, or intimidated during the period of the general strike in the spring of 1982. Under Sharon there was no freedom of the press on the West Bank, no freedom of assembly, no freedom to organize political parties. Nearly every elected mayor was deposed by the military government. Instead of enjoying municipal government, the towns have been firmly controlled by IDF patrols. During strikes, shops have been forced to open, campuses closed down.

The Arab town of Nablus has some 70,000 residents. It is nestled in a valley surrounded by several eroded mountains, and as of 1983, there were Jewish settlements on every summit. Some are pathetic, isolated outposts, to be sure, but the roads to the settlements are more impressive than the housing, and they entirely bypass the Arab dwellings. Settlements and housing are portents of a Jewish presence that does not so much annex the territory as graft a thin layer of control over the top of it. (In Nablus, some of the Gush Emunim have taken over the "Tomb of Joseph," yet another symbol of their misguided messianism. Next to the tomb is an Arab school, and there have been many fights. On the wall nearby, during much of 1983, DEATH TO COLLABORATORS was painted in red Arabic letters.) Ever since the mayor of Nablus, Bassam Shaka, was fired by Professor Milson, the town has been run by low-ranking Israeli officers. Public housing construction has been stopped. Roads are deteriorating. Families who protested by not paying taxes had their electricity shut off. Arab youths (including Shaka's own teenage son) have been political prisoners, and they report living with fifteen others in rooms seventy-five feet square, with a few blankets, no books, nothing but time to talk about the "struggle." Israeli investors and contractors, meanwhile, have not failed to profit from the situation. Benvenisti points out that hundreds of private speculators and builders have made fortunes here; the total amount of private capital invested may add up to some $250 million a year, according to the government's own reckoning.

Granted, the rhetoric of former Justice Minister Shapiro may have been too much. Patrols, settlements, interrogations, profiteering—this is the stuff of the British Raj, not Fascism. Indeed, if the Palestinians had one Gandhi instead of a hundred Garibaldis, the Israeli occupation might be put in serious difficulty. There are few well-documented cases of torture in Israeli military prisons, and no executions; when two terrorist prisoners were discovered to have been beaten to death in custody, their assailants were arrested. Nor has the Israeli government allowed all semblance of liberal decency to disappear. In the winter of 1984, an Israeli commission, under Assistant Attorney-General Judith Karp, reported to the Defense Ministry about the risks of vigilantism in the territories, and Defense Minister Moshe Arens took concerted action against it. Emile Greensweig's murderer was put behind bars in 1984, as were twenty Jewish terrorists connected to Gush Emunim.

Still, it would be terribly complacent of Israelis to take satisfaction in Israel's comparatively humane record of occupation. Fascist states did not have a democratic character to lose. IDF patrols and Gush Emunim vigilantes became increasingly trigger-happy during Rafael Eitan's tenure as Chief of Staff; the Israeli government extended Israeli law to Jewish settlements on the West Bank, and it also extended its high-handed control of West Bankers to some Israeli dissidents. Groups of Israeli professors and students who demonstrated for academic freedom at Bir Zeit University during the winter of 1982 were arrested and beaten. The head of the state television authority, the Likud-appointed Yosef "Tommy" Lapid, ran a campaign against "non-Zionist" reporting. One correspondent, Rafik Halabi, an Arab graduate of Hebrew University, claimed that as many as 120 people were on unpaid leave from the broadcast authority around the time of the Lebanon War, many of them in protest against political restrictions. In this atmosphere, Israel became a meaner place to live. A new extremist discourse emerged from the war, but also from the daily confrontation of Arab laborers and Jews, the first walking to jobs, while the latter averted their eyes. In Jerusalem, Israelis feared to walk near Arab neighborhoods at night. Soldiers were mobilized as if part of a deadly routine. Begin, and especially General Sharon, brought out the very worst instincts of Israeli young people: the desire for domination, lock-step, revenge. (Defending Sharon's role in the Sabra and Shatila massacres during the winter of 1983, one taxi driver insisted that the only way to deal with the Palestinians was to shoot them: men, women, and children. "I was in Lebanon," he said. "Twelve-year-old boys can kill you with an RPG [a rocket-propelled grenade] as easily as a man." True, a little resistance, a little scolding, and the cabbie took much of it back. The point was that this rhetoric was not an embarrassment to him.)

Before the October War of 1973, one well-known Israeli political scientist suggested that Israel could remain immune to the militarism which seemed to go along with military government in other countries. Israel, he said, could be the Athens of the Middle East ready to fight but culturally free. Tragically, Thucydides' cautionary evocation of life during the Peloponnesian War is also in many ways a depiction of trends in Israeli political culture since the 1967 war:

> Words had to change their ordinary meanings, to take those which were now given to them. Reckless audacity came to be considered the courage of a loyal ally; prudent hesitation, specious cowardice. Moderation was held to be a cloak for unmanliness; ability to see all sides of a question, inaptness to act on any.
> Frantic violence became the attribute of manliness; plotting, a justifiable means of self-defense. The advocate of extreme measures was always trustworthy; his opponent, a man to be suspected . . .[6]

Another political scientist, Yoram Peri, has convincingly shown that political life in his country has been profoundly affected by militarization and that the *institutions* of the military have actually encroached on civilian standards of justice.[7] Since the occupation is run entirely according to military law, Israeli soldiers, many of whom are civilian reservists, have not been subject to normal civilian penalties for the crimes they commit in uniform. Several times during his tenure as Chief of Staff, General Eitan arbitrarily lowered the sentences of soldiers; in two notorious cases, he pardoned murderers. Nor are civil prosecutors able to appeal such decisions, and there are no civil-rights laws by means of which an Arab victim's family might seek redress.

What of the corporate interests of the army? Peri makes it clear that the officer class is diverse and hardly represents a unified interest to be pressed against the civilian government. There will be no military coups; if anything, civilian leaders since the Lavon Affair have continued to undermine the professionalism of Israeli officers, with promises of promotion, of plum jobs in the party, or in some public corporation, after retirement. Yet the army's top command has grown used to the security arrangements afforded them by occupation of the West Bank, including training bases, military installations, easier communications. Future chiefs of staff may not be as outspoken as Eitan in defending annexation on Zionist grounds, but he reflected a widespread sentiment among career Israeli officers—more and more of whom are from the Second Israel—that the West Bank is crucial for the defense of the country in case of general war. To be sure, officers are paid to think in terms of the worst case and prepare for war. But the influence of the IDF may inhibit the political courage civilian leaders must show when they undertake the diplomatic initiatives for peace. (Thucydides added: "To succeed in a plot was to have a shrewd head, to divine a plot, still shrewder; but to try to provide against having to do either was to break up your party and to be afraid of your adversaries.")

During the negotiations over the Sinai withdrawal, the IDF leaked to reporters that giving up the Sinai would profoundly undermine the training programs of the Israeli Air Force. This proved a highly exaggerated claim, but it helped stall the talks. Making matters worse, Peri explains, is that the Ministers of Defense and the Chiefs of Staff no longer had clear boundaries between them. During the Lebanon War, for example, the Cabinet was completely at the mercy of reports supplied to it directly by Chief of Staff Eitan. The latter had Sharon's full support and encouragement; about the war, at least, he was Sharon's man. But what if, as was quite possible, a more moderate and less well-informed civilian had been Defense Minister during the summer of 1982? What standard procedures would have assured civilian control of Eitan's actions in the field?

iv

If the drive to annex the West Bank exacted an indeterminate price from Israeli civil institutions, its cost to the Israeli treasury can be all too easily measured. After 1982, Israel went through the hardest economic times in its history. The defense burden was at least partly responsible for this; military spending costs were about $5,000 per family per year. But even if the Likud government was in no way to blame for the arms race in which Israel competed, can it be said that Begin's ministers chose a prudent economic course over the demands of the new Zionism? In fact, since 1981, the Begin government viewed rapid consolidation of Greater Israel as its number-one priority, and so it acted as if its own short-term prospect of reelection was more important than any responsible economic policy for the long run. Begin's finance ministers spent about $200 million a year to build housing, commercial centers, and industry on the West Bank. But between 1981 and 1984 they spent perhaps ten times that sum to produce an illusion of prosperity, so that Likud's major constituencies—the young, the least educated, the North African Jews—would continue to go along with the new Zionist triumphalism.

During the election campaign of 1981, after it became clear that the Likud was in trouble in the polls, Finance Minister Yoram Aridor cut tariffs on cars and other much-sought-after goods, and linked salaries to 100 percent of the cost-of-living index. He raised subsidies on staples (bread, gasoline, eggs, milk, etc.) to some 6 percent of the GNP, though subsidies were never more than 3 percent under Labor. Such fiscal policies kept the inflation rate at around 150 percent, which promoted a buying spree such as the country had never seen. And the wild consumption was abetted by government instructions to the Bank of Israel, putatively as independent as the American Federal Reserve, to keep the Israeli shekel about 20 percent above its actual value, so that luxury imports would be cheaper. In consequence, consumer imports for 1982, were, in fact, 17 percent more than in 1981, and rose from $7.8 billion to $8.5 billion in 1983. Artificial support for Israeli currency put Israeli exporters at a serious disadvantage, which the government tried to make up for with costly export subsidies.

The Likud was reelected in 1981, but all this importing and government spending took its toll, and the invasion and occupation of southern Lebanon only added to the burden. By 1983, the Israeli economy was growing not at all for the first time since 1966. The balance-of-payments deficit was running at an astonishing $4.9 billion a year, only $2 billion of which was for military procurement. Inflation began to climb to over 200 percent a year. Obviously, normal conceptions of fiscal management had been jeopardized where the new Zionist agenda precluded all others. Indeed, the mutual confidence Israeli citizens needed to support democratic institutions may itself have been undermined. Amos Elon put the matter this way:

> We are not the first society in modern times in which real dangers have given birth to paranoia, in which chaos and anarchy breed irrationality, in which inflation fuels fanaticism, and vice versa . . .
>
> Thomas Mann, speaking of the Germans in the 1920s and '30s, remarked that during the days of the great inflation following the First World War, all their common values had changed and all their normal inhibitions went by the board: with the loss of their savings, they became accustomed to recognizing only force and violence; they forgot to rely on themselves and came to rely on the state and on blind fate.[8]

Where did all the money come from to make up the deficit? To be blunt, Aridor either covered the shortfall with American aid and the proceeds from the fund raising of Jewish organizations abroad or sold off accumulated foreign-exchange reserves crucial to the country's future economic development. One Israeli treasury official, who was appalled like most of the country's responsible economists by what the Likud government did under the Begin-Aridor policy, revealed that, by the end of 1983, Israel had some $3–$4 billion in gold and other hard reserves left. Nearly all the aid that did not go for military hardware in 1983, about $900 million, was used to service Israel's accumulated debt to the United States. Incidentally, Israel's older, marginal industries—textiles, agriculture, electronics, which are not high-tech industries—had borrowed some $650 million a year from American banks, and those lending institutions carefully watched U.S. government policy to establish Israel's credit rating. Aridor's reckless use of credit thus put Israel in a position where any future cut in American aid not only threatened the solvency of the Israeli government but threatened to put tens of thousands of Israelis out of work. At least 10 percent more Israelis were under the poverty line when Begin resigned in 1983 than before the Likud government took office.

v

Before 1984, some observers had pointed with relief to the surprising number of Israeli Arabs who voted for the Labor Alignment in the 1981 elections, accounting for nearly three of its electoral mandates. The Communist Rakah Party and small Arab lists lost an equal number of seats, which meant that about a quarter of the Arab voters switched to Labor. Did this shift reflect the increasing faith of Arab citizens in the conventional politics of the state, in spite of the extreme atmosphere? In fact, the rate of Arab participation in the voting dropped from 83 percent to 65 percent in 1981, and the swing away from Rakah reflected the radical estrangement of more and more Arabs from Israel's future. Jellal Abu-Tuami, who headed an exceptionally active Citizens for Peres committee in the Arab sector, claimed that the Arab vote for Labor was a desperate act of revulsion against the growing power of the Israeli right: indeed, several weeks into the 1981 campaign, Meir Kahane, leader of the Fascist Kach movement, called for jailing Arabs who had sexual relations with Jews.

There would be more. During the Lebanon War of 1982, an officer of the Jewish National Fund issued this "urgent message to American Jews":

> As Israeli soldiers fought to secure the Galilee by pushing beyond the northern borders into the enemies' midst, Jewish national fund planners and builders embarked on an intensive program to consolidate the Jewish presence inside the Galilee by widening the network of outpost settlements in sparsely populated areas. The settlers at these hilltop outposts are guardians of Israel's future, preventing illegal land grabs, and curtailing the expansion of Arab villages which breed and harbor terrorists.

Of course, the Arabs referred to in this message are citizens of Israel; many had had their own land expropriated and virtually none had perpetrated acts of terror. (Ironically, the Israeli film director Danny Waschman was making his deeply moving and critically acclaimed film depicting Israeli government expropriations of Arab land—entitled *Hamsin*—at the very time that this JNF fund raiser was issuing warnings about Arab "land grabs.") Besides, the Jewish Galilee suffered much more from neglect than from Arab expansion during Begin's era. While hundreds of millions of dollars were poured into West Bank settlement, very little went into such towns as Safad, though the climate, location, and natural beauty of the town rivals Jerusalem's. The population of Safad remains what it was twenty years ago, about 12,000. The town's artists' colony, which was vibrant during the late sixties, has become a ghost town; a mafia of immigrant families now smuggle in Oriental art from Amsterdam and pay off the tour buses to stop at their "galleries" in the town center.

None of this is to suggest that the animosity between Israeli Jews and Israeli Arabs was not reciprocal. Many of the 500,000 Arabs who are Israeli citizens had become increasingly militant supporters of the PLO. In the elections of 1977, over half the Israeli Arabs voted for Rakah, which claimed to be anti-Zionist and openly favored a PLO state in occupied territory. Arab student organizations at Hebrew University and other universities refused to stand guard duty on their own campuses, though these were the targets of terrorist attacks. Student groups issued statements endorsing the PLO as the sole representative of the Palestinian people. Thousands marched during the West Bank strike of 1982, showing the PLO flag. Tufik Zayat, the Communist mayor of Nazareth, always insisted that such sentiments are only the surface signs of an even deeper disaffection. Still, the more fundamental question is this: How can a democratic state not treat one sixth of its citizens as equals and remain democratic? How to avoid civil war? The new Zionists asserted: "If not Hebron, then not Tel Aviv!" Was it not inevitable that Israeli Arabs would say: "If Hebron, then not Nazareth!"

.

In 1948 the 175,000 Palestinian Arabs who stayed in the territory that became Israel were almost all peasant farmers. Unlike the professional people, merchants, workers, and other urban Arabs who fled cities such as Haifa and Jaffa in panic—or were driven out of towns such as Lod and Ramle by the Haganah—the Palestinians who became Israeli citizens lived mainly in rural villages in north-central Galilee or in the Little Triangle between Haifa and Nablus, which the fighting did not quite reach. With the exception of Christian Nazareth, these were among the most backward places in the territory that became the state of Israel. About half Israel's Arabs still live in nearly isolated towns and serve as a work force for Israeli Jewish industries. A quarter work on Jewish farms and construction sites.

These figures convincingly show that the Israeli Arabs are dependent upon and dominated by the Jewish economy, that Arabs have become a segregated industrial proletariat in Israel and will remain one unless some of Israel's political institutions are reformed. Yet the changes in the social conditions of the Arabs in these regions have not all been for the worse. In 1944 about 11 percent of the Arab population was employed in "commerce and services," as compared with only 8.2 percent in 1963. But most of the urban Arabs who had commercial jobs fled in 1948; a great many working in services in 1944 were clerks in the Mandate bureaucracy. In contrast, the number of Arabs working as "traders, [commercial] agents, and salesmen" in Israel actually doubled from 1963 to 1972 and was roughly equal to the proportion of Jews doing the same work during the same years.

Such comparisons tell us a good deal—not all—about Arab political power in Israeli society. In 1972 most of the powerful Israeli corporations, collectives, and unions were still ruled largely by an old-boy network of Histadrut managers and Labor Alignment politicians, few of them Sephardi Jews or sympathetic to them, let alone Arabs. Indeed, the crucial disparity between Arabs and Jews was that nearly 40 percent of Jews had technological, administrative, and clerical jobs in 1972, most of them not in private commerce, and only 6.7 percent were unskilled laborers. Only 12 percent of Arab workers were employed in such privileged fields.

To grasp the full implication of changes in the Arab sector, one ought to consider the resistance of rural Palestinians to modernization. One of the few Israeli academics to have done this successfully is Professor Sami Mar'i, an Israeli Arab whose major study, published in 1978, pertained to Arab education in the Jewish state.[9] Mar'i was born and educated in Israel; he attended Hebrew University, where he studied sociology. In 1984, he was one of a handful of Arabs teaching social science at Haifa University, the only university in Israel whose number of Arab students is proportionate to the Israeli-Arab population.

Mar'i's central point is that Arab citizens will have to have far greater social and economic opportunities in Israel if their children are to feel loyal to the state and their teachers are not to feel like quislings. Of course, it may be asked why the Israeli school system is not more fully integrated, why kibbutz schools still exclude Sephardi children from nearby development towns, or why Jewish urban schools exclude the Arabs from nearby villages. But Mar'i makes a forceful case that the Arab educational system ought to be run by Arab educators, that it should teach more about Palestinian national culture and history. Will cultivating Palestinian identity inevitably lead to anti-Zionism? Mar'i thinks not.

True, there is contempt among the Israeli Arabs for what Zionism represented and more for the spirit of Greater Israel. Israel's Arabs have had bitter claims against their government, arising out of the years of Israeli-Palestinian bloodshed. They often bore the brunt of the turmoil and have not forgotten the violence done them by Israeli forces: between 1949 and 1956, the state expropriated about half of all Arab land for Jewish settlement, often resorting to specious claims that the land was abandoned or was required for state security. During the Sinai War in 1956, Israeli soldiers shot forty-three people for breaking the curfew at Kfar Kassem. (The Israeli commanders were court-martialed, and pardoned after a number of years.) The Israeli defense apparatus resorted to high-handed "security regulations" to suppress the emergence of any national Arab party, such as the El-Ard ("the Land") Party of the early sixties, which threatened to field candidates for election to the Knesset. In 1976, six young men were killed by soldiers during demonstrations against new Israeli plans to expropriate land in the Galilee. The government would not hold public inquiries into these killings. (Mar'i has documented how, in addition to expropriating land, state officials discriminated against Arab municipalities and public schools during this period, denying Arabs the funds that might have helped them catch up to standards in the Jewish sector. He is particularly hard on the record of the state's Arab Department, which reports directly to the Prime Minister and the Defense Ministry but claims to be a bureaucracy set up to serve the Arab community.)

Yet Mar'i has pointed out that Israeli Arabs appreciate what they can share of Israel's libertarian style of life. If Hebrew culture falls short of English with respect to liberal freedom, it is incomparably more liberal than that of the Arabs; Zionism may be conquering, humiliating, and hostile, but Israel has been a source of rapid progress for some Arabs in their knowledge of technology and their sense of women's rights, economic equality, and the values of individualism. So whatever their current enthusiasm for the "Palestinian cause," Arab students have taken a place in the modern world by means of a Hebrew education. They have ceased viewing membership in a powerful, patriarchal clan as central to their lives and have grown accustomed to co-educational arrangements outside school as well as within it. According to the research Mar'i cites, Israeli Arab children have become impatient with rote learning and have shown a much stronger predisposition for independent and creative thinking when compared with children in West Bank schools. There is, moreover, an ambivalence toward Hebrew literature itself since, during four years in high school, Arab students have to study 768 hours of Hebrew language and literature (including Bialik, Alterman, and leading Zionist writers), as compared with only 732 in Arab studies. However, Israeli Arabs have developed an affinity for the Hebrew culture they have had to master; they are certainly more drawn to actual Israeli life than Diaspora Jews.

Mar'i's most discouraging finding is that, nevertheless, 90 percent of the Arab students he interviewed in 1977 doubted they had a future in Israel. (Some 40 percent of young Israeli Jews concurred with this assessment of Arab prospects. More recent studies have found that 60 percent of Israeli Jewish teens would refuse to live in the same apartment building as an Arab, and 40 percent would not want to work with one.) Such attitudes might change if progress could be made on peace between Israelis and the Palestinians beyond Israel's border. Still, a less dramatic finding of Mar'i's shows the severe obstacles that would exist for Israeli Arabs even if peace became possible. It seems that Arab high-school seniors who major in science believe their future in Israel will be especially grim, and some 90 percent choose to major in the humanities. At first this seems odd. Most students, Mar'i found, consider the humanities curriculum in Arab schools degrading, due in part to its emphasis on Hebrew literature. Besides, one would expect the young members of a minority to advance most rapidly in technical jobs, where knowledge of mathematics and science counts for more than, say, a grasp of the majority's literature. What these figures reveal, precisely, is that Israeli Arabs lack the independent industrial base which could absorb their young scientists and professionals. Jewish managers of Israel's advanced industries will not hire Arabs, whether because of misplaced feelings of patriotism, fear of espionage, or common racism. Another reason for the discouraging views of Arab science students is that secondary-school programs are very expensive to develop. Arab municipalities, which carry little weight with Israeli political leaders, and have a small tax base, cannot afford them, even though a majority of Arab parents, albeit a small one, favor technical training for their children. Mar'i's conclusion, that students choose the humanities because they've grown resigned to exclusion, to a career in schoolteaching within their own towns, seems inescapable.

Israel's industrial bureaucracy and the state's Arab Department have broken up the Arab community by encouraging the pre-eminence of local *hamulas*. To that end, Israeli leaders have made separate and unequal arrangements with the Druze communities, whose young men serve in the IDF while most Israeli Arabs do not. During the 1960s and 1970s, the established political parties gave small numbers of the most promising young Arabs jobs in the government and the Histadrut, where they would have to be politically circumspect. Such sinecures no longer exist. (That the Rakah Party receives an independent subsidy from Moscow has helped to make it a singularly effective forum for Arab dissidents, who would otherwise have no sympathy for Communist social theory.)

Israeli citizenship is of no advantage to Arabs who want to live in Israel so long as the governing apparatus does not reapportion the power held by the semiofficial Zionist institutions established during the years of the Yishuv. These bureaucracies—the Jewish Agency, the Jewish National Fund, the organized rabbinate—have routinely violated the democratic standards which must be upheld for the Arabs if they are to gain anything like equality. One crucial reform would be a written constitution, through which Israeli Arabs could obtain judicial relief. The example of American blacks seems relevant here inasmuch as Israel, too, will need affirmative-action programs, laws guaranteeing equal pay, fair-housing legislation, and so on. The Knesset has periodically debated whether the Law of Return should redefine who is a Jew by Orthodox criteria. But from the Israeli Arab perspective, it is difficult to see why the law itself should not be terminated, or how its attendant economic benefits could survive any impartial judicial review if Israel enacted a bill of rights.

The problem obviously is not simply that Israel is a Zionist state, as some ultra-left critics of Israel have charged. Israeli Arabs know better than most that they live in an incipiently democratic state which accords important civil rights to all. Yet old Zionist institutions still reserve the principal economic benefits only for the Jews, and this must stop if Israeli Arabs are to be integrated. By 1980, for example, the Jewish Agency had spent some $5 billion to develop the Jewish economy and advance the prospects of Jewish families. No Arab had access to any of those funds. Land expropriated from Arabs by the Israeli Land Authority for "public use" is still consigned to Israeli citizens according to the exclusionary regulations of the old Jewish National Fund. Again, Israeli Arabs may not reside on about 95 percent of cultivated Israeli land.

Regulations of this sort create a particular hardship for Israeli Arabs in towns such as Nazareth and Acre, which are critically short of housing. But the Israeli state apparatus itself has not been free of overt discrimination in favor of Jews—a pattern which intensified under the pressure of the new Zionism. In the 1984 budget for Arab and Jewish areas, the Arab city of Nazareth received the equivalent of $629.40 per capita, compared with $1,688 per capita for Upper Nazareth, the largely Jewish town next door. The Arab town of Kfar Kara got $231.17 per capita, while the neighboring Jewish town of Pardes Hana received $1,540.90 per capita.[10] The state still refuses to draft Arab men into the Israel Defense Forces, though Israeli Arab youths have paid a high added cost for their military exemptions: national service is not only the prerequisite for being socially accepted in Israeli cities; it is also necessary for benefits upon discharge, such as low-interest mortgages, jobs which require security clearance, welfare payments to parents with many children, and so forth.

In fairness, since Israeli Arabs live in a rural economy they have often avoided paying full income tax; they can eat better than poor Jewish Israelis and get services for less. Would they move to the cities and go to work in the advanced economy? And would Israeli Arabs want to take an active part in the life of Israel while receiving a greater share of social benefits as they did so? After all, conscripting them into the IDF would mean that they would have to fight other Arabs; perhaps the state deserves some credit for refusing to insist that they serve. Still, it seems of critical importance to reiterate here what some Israeli Arab intellectuals—the television journalist Rafik Halabi, for instance—have insisted all along: that the loyalty of Israeli Arabs to Israel derives from what democracy it has achieved. Halabi, who served in the IDF, loves Israel for the spirit of the journalists who stood with him during his *contretemps* at the Broadcasting Authority. Though he studied Hebrew literature, he would never call himself a Zionist; his career proves that more perfect democracy is the only incentive for Israeli Arabs to keep faith with the national life.

vi

Ever since the Lebanon War, Israel's military and West Bank journalists have been particularly admired in the West, and deservedly so. Such reporters as Halabi, Rubinstein, Yehuda Litani, Zeev Schiff, and Hirsh Goodman have not only chased the facts of the occupation but have implicitly given their countrymen the democratic standards to judge the facts by. In fact, the larger cultural phenomenon these reporters represent may be reason to hope that the new Zionism will yet be superseded by a culture of liberalism. The least that can be inferred from the growth of the liberal Israeli middle class, its domination of the popular culture of the country, is that—were the occupation to end, even abruptly—a community of Israeli artists and intellectuals would know how to make the most of peace. Some of the country's most admired songwriters, novelists, and playwrights have implied a post-Zionist culture.

Israel could become a sophisticated and Mediterranean democracy—a "nice tropical country," as the singer Mati Caspi put it. Since 1973, Danny Sanderson has performed dozens of idiosyncratic and satiric songs, paeans to his "little country, evading sorrow." Chanoch Levin has openly defied the government's pieties. Chava Alberstein and Arik Einstein have sung elegies to the Golden Age. In spite of the reactionary tone of their politics, Israeli youth are deeply devoted to the home-grown, highly individual rock of Tzvika Pik, or the softer Sephardi rock of Ha'Breira Ha'Tivit. Interestingly enough, A. B. Yehoshua's novel *The Lover* sold about 40,000 hardcover copies in 1977, the equivalent of 3 million in the United States. No one else has ever succeeded as brilliantly in depicting the dilemma of the new Israeli's interior life.

In *The Lover*, for example, we encounter Adam, a protagonist of great complexity. Crushed by the oppressive atmosphere of the October War, he sets out in search of his wife's lover, a callow fellow who failed to return from the front. Adam is by no means unscathed by his wife's infidelity. But the author wanted his readers to understand the urgency with which some Israelis want to reconstitute the private space which war and sacrifice seem constantly to obliterate. Incidentally, Yehoshua wrote the novel in many different voices, as if to underline how hard it has become for typical Israeli characters to reach each other. The only ones who do find each other, though in a tense and reckless way, are Adam's teenage daughter and a young Arab employee, who fall in love and have a brief affair. (Yehoshua has since conceded that writers of his generation are having difficulty finding their old moral center; it seems, he says, there are too many dreams and voices now stirring in the population to be defined by pioneering, the wars, the Zionist struggle for identity.)

The Lover's success was matched in 1981 by the acclaimed play *Adam's Purim Party*, an adaptation of Yoram Kaniuk's novel *Adam Ben Kelev* (*Son of a Dog*). The action is set in a mental institution; most of the inmates have been driven to madness by experiences in the death camps. At the play's climax, an elderly lady with a heavy Yiddish accent tells in a voice suggesting autism how when she came to Israel she had been "reborn" in *chalutziyut*, in pioneering. Slowly it becomes clear that her Zionist enthusiasm is disingenuous, that her happiness is a guilty bow to state propaganda. Then she clumsily begins a hora, stumbling over the words of a song of praise to the Negev, the location of which (one suspects) she would be hard-pressed to give.

It should be stressed that the liberal, post-Zionist curve of Israel's leading writers does not imply their domination of the politics of the country any more than the Canaanites dominated the politics of Ben-Gurion's Israel after the Sinai campaign (or, indeed, Robert Redford and William Styron have dominated American politics during the era of Ronald Reagan). Yehoshua and Kaniuk represent minority political views in the new Israel; indeed, while Yehoshua's novel was selling out, Begin was elected for the first time; while Kaniuk's play was being performed, Begin was elected for the second. Still, the success of these writers and artists shows another side of Israel's social fabric, and their influence attests to the extent that messianic nationalists—Naomi Shemer or the poet Uri Tzvi Greenberg—may have failed to dictate what Israel must become.

The educated public at least seems intuitively to disdain artists who refuse to define the nation in a spirit of post-Zionist pluralism. During the 1960s, Shmuel Bak's canvases were very popular. They were surreal, lugubrious, full of color and cunning: stony pears in barren landscapes, gruesome pear presses squeezing out juice from baby pears. Yet after 1973, Bak (himself a refugee from the Nazis) tried to rally Jews to the new Zionism with Stars of David—half-constructed, half-demolished—or with scenes of biblical tablets stacked up in graveyards, scenes pervaded with the soot of the crematoria. It is curious how much less popular he's become, in spite of the majority willingness to vote for the people endorsing his political message.

.

One historian, whose parents were old Labor Zionist veterans, claims he lives the life of an "internal exile." This is not to say that anyone can retreat from politics; there are children in the army, enemies at the gates. Yet particularly during the Lebanon War, it was hard for Israeli liberals not to be bitter watching the new Israeli majority burying Labor Zionist achievements under roads, apartment houses, and shopping centers in the West Bank. Since Begin was elected for the first time, most Israeli liberals have been distressed to see their society inherited by fringe romantics and Torah messi-anists who could never have built the state, distressed to see how the old leadership of Revisionism was buoyed up largely by the very flood of immigrants their parents sacrificed to "ingather." True, political power in a democracy is not an inherited right. The coalition of Zionist leaders and urban intellectuals that brought Hebrew life back from the brink of extinction finally grew corrupt and bureaucratic—inevitably spoiled, perhaps, by its own success. The old Labor Zionist establishment, including the rank and file, refused to admit before it was too late that they lived in a plural society. They endorsed a style of democratic centralism which was fit only for the old Zionist Yishuv, and treated the public culture as if this, too, were a mere extension of their power. Their attitudes were reflected in school curricula, industrial relations, approaches to welfare and electoral politics—also in a certain snobbery.

In fact, the same Sephardi and youthful voters who have kept the

Likud in power and have applauded its high-handed ways on the West Bank may ultimately become a sincere constituency for a more genuine pluralism than what the Labor establishment had ever managed; laissez-faire in culture as well as in industry. By integrating the Israeli middle class, Sephardi immigrants may have inadvertently prepared the ground for greater liberalism; the rate of intermarriage between Sephardi and European Jews is approaching 30 percent. Putting Arab difficulties aside, Greater Israel *has* been more encouraging to private initiatives than laboring Israel, at least to the Sephardi's sense of family loyalty, commercial freedom, and artistic dignity.

Yet the Arab question *cannot* be put aside, and the Second Israel's incipient social liberalism is unfocused; it has not yet taken on political form. Sephardi youth have particularly counted on the strong, triumphal state of Likud's rhetoric to protect their new gains from the old Labor Zionist elites. Begin seemed paternal, not a sectarian—not a Sephardi or an Ashkenazi, but a good Jew. Certainly the Second Israel has come to consider the national self-determination of Palestinians a merely abstract, threatening desire, and many worry that the fulfillment of Palestinian rights will force the Sephardi community back into the position of being subject to European bosses.

In response, most veterans among Israel's old Zionists—especially kibbutz members associated with Mapam—have proposed reinvigorating the Zionism of their youth. Secretly, they disdain the new Israel and even their own younger generation for the habits of urban and commercial society. They dislike the Sephardi family, American music, the religiosity which fills up the spaces which secular revolutionary litanies have vacated. Labor veterans will openly decry the selfishness, the *enochiyut* of their children, of the "immigrants," without quite grasping why those children and newcomers are committed to the ordinary pleasures of the middle class and take *enochiyut* to mean defensible individualism. (One former resident of a Mapai collective farm recalls with some bemusement how when he wanted to hire some workers to help him with seasonal crops, his mother accused him of "going back to the Diaspora.")

But one cannot simply revive an ideology, however noble, without also reviving the resentments inspired by the power of its historic institutions. There is no sense speaking of a Labor Zionist ideology or movement as if either could exist apart from the historic circumstances engendering them. Indeed, the question is not whether good Zionism or bad Zionism will prevail in Israel but whether democratic tendencies—some of which, to be sure, were inherent in historic Labor Zionism—will prevail against the anachronistic institutions which Labor Zionists once made; prevail against the new Zionist ideology of a Greater Israel. An Israeli need not be a Zionist of any kind to want democracy for his or her country. For Israeli democrats, Arabs included, Zionist ideas are at best a distraction, at worst, an invitation to authoritarian forces to set the terms of national debate.

That Zionism is tragically obsolete can be hard to understand, what with the wars, the increasingly uncertain economic situation, the conviction that the "civilized" Jews of the West could, if they would only come, contribute to some great social healing. American Jews have certainly made what they call Zionism the center of their institutional life. Perhaps the hardest thing for old Zionists to concede is what Ben-Gurion at once perceived and suppressed: that a profession of Zionism in the West, and especially in America, is not so much resistance to assimilation as a symptom of it.

Conclusion / The Divisions of Unity and Beyond

For those disheartened listening to Menachem Begin and Yitzchak Shamir speak for Israel from 1977 on, the reemergence of Shimon Peres must have been something of a relief. Peres pushed through a plan for Israel's unilateral withdrawal from Lebanon. Instead of condemning the United Nations, Peres asked for an expanded peacekeeping force of UNIFIL troops "in order to provide security for Israel's frontiers."[1] When he spoke to the American press about his country's requests for aid, he said little about Israel's virtues as an American strategic asset, but emphasized his government's plans to cut Israel's budget and imports and increase the productivity of Israeli industry.

When he met with Jewish writers and editors in New York, Peres explained how the new government would improve the "quality of life" in the West Bank and Gaza. Many of the Likud's former restrictions in the territories would be lifted: an Arab bank would be allowed; nearly all the books that had been banned would be permitted to circulate. The pro-PLO writer Raymonda Tawil would be permitted to publish a magazine. Peres said that Arab mayors would be appointed for the five Arab towns now run by Israeli army officers—though the mayors who had been fired or deported would not get back their posts. Peres also spoke of accommodation with Jordan, of strategic cooperation with the Hashemite regime. Israel, he said, had "changed its settlements policy."

Though Peres spoke for a government composed of ministers from the Likud, he never made a part of himself over in Begin's mold. Have the principles of Ben-Gurion's Labor movement outlasted the Likud? Just forming a "unity coalition" gave the Israeli government an ability to tackle problems that had seemed beyond reach only a few months before. Did this mean that Israel could be expected to solve its deepest problem—its conflict with Palestinians and Arab states?

i

Two weeks before the July 23, 1984, elections, when Shamir surprised Peres with an invitation to form a "national unity government," Peres dismissed the suggestion as a publicity stunt. Shamir was then trailing badly in the polls. The Likud government had started a questionable war and had obviously mismanaged the government's budget. Likud was running without any help from Begin himself. Shamir had been severely criticized by both major newspapers, *Ma'ariv* and *Yediot Achronot*. Labor was united, well financed, and tightly organized; the long feud between Peres and Yitzchak Rabin was submerged.

Peres confidently replied to Shamir that a coalition of the major parties would undermine the parliamentary system. The very idea offended some Labor supporters. When Revisionist Zionist politicians from Jabotinsky to Begin called for national unity, they usually meant their ideal of a militant corporate state.

The day after the elections, however, left-wing writers including A. B. Yehoshua and Amos Oz published a statement endorsing Shamir's offer. What liberal convictions could not justify, Yehoshua wrote, Israeli voters had made necessary. Of the 120 seats in the Knesset, Labor won 44, a plurality, but only three more than the Likud won. Two dovish, "civil rights" lists had 6 seats, while the ultranationalist Tehiya movement won 5. The rest of the seats, 24, were divided among thirteen other parties—religious factions, Communists, annexationists, *laissez-faire* militants. That Labor did not win, Jerusalem's mayor Teddy Kollek confessed, came as a bigger shock than the losses of 1977 and 1981. The alternative to a "unity" government, Yehoshua insisted, would be growing cynicism about the democratic process—a "nation torn and split."

According to a poll in the daily *Ha'Aretz*, 81 percent of Israeli Jews agreed that a unity government should be formed, above all to deal with the collapsing economy. The Gross National Product had not grown for two years.[2] Inflation, already at 400 percent, began to climb higher after the election; foreign-exchange reserves, already dangerously low, dropped by a third. There had been ninety-three strikes in 1983, causing the loss of an estimated million days of work. Investment of all kinds, even in real estate, had largely ceased; volume on the Israeli stock exchange was down to less than one sixth of what it had been the year before. Reckoned in dollars, tax collection had dropped by 15 percent.

By the end of July, fearing economic breakdown, Israelis converted some 300 billion more shekels into $900 million. As soon as the vote was counted, economists at the Ministry of Finance, now able to speak freely, warned that any further drop in reserves of hard currency would put in jeopardy Israel's ability to import grain and fuel. It would also threaten the government's ability to borrow short-term funds at favorable rates in American capital markets. Larger interest payments would, in turn, augment the foreign debt, which had already reached some $22 billion, nearly 40 percent of the government budget and a major cause of the inflation.

Shamir's Cabinet, acting as a caretaker government, proposed reductions in government spending. But the general secretary of the Histadrut labor federation broke off negotiations with Shamir's Finance Minister over a new wage contract for government workers. The Histadrut would consider a wage-price freeze, the secretary announced, but he would not deal with a government that had no authority. In private, he doubted that a narrow Labor-led coalition would have any more authority than the Likud. Could any narrow coalition restrain the unions and reassure industrialists, shopkeepers, or farmers that Israeli money would be worth making?

There was also Lebanon. Contrary to the impression given in the American press, the war itself had not been unpopular. Israeli journalists had turned against Ariel Sharon mainly for the way he had fought it: by July 1984, nearly six hundred Israeli soldiers had been lost, and many more had joined peace groups in protest. But even after the Kahan Commission forced Sharon to leave the Defense Ministry for his part in the Beirut massacres, some 60 percent of Israelis supported the invasion.[3] If asked by the polls, they would say that the PLO was severely weakened.

But the occupation of southern Lebanon was something else. Every week, several more Israeli soldiers, including reservists with wives and children, were killed or injured in routine patrols. Fewer young Israelis than ever before were volunteering for career service or officer training.[4] The occupation was costing about $1 million a day. Israelis wondered if either party would have the courage to pull the Israel Defense Forces from advanced bases in areas dominated by Shiite militants. Wouldn't a narrow Likud government fear the charge of failure, a Labor government the charge of treachery? A few months before the election some 32 percent of Israelis polled by a monthly magazine said they wanted a "government of strong leaders, not beholden to any of the political parties."[5]

Liberal critics such as Yehoshua had opposed the war from the start and certainly wanted the IDF brought home. But they could take no comfort from that poll on leadership, and still less from the elections themselves. Meir Kahane's movement, Kach, for example, drew some 26,000 votes from all segments of the population and double the national average from the army. Not only was Kahane to be a member of the Knesset, but a survey on August 3 confirmed what previous polls had revealed, that some 15 percent of Jewish Israelis endorsed his idea that Palestinians should be deported to Arab countries and Israeli Arabs induced to emigrate.

Kahane, it could be said, won only 1.2 percent of the vote. His election gave many other right-wing politicians, including Begin, the chance to criticize him for his racism. Yet many knowledgeable Israelis wondered whether the war against the PLO in Lebanon had irretrievably spoiled relations between Jews and the 600,000 Israeli Arabs. Labor and other moderate Jewish parties campaigned in the Arab sector as never before. But for the first time since the founding of the state, a majority of Arab citizens voted for lists endorsing the establishment of a separate Palestinian state under the PLO. The Communists won 4 seats, and 2 were won by the Progressive List for Peace and Freedom, led jointly by Mohamed Mi'ari, a radical Arab lawyer, and Mati Peled, a reserve general who had met with Arafat. Kahane's victory also raised doubts about the sympathies of the police. When his followers stormed through the Old City of Jerusalem after the election, smashing Arab shops, several border-patrol officers were seen embracing them. At subsequent Kahane rallies, police kept order. When he went to open an "emigration office" in the Arab town of Umm el Fahm, the police surrounded him. But they arrested only rock-throwing Arabs who, along with hundreds of Jews, protested Kahane's mischief.

The day after Kahane's raid on the Old City, a well-known novelist who had been in the Warsaw ghetto openly insisted that the time had come for democrats to take action. She supported Yehoshua's call for unity and wanted the police to be taken out of the hands of Interior Minister Joseph Burg, the leader of the National Religious Party. Still, she said, it was time to "bash the heads" of Kahane's supporters. But who would be bashing whom? The only Jewish Israeli to die at a political rally in the past several years was from Peace Now; while West Bank settlers had organized and were supporting a terrorist underground. Moreover, wasn't the hostility between the Sephardi Second Israel—now the majority—and Israelis from European families such as her own as strong as ever? The campaign was more courteous than in 1981. Still, 70 percent of Sephardi voters supported the parties of the right. Only 60 percent had voted for Likud this time, fewer than in 1977; the claim of the party's supporters that it could not be stopped from gathering more and more strength among Oriental Jews was shown to be wrong. But the greater part of Likud's loss had not been Labor's gain. Many Sephardi voters now chose the more extreme right-wing parties, though some voted for liberal splinter groups.

Deteriorating relations between secular and Orthodox Jews only exacerbated ethnic tensions. The largely Sephardi Shas religious party—the "keepers of Torah"—had won 4 seats. Its leader, Rabbi Yitzchak Peretz, demanded the release from prison of members of the Jewish terrorist underground, and the exclusion of women from the Cabinet. Peretz even expressed warm words for Kahane, who had, meanwhile, dismissed democracy as inconsistent with Jewish law. There were violent protests in the town of Petach Tiqvah when the Labor mayor tried to allow theaters and restaurants to open on the Sabbath. To Yehoshua, it seemed that fringe groups of all kinds were ready to drag more moderate people into street violence

—and would succeed in doing so if hard times hardened intolerant attitudes. "After the first skirmish," he said, "young people start fighting over the last one."

ii

By the beginning of August, public expressions of support for "unity" had become irresistible and Peres gave in to them. So did the Israeli President, Chaim Herzog, a former Labor politician, who asked Peres to work out a reciprocal coalition with Shamir. Although they started to negotiate, the party leaders, in fact, began to work to deny each other a parliamentary majority—not because they had changed their minds about joint rule, but because it was not clear to anyone, Herzog included, which party controlled the most seats from among the splinter parties, hence which man should become Prime Minister. By the end of August—after innumerable bargaining sessions and back-room deals—Peres and Shamir, remarkably, each controlled blocs of exactly 60 seats. The more closely one looked, the more irreconcilable those blocs seemed.

The Labor Alignment included Mapam, which still represented mainly the left-wing socialist kibbutzim and supported a policy of magnanimity toward the Palestinians. Peres also allied Labor with the two civil-rights lists led by Ammon Rubeinstein and Shulamith Aloni, both concerned to protect secular civil life from religious control. Peres got the support of former Likud Defense Minister Ezer Weizman, who claimed he had returned to politics to revive the "peace process" with Egypt and Jordan. Peres was even willing to rely on the tacit parliamentary support of the Communist Party and the new Progressive List for Peace and Freedom.

For his part, Shamir made an alliance with the five Tehiya deputies, who represented the new Zionist ideology of the West Bank settlers—the belief that military force should be used ruthlessly to consolidate Eretz Yisrael. He won the support of all religious deputies, including four from Shas, and two even more strident messianists of the Morasha Party. Only the National Religious Party leadership negotiated seriously with Labor, though its younger leaders insisted on an alliance with Likud.

Along with most other politicians, Shamir condemned the election of Kahane; but the Likud leaders, especially Sharon, were willing to count on Kahane's vote. Indeed, Sharon kept his position in the

Likud hierarchy by mobilizing the support of extreme Herut voters.
During the campaign Sharon crisscrossed the country, unaccom-
panied by any of Likud's managers, and drew enormous crowds
chanting "Arik! Arik!" Shamir invited Sharon to join Likud's negotiating team.

A new election seemed inevitable, yet neither Peres nor Shamir
saw any advantage in having one. Would not a new vote produce
virtually the same result? They began to meet privately and to seek
a compromise more earnestly. At the beginning of September,
finally, they announced that they had agreed on a formula for sharing power. Labor and Likud would contribute ten ministers each to
an inner cabinet of twenty, which would have final authority on all
matters of diplomacy and defense—though the government's first
concern would be to do something about the deteriorating economy.
Apart from the inner group, where there would be absolute parity,
some thirty deputies would have ministerial rank, including three
ministers from the religious parties. The government was to last
fifty months; Peres would assume the Prime Minister's job first,
while Shamir would be deputy prime minister and Foreign Minister;
after twenty-five months, the leaders would exchange positions.

The announcement surprised and excited Israelis. The deadlock
had been frustrating, the negotiations distasteful, accompanied as
they were by rumors that made the back-room dealings sound like
a political auction. By this time it seemed fair, if oddly contradictory, that Labor and Likud would each retain a veto over the
other's most intransigent policies. Labor could block Likud's demand
for more West Bank settlements in places heavily populated by
Palestinian Arabs, though Peres agreed to some five more settlements in places that would not, he said, impede Labor's strategy
of "territorial compromise" with Jordan. Likud could stop Peres
from making concessions to Jordan, though not from inviting
Hussein to negotiate "without preconditions."

Still, Labor had won greater authority in security matters, since
Labor's Yitzchak Rabin was chosen for the Defense Ministry for the
entire life of the government. Under Rabin would be a Likud deputy
minister; but Labor's Chaim Bar-Lev would be Minister of Police.
Correspondingly, Labor seemed preeminent in cultural affairs, since
Yitzchak Navon got the Ministry of Education. What Likud acquired

was greater control over economic policy, notwithstanding its disastrous inflation of the economy, often for its own political advantage. The Finance Ministry went to the liberal leader in the Likud, Yitzchak Modai, while Sharon—who criticized Shamir for conceding the position of Prime Minister to Peres—was appointed Minister of Trade and Commerce. Other Likud politicians were appointed Ministers of Science and Development, and of Tourism. A new ministry of "economic planning," with vague jurisdiction, was created for Labor's shadow Finance Minister, Gad Yaacobi.

iii

In putting together the "unity" coalition, Peres and Shamir saved their political careers. Peres had been a less popular Labor politician than Rabin and Navon; according to polls in November, 40 percent of Israelis wanted him for Prime Minister, more than four times the number before the unity deal. On the other side, Sharon and Deputy Prime Minister David Levy, Likud's most powerful politician from the Second Israel, openly competed to discredit Shamir. Even after the deal was announced, they demanded that further Cabinet appointments be made not by Shamir but by secret ballot in Herut; Shamir defeated them, but it is doubtful he would have been able to do so had it not been for his agreement with Peres. Yet aside from personal ambition and a fear of political deadlock, Shamir and Peres may have had more in common than either has with any of the more extreme ideological parties that backed them—including the small parties that have come to seem the consciences of the bigger ones but were left out of the coalition. The zealots of Tehiya refused to enter a government with Labor. Peres, for his part, was willing to enter a coalition without Mapam, whose six members broke from the Alignment and went into opposition with Aloni and the leader of Labor's doves, Yossi Sarid.

Before the election, Peres told *Time* that he wanted Israel to be "socially, like a kibbutz." But since the 1950s, when he was Ben-Gurion's favorite technocrat in the Defense Ministry, Peres has stood for values that are opposed to the old kibbutz vision. With Moshe Dayan, Peres called for market efficiency, meritocracy, urban development, and an end to the domination of collectivist ideals in Israeli society. It is worth recalling that in 1965 Peres and Dayan became leaders of the Rafi Party, which broke away from Mapai for reasons that may seem remote today but reflect ways of thinking that are still pertinent. Like Herut and the Liberal Party—though not in alliance with them—the Rafi leaders wanted to challenge the deeply embedded power and state syndicalist ideology of both Histadrut and the Mapai, which had been taken over by Levi Eshkol, Pinchas Sapir, and Golda Meir. Rafi leaders saw in the Israel Defense Forces, and the defense bureaucracies and industries supporting them, the modernizing dynamism that was needed to assimilate hundreds of thousands of new immigrants from North Africa. They favored taking hard action toward the Arab world, along the lines of the Sinai campaign of 1956.

Peres has spoken of compromise with the Arabs. But his first goal, he has said, is maintaining the IDF's technological edge over the hostile Arab states. He has also written enthusiastically about the coming of postindustrial society, of robotics, automation, of Israel's potential role as a retailer of services to Europe, including software and medical care.[6] To counter Mapam's threat to leave the Alignment, Peres maintained Labor's arithmetical parity with Likud by absorbing Ezer Weizman's three Knesset members and Yigal Hurwitz, the former Likud Finance Minister who had opposed the Camp David accords. Hurwitz had been a close associate of Dayan; and like Peres—and Yitzchak Navon and Gad Yaacobi— he had been a supporter of Rafi. Peres had a longstanding feud with Rabin and tried to cultivate such Israeli writers as Yehoshua. But Peres was drawn to men with Rabin's military background—such as Chaim Bar-Lev, Mota Gur, the Minister of Health, and "Abrasha" Tamir, a major general who left a high position as a strategic planner to join with Ezer Weizman and whom Peres appointed to direct the Prime Minister's office.

Peres's replacement of Mapam with Rafi people and former military men suggested that his coalition with Shamir would prove a resilient one. Indeed, when Shas threatened to desert the coalition later in the fall—and to pull the Likud with it—Shamir helped Peres settle the dispute and the coalition held. Peres, Rabin, and Weizman all worked with Shamir during the many years he commanded a branch of the Mosad, the Israeli intelligence apparatus. Peres collaborated with Shamir's former Defense Minister, Moshe Arens, to found the huge Israeli aircraft industry. Shamir and Arens have both expressed reservations regarding Peres's Lebanon policy.

Yet they have not bolted as a result. Though it will cost the Israeli government another half billion dollars, both Peres and Arens wanted to go ahead with development of the "Lavi" fighter. Correspondingly, Rabin and Weizman have been curiously close to Sharon, who served with them in the General Staff. Modai, too, was a major in the army, and the popular Likud mayor of Tel Aviv, Shlomo Lahat, was a general. Shared backgrounds, of course, do not determine political moves. One could expect much backbiting, disagreement, and jockeying for position among all these men. But of the new government's principal ministers only David Levy, who came from a Sephardi development town and made a success as a building contractor, seemed the product of the Likud's grass-roots politics.

.

Israel's military-industrial bureaucracy currently employs about 25 percent of the country's industrial work force and accounts for some 16 percent of its exports.[7] Labor's top men have been at its center since the 1960s, and have had much experience in common with most of Likud's leadership. Indeed, few of the latter shared much with the Herut rank and file, who tended to be workers, foremen, small businessmen, usually of Sephardi origins. Leaving diplomatic questions aside, if not for shared political and economic assumptions, how could the coalition ministers have come to terms so quickly on the tough monetarist policies which Modai unveiled the day after the government was sworn in? These included radical cuts of subsidies on essential commodities, the banning of luxury imports—cars, stereos, liquor—for six months, and higher unemployment in the public sector.

On November 4, with the agreement of the Histadrut *and* the Association of Manufacturers, the government took further action to reduce the rate of inflation, then running at about 25 percent a month. For the next three months wages and prices would be frozen and all prices would have to be fixed in shekels, not dollars. Because the government would continue to spend beyond its means—it employs some 35 percent of Israeli workers—inflationary pressures were expected to build at the rate of about 10 percent a month, although their effects were not registered until February. The Histadrut has conceded that, by then, workers would make up only about 80 percent of the erosion of their salaries caused by inflation.

Drastic as these measures would seem to Americans, they may not be harsh enough to shift workers from the government payroll to export industries that require more specialized skills. Such reputable economists as Meir Merhav of the *Jerusalem Post* have called for adopting the dollar as the official Israeli currency. For his part, Modai has spoken of a further 25 percent reduction in government spending, which would lead to much higher unemployment—though not as high as what adopting the dollar would bring.

The government's prudence is understandable. General unemployment would lead to higher Jewish emigration and greater Arab restiveness. Nor would a more severe reduction in spending do much to balance the budget in view of the higher unemployment benefits that would have to be paid. Still, the unity government's cautiousness cannot be blamed on a disagreement between Labor and Likud per se; indeed, class differences seem more potentially a source of tension than differences of party affiliation. Since the government was formed, the ministers who have most openly criticized Modai's economic policy are David Levy and Moshe Katzav, Likud's young Minister of Labor and Social Affairs—himself from the Second Israel. Levy and Katzav have accused Peres of indifference to the effects of austerity on the poor, who would now be unable to afford apartments or find jobs.

The criticism, no doubt, struck Labor leaders as hypocritical. But it may have insulated the Likud from the consequences of the Begin government's recklessness, and helped preserve for the Likud as a whole its image as defender of the common man. As the austerity measures become harsher, Levy and Katzav, as well as Sharon, could pose a deep threat to Peres. "The possibility remains," one close observer of Israeli politics explained, "that Peres will come to appear as a sort of Ramsay MacDonald. Some of the Labor politicians would have preferred to let the Likud form a narrow government and take the consequences of cleaning up the economic mess it created. Now Levy and Sharon and their followers, the hard core of the Herut Party, can attempt to dissociate themselves from the policies of Modai, a Liberal, and Shamir, whom they see as a has-been, and above all Peres, who will have to accept responsibility for unemployment. Peres has saved his position for the time being and he may get credit for taking charge at a difficult moment; but he may also have played into the hands of the Herut populists: no one should underestimate their ability to mobilize angry workers against Peres's leadership and discredit Labor."

It remained to be seen whether Shamir was indeed a has-been. For the first six months of their partnership, Shamir certainly seemed lost in Peres's shadow. Levy declared for the leadership of the Likud, and Sharon grabbed the headlines with his libel suit against *Time*. Nor did Shamir and Arens leave an unambiguous legacy. It was Shamir's government, after all, that had uncovered and indicted the Jewish terrorist underground. One of Israel's leading military correspondents, Eitan Haber of *Yediot Achronot*, believes that the army's General Staff under Arens had become far less mired in politics than it was under Sharon and the former Chief of Staff—now a leader of Techiya—Rafael Eitan. (Immediately after Kahane's election, Arens's chief education officer in the army announced an emergency program to teach recruits about the "virtues of democracy." Eitan, who has been openly bigoted toward Palestinians, had ordered courses on Zionism and the "love of Eretz Yisrael.")

Perhaps because of such changes, Gush Emunim concluded that even with Sharon in the government there was a potential for genuine cooperation between Labor and Likud, which would result in diminished government support for West Bank settlements. Sharon's ministry was expected to authorize many private development projects on the West Bank, where much of the land is privately owned. Still, a leader of Gush Emunim, Elyakim Ha'Etzni, greeted the formation of the coalition with the announcement that his movement would revert to tactics for illegal settlement that Zionist pioneers had used under the British Mandate—tactics the Gush Emunim actually used against Rabin's government in the 1970s. In fact, the government no longer had money for any development projects, on the West Bank or anywhere else.

iv

One useful result of the unity government was that Gush Emunim's threats were not taken as seriously as they would be under a narrow Labor coalition. But Ha'Etzni's warning suggested how characterless Israel's two major political parties had become and how much they were concerned to appeal to a broad Israeli public that was increasingly urban, youthful, influenced by television. Will parties that concentrate on short-term economic or diplomatic gains increasingly ignore grandiose ideas of extending the reach of Zionism? Will Tehiya's exhortations to settle in holy land eventually become as irrelevant to middle-class Israeli families—whether of Sephardi or European origin—as Mapam's Labor Zionism of agricultural collectives and dedicated socialist schools?

Perhaps. But Mapam defectors from the Alignment were justifiably concerned that a unity government would preserve a state of affairs more congenial to Likud's most strident supporters than to Labor's most moderate ones. Whatever may become of the ideal of Greater Israel, the fact of a Greater Israel has persisted since 1967. The unity government gave no promise of fundamental change; its main immediate effect was a new atmosphere of hope that the country's divisiveness, which the elections only confirmed, would not now lead to riots among Israelis who had the deepest sense of grievance—among West Bank settlers, say, or in poorer quarters and hinterland towns. (The uncertainty about how the government's economic policy would work has dimmed that hope somewhat.) The unity government leaders may agree to reform the electoral system in a way that would diminish the influence of the small religious parties. They could raise the minimum proportion of the vote necessary to enter the Knesset to, say, 4 percent, which would shut out Kahane and force all religious politicians into one camp. But a consolidated religious bloc in the Knesset would, in all likelihood, support the Likud. Navon may well call a halt to religious encroachments on secular education. But rule over 1.5 million Arabs is itself a kind of education for young Israelis and one over which he has no control.

.

During the campaign, Yitzchak Navon visited the development town of Yoqne'am Illit, in the Valley of Jezreel. Yoqne'am's residents are largely North African immigrant families who work in Haifa or in the well-to-do kibbutzim nearby, or in the ammunition factory that the state set up there. An armored infantry base is a mile away. Navon was Labor's most prominent Sephardi politician. Yoqne'am's residents welcomed him enthusiastically when he was President of the state. Would they welcome him as a representative of the Labor Alignment?

"Look how they humiliated Navon," a young man said. "First he was President, then they made him nothing, number three." Who were "they"? Alignment types—*Ma'arachniks*—the Ashkenazim, the well-educated, such as the members of the neighboring kibbutzim who once every four years—during an election campaign—turn out to demonstrate along the Yoqne'am roads. "Look at their demonstrations during the war," he went on. "Their signs were always full of English. What for? To embarrass the state in front of the Americans. If you had a wife and she publicly embarrassed you, would you keep her?"

He had read the Bible. He interpreted it as prohibiting the return of any part of Eretz Yisrael. "They'd give up the patrimony to others, like wicked brothers. They love the Arabs more than their own."

That night, a group from the high school came out to heckle Navon. In the stands next to them was a farmer who had been born in Kfar Yehoshua, a Mapai farming community nearby. He had had almost nothing to do with the Oriental Jewish town, though his daughter had just married an Iraqi boy she had met at Ben-Gurion University in the Negev. (He said that the overvalued shekel, which Likud had subsidized and with which Yoqne'am's residents had imported cars and television sets, had forced his neighbors to pull up and burn their orchards. Their crops could not be exported.)

Navon came to the podium, clapping his hands to the Labor campaign jingle—a tune curiously like melodies to be found in the Sephardi liturgy. He started badly. Labor people, he said, had "opened the gates" to North African immigrants. The students took this as a provocation. "Who else would have done your dirty jobs," a young man yelled back. Navon had doubtless heard this many times before, but it seemed to rattle him nevertheless. He was talking about the events of thirty years ago. Likud had governed for seven; why did these young people believe that Labor was still *Ha'mimsad*, the establishment? In fact, Israel's biggest industrialists —including David Moshevitz of Elite, and Uri Bernstein of Amcor, both prominent in the Association of Manufacturers—strongly supported the Labor Party in these elections. Though the Labor Alignment appointed Israel Kessar, a Sephardi, as head of the Histadrut, the managers of Histadrut-owned industry—which still accounts for some 25 percent of GNP—have done little to dispel the idea that Labor's method of "socialist" development during the 1950s and 1960s became corrupted by patronage, by favors for "them," and discrimination against the Sephardi immigrants. (Just as the campaign was getting under way last June, Yaacov Levinson, the former chairman of Bank Ha'Poalim—the Histadrut's most glamorous and profitable operation—killed himself in the middle of a Histadrut investigation into his affairs. In his suicide note Levison maintained his innocence and accused his colleagues of untold deceptions.)

Navon tried a different tack. As President, he grandly confided, he had met with Argentina's Raúl Alfonsín and they had talked about whose country's currency was losing value faster. "Argentinians count their money in the millions," Navon exclaimed. To which a young woman responded mockingly, "You see, this is an international phenomenon!" A boy of about eighteen interrupted Navon. Why had he called Arabs "brothers" in a television campaign spot? Why did he love the Arabs? Navon's face turned red. "What geniuses you are! What diplomats!" Navon shouted, causing the speakers to crackle. "Can't you understand simple arithmetic? Why, the very point of Labor's Zionist program is to have as much land as possible and as few Arabs as possible!"

That farmer from Kfar Yehoshua, who was appalled by the shouting, was hearing Navon make a familiar argument—for something like the Allon plan for "territorial compromise" with Jordan. But had these young people heard what he had heard? During his childhood, there was the struggle against Fascism; during theirs, the wars of 1967 and 1973 and the struggle against Palestinian terrorism. Navon's reply only seemed to confirm their belief that the West Bank should be annexed and its residents expelled. Was Kahane doing no more than carrying to its logical extreme what had become the conventional wisdom during the Begin years? Was this the fate of that "demographic" argument?

·

Begin is gone, but not the borders which Likud supporters take for granted as "realistic" and unchangeable. During the election campaign the party simply called itself National Camp—*Ha'-Machane Ha'Leumi*—and defended rule over "Judea and Samaria"; the PLO, scattered by Sharon's war, was no longer a matter for anxiety. For most young people in Israel, the territories seem as much a part of Israel as Arab Nazareth. Likud's vote in the army fell by some 15 percent. But Likud, Tehiya, and Kach together got 45 percent of the vote in the army, 60 percent including the religious parties. Labor and the civil-rights parties got about 39 percent. Again, some 60 percent of Jewish high-school students—two thirds of whom are of Sephardi origin—were unwilling to live in the same building as Arabs, and 40 percent were unwilling even to work with an Arab.[8] It is hard to see how the rightist groups will do worse with young voters once the IDF is out of Lebanon.

Young people whose families have been strongly attached to Labor are meanwhile confused and demoralized. In Labor youth movements, among the sons and daughters of the left-wing academic activists—even on the kibbutzim—one hears the expression *"Ani masea rosh katan"*—literally, "I am carrying a small head," that is, keeping a low profile. This helps to account for last year's decline of volunteers for elite units and officer training in the army. If one thinks how aware young Israelis have been made of war, Greater Israel, death camps, and the Bible, it is hard to believe they would not eventually want something more stirring from national leaders than Peres's dream of high technocracy. If the unity government were to fall apart, Peres might well be reelected. But there should be no doubt that Sharon's nationalism and Levy's populism will seem more powerful attractions in the long run, in the absence of peace.

•

Israel's leading high-technology industries may respond to a period of strong government. The Haifa-based Elron group projected sales of $350 million for 1985, $100 million more than 1984, and it even set up a branch plant on Boston's Route 128. Greater Israel's population is about 5 million; its entrepreneurs have capital to invest, and they will likely benefit from the recently negotiated free-trade agreement with the United States. There are many fine universities in Israel, though recent budget cuts have lessened their ability to meet the growing demand for computer engineers. But Peres's plan for recovery may ultimately lack the political forces to carry it out. Likud, not Rafi, finally emerged as the party to challenge the power of the Histadrut and repudiate the old Mapai's state socialism. Can a Labor Party making itself over in the image of Rafi compete with Likud? The Likud includes not only technocrats and the old Herut nationalists but also a young guard of leaders such as Katzav, or Meir Shitrit, the mayor of Yavne. Elections within the Likud have also brought forward Uriel Linn, an impressive young economist whose family emigrated from Morocco.

If they use their power competently, Peres, Rabin, and Navon may increase their personal prestige. If, as expected, there are new elections before the government's term expires, Peres might be a more popular candidate running as the Prime Minister, which is precisely why Sharon opposed the deal. But Labor is short of new leaders who can make the case for civil rights and territorial compromise to the new Israel. Jealous of its power, the central committee of the Labor Party has blocked the advance of such prominent liberal academics as Shlomo Avineri and Zeev Sternhel. Labor's most promising Sephardi intellectual, Shlomo Ben-Ami, has become estranged from the party.

The youthful head of the Jerusalem branch of the Labor Party, Uzi Baram, the son of the former head of the Jerusalem branch, Moshe Baram, asserted after the election that Labor's leadership should be opened up. Perhaps, he said, Labor should adopt an internal primary system like the Likud's, in order to elect Knesset members from the rank and file.[9] Reform seemed to him all the more necessary since elections to the Histadrut general council were coming up in 1985. However embarrassing Labor's connection to such powerful Histadrut corporations as Bank Ha'Poalim or Koor may be, they have been important in financing the party's organization and electoral campaigns. Labor's control of the unions, moreover, provides the party with its main base from which to sustain and possibly increase its appeal to Israeli workers. A takeover of the Histadrut by the Likud at any time in the future would be a strong sign that Peres's gamble on "unity" had failed to rehabilitate Labor in the eyes of the Second Israel.

As it happens, Uzi Baram eventually became Secretary General of the party, and Labor's Kessar won easy reelection as head of the Histadrut in May 1985. Yet without a trusted new leadership at the top, Labor's standing increasingly depended on the unity government's managing difficult problems; by June, Likud seemed poised for a comeback. The economy still showed few gains under Peres, despite new American aid amounting to $1.8 billion. More important, the government's decision—which was largely Rabin's decision—to exchange convicted Palestinian (and Red Guard) terrorists for Israeli soldiers captured in Lebanon ironically seemed to vindicate Sharon's view that cruelty was endemic to the struggle between Israelis and Palestinians and that military power was all.

Rabin claimed, plausibly, that the IDF could not send soldiers into battle and then tell them to "go to hell" if captured. But whatever its impact on the army's morale, the exchange gravely demoralized the public. Some of the terrorists returned to their West Bank homes and were greeted as heroes; the celebrations seemed to imply that Peres's effort to achieve some diplomatic breakthrough with the West Bankers was an illusion. Immediately, Likud leaders (most of whom had voted for the exchange) began to call for the release of the Jewish terrorists as well. At all events, less than a year after the unity government had been formed, Labor's prestige had come to depend on the success of the peace process.

v

By January 1985, the unity government had embarked on a policy of withdrawal from southern Lebanon, with UN forces having a part in the arrangements for peacekeeping. How could the government approach the question of the West Bank? Peres, Rabin, and Weizman clearly favored territorial compromise, but have committed themselves to achieving a consensus with the Likud. When in February 1985 King Hussein and President Mubarak called for new peace talks—including a Palestinian delegation acceptable to Arafat—Peres encouraged the initiative and Shamir denounced it. Moshe Arens has said that he favors annexation of the West Bank because he would rather fight for "pluralism" in Greater Israel than fight terrorism from a smaller Israel. Does this mean that he and other Likud military technocrats might be more open to a negotiation with Jordan? Probably not.

The West Bank Arabs, he said, don't present a problem essentially different from the Israeli Arabs'. "In either case, we must make it our business to be more open and pluralistic—though the effort could take a generation: they don't want us here." Eventually, Arens

said, the Israeli Arabs would have to be brought into the army.
But he could not say when.

> The younger generation of Arabs has undergone a process of "Israel-
> ization." The same is true around Jerusalem. They have mastered
> Hebrew, want to be accepted and enjoy equality before the law. But
> nothing much can be done during a state of war. We have started by
> widening the circles of opportunity for minorities such as the Druze in
> the army.

Some unpleasant questions lie beneath that reasonable-sounding
talk. The Druze are recruited mainly for the border patrol, which
is trained to keep the larger Moslem Arab community in line. And
if "Israelization" means accepting Israel as a secular, Hebrew democracy, then what about all the young Jews who seem drawn to
theocratic ideas—and the near-majority who say they don't want to
work with Arabs? Can Israeli Jews hope to develop a common
language with Israeli Arabs so long as the country maintains its
hold over a million more Palestinians?

"We are a nation still dragging our roots around with us," Arens
insisted. "There may be more elegant laws than, say, the Law of
Return, but this is still necessary so long as we provide a haven—
for Russian Jews and others. We must rule out a return of territory
so long as security is paramount. The Arabs would destroy us if
they could. The Middle East is a dangerous place: look at what has
happened to Lebanon."

Shimon Peres may be more sincere about the values of pluralism
and is, in any case, more enthusiastic about negotiating with Jordan
—though his views seemed identical to those of Arens when he
served as Rabin's Defense Minister between 1974 and 1977. In
1982, however, Peres supported the Reagan plan, which called for
"self-government by the Palestinians of the West Bank and Gaza
Strip in association with Jordan," and condemned Jewish settlement activity in the West Bank for the way it stifled development of
the impoverished regions in Israel, particularly in the Galilee.
Peres has encouraged King Hussein to create a joint Jordanian-
Palestinian delegation to peace talks, even though the Palestinians
—according to Arafat's agreement with Hussein—would have to

be approved by the PLO. Rabin has been equally constructive since becoming Defense Minister. In a private meeting with Gush Emunim settlers, Rabin warned them against any form of vigilante activity. (Rabin may still have to deal with more such episodes as the rocket attack on an Arab bus in November 1984, in retaliation for the killing of a Jewish couple the previous week.)

Sadly, however, the distinction between Peres's enthusiasm for an arrangement with Jordan and Arens's skepticism about it may not have the political importance it might have had when Sadat went to Jerusalem. Hussein has boldly reestablished diplomatic relations with Egypt. In Washington in June Hussein insisted that he and Arafat had agreed on the need for a joint delegation to enter peace talks with Israel and that Arafat, too, would be willing to exchange "peace for land." But the Hashemite regime is still dependent on the Gulf countries, which cut his $1.2 billion subsidy in half in 1984. To enter into serious peace talks with Israel, Hussein needs not only the reassurance from Israel of a freeze on settlements —which the unity government has not given him—but also some indication that Israel will permit Jordan to reestablish Arab sovereignty over Arab Jerusalem. Arafat has given Hussein a mandate to negotiate on behalf of the Palestinians—a terribly important development, since this will preclude the evolution of an independent PLO state and Arafat knows this. With Hussein leading a joint delegation, Palestinian intellectuals and West Bank elites will inevitably become more important to the Palestinian national movement than leaders who had prosecuted a futile armed struggle. Indeed, Hussein may finally succeed in playing Victor Emmanuel II to Arafat's Garibaldi, however much Arafat may want to yank his mandate back. But, in any case, given the large population of Palestinians in his country Hussein wants a virtual guarantee that peace talks, once started, will succeed.[10] Peres's Labor Party is uncompromising with regard to Jerusalem.

The United States might have intervened with some new plan for indirect negotiations. It may yet try to revive negotiations for an agreement on disengagement of forces between Jordan and Israel —like the one that nearly came about in 1974. Peres could probably muster a narrow Knesset majority for an interim settlement, especially if the U.S. government made it clear that economic assistance would be coordinated with a comprehensive American

Middle East policy. Some of the Liberals in the Likud—Arie Dulzin, the chairman of the Jewish Agency; Menachem Savidor, the former Knesset speaker; Shlomo Lahat—have already called for a split with Herut. But as of the spring of 1985 the Reagan Administration was more concerned that the Israeli government solve its economic difficulties rather than risk any peace initiative.

That seemed shortsighted. Arafat's prestige survived Sharon's blows, and may even have been enhanced by them; even after his bloody conflict with the Syrian government, Arafat managed to assemble a quorum of the Palestine National Council in Amman in December 1984. The proceedings were broadcast all over the region, including the West Bank and Gaza, by Jordanian television; Hussein promised the PNC that he would not act without their consent, though, pointedly, he would not promise to back PLO demands for an independent state and renewed his offer of a federation. Fatah's abortive terrorist attack on Tel Aviv during the 1985 Independence Day celebration—Palestinian commandos were captured at sea by the Israeli navy—may indicate that Arafat is still more determined to block Israeli–Jordanian *rapprochement* than endorse it. But Israeli attacks on the PLO have done nothing to help Hussein escape the limits of Arab consensus, much as they may have encouraged West Bankers to hope for greater PLO cooperation with Hussein. If America permits the Israeli government to use the time the IDF bought in the Lebanese war against PLO terror to consolidate new Zionist gains in the West Bank, increasing the Jewish population there to, say, 50,000 people—including thousands of fanatic, armed vigilantes—would there be anything left to negotiate?

Moreover, the Jordanians, the Israeli Labor Party, the West Bank middle class, moderate Palestinians with links to Fatah (which had to split away from Syrian control), the Saudis and Egyptians, the Americans—all these groups have no other basis for agreement than the one President Reagan proposed. Indeed, confederation is the only plan which could evolve reasonably from Camp David's transitional arrangements providing for Palestinian autonomy; in no other way than by means of autonomy can all sides test each other's sincerity and learn to live with peace. Autonomy would allow for the development of what Jordan's Crown Prince Hassan has called "regional" economic and political institutions which include Israel; institutions which seem the more necessary now that the economy and demography of historic Palestine are not as easily divided, or "partitioned," as in 1948.

Besides, leaders become hostages to the expectations for peace they raise as well as to the hatreds they inflame. The question of Jerusalem might also seem less intractable after a few years of peaceful autonomy. Some in Israel, people such as Yuval Neeman, the leader of the ultra-right Tehiya ("Renaissance") Party, accept the burden of permanent war and point to the deterrent power of Israel's nuclear potential. But all moral questions aside, can the Jewish state ever use such weapons on neighbors who live a few kilometers away? Neeman seems blind to the fact that Israel's nuclear weapons make nonsense of the very Arab threat his hard line presupposes; that is, the potential destruction of the Jewish state by Arab invasions. The Arab scholar Fouad Ajami insists that every Arab leader knows how a successful invasion of Israel, which threatens the massacre of Israel's citizens, would bring holocaust to Arab capitals. So nuclear weapons ought to reassure Israelis that radical Arab threats to destroy Israel are obsolete and hollow. What they cannot do, precisely, is deter the wars of attrition that have taken so large a toll in Israeli soldiers and embittered daily life.

Control of the West Bank *has* helped in the fight against Palestinian terrorism. It would, in any case, always be hard to let go of the tiger's tail. Yet the most proven way to check terror is to enlist Israel's Arab neighbors in the fight against it. There have been no terrorist attacks from Egypt or Jordan for years; there have also been no terrorist attacks coming from the Golan since 1973. Besides, however indefensible terrorism is in moral terms, it cannot be doubted that Palestinian terror has roots in political frustration. Nothing would undermine this so much as simple justice. Even if terrorism cannot be utterly eliminated, can terrorists kill nearly as many people as die in one day of high-tech war?

The new Zionist program has invited an ongoing war of attrition, first with Palestinians in the streets of the West Bank, then with Syria over the Golan Heights. Inevitably, too, there will be confrontation with the governments of Jordan, Saudi Arabia, and Egypt. Islamic fundamentalism is on the rise and may ultimately sweep away any or all of these regimes, but it is most likely to do so if the Palestinian problem continues to fester. On the Golan Heights there are arrayed more Syrian tanks than the number with which Germany attacked the Soviet Union in 1941. Israel is a country of 4 million people— 3.5 million of them Jews. About 18 percent of the country is of Palestinian Arab origin. The Arab world is 100 million people. Their leaders have an endless capacity to wage wars of attrition on Israel's margins. To be blunt, Israel's army can defeat or deter attacks, but it can never exact surrender of the West Bank and Jerusalem. Even in Lebanon, Israeli forces pulled back without a peace treaty, and with new terrorist problems—from Shiite militias —dogging its remaining forces.

One cannot conjure away the risks of peacemaking, however preferable they are to war. Withdrawal from the West Bank, even under Jordanian auspices, will inevitably lead to the return of some refugees and the kind of social turmoil that encourages anti-Israel terror. The PLO has been split and may—as Jordanian leaders hope—ultimately be put in eclipse, yet some PLO leaders and cadres will inevitably play a role in the West Bank's future whether or not they renounce their long-standing irredentist claims on Israel proper. Any peace will be fragile before it can be superseded by commercial routines, circles of private affection and libertarian spirit, and the precedent of cooperative enterprise. Indeed, any further efforts to make peace—no matter how they are buttressed by security guarantees, transitional arrangements, international support, and American largesse—will need leaders who are prepared to believe in a world where Jews are not merely victims or pariahs. After six Arab-Israeli wars—after the European Holocaust and the mass expulsion of Jews from Arab lands—are such leaders emerging from Israel's younger generation?

It is difficult to say; youths become parents and which parents do not pray for peace? What can be said is that, in 1985, Ben-Gurion's plan to partition the land is no less vital for Israeli democracy than before and that, during the elections of 1984, the Israelis of the coming generation seemed less open both to partition and to democracy than their own parents were. That may prove the tragedy of Israel.

Epilogue / An American Zionist?

So few American (and Canadian) Jews have tried to make their lives in Israel since the 1950s—most of whom, like myself, returned home—that one would expect from them considerable skepticism regarding historic Zionism by now. Yet this is not the case. When the state of Israel was proclaimed in 1948, Churchill cabled Weizmann what a fine moment it was "for an old 'Zionist' like me!" In Churchill's sense, at least, Israel has been a continuing source of fascination and pride for American Jews, too—though they have never much taken to heart the claims of revolutionary Zionist ideology.

Since 1967, moreover, a good many Western Jews have been attracted to the new Zionist rhetoric of the Israeli right. I am speaking here not only of the Orthodox thinkers who (together with Christian fundamentalists, ironically) have been drawn to the messianic prospect of an Israel ruled by Mosaic law, but also of self-defined secularists, former liberals, neo-conservatives. American Jews make up a disproportionately large number of the thousands of people who have settled the West Bank. Less intrepid American Jews—indeed, the majority of Jews who strongly support Jewish defense organizations and social societies—have come to treat political action on behalf of Israel's diplomacy as a kind of self-evident corporate responsibility. According to the prevailing view, their Zionism is a disciplined public service in common institutions such as the United Jewish Appeal, the Jewish Agency, and the World Zionist Organization. Vaguely articulated images of the achievements of the old Zionist Yishuv reinforce this trend and inspire secret yearnings. One might almost say that fund raising on behalf of Israel has superseded as public duties the Orthodox legal and ritual obligations modern Jews have typically been unwilling to perform.

The very notion of the "modern Jew" is a daunting one, and the classical Zionist writers have shown how hard it is to understand it. Before 1967, many American Jews were willing to acknowledge that Jewish tradition had become a kind of civil religion for them in *this* country, a complement to American liberal democracy rather than a "national" affiliation or a dependence on Hebrew-cultural activity. American Jews had emphasized Judaism's ethical side almost to the exclusion of what was more strictly cultural and aesthetic. Moses Hess had discovered that, to be sure, the historical and biblical models of normative Judaism—out of which the ethics of the Jews emerged—were difficult to separate from the incipiently national character of the Eastern Jewish people; it was that national character which gave rise to Zionism. But the Eastern Jewish people are no more, and common ancestry does not necessarily mean an Israeli and an American Jew have as much in common as the new Zionist rhetoric demands. There has been pride in one another—Israelis in our Bellows, American Jews in their Ben-Gurions—and generosity to each other when this is possible. Yet would Achad Haam have expected American Jews and Israelis to define themselves by means of the other?

In fact, when Zionist pretenses are put aside, Israelis and American Jews are often deaf to each other. One hears Israel's most intelligent and tolerant writers complain about American Jewish visitors who have the temerity to assert how Israel is not "Jewish" enough, not good-natured enough, not keeping faith with the prophetic imagination of Isaiah—"these people," as A. B. Yehoshua puts it, "who cannot even read Hebrew." Even radical Israeli doves, who would otherwise have no compunctions about American Jewish intellectuals attacking the Likud (or pressuring the U.S. government to condition its aid), cringe when they hear the same people talk about the Jewish "ethical vocation," or, worse, lecture

Israelis about how Judaism mandates a peculiarly open-spirited morality, a sense of history. Equally, American intellectuals have little patience for Israeli writers and critics who treat American Jews as nothing but Arnold Toynbee's "fossils." In Boston, in 1984, Amos Oz used a podium provided for him by the American Friends of "Peace Now" to lecture his audience about how American Jewish life is bankrupt, doomed—a "museum, not a theater." Israeli democracy would work better, he said, if more of the audience went to Israel. (It never entered his mind, presumably, that Massachusetts would probably not have gone for Reagan if more Israelis like him had moved to Boston.) The point is that American Jews and Israelis are talking past one another, and how could this be otherwise?

American Jews are not living on Hebrew. They live on what Irving Howe has called "the questions." Amos Oz cannot turn Howe Jewish in any sense which will make sense to Howe, and vice versa. They each mean something quite different by the word "Jew," and will certainly be at odds when it comes to "modern Jew." It is for this reason, among others, that Israeli immigrants to the United States often live in neighborhoods almost entirely divorced from those of American Jews and will have little to do with American synagogues or organizational life. The new Zionist rhetoric only obscures these divisions and locks Israelis and American Jews in a debate in which both sides must necessarily become increasingly disillusioned. Why, then, do American Jews who still bother with their origins add to the confusion by paying lip service, and more, to Zionism?

.

The shocking events of 1967 certainly had something to do with this; like my father, a great many American Jews could not refrain from reassigning the images of the Holocaust to the Arab-Israeli dispute. Since 1948, professions of Zionism have, again, been a kind of effort to keep faith with the victims of the death camps. Israel's difficulties seemed to sustain the idea that being a Jew requires little more than a sense of oneself as victim in the Gentile's scheme of things, and so much so that post-1967 Zionism may have become the new "unifying myth" of the Jews—of power, survival, of a kind of secular redemption. Of course, few American Jews actually confronted Nazis. Only people who are now over sixty would have even read newspaper reports of Nazi atrocities or Haganah victories with some mature sense of what was happening. Most Jews have partial evidence, books and testimony, the stare of relatives in old snapshots. It is for these reasons, perhaps, that American Jews have recast Zionist history in terms of absolute moral, even theological categories, the ones suggested by an increasingly idealized rage. The philosopher Emile Fackenheim wrote after the Six-Day War:

> Auschwitz is a unique descent into hell. It is an unprecedented celebration of evil. It is evil for evil's sake. Jews must bear witness to this truth . . . They were and still are singled out by it, but in the midst of it they hear an absolute commandment: *Jews are forbidden to grant posthumous victories to Hitler.* They are commanded to survive as Jews, lest the Jewish people perish. They are commanded to remember the victims of Auschwitz lest their memory perish. They are forbidden to despair of man and his world, and to escape into either cynicism or other-worldliness, lest they cooperate in delivering the world over to the forces of Auschwitz. Finally, they are forbidden to despair of the God of Israel lest Judaism perish.

A secularist Jew, Fackenheim continued, "cannot make himself believe by a mere act of will, nor can he be commanded to do so. Yet he can perform the commandment of Auschwitz."[1]

Before I lived there, Israel certainly seemed to me a kind of risen victim and, like someone born again, I rushed to assume its blamelessness with a certain ecstatic passion. (Fackenheim went on to write: "No decent anti-Zionism can be possible after the Holocaust.") It did not occur to me then that Fackenheim's formula for converting modern Jews to Judaism—the "commandment of Auschwitz"—was itself a kind of victory for Hitler's apocalyptic ideas. An Israeli official I know, a former American, gave a series of Israel Bond dinner speeches in the aftermath of the Lebanon invasion which were strongly critical of the American media for their allegedly biased coverage of the war. When his tour was completed, he confessed his astonishment to me at the response of his audiences to his lectures. He had been a supporter of Begin and knew a demonstration of Jewish power when he saw one. "Yet they kept raising the Holocaust," he told me. "Is anti-Semitism so bad here?" he asked.

No doubt American Jews—indeed, all Americans—need to be

vigilant in defense of civil liberties. But that Israeli official was inadvertently suggesting an even better question than the one he
asked. If American Jews were denied such opportunities to act out
vigilance for Israel, what would be left of their Judaism? Recall
Sartre's observation that where Jews do not exist anti-Semites invent
them. Is it possible that American Jews now need to invent anti-
Semites to feel like Jews, to perform the commandment of Auschwitz? The real question, the one American Jews (who are not
Orthodox) are most reluctant to confront, is: In what does contemporary secular Jewish cultural life consist? The American-born
Israeli writer Hillel Halkin put it this way a few years ago: "A
smattering of Yiddish or Hebrew remembered from childhood, a
nostalgia for a parental home where Jewish customs were still kept,
the occasional observance of an isolated Jewish ritual, the exclusion
of some non-kosher foods from an otherwise non-kosher kitchen, a
genuine identification with the Jewish people combined with a
genuine ignorance of its past history and present condition."[2]

Halkin may have overstated the case, but it is certainly true that
most American Jewish families left behind the Torah and Yiddish
when they moved to the suburbs. In view of so much attenuation,
what else but the commandment of Auschwitz makes sense? So
there are bar mitzvah boys who have never heard of Maimonides
but know just how to despise the old Mufti of Jerusalem; every
day, Jewish scholars feel compelled to search for nuance and intent,
not in the pages of the Talmud, but on the Op Ed page of *The New
York Times*. According to neo-conservative observance, American
Jews who promote liberal-democratic standards in the Middle East
over "Jewish power" or—what seems the same thing—the new
Zionist explanations, invite assimilation, anti-Semitism, and worse.
The commandment of Auschwitz inspires sermons of solidarity from
suave rabbis, even media events. It seems to mandate that Israeli
politicians, including the guilty General Sharon, should be received
in American synagogues with a reverence justly denied them at
home.

·

If Halkin is right about the demise of Old World Jewish culture
among American Jews, he may also be right that this prefigures the
collapse of once vigorous Jewish social institutions and self-help
societies in this country. Yet it is hard to see how acknowledging

Halkin's perceptive claims will benefit any version of Zionism that is not merely vicarious. (This is why Halkin's appeal to American Jews—that they adopt Israel and not merely support it from afar —had little impact on immigration figures.) The pace of American Jewish breast-beating has quickened—checks have been written, congressmen lobbied. None of this suggests that American Jews will choose to become Israelis: the decline of Jewish "ethnic" culture that Halkin laments, along with the increasing tendency toward intermarriage and assimilation he identifies, make a move to Israel all the more implausible. In a 1982 survey, Professor Steven M. Cohen found that over 80 percent of American Jews deny that they ever give serious thought to settling in Israel.[3]

Achad Haam once implied that secular Jews needed to know the laws even more than pious Jews needed to observe them. Halkin was certainly shrewd to suggest that American Judaism itself will now be very difficult to develop and sustain. He was probably right that only about a million of America's 5.7 million Jews still know something about the practices of traditional Judaism, or find much that is deeply illuminating in Jewish texts. In consequence, it is easy to conclude that the new Zionism is all American Jews have left, not only as an ideology, but as the basis for an institutional life. In lieu of Zionism, a friend of mine once quipped, can American Jews just present their children with a catalogue of Schocken books? Can the terms of Judaism be taught to modern children without the reinforcements of national culture?

The answer, I believe, is a qualified yes, though the question is too difficult to receive more than passing treatment here. What seems obvious, however, is that there is a perverse notion of identity lodged in my friend's challenge, and this ought to be addressed first. If it is true that the texts, ethics, and poetics of Judaism *cannot* be taught to American children, what should we teach them about Zionism? That the Jewish people survived two thousand years of exile for spite? The night terrors of the Holocaust, which are at the heart of current American Zionist myths, are at odds with the ordinary experiences of young Jews in this country, and even more at odds with the manifest power of the state of Israel. (As his plane banked over Tel Aviv, Alexander Portnoy could concentrate his mind only on shagging fly balls in center field with a dream of freedom that would have silenced Nietzsche.) But this is just why

Americans who want to stay Jews will need the Schocken list and a lot more besides. Think of what it takes to keep up the tradition of symphonic music in this country.

The vitality of Jewish life depends on the gradual building up of day schools, journals, university programs, and cultural centers, all of which require money and stamina. Yet—and here is a double irony—over half of the $500 million raised by the UJA apparatus each year (some $300 million) goes directly to Israel, some of it indirectly to the West Bank. The Yiddish research institute, YIVO, now based in New York, survived the 1970s at the pleasure of the National Endowment for the Humanities. I can personally attest to the financial burden of providing tuition for Hebrew day schools. Jewish homes for the elderly are increasingly decrepit. Scores of Jewish scholars, graduates of Jewish Studies programs at great universities, cannot find teaching posts. Nor is the money raised for Israel even accounted for properly. I do not claim any special knowledge about this, but it seems obvious that the mere existence of the old Zionist *apparat*, the Jewish Agency, allows for some serious corruptions of purpose. (A most flagrant example is the millions of dollars—we do not know exactly how many millions, since the Jewish Agency will not account precisely for its budget—which flow directly into the coffers of the Israeli political parties, as if these were still competing Zionist movements.)

Of course, tens of millions are eaten up by the *aliyah* bureaucracy, from Rehov Straus in Jerusalem to Park Avenue in New York, despite the fact that few Americans move to Israel. Hundreds of *shlichim* ("emissaries of Zionism") still come to the Jewish suburbs of Toronto or Los Angeles hoping to capture the imaginations of American Jewish children they barely understand. Most of the *shlichim* I have known are fine people, and would readily acknowledge that the money spent on them could be better spent in Israel or, indeed, in America. A few will concede that, since ten times more money comes to Israel nowadays directly from the American government than from the UJA, the role of the *shaliach* is increasingly expected to be that of apologist for Israeli government policy to the American public at large, even if this means trying to stifle free debate in the very American Jewish community that supports them.

All Americans and not only American Jews should help Israel

defeat or deter enemies sworn to the state's destruction. But Israel's political dilemmas have not been so clear-cut since 1967, and certainly not since President Sadat went to Jerusalem. What is often lost in that increasingly demeaning debate about when or whether it is "appropriate" for American Jews to dissent publicly from Israeli policy is that American Jews, like Israelis, are citizens of a democratic country; that in democracies, political decisions are almost never clear-cut. It is not a question, after all, of being "for" or "against" Israel, though taking pleasure in the Zionist saga has been every Jew's privilege. On the contrary, all that remains for Americans is to be for one group of Israelis over another, one version of justice over another. And Americans should be for Israelis who want to preserve democratic ideals.

Not that American Jews have had much influence over the institutions they support. Eliezer Jaffe, a Hebrew University sociologist who has made a study of Jewish Agency politics, notes that the agency's executive committee, with thirteen members, can hardly escape Israeli political control, since the non-party American and European representatives (the fund raisers) account for only six votes. By agreement, the chairman of the World Zionist Organization also serves as chairman of the Jewish Agency assembly and executive. The major horsetrading for agency plums, such as department portfolios, control over governing bodies and over $450 million of charitable funds annually (for four years), takes place not at the meeting of the agency assembly but at the World Zionist Congress.

"The political preparation of the WZO's delegates to the assembly votes," Jaffe writes, "makes the American delegates look like tourists in Disneyland."[4] Few of them understand the politics of the agency or the WZO, and most of them will never attend another assembly meeting. Ironically, the Americans fund over 65 percent of the agency's budget, yet they have only 30 percent representation at the assembly and on the board of governors. They are also unaware that they indirectly fund the activities of the WZO, an organization of old Zionist political parties moribund in the Diaspora, but which, again, funnels vast sums to political parties in Israel. Agency income in 1981–82 came primarily from contributions to the UJA ($247.2 million) and from the Keren Hayesod ($35.9 million), which operates in areas other than the United States, such as South

America and Europe. However, Keren Hayesod funds are not restricted to non-political, charitable work, as is the case in the United States. Thus, Keren Hayesod allotted an additional $36.5 million to the WZO, which, together with another grant of $15.5 million from the Israeli government, made up the entire income ($52 million) of the WZO in 1981–82. Forty-nine percent of Keren Hayesod contributions, Jaffe concludes, fuel the politics of the WZO, while only 51 percent goes to the Jewish Agency. This siphoning-off of funds forces the UJA to spend hard-raised millions to cover the lion's share of the Jewish Agency's debt repayments, which totaled $60.8 million in 1981–82 alone. Of this, the UJA covered 75 percent ($45.6 million), while Keren Hayesod covered only 25 percent ($15.2 million). These are huge sums of money presided over by politicians who are mere surrogates of the larger Israeli parties, and are certainly not people responsive to the Western Jews they tax.

Would it be wrong for thoughtful Western Jews who are anxious about Israeli democracy to abandon the WZO's structure altogether, to support Jewish Agency welfare work and their own welfare funds—or, indeed, whatever social and educational institutions they please, in the United States or Israel—without WZO intermediaries? That question seems especially pertinent, considering the political intrigues which have afflicted the Jewish Agency's disbursement of its huge amounts of money. When, for example, American philanthropists wished to oppose some of the policies decided in Jerusalem, the WZO executive committee blocked them in a most high-handed manner: the thirtieth and largely unelected Zionist congress met in Jerusalem during December 1982, and an unlikely coalition of delegates, led by American Hadassah women, put through a majority resolution to suspend funding of Jewish settlement of the West Bank. They underestimated their adversaries and overestimated their movement's residual power, for the plenum was promptly suspended by Arie Dulzin, the chairman of the Zionist executive and a leader of the Likud.

·

My claims against the new American Zionism will probably offend many people who would otherwise agree with their logic. This is not really surprising in view of the anti-Zionist rhetoric which was so fashionable during the seventies among New Leftists and which persists, though in less strident form, among the major European Social Democratic parties. In the Soviet Union, there is the terrifying revival of old Bolshevik slanders against Zionism: that it is inherently racist and the tool of imperialism; the Soviets have wedded this attack to a vicious campaign of anti-Jewish repression at home. Anti-Zionism has been common at the United Nations since 1974 and is incorporated into some of its important resolutions. No thoughtful person wants to appear sympathetic to anti-Zionist claims of this kind, and Jews will be tempted to profess Zionism out of outrage, fear, and confusion.

But defiance only cedes to terrorists, commissars, and ayatollahs the right to define how modern Jewish purposes should be debated. The young Eastern Jews who invented Zionism one hundred years ago did not waste energy disputing czarist blood libels. Instead, they honored the Orthodox culture of their rabbis by criticizing it ruthlessly, writing themselves free of the failing prejudices that trapped them along with the Czar's edicts. In this excellent sense, the Zionists earned their tragedy, as Israelis may yet earn what Zionists once called "normalcy." Can so much be said for American Jews?

In the book of Leviticus, after animal sacrifices were abandoned, the children of Israel were ignorant and impulsive, yet they yearned, as men and women will, to approach God as Moses had done. It fell to the priests, the text relates, to try and make the sacred possible; they separated out a portion of the food, or the cloth, in order to create a symbolic "distinction" between the holy and the profane. When there were no more prophets to convey God's will, the Jews in exile all took on the practices of the priests, accepting the distinctions implied by the law. It then fell to the rabbis to find what was more sacred in the very act of interpreting the law—"tumbling and tumbling in the Torah," as the sages put it.

American Jews, with their love of secular science and art, will not all be priests or rabbis, and much as they might envy Moses for his faith, they cannot all go about like prophets. Yet, as the great American Jewish historian Salo Baron has said, America is the Jews' first real experience with "emancipation" and, though this may not be as spectacular as national self-determination, it can be more interesting than it is. New generations of American children will not be Jewish for the sake of fund-raising institutions

—or even for the sake of "survival"—but some, not millions, may decide to be Jewish for the sake of normative Jewish ideas, which America's Zionist leaders often obscure. American Jews may study texts, meet together in lectures and concerts. They may observe festivals, study Hebrew, history, melodies. In a way, an American Jew may have nothing more to look forward to than being a critic whose subject is the Torah; if spiritual life in the modern world *must* be vicarious, then better to struggle along with the children of Israel at Sinai than to dance even with the pioneers at Degania. To be sure, deciding to be Jewish because this is interesting is itself an American conceit: Abraham intended to sacrifice Isaac to something more terrible than the pursuit of happiness. But Jewish life will either become more interesting in this country or it will disappear. American Jews will have to retrieve or get at something more skeptical in the Jewish spirit. And some will have to write elegies to the Zionists' tradition, just as the Zionists once wrote elegies to Orthodoxy. This was mine.

Notes

Acknowledgments

Index

Notes

Introduction / The Jewish Problem

1. General reviews of the history of the Eastern Jews in the nineteenth century are to be found in Howard M. Sachar's *The Course of Modern Jewish History* (New York: World, 1958) and Solomon Grayzel's *A History of the Jews* (Philadelphia: Jewish Publication Society, 1947). Readers who wish a more intensive study can read Simon Dubnow's classic *History of the Jews in Russia and Poland*, Vol. III (Philadelphia: Jewish Publication Society, 1946). A vivid picture of Jewish seclusion is provided by Chaim Weizmann in his memoir, *Trial and Error*, especially "Earliest Days" (New York: Schocken, 1966). The flavor of the Eastern Jews' daily life is nicely captured in *The Shtetl Book*, by Diane K. and David G. Roskies (New York: Ktav, 1975, 1979). See also Hans Roggers's article "Russian Ministers and the Jewish Question," *California Slavic Studies*, Vol. VIII (1975).

2. Ezra Mendelsohn, *Class Struggle in the Pale* (Cambridge University Press, 1970), p. 109.

3. Ber Borochov, *Essays on Nationalism, Class Struggle and the Jewish Problem* (London: Mapam, 1971), p. 47.

4. New York: Avon Books, 1964, p. 16.

5. *World of Our Fathers* (New York: Harcourt Brace Jovanovich, 1976), p. 236.

6. Gershom Scholem, *Shabbetai Sevi* (Princeton, N.J.: Princeton University Press, 1973), pp. 8–15; for an analysis of the meaning of Eretz Yisrael in normative Judaism, see W. D. Davies, *The Territorial Dimension of Judaism* (Berkeley: University of California Press, 1982), pp. 108–9.

7. "Call to Jewish Youth," in Marie Syrkin, ed., *Nachman Syrkin: Socialist Zionist* (New York: Herzl Press, 1960), p. 299.

1 / Political Zionism

1. *Auto-Emancipation* is published in full in Arthur Hertzberg's indispensable book, *The Zionist Idea* (New York: Atheneum, 1969), pp. 181–98. See also David Vital's analysis of Pinsker's life, in *The Origins of Zionism* (Oxford University Press, 1975), pp. 122–32.

2. Vital, *The Origins of Zionism*, pp. 78–81.

3. Ibid., pp. 155–9.

4. In *Collected Works of Achad Haam*, in Hebrew (Jerusalem: Jewish Publishing House, 1955), p. 30.

5. Quoted from Amos Elon's *Herzl* (New York: Holt, Rinehart, and Winston, 1975), p. 23.

6. *Rome and Jerusalem* (New York: The Philosophical Library, 1958), p. 50.

7. *Confessions*; quoted from Heinrich Graetz, *The History of the Jews*, Vol. V (Philadelphia: Jewish Publication Society, 1894, 1941), pp. 553–5.

8. *Fin-de-Siècle Vienna: Politics and Culture* (New York: Knopf, 1980), p. 148.

9. Quoted from Elon's *Herzl*, pp. 57–8.

10. Jacques Kornberg, "Theodor Herzl: A Reevaluation," *Journal of Modern History*, Chicago (June 1980), pp. 229–31.

11. A fine translation of *The Jewish State* appears in Hertzberg's *The Zionist Idea*, pp. 205–30.

12. *Old-New Land*, trans. Lotta Levensohn (New York: Herzl Press and Bloch Publishing Co., 1941, 1960), pp. 80–1; see also p. 125.

13. *Zionist Writings* (2 vols.), ed. and trans. Harry Zohn, Vol. 1 (New York: Herzl Press, 1973), p. 154.

14. Ibid., pp. 164–5.

2 / Cultural Zionism

1. The *Autobiography* is as yet not translated into English. It was published in Russian in three volumes between 1934 and 1940, in Riga. This quote is from Volume I. I am grateful to Professor Jacques Kornberg at the University of Toronto for showing me fragments from his own translations.

2. "The Jewish State and the Jewish Problem," *Ten Essays on Zionism and Judaism*, Leon Simon, ed. (New York: Arno Press, 1973), pp. 43–4.

3. Leon Simon, *Achad Haam* (New York: Herzl Press, 1960), p. 35.

4. Ibid., p. 143.

5. Herbert Spencer, *Structure, Function and Evolution*, edited, with an introductory essay, by Stanislav Andreski (New York: Scribner's, 1971), p. 81.

6. Translated as "Imitation and Assimilation," in *Selected Essays of Achad Haam*, Leon Simon, ed. (New York: Atheneum, [1912], 1970), p. 116.

7. Simon, ed., *Ten Essays*, p. 239.

8. Quoted by Achad Haam in "The Supremacy of Reason," in ibid., p. 207. (An especially rewarding approach to Maimonides may be found in the work

of Professor Yeshayahu Leibovitz, whose book, *Essays on Jews and Judaism*, is available in Hebrew from Schocken Books, Tel Aviv. See especially Chapter 1, "The Significance of Halacha." A useful companion to Maimonides's *Guides of the Perplexed* is David Hartman's *Maimonides: Torah and the Philosophic Quest* (Philadelphia: Jewish Publication Society, 1976); see especially pp. 166–7, and *passim*.

9. "Summa Summarum," *Ten Essays*, p. 155.

10. See "Flesh and Spirit," in Simon, ed., *Selected Essays*, p. 139.

11. "The Transvaluation of Values," ibid., p. 231.

12. "Judaism and the Gospels," *Ten Essays*, p. 229.

13. "Slavery in Freedom," *Selected Essays*, p. 193.

14. Ibid., p. 194.

15. Quoted from Tudor Parfitt's essay "Achad Haam's Role in the Revival and Development of Hebrew," Kornberg, ed., *At the Crossroads* (State University of New York Press, 1983), p. 23.

16. "Zionism and Jewish Culture," *Philosophica Judaica*, Leon Simon, ed. (Oxford: East and West Libraries, 1946), pp. 92–4.

17. Ibid., p. 282.

18. "The Truth from Eretz Yisrael," *Collected Works of Achad Haam*, p. 30.

19. *Trial and Error* (New York: Schocken, 1966), p. 54.

20. "The Jewish State and the Jewish Problem," *Ten Essays*, pp. 40–1.

21. Zohn, ed., *Zionist Writings*, Vol. II, p. 131.

22. Quoted from Jonathan Frankel, *Prophesy and Politics, Socialism, Nationalism, and the Russian Jews, 1862–1914* (Cambridge University Press, 1981), p. 140.

23. These matters are taken up in Professor Jacques Kornberg's "Achad Haam and Herzl," *At the Crossroads*, p. 125.

24. See Elon's *Herzl*, p. 402.

3 / The Conquest of Labor

1. Mendelsohn, *Class Struggle in the Pale*, p. 85.

2. Ibid., p. 33.

3. Frankel, *Prophesy and Politics*, p. 205.

4. Mendelsohn, *Class Struggle*, p. 109.

5. Frankel, *Prophesy and Politics*, p. 140.

6. Syrkin, ed., *Nachman Syrkin*, p. 276.

7. Ibid., p. 34.

8. Frankel, *Prophesy and Politics*, pp. 294–6.

9. "The Socialist-Jewish State," Syrkin, ed., *Nachman Syrkin*, p. 282.

10. Ibid., p. 270.

11. Ibid.

12. Ibid., p. 288.

13. "Moses Hess," ibid., p. 307.

14. "The Socialist-Jewish State," p. 261.

15. Ibid., p. 106.

16. Ibid., p. 283.

17. Ibid., pp. 290–3.

18. These essays are collected in *Essays on Nationalism, Class Struggle, and the Jewish People* (London: Young Mapam, 1971); this statement is from "Our Platform," p. 40.

19. "Nationalism and the Class Struggle," ibid., pp. 3–18.

20. "The Economic Development of the Jewish People," ibid., p. 49.

21. Herbert H. Rose, *The Life and Thought of A. D. Gordon* (New York: Bloch Publishing Co., 1964), p. 37.

22. Quoted in Howard Sachar's *A History of Israel* (New York: Knopf, 1976), p. 71.

23. "Summa Summarum," *Ten Essays*, pp. 151–2.

24. See *Arthur Ruppin; Memoirs, Diaries, Letters*, Alex Bein, ed. (New York: Herzl Press, 1971), especially Chapters 10 and 11, which give a vivid picture of the purchase and development of agricultural land; this quote is found on pp. 102–3.

25. Arthur Koestler, *Thieves in the Night* (New York: Macmillan, 1946), p. 17.

26. *Selected Essays* (New York: Arno Press, [1938], 1973), pp. 52–5.

27. Ibid., p. 60.

28. Ibid., p. 81.

29. Ibid., p. 93.

30. Ibid., pp. 23–8.

31. *The Israelis: Founders and Sons* (New York: Holt, Rinehart, and Winston, 1971), p. 144.

32. Rose, *Life and Thought*, p. 41.

33. From an unpublished interview with Esther Fuchs.

34. See the *Encyclopedia of Zionism and Israel* (New York: Herzl Press/McGraw-Hill, 1971), p. 792.

35. Hertzberg, *The Zionist Idea*, p. 548.

36. *Trial and Error*, p. 531.

4 / Class to Nation

1. Shlomo Avineri, *The Making of Modern Zionism* (New York: Basic Books, 1981), p. 205.

2. The events surrounding the promulgation of the Balfour Declaration are covered stirringly by Christopher Sykes in his book *Crossroads to Israel* (Cleveland: World, 1965), especially Chapter 1; see also Peter Grose, *Israel in the Mind of America* (New York: Knopf, 1983).

3. Quoted in Michael Bar-Zohar's *Ben-Gurion: A Biography* (New York: Delacorte, 1977), p. 37.

4. Quoted in Sykes, p. 11.

5. Quoted in Hans Kohn's essay "Zion and the Jewish National Idea," in *Zionism Reconsidered*, Michael Selzer, ed. (New York: Macmillan, 1970), p. 202.

6. See Weizmann's attitudes toward the Labor movement in *Trial and Error*, pp. 298–303.

7. Yonathan Shapiro, *The Formative Years of the Israeli Labor Party* (Los Angeles: Sage, 1976), p. 16. Shapiro's book is the source of most of the data on the early Labor movement. See especially Chapters 1 and 2.

8. Ibid., p. 27.

9. Quoted in Avineri, p. 200.

10. See Noah Lucas, *The Modern History of Israel* (London: Weidenfeld and Nicolson, 1974), p. 83 and *passim*. Lucas's is perhaps the best history of Israel now in print.

11. Shapiro, p. 57.

12. I am grateful to David Argaman, of Kibbutz Ramat Hashofet, for sharing this with me. It is a part of his M.A. dissertation for Haifa University, 1978.

13. Simon, *Achad Haam*, p. 263.

14. Walter Laqueur, *A History of Zionism* (New York: Holt, Rinehart and Winston, 1972), p. 342.

15. Ibid., p. 341.

16. Avineri, p. 163.

17. Ibid., p. 164.

18. Laqueur, *A History of Zionism*, pp. 340–1.

19. Avineri, p. 167.

20. Ibid., p. 168.

21. Ibid., p. 172.

22. From Joseph B. Schechtman, *The Jabotinsky Story: Fighter and Prophet*, Vol. II (New York: Thomas Yoseloff, 1961), p. 531.

23. See Arthur Koestler's *Promise and Fulfillment* (New York: Macmillan, 1949), pp. 312–13.

24. Schechtman, p. 243.

25. *Trial and Error*, p. 338.

26. Quoted in *From Haven to Conquest*, Whalid Khalidi, ed. (Beirut: Institute of Palestine Studies, 1971), p. 153.

27. *The Autobiography of Nachum Goldmann* (New York: Holt, Rinehart, and Winston, 1969), p. 117.

28. Avineri, p. 206.

5 / *Independence or Colonialism*

1. Schechtman, *The Jabotinsky Story*, p. 240.

2. Michael Bar-Zohar, *Ben-Gurion: A Biography* (New York: Delacorte Press, 1978), pp. 82–3.

3. Hertzberg, *The Zionist Idea*, p. 561.

4. *Trial and Error*, p. 385.

5. Official Summary of the Betar Congresses, Jabotinsky Archives, Tel Aviv; quoted in Eric Silver's *Begin* (New York: Random House, 1984), Chapter 2.

6. Avineri, p. 548.

7. *The Economic Organization of Palestine*, Said B. Himadeh, ed. (Beirut: American University Press, 1938). See Himadeh's Chapter 5, "Industry," pp. 215–99, especially p. 290 and *passim*.

8. See Marie Syrkin's essay "I. F. Stone Reconsiders Zionism," in Walter Laqueur, ed., *The Israeli-Arab Reader* (New York: Bantam, 1969), pp. 337–8. The issue of Arab immigration has been taken up also by Joan Peters in her highly controversial book, *From Time Immemorial: The Origins of the Arab-Jewish Conflict over Palestine* (New York: Harper and Row, 1984), especially Chapter 11. Peters's data have been challenged by Norman G. Finkelstein, in an as-yet-unpublished paper entitled "Protocols of Joan Peters: The 'True Believers' History of the Middle East," which he kindly sent to the author. In any case, the number of Arabs who came, and their actual place of origin, beg the question of the subjective feelings of the people who came to call themselves Palestinians. It is with these people that Israelis have to make peace, and claims against any Arab's right to call himself Palestinian seem more fit for testimony before the Peel Commission than for serious discussion of the Arab-Israeli dispute in 1985.

9. Quoted in Laqueur, *A History of Zionism*, p. 246.

10. Ann Mosely Lesch, *Arab Politics in Palestine, 1917–1939: The Frustration of a Nationalist Movement* (Ithaca, N.Y.: Cornell University Press, 1979), pp. 68–70.

11. See Kenneth Stein's *The Land Question in Palestine, 1917–1939* (Chapel Hill: University of North Carolina Press, 1984).

12. Koestler, *Promise and Fulfillment*, pp. 25–35.

13. *My Life* (New York: G. P. Putnam's Sons, 1975), p. 158.

14. Prof. Bella Vargo (of Haifa University), "The Attitude and Activity of Yishuv Leaders during the Holocaust," a lecture at the City University of New York, Graduate Center, 1981.

15. Bar-Zohar, *Ben-Gurion*, p. 96.

16. See Sachar, *A History of Israel*, pp. 230–46. Sachar's book is by far the most comprehensive work on Israel, an invaluable source of social and economic data.

17. See Edward Luttwack and Dan Horowitz, *The Israeli Army* (New York: Harper and Row, 1975), especially "Origins," pp. 16–18 and *passim*.

18. "The Imperatives of Jewish Revolution," in Hertzberg's *The Zionist Idea*, pp. 606–17.

19. Arendt's charge is from "Zionism Reconsidered," *The Menorah Journal*, Vol. XXXIII, no. 2 (Autumn 1945); Chomsky makes his case in his *Peace in the Middle East?* (New York: Pantheon, 1974).

20. Yehuda Bauer, *From Diplomacy to Resistance* (New York: Atheneum, 1970), p. 233.

21. Hertzberg, *The Zionist Idea*, pp. 307–12.

22. *Trial and Error*, p. 434; an account of the Bermuda Conference can be

found in Arthur D. Morse, *While Six Million Died* (New York: Random House, 1967, 1968), pp. 47–52; the case of Joel Brand is taken up in Yehuda Bauer, *The Jewish Emergence from Powerlessness* (University of Toronto Press, 1979), pp. 16–19.

23. *Problems of World War II and Its Aftermath: Part 2*, Committee on International Relations, U.S. House of Representatives, Select Hearings, 1943–1950 (Washington, D.C.: U.S. Government Printing Office), p. 232.

24. *Pillars of Fire*, a film documentary of Zionism; quoted in Silver's *Begin*, Chapter 1.

25. See Begin's poignant memoir, *White Nights* (London: Futura Publications, 1957, 1978), p. 91.

26. Bar-Zohar, *Ben-Gurion*, p. 123.

27. *The Revolt* (Los Angeles: Nash Publishing, [1948], 1972), p. xi.

28. Bar-Zohar, *Ben-Gurion*, p. 137.

6 / State and Revolution

1. Sykes, *Crossroads to Israel*, p. 353 and *passim*.

2. Ibid., p. 347.

3. Silver, *Begin*, Chapter 10.

4. Meir, *My Life*, p. 279.

5. Silver, *Crossroads to Israel*, Chapter 11. A balanced account of the affair can be had by reading, in tandem, Koestler's *Promise and Fulfillment*, and Bar-Zohar's *Ben-Gurion*.

6. Norman L. Zucker, *The Coming Crisis in Israel: Private Faith and Public Policy* (Cambridge, Mass.: MIT Press, 1973), pp. 63–5.

7. Koestler, *Promise and Fulfillment*, p. 321.

8. Two excellent discussions of religion and state in Israel are Zalman Abramov's *Perpetual Dilemma* (Fairleigh Dickinson University Press, 1976), and S. Clement Leslie's *The Rift in Israel* (New York: Schocken, 1971).

9. See Lucas, *The Modern History of Israel*, p. 339.

10. Bar-Zohar, *Ben-Gurion*, p. 219.

11. *Israel: Years of Challenge* (London: Anthony Blond, 1963), p. 211.

12. *My Life*, p. 283.

13. *Yoman Ishi*, in Hebrew (Tel Aviv: Ma'ariv, 1979).

14. Bar-Zohar, *Ben Gurion*, p. 216.

15. Lucas, *The Modern History of Israel*, Chapter 14.

7 / The End of Zionism?

1. Shabbetai Teveth, *Moshe Dayan* (London: Weidenfeld and Nicolson, 1972), p. 331.

2. Meir, *My Life*, pp. 258–68.

3. Ibid.

4. Quoted from Lawrence Meyer's lively book, *Israel Now* (New York: Delacorte Press, 1982), p. 161.

5. From an interview with Shimon Shofti, former managing editor of the Kibbutz Ha'Artzi newspaper *Al Hamishmar* and past secretary of Kibbutz Ramat Hashofet, June 1974 and April 1983.

6. See Howard Sachar's whole discussion in *A History of Israel*, pp. 386–9.

7. *My Life*, pp. 278–9.

8. Shlomo Swirski, "The Oriental Jews in Israel," *Dissent* (Winter 1984).

9. *The Modern History of Israel*, p. 310. Lucas's book is an invaluable source of economic data and analysis. See especially Chapter 14.

10. See Asher Arian's "The Electorate in Israel: 1977," in *Israel at the Polls*, Howard R. Penniman, ed. (Washington, D.C.: American Enterprise Institute, 1977).

11. The September 1, 1954, entry in Sharett's diary reads: "Teddy [Kollek] painted a horrifying picture of relations at the top of the security establishment. The Minister of Defense [Lavon] is completely isolated—none of his collaborators speaks to him. During the Olshan-Dori Inquiry . . . *some of his collaborators plotted to blacken his name and trap him. They captured the 'man who came from abroad,' who escaped from Egypt . . . and instructed him in detail how to answer, including how to lie to the investigators . . .*"

12. *My Life*, p. 290.

13. Author's interview with Mr. Navon, January 1983.

14. Bar-Zohar, *Ben Gurion*, p. 295.

15. Avraham Avi-hai, "David Ben-Gurion's Political Philosophy," *Encyclopedia Judaica Yearbook* (1974), p. 89.

16. Quoted in Walter Eytan, *The First Ten Years* (New York: Simon and Schuster, 1958), p. 195.

8 / *A New Zionism for Greater Israel*

1. Nadav Safran, *Israel: The Embattled Ally* (Cambridge, Mass.: Harvard University Press, 1978), p. 387.

2. Quoted in Theodore Draper's *Israel and World Politics: The Third Arab-Israeli War* (New York: Viking Press, 1968), p. 65.

3. Ibid., p. 113.

4. Teveth, *Moshe Dayan*, p. 394.

5. Sachar, *A History of Israel*, p. 673.

6. Ibid., p. 674.

7. Teveth, *Moshe Dayan*, p. 411.

8. *My Life*, pp. 368–9.

9. Quoted from Rael Jean Isaac's *Israel Divided: Ideological Politics in the Jewish State* (Baltimore: The Johns Hopkins University Press, 1976), pp. 65–6.

10. Teveth, *Moshe Dayan*, p. 205.

11. Meir, *My Life*, p. 378.

12. Ibid., p. 405.

13. I am grateful to Arie Ben-Shachar, an administrator at Hebrew University, for sharing this and other compiled data with me. Mr. Ben-Shachar composed this table from *Government of Israel Yearbooks*, for his doctoral studies at the University of Toronto.

14. See my article "Three Months of Yom Kippur," *The New York Review of Books* (January 24, 1974).

15. See my articles "The Last Hurrah" and "The Threat from the Right," *The New York Review of Books* (May 2 and May 16, 1974).

16. See my article "Israel Letter: The New Trap," *The New York Review of Books* (October 30, 1975).

17. See my full election report, "A New Israel," *The New York Review of Books* (June 23, 1977).

9 / The West Bank Tragedy

1. For complete data, see Brian Van Arkadie's *Benefits and Burdens* (Washington: Carnegie Endowment for International Peace, 1977) and *Judea, Samaria, and Gaza: Views on the Future*, Daniel J. Elazar, ed. (Washington: American Enterprise Institute, 1981).

2. The full story of West Bank violence can be found in Rafik Halabi's *West Bank Story* (New York: Harcourt Brace Jovanovich), 1982.

3. This report has been published by the American Enterprise Institute. I am grateful to Mr. Benvenisti for sharing some of his preliminary findings with me.

4. See my "Israel Letter," *Dissent* (Winter 1979).

5. See my article "Whose Peace Now?" *The New York Review of Books* (Christmas Issue, 1979).

6. Jimmy Carter, *Keeping Faith: Memoirs of a President* (New York: Bantam, 1982), p. 300.

7. See my reports "Looking over Jordan," *The New York Review of Books* (April 28, 1983), and "Can Begin Be Stopped?" *The New York Review of Books* (June 2, 1983).

8. Menachem Milson, "How to Make Peace with the Palestinians," *Commentary* (May 1981).

9. See Ze'ev Schiff and Ehud Ya'ari, *Israel's Lebanon War* (New York: Simon and Schuster, 1984), pp. 11–46.

10 / Democracy or Zionism?

1. Mina Tzemach and Ruth Tzin, "Attitudes of Adolescents toward Democratic Values," a paper presented to the Van Leer Jerusalem Foundation in conjunction with *DAHAF* research, September 1984.

2. *The Beirut Massacre: The Complete Kahan Commission Report*, with an introduction by Abba Eban (New York: Karz-Kohl Publishing, 1983), p. 57.

3. Philadelphia: Jewish Publication Society, 1974, p. 4.

4. Meron Benvenisti, "The Turning Point in Israel," *The New York Review of Books* (October 13, 1983).

5. *Every Sixth Israeli*, Alouph Hareven, ed. (Jerusalem: The Van Leer Jerusalem Foundation, 1983). See especially Hareven's essay, pp. 6–9.

6. Revised, with an introduction by T. E. Wick, Modern Library College Edition (New York: Random House, 1982), pp. 199–200.

7. *Between Battles and Ballots: Israeli Military in Politics* (Cambridge University Press, 1983). See especially p. 282, and *passim*.

8. "The Way to Bedlam," *Ha'Aretz* (October 21, 1983).

9. Sam Khalil Mar'i, *Arab Education in Israel* (Syracuse University Press, 1978).

10. See David K. Shipler's report in *The New York Times* (December 29, 1983).

Conclusion: The Divisions of Unity and Beyond

1. See Peres's interview with Lally Weymouth, *Los Angeles Times* (October 14, 1984).

2. See my article "Can Begin Be Stopped?"

3. Data are taken from Dalia Shekhori's paper "Public Attitudes in Israel toward the War in Lebanon," which she presented to the Kennedy School of Government at Harvard University, February 1984.

4. Michael Grati, *Ha'Aretz* (July 26, 1984).

5. *Monitin* (April 1984).

6. See Peres's contribution to *Israel Toward the 21st Century*, in Hebrew (Jerusalem: The Van Leer Jerusalem Foundation, 1984).

7. Yoram Peri and Amnon Neubach, "The Military-Industrial Complex in Israel," published by the International Center for Middle East Peace (Tel Aviv).

8. See Hareven's study in *Every Sixth Israeli*.

9. Peres is known to favor a new electoral system along Scandinavian lines, by which the country would be divided into three-member constituencies. Younger people who were elected would not be so tied to the party *apparat*. The plan suggests Peres's capacity for fresh thinking; but since it would antagonize the NRP, its chances of being adopted by the current Labor leadership are small.

10. See my article "Jordan: Looking for an Opening," *The New York Review of Books* (September 27, 1984).

Epilogue: An American Zionist?

1. *Commentary* (August 1968).

2. *Letters to an American Jewish Friend: A Zionist Polemic* (Philadelphia: Jewish Publication Society, 1977).

3. *Moment* (July–August 1982).

4. *Jerusalem Post*, International Edition (June 26–July 2, 1983).

Acknowledgments

A great many people have contributed to this book, some deliberately, some inadvertently; I should at least like to thank the former. Early drafts were read by Elzbieta Chodakowska-Ettinger, Irving Howe, James Paradis, Kenneth R. Manning, and Susan Avishai; they did not so much save me from mistakes as from myself, though the last, it must be said, has had the most practice doing so. Menachem Brinker read through a more nearly finished draft and, as always, taught me many things I didn't know. Parts of the manuscript benefited from the comments of Jacques Kornberg, Leonard Fein, Sheldon Schreter, and Bruce Mazlish. Sections taken from my essays for the *New York Review of Books* received the indulgent attention of Robert Silvers, who more than anyone else over the last twelve years has encouraged me to think boldly about Israel and the Middle East, and to write. Finally, thanks are due to David Rieff, Roger Straus, and Lynn Warshow, editors who make it their business to become one's friends.

Index